"*Baptistland* is a story of al[...]ese things, it is a story of resi[...]ost, Christa Brown has worked for decades to press for accountability [...]hin the Southern Baptist Convention. In the face of vicious opposition and widespread complicity, she persists to this day in calling for truth, demanding follow-through, and pressing forward with unwavering conviction and hard-earned hope."

—Kristin Kobes Du Mez, PhD, author of *Jesus and John Wayne*

"*Baptistland* is a searing yet inspirational memoir and sorely needed guide to all who try to expose any corrupt institution. I just can't convey how incredibly impressed and grateful I am for Christa's groundbreaking work . . . She opened the door for so many other survivors to start speaking up."

—David Clohessy, activist and former executive director for the Survivor's Network of those Abused by Priests (SNAP)

"In this steady, harrowing account, Christa Brown details the brutality of the social hierarchies of the Southern Baptist Convention, as evinced in the SBC's leadership, its clergy, and the teachings from its pulpits. In almost fractal-like fashion, the dominance and patriarchal aggression of abusive pastors is recreated in smaller and smaller settings, between husbands and wives, parents and children, older and younger siblings. The one constant is the requirement that no one speak truth to power. To be an abuser is to remain at the heart of the fold; to speak up as victim or ally is to be exiled, or worse. Christa Brown took that deal, and the result is clarity and candor that no doubt has saved lives, and might, if given the audience her voice deserves, lead to lasting change."

—Lacy Crawford, author of *Notes on a Silencing: A Memoir*

"*Baptistland* is the moving story of how Christa Brown broke cycles of intergenerational trauma, helped her fellow abuse survivors, and kept her sense of empathy and truth. The work of reform continues, and Christa has given advocates a powerful place to start."

—Rev. Nathan Empsall, Executive Director of Faithful America

"Christa Brown has long been a crucial voice speaking out against clergy sexual abuse and its systematic cover-ups within the Southern Baptist Convention. Her beautifully written memoir offers a stunning portrait of how Baptist culture and theology have shaped evangelical children and family life over generations, creating the "what happened didn't happen" stance embodied by both her childhood church and her family . . . *Baptistland* is a powerful and truly inspiring read!"

—R. Marie Griffith, author of *Moral Combat: How Sex Divided American Christians and Fractured American Politics*

"Overcomer. This word effectively describes Christa Brown ... When I read *Baptistland*, I was overwhelmed as I read of her emotional and physical abuse ... She went on to become an appellate court lawyer and the most well-known advocate for change in how the SBC deals with sexual abuse. She persisted and triumphed."

—Dee Parsons, *The Wartburg Watch*

"In *Baptistland*, Christa Brown bravely summons her own experiences of child abuse in her family and church as she stares down the abuse crisis that is rotting evangelicalism from the inside out. With lawyerly precision, she dissects the lies underlying evangelical obsession with authority and power. You are your own, Brown insists, and you have one wild and precious life."

—R. L. Stollar, author of *The Kingdom of Children: A Liberation Theology*

"*Baptistland* will make you weep. It will make you angry. It will break your heart. It will open your eyes. Christa Brown is not just a survivor—she is a hero we don't deserve. Every Southern Baptist needs to read this story, and every Southern Baptist leader needs to account for what it reveals."

—Karen Swallow Prior, PhD, author of *The Evangelical Imagination: How Stories, Images and Metaphors Created a Culture in Crisis*

"I'd highly recommend it to anyone who cares about sexual abuse survivors, the problem of clergy abuse, and the need for churches to make structural changes to prevent abuse and support survivors."

—Susan Shaw, author and professor of Women, Gender, and Sexuality Studies at Oregon State University

"Christa Brown is renowned as a fierce and resilient advocate, someone who has demanded truth and justice from one of the most influential church bodies in the United States. In *Baptistland*, we see Brown's origins: coping with a family legacy of fear and dysfunction, childhood clergy abuse, and the painful, vital work of learning how to demand a better life for oneself and those who will follow. There is vulnerability and courage in these pages."

—Sarah Stankorb, author of *Disobedient Women: How a Small Group of Faithful Women Exposed Abuse, Brought Down Powerful Pastors, and Ignited an Evangelical Reckoning*

BAPTISTLAND

BAPTISTLAND

*A Memoir of Abuse,
Betrayal, and
Transformation*

CHRISTA BROWN

lakedrivebooks.com

Lake Drive Books
6757 Cascade Road SE, 162
Grand Rapids, MI 49546

info@lakedrivebooks.com
lakedrivebooks.com
@lakedrivebooks

Publishing books that help you heal, grow, and discover.

Hardcover ISBN: 978-1-957687-42-1
Paperback ISBN: 978-1-957687-44-5
eBook ISBN: 978-1-957687-45-2

Library of Congress Control Number: 2024931270

Cover design by Laura Duffy Design
Cover photo by Jim Hill
Author photograph by Michael Ciaglo

This book is a memoir. It reflects the author's present recollections and information gathering of experiences over time. Some of the names of individuals or institutions and their characteristics have been changed, some events have been compressed, and some dialogue has been recreated.

*For Jim, my love and my rock. So much of life's
goodness begins with him.
For Stacy, with fierce love. From her first breath,
she was an inspiration.*

*And for all those who have experienced faith-based
sexual violence and religious institutional betrayal.
You are not alone. You matter.*

The land you grow up in is a forever thing, remembered when all else is forgotten, whether it did you right or did you wrong. Even when it flat near kills you.

—Lynda Rutledge

CONTENTS

THE FOURTH DEATH

FOREWORD

I GREW UP believing that the church is supposed to be a refuge—a safe place. My years as a child sexual abuse prosecutor opened my eyes to the deeply painful truth that abuse is all too prevalent *inside* of the church. Tragically, it is not a refuge for many.

Over the following years, I started an organization whose primary purpose was to address abuse within the church, with the hope that one day it would truly become that refuge I had once believed it to be. A few years later, I found myself really struggling with the painful reality that the most horrific consequence of sexual abuse within the church was not its tarnished reputation or even the fact that it had turned so many people away from God. What increasingly horrified me about this evil reality were the decimated lives of countless individuals who had been abused by a "Christian" leader and then betrayed by the very institution they had hoped would be their greatest advocate.

These precious people are the beaten and bruised who lie on the side of life's roadways having given up hope. Their stories understandably haunted me; however, I increasingly realized that their stories didn't seem to haunt or even concern so many who called themselves Christians.

Eventually, I too began to lose hope. And then I met Christa Brown.

I first met Christa through her powerful and sobering life story found in the pages of her first book, *This Little Light*. The abuse perpetrated on her by a "trusted church youth leader" and the subsequent betrayal, marginalization, and eventual vilification of Christa by her church, the Texas Baptist Convention, and eventually the Southern Baptist Convention and beyond angered me, grieved me, and most importantly, prompted me to reach out and meet this hero over a decade ago. Since then, Christa has become a dear friend, teacher, and confidante.

Christa Brown was one of the first survivors I met that prevented me from losing hope. In fact, her tireless advocacy on behalf of abuse survivors within the Southern Baptist world inspires me and so many others on the front lines of advocacy work to keep pressing forward.

One thing I've learned in almost thirty years of advocacy work is that it truly takes a village to help the hurting and to work toward transforming the church into the refuge it was always supposed to be. In many ways, I consider Christa Brown to be the glue that keeps this village together as we keep pressing forward.

Baptistland is a book that tells the rest of Christa's story. She dives deeper into the world of her dysfunctional childhood and the Christian fundamentalism and patriarchy that was the bedrock of her religious upbringing and early church life. We learn how that toxic culture stole her individuality, her voice, her agency, and in many ways, her life. It was only after Christa made the monumental decision to report the abuse and to expose those who protected her abuser that she finally began down the road of reclaiming what had been stolen from her.

Baptistland is the story of that journey and what happens in many religious communities when a woman steps forward and uses her voice, her agency, and her life to speak out to bring light to dark places. At first, the institutions ignored her. When that was impossible, they attempted to marginalize her. When they realized that Christa Brown is not one to be marginalized, they took private and public steps to vilify her. Needless to say, they failed.

I believe that Christa Brown would be the first to acknowledge that all of this has come at a significant emotional, physical, and spiritual cost. However, *Baptistland* is also a story of hope.

You can hear a voice of growing strength, especially as Christa emerges from Baptistland to become her own person in a career as a successful appellate attorney. And you can hear, especially today, a voice of gentleness, peace, and self-assuredness that has not lost any of its sharpness, as she has moved away from Baptistland, raised a family, and is now enjoying her grandchildren.

I did not really know where that voice came from, but now I know, and I dare say that Christa's example shows that such a voice can rise within anyone who needs to speak truth.

Christa Brown remains my hero, and I think she might become your hero by the time you've finished this beautiful book.

Boz Tchividjian
Attorney advocating for abuse survivors inside and
outside of courtrooms

AUTHOR'S NOTE

CLAUDE MONET PAINTED the same waterlily scenes over and over. Each time, the truth of the waterlilies appeared slightly different, depending on the light.

The truth of a person's trauma story is similar. It may appear slightly different with each telling, depending on the light in which it is captured.

I've done my best to tell the truth as I know it, as it lives in my body, mind, and spirit. But necessarily, like most memoirs, the book derives in large measure from my memory, and memory isn't perfect.

Many of the dialogues have been reconstructed according to my memory, and some have been edited, condensed, or paraphrased.

I've changed the names and identifying characteristics of many of the people in the book. But they are all real.

And if you're wondering about that blue tree on the cover, that's real too. As a kid, I wanted to slither out of my skin, to become invisible. But now, I've put my skin onto a book cover. So much that was so terrible was done to my body—to me—and the tattoo was my way of reclaiming my own self. This is an intimate story.

PROLOGUE

When despair for the world grows in me . . .
I feel above me the day-blind stars
waiting with their light . . .

—Wendell Berry

DAD TAUGHT ME to see patterns in the dark. On the rare nights when he wasn't working, he'd hold my hand and take me out into the yard where I would watch in wonder as he looked up into the darkness, extracted a pattern from the points of light, and then shaped that pattern into a picture. At first, feeling swallowed by the inky enormity overhead, I struggled to see what Dad saw. But over and over, he would drop to one knee, wrap an arm around my shoulder, and with his other arm outstretched, he'd point to each of the seven stars of the Big Dipper, and one by one, I would follow his line of sight out beyond his index finger to mentally connect the sparkling dots. Eventually, I managed to see it, and over time, I learned to spot the pattern all on my own. After that, I never lost it. The Big Dipper was always there waiting for me.

As Dad moved on to the Little Dipper, Orion, and the Milky Way, the patterns of the dark grew familiar, and together, we made wishes on shooting stars. Usually, it was just the two of us. I guess my sisters weren't interested. Or maybe they were afraid of the dark. So was I—and still am—but leaning up against Dad and wafting in the smell of his Old Spice, I felt safe.

After we moved to Farmers Branch, those magical nights ended. Maybe the big-city lights of neighboring Dallas made the sky too bright, or maybe Dad was just working too much overtime. But many years later, when I was out in Marfa, I looked up and saw the Milky Way stretched like a wide white ribbon across the sky, and I swear I suddenly caught a whiff of Old Spice. I felt the warmth of Dad's arm, and the stars seemed like old friends.

Whenever I think of Farmers Branch, a host of memories fills the air around me. Like stars on a West Texas night, they shine so bright that, eventually, I can hear the voices in the memories and see the patterns in the points of light.

It's not always easy. There is little that is linear in my memories. Time to me seems more circular and associative. Many of my memory fragments are a chaotic mess, but I try to impose order on them anyway because how else could I talk about them? I navigate into narration, but really, the memories are more like stars in an endless night sky.

When you're raised in a "what happened didn't happen" sort of family, things aren't necessarily what they seem and the patterns aren't always apparent. Even the bare bones of figuring out what's true and what's not is fraught. So let me just tell you up front that at least two of my sisters, and maybe all three, would see family patterns differently from me. Their views would tell different stories, as though they were seeing the sky in some alternate universe. All I can do is tell you my *own* story and tell it from the vantage point I hold at this moment.

I died four times. Four times when the elemental structure of my being was flung into the dark void. This book is my attempt to make sense of those deaths. Rather than fleeing from that darkness, I have chosen to walk into it, following the threads of my memory through the labyrinth of my life—and my deaths—connecting the points of light as best I can. The labyrinth was long and arduous, but as each death rebirthed me into a new self, it ultimately led to a center of peace.

My first life ended when a Southern Baptist pastor took an unholy hankering to my young Lionette legs. Of course, I didn't know my life had ended. I was just a naive, far-too-trusting church girl. But everything my life had been before his hankering came screeching to a halt, and I was never a kid again. My second life ended when my lousy brother-in-law decided he had "married the wrong sister" and made a move on me. In some ways, that second death was sort of like the first, but maybe that's just the nature of death. There's a before and there's an after, but even though there's no blending of the two domains, it's only much later when you realize you're in a different place. My third life ended when I started talking about what that predatory preacher-man had done to me, and I was confronted with the truth that no one gave a flip, except for trying to shut me up. Stepping into that reality was like stepping into an alternate no-exit universe in which the Dantean layers just kept going deeper. It was a death so hellish that my very cells mutated in rebellion. Then, just a few days after Mom died, my fourth life ended when all three of my sisters stood in front of the credit union and decided to split the money without me—as though I never existed. They swore each other to secrecy, but since I refused to die quietly, their secrecy didn't succeed.

Of course, the devil is in the details. This is the story.

The First Death

1

The Good Days

What we remember from childhood we remember forever—permanent ghosts, stamped, inked, imprinted, eternally seen.

—Cynthia Ozick

THAT FIRST SUMMER in Farmers Branch, tar bubbled up in the street like some sticky, stinky ooze from the underworld. Judy and I took turns riding our shared hand-me-down bike up and down the block, popping tar bubbles with the tires. Our rules were that we had to keep pedaling forward and we couldn't put a foot down. So we would twist and turn the handlebars, trying to stay upright while we followed the black lines that filled the asphalt's cracks in chaotic patterns. At the end of each turn, we would report back on how many tar bubbles we had popped. Judy always won.

Of course, it was really the Texas heat that always won. No matter how many tar bubbles we popped, more kept boiling up. Dad hadn't yet put the window units in, and Mom could hardly bear the heat. She had shut all the blinds to block the sun and was trying to get some unpacking done, but every time we stepped in the kitchen for Kool-Aid, she'd be sitting with some iced tea and a folded paper fan. The air inside our west-facing house was flat-out stupefying. So we'd hustle back outside just as fast as we could. Besides, we knew it was better to stay out of Mom's way.

I wasn't happy about the move, but still, I'd seen one good thing right away. Dad had found us a house right across the street from a school, and as soon as we pulled into town and turned a corner around the school's back side, Mom pointed out that it was where I would go for fifth grade in the fall: Valwood Elementary. It was a long, low, flat building.

No stairs. That was the first thought I remember having in Farmers Branch as we drove past the back side of the school on the last couple blocks of our road trip from Wichita. I stared at the building even as Mom claimed victory on the game we'd been playing. Ever since we'd crossed the Texas border, she'd been egging me on to guess the name of our new street. "Think about faraway places," she'd said, her arm thrown over the back of the front seat. So, while staring at her hand as she picked at the skin around her thumbnail, I'd guessed names like "Paris Lane" and "Taj Mahal Boulevard."

"Think about the last report you did," she'd hinted. It was a school project Mom had helped me with, clipping pictures of Egypt from old copies of *National Geographic* that we got at the thrift store. "Camel Street? Nile Way? Red Sea Road?" With every guess I tossed, Mom just smiled like the Sphinx. Somehow, I never guessed Pyramid Drive.

"You see, I told you you'd like it," she exclaimed, pointing to the street sign. But I was still fixated on the school. *No stairs.*

To this day, I can hear the cackle that Judy would let loose whenever she managed to shove me on the stairs in that two-story schoolhouse in Wichita. I was always so afraid I might tumble all the way down, yet I could never manage to keep an eye out for Judy and look where I was going at the same time. So I just held my breath and held the rail. Not that it ever made any difference. If Judy was in the mood for a laugh, she would find me. That was pretty much the core of our relationship.

In Wichita, we had always been in the same school, and even the same classroom for a couple years. That was because I'd been placed in an experimental program which kept me at the same grade level but put me, and a half-dozen other kids, in a classroom with kids a year older. It meant I wound up in the same classroom with Judy.

That was the downside of being in the "gifted" program—no escape from Judy. The upside was that, for those early years in Wichita, the program kept me with the same small group of friends, and they got used to me. For a kid with a facial scar and a speech impediment, that continuity of friendships was invaluable.

Things changed in Farmers Branch. Not only would I never again be in the same classroom with Judy, but for a while, I wouldn't even be in the same building with her. Sixth graders went to junior high in Texas, which meant Judy would be at a different school. So she wouldn't be lurking around corners or shoving me against walls at *my* school. She simply wouldn't be there.

Another good thing about the move was that Mom decided to stop dressing Judy and me in look-alike clothes. I figure I'd better tell you the good things like this right away, because things went downhill fast in Farmers Branch, and once I start telling the bad things, I might forget the rest. I don't want to do that.

It was one of the few ways that Judy and I were alike. We both hated those matchy-matchy outfits Mom made us wear. She sewed them herself, and she always beamed with pride when people told her how cute we looked. But whenever I see old photos of Judy and me in our look-alike short sets with the rick-racked crop tops, what I see is how Judy is glowering at the camera, looking like she's ready to punch someone. She probably did just as soon as the picture was taken. That someone was probably me.

Occasionally, Judy would punch my younger sister, Nancy, but it was rare. Mom tended to protect Nancy, and Judy was simply more habituated to tormenting me. My oldest sister, Rita, was above the fray and untouchable. So I was the one on whom Judy dissipated her rage.

Sometimes I wonder if Judy was just born mad. Mom occasionally talked about what a difficult baby she'd been. When she got old enough to pull herself up, she would stand in her crib screaming while she held the rail and yanked herself back and forth, banging her head over and over until she exhausted herself.

"I wasn't going to give in to that," said Mom. "She just had to learn."

Whenever Mom recounted this, she seemed to have a measure of pride in her voice, as though she had won some battle by not letting Judy get the best of her. She would laugh at how hardheaded Judy was, extending her arms and bending her elbows back and forth to mimic how Judy would bang her head in her crib. I always laughed along and wished that I myself could win some battles with Judy. But for me, there was never anything to do but curl up in a ball and wait for my sister's rage to pass.

Nowadays, I try to keep that image of Judy in my mind—a child so desperate for attention that, incessantly and futilely, she kept banging her head against her crib. It's an image that helps to soften all the ugliness that came later. Besides, I figure I probably had something to do with Judy's deprivation. My birth came just one year after hers, and with my medical issues, I imagine I kept Mom busy.

My sisters and I were all born in Texas—I doubt that Dad would have had it any other way—but we moved to Kansas when I was barely three. Our house in Wichita had five huge cottonwood trees at the back of the lot where Judy and I caught lightning bugs on summer nights, and during the days, we'd sit there in the sandpile, conjuring schemes for getting rich off the tiny fluffs of "cotton" shed from the trees. We planned everything we'd do with the money we'd make from bunching all the little fluff bits together and selling them. After we'd exhausted our dreams for an extravagant future, Judy would get up and start singing "Waltzing Matilda." She'd throw her head back, thrust her chest to the sky, and weave circles in the grass, singing at the top of her lungs. I'd get up and join her, and we'd hold hands and twirl round and round, faster and faster, until finally we dropped, dizzy and exhausted. To this day, whenever I see cottonwood fluffs in the air, I hear "Waltzing Matilda" in my mind.

As far back as my memories go, there was always at least Judy to contend with—her pinching, punching, shoving, pushing, arm-twisting, hair-pulling, clawing, kicking, hitting, and terrifying tickling. She couldn't tolerate frustration. If she didn't get what she wanted, which was often, she threw a fit, and frequently her fits centered on lashing out at me. Heck, even my Woody Woodpecker coloring book wasn't safe from Judy. Just two days after Santa brought it to me, she tore it apart. No reason at all. That's just how she was.

I cried about that coloring book. I suppose that's why Judy destroyed it—because she could see how much I loved it. But with a raised palm, Mom just said, "If you keep on crying, I'll give you something to *really* cry about."

So, I learned there was never any point in complaining to Mom about Judy's torments. "Just don't rile her up," she'd say. Or worse, she'd make us *both* apologize. "Tell your sister you're sorry," she'd demand, and even though I never could figure out what I was supposed to be sorry for, I knew I had to do it. Then, after Judy and I had each taken our turn at phony contrition, Mom would insist we hug one another, and almost always, Judy would be giving me a good hard pinch where Mom couldn't see.

Up until I was about six, I shared a trundle bed with Judy in a room with animal print wallpaper. Every night, after Mom was through reading to us— *Five Little Peppers* was my favorite—we said our prayers:

Now I lay me down to sleep,
I pray the Lord my soul to keep.
If I should die before I wake,
I pray the Lord my soul to take.

Judy recited it as fast as she could, but I prayed it earnestly, terrified of the possible truth of it and always knowing that if I didn't wake, it would be because Judy had finally held the pillow over my face for too long. After my prayers, I would turn to whisper a second plea to the animals on the wall. They were the ones I counted on to protect me in my sleep.

Every day, from the moment I awakened, I was always scanning the air for danger. Whenever one of Judy's rampages started brewing, if I could spot it soon enough, I would crawl into the bottom of the pantry and tuck myself behind the bags of beans and rice. There, I would slow my breath and imagine myself invisible, suppressing my own life force so Judy wouldn't find me.

Eventually, when I got too big and couldn't cram myself into the pantry, I had to find other places and use other tactics. It was high-stakes hide-and-seek, and whenever I failed, the cost was painful. Hiding under the bed was fast but seldom worked; Judy would just drag me out. Inside the laundry hamper was better, but I needed a head start because it took a while to get into it. Once, I just flat-out locked her out of the house.

We were playing kickball in the backyard, and I'd sent the ball straight into a rose bush. Judy ran to retrieve it, and while she stood trying to hold her finger over the hole left by a thorn, I heard her low growl: "I'm gonna kill you." I turned and ran for the house. Judy was always way faster than me, but that was one time when I got enough of a head start. I locked the door behind me just as Judy flung her fists against the wood. She pounded and kicked at the door, and screamed at me to open it, but I didn't.

I inched back the curtain on the utility room's window and peeked at her face. She was transformed. A monster.

"I'm gonna kill you," she shouted, spewing spit on the window.

I hovered there behind the door, trying to decide what to do. Judy's murderous rage showed no sign of abating, so I went to my room and took out my New Testament—the little white one that Brother Morgan had given me when I got baptized—got on my knees, and began to pray. Since I was "saved" by then, I must have been at least seven, maybe a little older. "The Lord is my shepherd, I shall not want." While I held the holy book in my hands and pleaded with God to protect me, I recited the prayer I'd learned in Sunday school.

After a small eternity of recitation and prayer, I heard Mom's car in the driveway. Knowing she'd be mad if she saw that I'd locked Judy out, I ran to the back door, quietly turned open the lock, and scurried back to the bedroom. Clutching the New Testament to my chest like some magic amulet, I heard Judy open the back door just as Mom came in the front door. "Thank you," I whispered.

SO, IT'S NOT as if my life in Wichita was ever safe. But it was normal and predictable. Even the "duck and cover" drills at school seemed normal, although those images of nuclear bombs always terrified me, and even as a kid, I never could understand how my school desk would protect me against *that*. But "duck and cover" was what our teacher said we should do, so I did.

Our kickball games caused trouble more than once. When one of us accidentally kicked the ball into the backyard of our fearsome neighbor, Mrs. Smith, we couldn't figure out what to do. Whenever we walked to our friends' house, two doors down, we'd balance on the curb to avoid touching Mrs. Smith's grass and incurring her wrath. But Judy mustered up the courage to knock on her door, and when no one answered, we went around to the gate. It was locked, but Judy climbed over, found the ball, tossed it to me, and then started climbing back over the gate. Just when she was at the top, Mrs. Smith's face suddenly appeared in the garage window right next to the gate, and she was screaming bloody murder. Startled, Judy fell from the gate. She hit the pavement hard but scrambled right up, and we both hightailed it home.

By then, Mom was back, so we figured we were in trouble. But instead of yelling at us, when Mom saw how scraped up Judy was, she marched right over to Mrs. Smith's house, knocked on her door, and let loose a piece of her mind. We could hear Mom all the way from our own porch. "They're just kids! How dare you terrify them that way? She could've broken her skull!" It felt good to hear Mom sticking up for us.

On weekends, Mom would sometimes whip us up piles of pancakes, as many as we wanted, shaping them into elephants, camels, and giraffes. It was magical. My heart would skip a beat as soon as I saw her take the Aunt Jemima syrup from the pantry. Sometimes, while we ate our zoo-animal pancakes, Dad would take the newspaper and fold a pressman's hat for each of us. He'd work the toothpick in his mouth back and forth as he turned and folded the paper just so, until he plopped a hat onto each of our heads. If it was a Sunday, one of us would get a colored hat folded from the funnies.

Years later, when my own daughter was small, I tried like heck to pour pancakes into identifiable shapes and never could. But Mom had the knack for it. Whether with her batter-pouring artistry or her way with words, she made pancake shapes that came to life in my mind, just like the rabbits and fish that she sometimes pointed out in the clouds when we hung clothes on the line.

There was nothing I loved more than those rare times alone with Mom, handing her the clothespins and wafting in her scent of Aqua Net, talc, and Tabu. Sometimes she would recite Longfellow's poem "Hiawatha's Childhood" while she worked:

> By the shores of Gitche Gumee,
> by the shining Big-Sea-Water,
> stood the wigwam of Nokomis,
> Daughter of the Moon, Nokomis.

I had no idea where Gitche Gumee was, but I loved the sound of it in Mom's voice. In those moments I was in heaven.

I search my mind for memories of Mom holding me, and I comb old photos looking for myself in Mom's lap. I can't find any. Instead, I find an old image of my oldest sister, Rita, holding me when I was a baby, and I wonder whether she wound up taking the role of a surrogate mom for me. Or was it just a single snapshot? You might think I would at least hold some vague body-memory of feeling safe and loved in Mom's arms. Yet, that scarcely exists either. What I can summon—and what I cling to—is the memory of standing next to her while she hung laundry on the line. Sometimes I'd slide up against her leg and she wouldn't step away.

Mom had honeysuckle, morning glories, roses, gladiolus, and bells of Ireland growing along the fence in Wichita. "Can you hear the tiny bells?" she'd ask me. Then she'd conjure a whole magical world of fairies who lived among the bells of Ireland, eating the honeysuckle nectar and using the lightning bugs to illumine the night. Before we finished up and carried the clothes inside, we'd always stop to pull out the stamens of a few honeysuckle flowers and lick some of the fairyland nectar for ourselves. Sometimes we'd stop to watch a roly-poly, or she'd gently lift a ladybug from a leaf and tell me they brought good luck.

With her words, Mom could also conjure faraway places. Every so often, we'd all pile in the car and go park near the airport to watch planes take off. That was Mom's favorite thing. She would imagine where the planes were going and then bring other lands to life with her stories. I've often wondered if my wanderlust got its start on those nights with all of us together watching the planes.

Other magical moments materialized on days when the bookmobile came. Mom would walk us to the end of the block where the wheeled cave of wonder was parked. The anticipation of what I might find always had me skipping. When we got there, we'd wait our turn and then enter the cave where Mom would help us explore. She'd let us take our time, and each of us got to pick two books. We'd print our names on lined cards and then carry home our precious cargo, which we got to keep as though our own, until the bookmobile came around again.

Books: They were what allowed me to glimpse a world beyond the constrained boundaries of family, school, and church. They were also the only safe thing to care about. Judy couldn't destroy them because they belonged to the library, and in our family, library books were practically sacred.

Though a measure of fear was always part of the normalcy in my family, it wasn't until Farmers Branch that everything got really catawampus. Ironically, I often wondered whether Dad moved us there because the bucolic-sounding name of "Farmers Branch" gave him some vague feeling of familiarity and safety. Raised by a ferociously violent father and left for dead on a World War II battlefield, he had little trust in anything or anyone. But the land and all it brought forth was true for him. He remained a farmer at heart—a man who could take one look at the clouds and know what kind of weather was on the way.

IT WAS 1962, and with the country having moved on from the McCarthy era, the *Dallas Morning News* finally had a union shop. So Dad wanted to return to Texas. He started a pressman's job at the *News*, while we all stayed in Wichita to finish up the school year.

After a few weeks, he put up a down payment on a 1,300-square-foot house in Farmers Branch without Mom having ever seen it—a fact that makes me catch my breath. Mom wound up living fifty years in a house she'd had no say in selecting. But it had two bathrooms, and when we first got there, Mom oohed and aahed over that like she'd died and gone to heaven. The house was across from a school, and just a block away from a library, a rec center, a pool, and a park. That was so like Dad—always wanting to make sure his kids would have more opportunity than he had.

When we first moved in, the yard was flat and bare, without a single tree. So, at Mom's urging, my three sisters and I drew diagrams of how we'd like the yard to look and what we'd like to plant. I drew the yard with lots of fruit trees, a vegetable garden at the back, and flower beds on the sides, with gladiolus, hollyhocks, morning glories, and bells of Ireland—just like Mom's flower beds in Wichita.

Dad went right to work on it, and for the next forty years, he spent every minute he could working in that yard, transforming it into an urban oasis. Right away, he planted a couple pecan tree sprouts at the back, even knowing it would probably be ten years before they produced. Then he planted pear, apple, and fig trees, and put in a mounded berm for spring-blooming bulbs. He never had any kind of irrigation system; he'd just stand out there holding the hose, watering things by hand. That yard may have been the only place where Dad was truly happy.

When he got a load of sand to loosen up the garden patch, Judy, Nancy, and I used it to build a giant fort. We spent a couple of days working on it, and it was as fine a fort as any you would ever see. But just about the time we finished it, the Harrison twins leaped over the fence and body-bombed it, flinging themselves into our fort every which way. We yelled at them, but they thought it was great fun, and in any event, the fort was destroyed. It didn't seem like there was much we could do about it.

Mom thought otherwise. "Why didn't you stop them?" she demanded. She had wanted to take a photo and we had spoiled things by letting the boys demolish the fort. We tried to explain, but she wouldn't hear it. "You could've stopped them if you'd wanted to," she insisted.

Seeing how angry Mom was, I prayed fervently before going to sleep that night, imploring God to please restore our fort so that Mom wouldn't be so upset. I knew God was busy, of course, but I figured if he could part the Red Sea, he could surely rebuild a sand fort so that my mom might feel better. But of course, the next morning, when I hopped out of bed to run and look out the back window, I could tell that God hadn't come through.

ıER, Judy and I would often play in an empty lot by the rec
ıe doing construction work and had blocked off the whole cor-
neı . of thick wooden posts whose tops were cut on the diagonal. One
day, Judy decided to jump from post to post, and she taunted me to do the
same: "Scaredy cat, scaredy cat!"

Finally, I climbed on top of one of the angled posts, sized it up, and jumped.
I made it, but it was tricky. You had to land your foot at an angle, heel down.

Then Judy challenged me to see who could keep hopping post to post the
longest. For Judy, who had more agility, it was no problem. But I overshot a
jump and my leg came down on the far side of a post with the pointy part sticking into the back of my thigh. It tore a long gash behind my knee and left wood
bits and splinters up and down the back of my thigh. I hobbled home, afraid of
how mad Mom would be, and sure enough, she was.

I spent the next couple hours on my belly with Mom berating me while she
dug all the bits of wood out of the gash and all the splinters out of my thigh.
There was no such thing as going to the doctor for something like that; Mom
just took care of it. Once, in Wichita, when a spider popped out of my toy
sewing machine—Mom said it was a brown recluse—the bite swelled into a
large boil and Mom just lanced it herself.

The gash behind my knee left me with a long, wide scar. A few years later,
when I became a high-kicking Lionette on the football field, I sometimes felt a
slight catch there. But though the catch would conjure the memory of how
much it hurt when Mom was digging around in the gash, mostly what I remembered was how much Mom yelled at me while she did it.

THE HARRISON TWINS—Phil and Bill—were part of the neighborhood gang that
we hung out with for a couple years. We all played kickball together and always
in the yard of the kids next door since Dad had made it clear he didn't want the
neighborhood kids in *our* yard. Once, when I missed a ball and failed to get a
player out on first, Judy marched over from her spot as catcher and kicked me
in the shins so hard I fell to the ground. Then, with me on the ground, she
kicked me a couple more times for good measure while screaming that if I

missed any more balls, she'd teach me a *real* lesson. The neighborhood kids watched in stunned silence.

By then, I was already taller than Judy, so you might think I would have fought back. But I didn't. She had always been scrappier and stronger, and I was habituated to simply enduring.

As I struggled to my feet, I half-glimpsed the other kids' wide eyes, but I kept my head down, clenched my teeth, and resolved not to cry. Judy shoved me and told me to get back on my base. "You better not miss again," she growled, stomping her way back to home plate. It was then, with Judy's back turned, that I made the mistake of raising my chin and looking full-on at the faces of the other kids. Even Phil and Bill, rough as they were, had mouths agape.

I started to cry, and as I turned to run toward home, Judy yelled after me, "Crybaby!"

I always hated myself for crying and wished I could be more like Judy. Mom could spank Judy until her wrist hurt, but Judy would never give Mom the satisfaction of seeing her cry. She'd just grit her teeth all the harder. But I couldn't stop the tears. So I waited in the garage for a few minutes before going into the house.

When Mom saw me, she asked why I wasn't out playing, and I tried to tell her about Judy kicking me. But Mom just said, "If you want to play kickball, then sometimes you're gonna get kicked."

"But, Momma, it wasn't like that."

She cut me off. "Stop being a tattletale and learn to get along."

What I learned was that there was never much point in trying to get help from Mom. There was no such thing as "getting along" with Judy; there was only getting out of her way. So I learned not to play kickball anymore. Instead, I stayed inside and devoured Nancy Drew books. With the library just a block away, I had an unlimited supply.

It wasn't as if Mom was any easier on Judy. The next summer, Judy went tearing around the bases and flung her arm against a metal play-set as she ran past. In pain, she left the game, walked home, and lay down on the couch, where she stayed for the rest of the evening. Occasionally, I'd hear her whimper.

Never before had I ever heard Judy whimper, but Mom didn't even seem to notice. She was bustling around as though Judy were invisible, and I could tell she was set on ignoring Judy.

I thought back to when Judy had broken her nose and split her face open on the school playground in Wichita. She'd gone tearing out for recess and had run full-on into the lowest of the metal pull-up bars. She fell unconscious and bled so much that kids came running in from the playground yelling, "Judy's dead!" For just a bit, I was distraught. But then a teacher thought to find me, and she said they had called my dad who was going to take Judy to the doctor. She wasn't dead, the teacher assured me.

That was so like Judy—hardheaded to the nth degree. She ran so headlong into that metal bar that she broke her face wide open, yet even when kids said she was dead, she didn't die. For a long time after that, I regularly asked God to forgive me for all the times I'd wished for a life without Judy.

"Momma, I think maybe Judy might need a doctor?" I finally ventured ever so tentatively, hoping not to make Mom mad. "It seems like she's really hurt."

"Well, if it hurts, then maybe that'll teach her not to go flinging her arm around." Mom turned back to her broom, and I knew not to say more.

Judy continued to whimper. She didn't get up to go to bed but just stayed there on the couch in her clothes. I brought her some water, but she refused it. And Mom just acted like Judy didn't exist and then went to bed herself.

I was so worried about Judy that I was lying awake when Dad got home from his night shift. As Mom and Dad talked, I listened as best I could. Dad wanted to know why Judy was on the couch, and Mom kept saying that Judy just needed to learn to watch where she was going. "She doesn't need a doctor," Mom insisted. But after a little while, Dad changed out of his inky work clothes, gathered up Judy, and drove off. When they came back, Judy had a cast. "It was broke," he said.

Of course, doctors were expensive, and money was always tight. Those realities had no doubt factored into Mom's reluctance to take Judy to a doctor. Mom herself went several years with a gap-toothed smile because when she had a couple teeth go bad, rather than spending the money to get crowns, she had the teeth pulled. Eventually, she got a partial plate, but those gaps were part of her smile for quite a while. There was always something else the money was needed for, and Mom put herself last. That's just how it was; doctor visits were a rarity.

Mom and Dad were both children of the Depression. Dad grew up on a cotton farm in North Texas, a few miles west from the then-tiny town of

Sanger. He was the seventh of nine siblings, one of whom died in infancy, and all of them born in a house without electricity, running water, or indoor plumbing. Dad walked into town to go to school, cutting through the fields when he could, and was always careful to skirt wide around some mean dogs on a neighbor's property. Even decades later, when we'd occasionally drive out on those country roads, just to reminisce or visit the old cemetery, Dad never failed to mention those dogs, their fearsomeness having cut a deep rut in his memory.

Except for the squirrels and rabbits they shot in the fields, the family of ten grew or raised almost all their own food. They grew their own vegetables, butchered their own hogs, milked their own cows, churned their own butter, and gathered their own eggs from their own chickens. Nobody else did much of anything for them. Dad's mom and four sisters sewed the family's clothes along with the quilts on the beds, and they still picked cotton in the fields too. By the time Dad was eight, his three older brothers had left home, so most of his memories were of picking cotton in rows alongside his sisters. He talked of picking as much as three hundred pounds a day, and for his whole life, it seemed he never forgot the stooping weight of that cotton sack on his back.

Schooling took second place to working on the farm. September after September, Dad would start the school year late so he could work the harvest, and then on his own, he'd have to catch up on all the schoolwork he'd missed. In the spring, he'd miss school again for the planting season. Dad often reminisced on how much he had envied the "city kids"—the kids of small-town Sanger—because they didn't always have to start out behind.

The family's farmhouse burned to the ground when Dad was eight, an event that, for his entire life, remained vividly present in his psyche. As he always recounted it, the family lost everything except "one old rickety rocking chair" that a neighbor managed to pull out from the fire. The family had gone into town for provisions, and just as they were returning, they saw the flames and smoke in the distance, knowing it was the direction of their house. "By the time we got there, it was all gone," said Dad.

The fire was determined to be arson, with speculation that it was done by someone whom Dad's hot-tempered father had offended. But no one was ever charged with the crime. Dad went to live for a while on an older brother's nearby farm, and the whole family set to work building a new house. When they had a roof and walls, they set to work building some beds, a table, and chairs. The family did it all themselves, and still tended the farm at the same time.

By contrast, Mom grew up as a city girl. During the Depression, her family raised rabbits for food and recycled every scrap of everything. Her family had left Illinois with nothing more than what they could pile in their car and had driven west with the desperate hope of starting a new life in California. Her older brother, Jack, had dropped out of high school to work with his dad in building houses.

Mom and Dad's Depression-era habits carried forward into our own household. We darned socks, patched shirts, and mended moth holes in our sweaters. Mom kept used pieces of aluminum foil on a shelf, and none of us ever dared use a piece just once. We shopped day-old bread and drank home-made iced tea—never sodas. Potato chips were unthinkable, something rich people ate. Once a month, when Mom would roast a chicken, she'd carefully pick all the tiny pieces off the carcass to make a casserole with the leftovers, and then she'd boil the neck and back to make a soup. Three meals for a family of six from a single chicken.

Judy was a picky eater, and often Mom would decide to teach her a lesson. "You'll sit at the table 'til you eat what's on your plate," she'd command. So Judy would sit there. Mom would launch into one of her lectures about the starving children in China, admonishing us to "be grateful for how good you've got it." I'd listen quietly and clean my plate, mentally vowing to take food to China someday, but Judy would sit with her jaw set in stone. Mom never won those battles.

The only time I joined Judy in her refusal to eat was when Mom served spinach. It was always the canned stuff—slimy, salty, and stringy. Judy and I would sit for what seemed like forever until, finally, when Mom had gone back in the kitchen, Judy would slop her spinach onto my plate, and with a grin, reach over and pinch me—hard. It was her way of saying "you better not tell or else." By then, the spinach was cold and even more awful than it had been at the start, but eventually, I would eat it.

Dinner time was often difficult for other reasons. Dad sat at the head of the table and everything turned on his moods. If he was in a good mood, things went smoothly. If he was in a bad mood, then we all lived and breathed with only one purpose—to avoid anything that might escalate his anger into rage. In truth, Dad's seething anger was almost worse than his rage, because it carried the anticipation of what would follow. But no matter how much the tension grew, we would all sit, heads down, and continue eating as though everything were perfectly normal, all the while waiting with dread for the full-on explosion that we sought to avoid but knew for sure was coming.

YEAR AFTER YEAR, Mom lined the four of us up for stair-step style photos, always in the same order based on our ages—Rita, Judy, Christa, and Nancy. She often talked about how the four of us could be like the singing Lennon Sisters on *The Lawrence Welk Show*. But of course, that was Mom's little fantasy, not ours. I was more enraptured with the magic sound of Myron Floren, Welk's longtime accordionist. Sometimes, Dad would even get up out of his chair and dance a little jig with me.

As our bodies began to change with adolescence, so too Judy's torments changed as she found new ways to humiliate me. She would often kick me in the crotch, pinch my nipples, and punch at my budding breasts. Since she was a leftie, it was the outer side of my right breast that often bore the bruises.

When I started wearing a bra, Judy would pop the back of it endlessly, and if I got annoyed, she'd reach around front and shove her hand under it for a painful squeeze. I learned that it was better to just let her pop the back.

Judy loved to follow up her torments by telling me that I didn't have any sense of humor, that I couldn't take a joke, that I was too sensitive. No matter how much she pinched, hit, jabbed, and taunted me, the problem was mine because, after all, she was just playing. If I cried, it only fueled her to hit me harder and then to follow up by calling me a crybaby.

To escape the worst of her, I learned avoidance tactics. For example, I gave up playing the card game Battle with her, because if I won, she'd punch me, and if she won, she'd punch me. Either way, I'd be bruised, so it was better not to play. Even years later, as adults, whenever Judy would want to play a card game at Thanksgiving, I would always bow out. I carried in my body and mind the near-constant threat of harm from her in childhood and adolescence, and the certainty that no one was ever going to protect me.

Birthdays were particularly bad. Judy twisted the notion of birthday spankings into a full-on license for unrestrained birthday beatings. Invariably, I'd wake up on my birthday with a clenched stomach, knowing what awaited. One birthday "spanking" was never enough. She felt fully entitled all day long.

So, I tried to be like the roly-poly bugs that I sometimes gathered into jars. I'd curl into a ball to protect myself, but of course, I didn't have an armored shell. And at nighttime, in our shared bedroom, there was nothing I could do. Sometimes, in the dark, I'd awaken in a panic, unable to breathe, with Judy holding the pillow over my face, growling in my ear that no one would ever know how I died. Then, she'd suddenly lift it, tell me to stop snoring, and slip back into her bed as though nothing had happened. One time, when she lifted the pillow, she explained how she had read that, without oxygen, a person would turn blue. While I lay gasping, she said she had wanted to see whether it was true—whether I would really turn blue.

There were other times when I'd wake up on the floor, flailing and crying because Judy had shoved me out of the bed. Smirking, she would pinch the skin over my ribs, twisting till she saw the pain in my face, and then she'd whisper, "You better not tell." So I didn't.

Judy had a knack for zeroing in on the most sensitive spots. For example, she knew how to target the most painful place on my knee where she would squeeze to the point of agony. Of course, she was also trying not to leave any visible marks. Not that anyone was looking. Once, she gouged out three deep bloody grooves on my shoulder with her fingernails. Usually, she just left small thin crescent moon bloodlines on my arms, but that time, she left long furrows and knew she'd made a mistake. I could see it in her face. But all it took was her threatening to kill me and I wore sleeves in the heat all summer long so that Mom wouldn't notice.

Even the dog was on Judy's side. If she took a notion, she'd provoke him to attack me. She'd yell, "Sic her, Frisky, sic her," and Frisky would immediately obey, while I would scurry on top of the dining table in terror. I'd stay there, thinking of all the homework I needed to be doing and hoping Mom would get home soon, while Judy would laugh in glee at my fear of the small pug, growling and leaping as if he would eat me alive.

I always wondered if Judy had gotten the idea to sic Frisky on me from listening to Uncle Jack and Mom talk about Oakie, the Doberman pinscher they'd grown up with. Jack loved to regale us with the story about how he'd trained Oakie to charge people. "He'd go running toward someone, his teeth bared and barking like he was gonna tear them apart," he'd chuckle. "Their eyes would get as big as saucers! They'd be terrified of this big lunging Doberman, and then Oakie would just skid to a stop right in front of them."

Jack invariably laughed himself to tears whenever he told this story, and Mom would join in. I always thought it sounded awful and imagined how I would feel if a big Doberman came charging toward me. But whenever I said anything, they would just dismiss me: "Oh, but he never actually hurt anyone."

Even when Judy wasn't inflicting pain, she was always messing with me. The notion of bodily boundaries simply didn't exist. For bath time, we weren't allowed to lock the bathroom door because, with five females sharing one bathroom, Mom said we needed to leave the door unlocked so that if someone had to pee, they could. As a practical matter, this meant Judy could come in any time she wanted and shove my head underwater. And if I locked the bathroom door, contrary to Mom's rule, Judy would just pick the lock with a paper clip.

Basically, Judy just did whatever she wanted to me. She would reach out to pop one of my pimples as though it were one of her own, and Mom practically encouraged her. "Let her help you," she'd say. "You don't want to walk around looking like that." Of course, more often than not, Judy's pimple-popping efforts just made things worse. She seldom washed her hands, and so, what started as an ordinary pimple would often become an angry infected blob.

WE DIDN'T KNOW why at the time, but Dad's rages grew more frequent in Farmers Branch, and Mom, not yet forty, began breathing into paper sacks to try to deal with her panic attacks. As kids, we often ended our days in fitful attempts at sleep, wondering whether the terror of the evening would wear off while Dad worked his night shift, or whether he'd arrive home in the early morning stomping his feet and slamming doors. Sometimes his rages would dissipate quickly, as though his demons just got tuckered out, but usually they lasted for days at a stretch. We were always holding our breath, waiting for the next volcano. Even Frisky, the dog, learned to stay under the table, out of reach from Dad's kicks.

I dealt with it all by playing the piano. But strangely, when I started getting serious about it, Mom became discouraging. "It's not practical," she'd say. "You're living in a fantasy."

I couldn't understand. Whenever some relative would visit, Mom would brag on me and insist I play for them. Though I played well, I never imagined the relatives really liked it much—they just sat politely with stiff smiles. Then afterwards, Mom would berate me. "What are you thinking, Christa? That you're going to be a concert pianist?" She said it was time for me to "grow up" and live in the "real world," and eventually, she insisted that if I wanted to take more lessons, I'd have to pay for them myself. That was hard to do with babysitting money and some cash-off-the-books work at the local five-and-dime. But I managed. And while Mom still demanded that I perform whenever anyone came by the house, behind the scenes it was another story. "How much longer are you going to keep up this fairy tale?" she'd ask.

WHEN MOM'S AUNT Dora died, she left Mom $500, and Mom decided to use that money to start taking classes at North Texas State. It was *her* money, she announced, and she was going to use it to fulfill her dream of getting a college degree.

Mom had only one semester at a junior college before marrying Dad, and she'd taken a couple more classes when we lived in Wichita, so she had a long way to go to get a degree. But Mom stuck with it, and three years later she graduated. Though the three of us younger kids missed her a lot—she stayed busy with schoolwork—I understood that she was doing something important, and I felt proud of her. Of course, she wasn't around much to intervene with Judy, but since she had seldom intervened before, I didn't notice any difference. Judy's brutality had *always* gone unchecked.

Nowadays, I look back and marvel at Mom's gumption. She was a woman in her forties who had already raised one kid to full-grown and had three more still at home, and she was a woman in a deeply troubled marriage who was often profoundly depressed. Still, she set her mind to getting a college degree. And she did. After she graduated, she got a job teaching second grade—by then I was halfway through high school.

2

God Loves You, Christa

*It's wrong what they say about the past . . . about how you can bury it.
Because the past claws its way out.*

—Khaled Hosseini

MY FIRST LIFE ended with an assault on a dark dirt road near the old Addison airport north of Dallas. There were many more assaults that followed, but that's where my mind returns most often. For fifty years, I have pictured myself on that dark road, pinned between the pastor's body and his baby-blue station wagon. Over and over again, the past keeps clawing its way out from the hellhole of Farmers Branch.

There's the me who existed *before* the dark road and the me who existed *after* it—the dehumanized ghost girl. But at the time, I didn't even realize I had died. And I didn't have a clue why I struggled so much for so many years to follow, constantly trying to figure out how to be human and whole again.

I think of that dark road as when it all began. It's a marking point. But really, I don't know when it began. *When did I become prey for the pastor?* Probably much sooner.

How many times did it happen? How many people knew? How many Bible verses did he weaponize?

By reducing my story to these kinds of calculations, it helps me detach from it, which helps because no one would ever want to be stuck inside *this* story, least of all me. Detached is far better, so I use tricks like this to force my mind out of the rut.

Despite the way my brain tends to fixate on that dark dirt road, maybe it all really began with his off-color jokes. Before the church bought him that baby-blue station wagon, he used to drive a '66 stick-shift Mustang, and after church, my friends and I would cram in to go to the Taco Bell or Baskin-Robbins. One of us always had to sit in the middle and scrunch up our knees in between the bucket seats, and invariably he'd crack a joke about how he was going to put his stick between our legs. It was the same joke every time, and we all just laughed. All of us. He was the pastor and we were just giggly girls.

Heck, we were such naive girls that when Cindy, age fifteen, announced she was getting married to a young soldier, we all thought it was romantic. When it turned out she was pregnant and had to drop out of school, we again imagined it as a fairy tale. But when I went to her baby shower, Cindy had a black eye. She said she'd bumped something or other, but I knew it wasn't true. Still, we all carried on, giggling and laughing, as though getting married at fifteen, dropping out of school, and wearing a black eye were the most exciting things in the world.

Worried, I tried later to tell Mom about Cindy's black eye, but Mom didn't want to hear about it. "She made her bed and now she's got to lie in it," she said.

"What does that mean?" I asked.

"You know. She's the one who got herself into this, so now she's got to take what goes with it. Just let that be a lesson."

I had no clue what kind of lesson Mom thought I was supposed to learn, but I knew she didn't want to talk about it, and after that, she forbade me from going over to see Cindy.

"What about when the baby comes?" I protested. "Can't I go see the baby?"

Mom said no. "She's a married woman now, and you don't need to be around that kind of influence."

Still, I continued to worry and decided to talk about it with the youth pastor, Tommy Gilmore. Before she got married, Cindy had been going to our church regularly—always catching a ride with a neighbor—and hanging out with our youth group. So Tommy knew her, and I thought for sure he'd figure out some way to help her. He didn't.

"She's not even a member," he said.

"But she has a black eye!" I told him again.

"Doesn't matter. She's not a member. So she's not our problem."

SINCE TOMMY WAS a touchy-feely kind of pastor, I didn't think much of it when an arm around my shoulder became a hand massaging my neck. Or when ordinary hugs became longer, pressed-in hugs. Or when holding hands in group prayer circles became holding hands in solitary prayers. Should I have realized something was amiss? We were praying, and he was the pastor.

Then came a hand goosing my butt when I got a drink at the water fountain, and then a hand on my knee, and then a hand going up my thigh. Though I sometimes felt uncomfortable—and even refrained from practicing the piano in the sanctuary because he interrupted me so often—never once did I imagine there was anything inappropriate going on. He was, after all, my pastor.

Then there were the times when he seemed to be all over me while we played Twister. It was a game he often brought out at youth group gatherings, and it never occurred to me—and apparently to no one else—to think there was anything inappropriate about the pastor playing it with the kids, twisting his body and pressing against us as he did. I thought it was just good clean Christian fun.

It was the same sort of thing when we played flag football. Somehow, he always wound up pushing me to the ground and then lying on top of me, as if he couldn't manage to just pull the flag. I didn't like it, but I didn't want to be a whiner. Everyone else acted as though it was just part of the fun. So I played along and laughed it off.

To this day, I still tend to mentally discount all that handsy stuff—maybe only because it was less horrible than all that followed—and I tell myself that things didn't really begin until that dark road near the Addison airport, where I jumped out of the car because I suddenly felt so afraid. But of course, he was way ahead of me, as though he had calculated in advance every move of that first unabashed assault.

"GROOMING": IT'S THE word everyone uses, but it doesn't begin to convey the full premeditated ferocity of what actually happens. Strangely, it's a word that carries a connotation of care. You might imagine someone tending to a horse and giving attention to its coat. But for the horse, there is no ulterior motive. By contrast, with the "grooming" of human children, there is profound conniving evil.

It began when I was fourteen or fifteen—it's hard to know. Apart from all the lewd jokes and handsy stuff, sometimes I think every single thing that ever happened in that church was a setup and part of the grooming for abuse. After all, as far back as I can remember, I was taught to be submissive and trusting of pastoral authority. "Trust and obey, for there's no other way." It was a hymn I'd sung a thousand times, and even though I knew it was about trusting God, it was the pastors who carried the authority to tell us what God wanted. My role was to "trust and obey."

Maybe it runs even deeper. The very essence of evangelical faith is the relinquishment of personal autonomy with an all-encompassing surrender to a higher authority. True love for Christ meant "dying to self." It's what that nauseating "I Surrender All" hymn was all about:

> All to Jesus I surrender
> All to Him I freely give

On countless Sundays, I'd stood singing every verse through interminable altar calls, sometimes weeping as I sang, praying others would find the path of surrender, even as I fervently renewed my own determination to live surrendered.

Of course, despite the words of the song, it's not really a "surrender" that you "freely give"; instead, it's a "surrender" given to avoid eternal hellfire. Sometimes I think this single hymn may say everything anyone needs to know about the faulty foundation for evangelical notions of consent: give everything or get damned for all eternity. Talk about a power differential. And once you "surrender all," that singular decision gives tacit consent, not only to God, but to the whole God-ordained chain of command: God, pastor, husband, wife, child. Kids are at the bottom, so kids are expected to surrender to pretty much everyone. Faith demands it. And I was a girl of infinite faith. Heck, if Abraham had told me to lie down on the sacrificial altar because God said he should plunge a knife into me, I might have hopped up onto that altar and shouted "Hallelujah!" That's how surrendered I was.

Like some indoctrinated Young Pioneer of the Soviet Union, I'd marched into the church sanctuary every summer from my earliest years, singing "Onward Christian Soldiers" at the top of my lungs. That was me, a soldier in the cause of Christ, determined to do whatever it took to further the mission.

And how many times had I recited Hebrews 13:17 in some Training Union memorization drill? "Obey them that have the rule over you, and submit your-selves, for they watch for your souls." That was God's word telling me that the pastors were the ones watching out for my soul, keeping me from eternal dam-nation in a literal hellfire. Disobedience was unthinkable.

Of course, back then, it never occurred to me to consider how conve-nient it was for the pastors that they got to channel God into telling every-one they should be obedient to *them*. Instead, that "trust and obey" stuff was so embedded it was as though the church had implanted some chip in my brain to control me from within. Nowadays, I find it impossible to seg-regate any part of my faith that didn't somehow factor into the grooming for abuse.

So, I have trouble pinpointing when it all began. If I count all the handsy stuff, it started sooner, and if I count all the grooming for submission, it started *a lot* sooner. But if I start counting at the dark road near the Addison airport, it began just after my sixteenth birthday. I choose the dark road, because the cal-culation from that point yields a smaller number of assaults and because the dark road was an overt, wholly unambiguous assault.

OF COURSE, I knew it had been wrong of me to be out there dancing on the football field in that short-skirted uniform. Brother Hayden preached that women who wore short skirts were "harlots" who would be cause for their "brothers" to sin. So, all on its own, the short skirt would have been bad enough, but I was also *dancing*—and in public. Brother Hayden regularly railed against dancing along with other sins like drinking and gambling and cards and spinner games—all the things good Christians weren't supposed to do.

Really good Baptists played dominoes, not cards, but even as a fervently faith-filled kid, I never could see how there was much difference. How could

Canasta be sinful when 42 wasn't? So, I never worried much about the card games. But I *did* worry about the dancing—maybe because I loved it so much. Or maybe because it made me feel rebellious and free.

Dancing with the other girls on the drill team took me outside my usual fretting. Moving in unison to the music—marching, kicking, and swaying—I felt as though I belonged. And as we performed under the Friday night lights, I sensed I was part of something bigger than myself. This was Texas, after all, where high school football was the be-all and end-all. So even though I knew it was wrong, I kept right on. Whenever Brother Hayden chose the sin of dancing as his Sunday night sermon, I just slunk down in my pew and waited for it to be over.

It was strange how Brother Hayden never preached against smoking cigarettes. Maybe it was because so many of the deacons smoked, and he didn't want to bite the hand that fed him. The deacons, after all, were the ones who recommended his annual pay raise to the congregation.

It used to drive Dad nuts to see Deacon Green out there in front of the church, chain-smoking one cigarette after another. "What kind of example does he think he's setting for all our kids?" he'd ask. Mom would tell him to let it go, but of course, that wasn't something Dad was good at.

"He could at least go sit in his car," he'd grumble. "Or he could go out back *behind* the church. But he stands right there in front, glad-handing everybody with that phony smile of his and all the while blowing smoke."

I used to worry that Dad might say something to Deacon Green, but fortunately, Dad didn't go to church very often because, usually, he slept in on Sunday mornings after having worked the Saturday night shift, running the presses at the *Dallas Morning News.* But even though Dad missed church services, he often read from his book of devotionals on Sunday afternoons. He kept it right by his chair along with a New Testament, and after our Sunday meal—often a big pot of pinto beans and cornbread—he'd take to his chair to read. Dad also liked to watch Billy Graham on TV, and sometimes Oral Roberts too.

During those years, Mom sought to honor the Sabbath by cooking up our Sunday beans the day before. That way, she wouldn't be doing the work of it on Sunday. She always used lots of bacon grease—scooping it out of a red Folgers can at the side of the stove. If there's one thing Mom taught me, it's that almost anything tastes better with bacon grease.

FROM MY EARLIEST memories, I'd been at the church whenever the doors were open. Sunday school and Sunday morning worship were only the beginning. There was also choir practice, Training Union, and the Sunday evening service. Then on Wednesdays, we had Girls' Auxiliary, and after that, Wednesday night prayer meeting. On Thursdays, there was "visitation," when we'd go out knocking on doors to invite people to our church. Occasionally, we had week-long revivals when I went every night, and in the summers, we had vacation Bible school, which I still went to as a teacher even when I got a bit older. In high school, I had piano lessons in the church sanctuary, taught by the church's music minister. I thanked him a hundred times for giving me lessons I could afford, but strangely, it wasn't until many years later when it occurred to me to wonder whether perhaps it was the church that owed *me* a thank-you. After all, they paid for the services of the Sunday morning organist and pianist, while I played for Wednesday nights and sometimes Sunday nights—and also occasionally for choir practice—without ever receiving a dime. But they allowed me access to the sanctuary whenever I wanted so that I could practice on the baby grand, and that was one more reason why I was always there.

The church was my life. It was the very air I breathed. And with that constrained perspective, I had no capacity to see the warning signs of what was to come.

In the months before it began, the two big debates at the church's business meetings—after Wednesday prayer meetings—had been whether to buy cushions for the pews and whether girls should be allowed to wear slacks at church camp. Of course, the men were the ones who actually did the debating while the women sat and nodded. The cushion question was decided quickly: there wouldn't be any. They were too expensive and, besides, as one of the deacons noted, since Christ had suffered so horribly for us, surely as Christians we could bear sitting on wooden pews for him. Maybe it would even help to remind us of Christ's suffering, he said.

The issue of girls wearing slacks was tougher. I sat in a hard pew and listened to the men debate about whether the immodesty of girls in slacks could be tolerated. Finally, it was decided that we could wear slacks on the bus to get to the camp, and for hikes at the camp, but not for chapel events. And they had to be slacks, not jeans. It was a decision that made me feel like we were a modern, progressive kind of church.

FROM MY EARLIEST days, I grew up singing about a Jesus who "loves the little children, all the children of the world; red and yellow, black and white." But of course, the children I saw in my Sunday school class were always and only white. Still, I unthinkingly believed the song. So, when I invited a Black friend to come to church with me, his reaction took me by surprise.

Ray shook his head. "Can't. They won't let me in the door," he said.

Stubbornly, I insisted he was wrong. "My church isn't like that," I argued. But of course, Ray was way more savvy than me. Patiently, he tried to tell me the reality of his world, but I remained unconvinced. So, the next Sunday, I stopped Tommy, the youth pastor, and asked him straight-up what would happen if I brought a Black friend to church with me. "The deacons will stop him at the door," he said, "and suggest a different church for his kind."

Stunned, I commenced to arguing. But Tommy just laughed at me. It was the same sort of condescending laugh Brother Hayden had given me a year earlier when I'd told him I felt called to be a pastor. "Girls can't be pastors," he'd said. "Maybe you can be the wife of a pastor." Now Tommy was stopping just short of patting me on the head like a four-year-old. "When you get older, you'll understand," he said. "They've got their own churches."

"But why?" I wailed. "He's my friend. Why can't I bring him *here*?"

"You're cute when you get mad," he snickered, "but you're just gonna have to wait 'til you grow up to understand. This is the way the *real* world is."

I kept on arguing, but Tommy just kept grinning. "There are lots of good churches for *his* people," Tommy said, "and he'll be more comfortable with his own kind anyway."

IT WAS ANOTHER day at home of curses and yelling and sending us all to hell. I was in the living room, trying to drown it all out by pounding out some Rachmaninoff, but even as I tried to ignore what was happening in the den, I could tell from the sound of it that things were bad. Rita was screaming. She was married by then but had moved back in with us while her husband was in Vietnam. When Mom started screaming too, I got up from the piano and peeked around the edge of the door frame.

Dad had Rita in a chokehold with her neck in the crook of his elbow. Mom and Judy were trying to pull him off; Nancy was cowering in the corner. Frozen, I took in the scene and then suddenly, I did the unthinkable. I ran for the phone. Not the one in the kitchen—it was unreachable—but the one that sat by my parents' bedside and that none of us kids ever used. I called the police.

I still remember how it felt, waiting as the rotary dial went around in surreal slow motion, unbelieving of what I was doing even as I was doing it, and thinking Dad would probably kill me.

After I hung up, I stepped back to the edge of the den and yelled that the police were on the way. Dad let go of Rita and skulked back to his bedroom. Rita took a deep breath. And everyone looked at me as if I'd gone berserk. By the time the police got to the house, none of us had much to say. The police didn't say much either; they just asked which church we went to. When we told them First Baptist, they called Brother Hayden.

He showed up right away and we all six sat around the table with him. Though Dad was sitting right there, looking steamed but acting calm, Brother Hayden directed his remarks mostly to Mom and the four of us. "Don't give him reasons to get angry," he counseled, and then he prayed for us. He also instructed us that we shouldn't talk about it with anyone else, and he assured us that he wouldn't tell anyone either. He said that taking care of our problems privately was important because it would be "a bad witness" to the community if people knew the police had been called to the home of a good Christian family like ours. "Think about the effect it would have on others," he said, looking straight at me when he said it.

Even then, some part of me knew it was crazy. My father was choking my sister, and Brother Hayden's advice was that we should worry about what others might think? Yet, he was our pastor. I felt duly admonished.

After Brother Hayden left, I went to my piano lesson at the church and pretended as though nothing had happened. But afterwards, Tommy came up behind me when I was at the water fountain. "I heard the police were at your house," he said, and he asked me to come to his office. There, he pried me with questions, and in truth, it didn't take much prying because it felt a relief to talk to someone.

In our house, we had the Brown version of the Vegas rule: What happened in the Brown house stayed in the Brown house. It was nobody else's business. So, for years, I had lugged around family secrets, carrying their weight like a sack of rocks on my back.

It was a sack whose existence I never even acknowledged. For example, it had never occurred to me to tell anyone that my sister beat up on me and my mom did nothing. Why would I? It was what was normal. Even as I got older and suspected that maybe some things *weren't* so normal—like Dad's rabid foaming-at-the-mouth rages—the familial code of silence still *felt* familiar. Pretending that nothing was happening was how we all got by.

This meant I was isolated emotionally and didn't allow myself any true closeness with anyone. Even with my best friends, I never talked about my family. But with Tommy, I finally broke the family code of secrecy—our omertà. And rather than yielding safety, it yielded only an even more stringent omertà—to not talk about Tommy either.

He said he wanted me to come talk with him every Sunday, in between my piano lesson and the start of choir practice. But he said I shouldn't tell anyone. "It would probably just make your parents mad if they knew you were talking about them," he cautioned. That made perfect sense to me.

Week after week, I went straight to Tommy's office after my piano lesson. The music minister—my piano teacher—had his office right next to Tommy's, so he almost certainly would have noticed, but he never said a word about it. Meanwhile, little by little, I grew more at ease in being alone with Tommy. Of course, to call it "counseling" would be a misnomer. He was the one who did most of the talking, all about the great things he was going to do for God. I just felt honored to be listening to a man whom God was going to use for accomplishing so much good.

Over and over, when he'd take us all home after church youth events, I wound up being the last one in the car. Then, after having dropped off everyone else, he would drive around in the dark, with him talking and me listening. As with his "counseling" sessions, they were always one-sided conversations, typically about his plans for furthering God's kingdom. But sometimes he veered onto other topics. Once he told me I reminded him of *Barbarella*, a movie he said was about "sex in space." Then he pulled over and took out a photo. It was a picture of the film's poster with Jane Fonda. I couldn't help but blush and he noticed. It was probably the first time I'd heard the word "sex" spoken out loud, except during health class. But Tommy told me it was wrong for me to get all nervous about it since sex was a gift from God. Other times, he would recite passages from the Song of Solomon, saying that I too had "doves' eyes" and a neck like "a tower of ivory." I was embarrassed, but mostly I just kept my head down and my mouth shut. When he started telling me I had "breasts like clusters of grapes," I was mortified to even hear the word "breasts" spoken out loud. But again, what could I say? He was reciting from God's holy word, and he was the pastor.

Nowadays I look back and see such a stark contrast between who he was—a grown married man who talked about *Barbarella* and sex in space—and who I was—a naive, nerdy, idealistic, true-believer church girl who went around singing "The Impossible Dream," believing that she herself would be "willing to march into hell for a heavenly cause."

JUST AFTER I turned sixteen, Tommy drove a bunch of us home after the first football game of the season. Since I was on the school drill team, I was still wearing my Lionette uniform with its tasseled white boots and sequined cowgirl hat. As usual, I was the last one left in the car.

He drove out on a dark road and pulled over. "Do you know what 'obsession' means?" he asked. Then he proceeded to explain it and told me he was obsessed with wanting to kiss me. He said that he thought about it all the time and that God wouldn't keep putting the thought into his mind if God didn't want him to act on it.

I didn't know what to say. I guess I was a late bloomer, but I had zero experience with boys, other than riding bikes and playing kickball with them. Until just a few weeks earlier, I'd had a full mouth of metal for four years of wearing braces—the old-fashioned kind. And the only experience I had with kissing was my bedtime pecks on the cheek for Mom.

So I sat there in the dark silence, feeling my sweat and trying to figure out what to say. As I stared down at my lap, I became hyper-focused on my exposed legs, so white they seemed to glow in the dark. Self-consciously, I tugged down the skirt of my Lionette uniform.

Finally, after I'd squirmed a while, he asked me directly, "Will you let me kiss you?"

"No."

When I hold that snapshot in my mind's eye, I feel proud of that girl. She said "No." She'd been raised from toddlerhood to be deferential and submissive to adults, and especially to pastors, and she still managed to say "No."

But of course, it didn't end there. I was no match for his persistence, and the outcome was inevitable.

Immediately, I felt that perhaps I'd been too abrupt. Or impolite. Maybe even rude. Since I didn't want to hurt his feelings, I tried to soften it. "You're like an uncle to me," I said, "or a big brother. I just don't understand."

"Silly goose." That's what Tommy sometimes called me. "Go home and pray about it. We'll talk again." So I did. Tommy instructed me to pray that God would empty me of myself and all my doubts, and would instead fill me with "Him." So that's what I prayed, but the questions and doubts didn't go away.

Neither did Tommy.

After that night, he asked for a kiss on every ride home. "What would be the harm with just one kiss?" he kept asking. And in "counseling" sessions, he would stand over me, gripping my shoulder and praying aloud: "Lord, please help Christa know and accept your will for her life so that she will submit to becoming my helpmeet in accordance with your holy plan."

I couldn't make sense of it, but even though I was a Bible drill champion and had memorized countless verses, I was no match for the pastor. If anything, it was my reverence for scripture that made me all the more susceptible to his twisting of it, as he launched a barrage of Bible verses to compel my balking teen self to stop resisting what God wanted of me.

"Lean not unto thine own understanding," he always recited, as he insisted it was a sin for me to keep trying so hard to understand. He said I needed to stop resisting and "let go and let God."

Finally, I did just that: I let go. I said "Okay." I thought one kiss was all he wanted and that, afterwards, everything could go back to normal. I thought that if I let him kiss me—just once—it would put an end to things and we wouldn't have to keep talking about it.

So Tommy drove that baby-blue station wagon out on that dark road near the old Addison airport. When he pulled over, I felt so fearful that I leaped out of the car. Having heard friends talk about making out in cars with their boyfriends, I knew I didn't want anything like *that*, and I thought it would be more formal—safer—if we were standing. Silly me.

There was no safe place, and I was already a cooked goose. With me trapped between the car and his body, his hands went everywhere—as if he had a dozen—and he invaded my mouth with his tongue. I pushed back at him, but neither the car nor his body would budge. Then he began licking my face— licking me! I stood as a frozen pillar, arms pressed against my sides, as he whispered in my ear, "It's all right. Nothing's happening. There's nothing wrong with this." Then he told me how much he loved me and how long he had waited for me and how much he had prayed about me. "God loves you, Christa."

From there, things went off the cliff and into the abyss. The abuse escalated. Each time, when he was done with me, he always ended by saying "God loves you, Christa." Nowadays, those words are so tainted that if someone tries to talk to me about "God's love," I'll catch a nauseating whiff of a sour, garlicky tobacco odor overlaid with a sickening mint sweetness—the smell of his breath. I recoil.

How many times did it happen? I feel like I should be able to answer this, as though I owe my body an accounting. So my mind goes through all sorts of landmarks for figuring out how many weeks the nightmare endured. It began in early September at the start of football season. Then in October, or maybe November, he drove me to the convention center in Fort Worth where the Baptist General Convention of Texas was having its annual meeting. *Didn't anyone wonder about a pastor showing up with a solitary young girl?* During the Christmas holidays, he recommended me to the Phipps as a babysitter and came over to get his fix after the kids were asleep. In January, on his birthday, he wanted "special favors" because he was feeling old. (He claimed he was turning thirty, but years later, I figured out he wasn't even honest about something as simple as his age.) On Valentine's Day, he left a small golden pin in my locker at school.

I never once wore it because I couldn't imagine what I would tell Mom about where I got it. In mid-March, he became enraged after I cut my hair. It was right before the Girls' Auxiliary convention in Brownwood, and his anger made me so distraught that I wound up talking about it with my best friend, Barb, while we stayed awake lying on mats in a school gymnasium surrounded by a hundred other girls there for the convention. Barb told me Tommy was right— that I should have asked his permission—and she took the fact of Tommy's "love" for me totally in stride. "If Tommy says it's God's will, then it's God's will and you shouldn't doubt him." Those were her words of wisdom; she was a born and bred fifteen-year-old Southern Baptist girl whose dad was a deacon. Finally, in late April, or maybe early May, there was the Girls' Auxiliary coronation ceremony, when I attained the highest rank of Queen Regent in Service—it was sort of like being an Eagle Scout for good Southern Baptist girls. After months of "servicing" the pastor, there I was walking down the church aisle in my long white gown, crown on my head, scepter in hand, and cape on my shoulders, receiving the pinnacle regalia.

So, I count from September through April as the time when he was sexually abusing me. At least seven and maybe eight months—almost all of my junior year in high school—when it was happening at least once a week, almost always on Sunday evenings. That adds up to about thirty times.

But sometimes it happened on *both* Wednesday and Sunday evenings. And sometimes he took me with him on Thursday visitation nights, when we'd go out telling people what a great church we had, and afterwards, he'd drive me out on some dark road. Then there were Saturday nights when he'd sometimes hire me to babysit while he took his wife, Sue, out to a movie. When it came time to drive me home, he'd tell Sue that he was going to drop by his office and would be late getting back. It wasn't necessarily a lie because sometimes he did indeed drop by his office, and he took me there with him, but other times, he drove me out on another dark road. He seemed to know where every dark road in the county was.

If I could add up all these other times, when it was *more* than once a week, I know that, in actuality, it would amount to *more* than thirty assaults. But does it really matter whether it was fifty times, or maybe only thirty, when my young body was rendered into a robotic sex toy? I tell myself it was "maybe only thirty," because even that number is too much for me to handle. The garish awful images that flash into my mind are too overwhelming, and the more I focus on them, the more my brain tries to white them out. Trying to recall every event—every sexual assault—is like driving headlong into a blizzard, disorienting and dangerous.

TOMMY ALWAYS HAD a Bible verse at the ready, and how could I argue with the Bible? I had known it always and only as the word of God. To have run from it would have been like trying to run from my own soul. So, little by little, I became compliant and numb. Still, I kept trying to understand, and in my stubborn efforts, my adolescent grandiosity collided with my boundless faith. He said that this was God's special role for me—I was "chosen"—and that I was predestined to be a helpmeet for him in his holy work of advancing God's kingdom. I believed that, in part, because I *wanted* to believe it. Doesn't every teenager want to be special? In my girlish, hyper-religious brain, I even imagined there was something holy going on.

"Ye are not your own." That was another one of the weaponized Bible verses that he would berate me with. In his translation, it meant that my body existed for the service of God and that it didn't belong to me. Of course, he was the one to tell me what God wanted because he was an "anointed one"—an ordained pastor, a man of God. No doubt many would say the verse is metaphorical, but I'd grown up in a faith that preached the Bible as the *literal* word of God. "The Bible says it, I believe it, that settles it." Raised with that mindset, biblical authority held enormous power.

So when Tommy hammered away at "ye are not your own," and chastised me for not turning my body over to "God's will," it started to make sense in my faith-addled brain. And it meshed with other lessons. From way back, I'd been taught that if I truly loved Christ, I had to be willing to "die to self." So, that's what I tried to do—to die to my own self. And the pastor took my sacrificial body and savaged it, all in the name of God.

For months, I still kept struggling to understand. *How could he and I be "married in God's eyes," like he said we were, when he already had a wife right here on earth—and a child too?* But Tommy said I needed to attune my imagination to "God's possibilities," because God's way would bring freedom from fretting. And always, there was his incessant drone of "live by faith."

"Be not conformed to this world," he'd recite, "but be ye transformed . . . that you may prove what is that good and acceptable and perfect will of God." It was still another verse that he'd use to insist I shouldn't consider the standards of "the world" and should instead place my trust in God's will for our relationship, because God's will was perfect. This was Tommy's way of telling me it didn't matter that he was already married, because the idea of one-man-one-woman was a standard of "the world," and God's will wasn't limited like "the world" was.

Yeah, it was twisted. All these years later, I still find it painful to realize that I actually believed it. *How could anyone be so stupid?* And yet, I was not in fact a stupid girl. Instead, I was a faith-filled girl, and that's different.

Tommy didn't like it when I asked too many questions. He would chastise me, asking, "Where would we all be if Mary hadn't trusted God even when her special role was something she couldn't understand?" For anyone raised evangelical, the answer to that question was "hell." If Mary hadn't been willing to trust in what God wanted of her, however crazy it seemed, then human beings for all time eternal would be in hell without a Savior. And we aren't talking some mere metaphorical hell. The church I grew up in dished out a constant threat of a hyper-violent hell where those who rejected God would burn forever in a fiery inferno without ever getting the relief of burning up.

So, the admonition to be like Mary weighed heavily. Not that I ever specifically imagined I would give birth to a Christ-child. I only believed what the pastor told me—that just as God had decreed a special role for Mary, so too did God have a special role for me. It wasn't my place to try to understand but to simply live by faith in submission to God's will. So that's what I did.

As a girl who loved God, how could I have done otherwise? The first time I ever held a whole quarter in my hand, I spent it at the five-and-dime to buy a tiny ceramic baby Jesus—"the babe, wrapped in swaddling clothes, lying in a manger." The option of saying no to God wasn't within the realm of possibility. Like a fish in a barrel, I was trapped by the immutable boundaries of my own faith-based identity.

Nowadays, I often think about Mary. Did she truly have the option and the power to say no? How could a naive young girl—fifteen at the oldest—consented to have her body "overshadowed" and impregnated by the ultimate authority figure, an all-powerful God? And if I believe that Mary consented to God's will, then how should I *not* believe that I too consented? After all, I too said "according to thy will," and I too was instructed by an emissary of God (albeit a pastor, not an angel), and I too answered the "call of God" on my life and complied, believing myself to be a servant of God. Yet today, if there's one thing I know for sure, it is this: compliance does not equal consent.

I expect some will consider me blasphemous to even imagine that I was somehow like the young Mary, or to imagine that Mary too was raped. But I wasn't the one who first came up with these comparisons. It was the pastor who specifically told me that I should be like Mary and have a faith like hers, trusting in God's will no matter how incomprehensible it seemed. So that's exactly what I tried to do—to have the kind of strong faith that Mary had. None of it made any sense, but I pondered it all in my heart, just the way Mary did.

Sometimes I *still* ponder it. The girl I was then—the girl of infinite faith—flat-out terrifies me. Yet she is a part of me. To feel even an inkling of her presence in my consciousness is for my whole body to feel itself at death's door and for my mind to sense a darkness so deep that I have to distract myself lest screams escape my throat. I feel I could be cousin to some religious terrorist somewhere, because a part of me understands—viscerally *knows*—the horror of how, for love of God, someone could be convinced to do almost anything. That's the girl I was—the girl who would do anything for God.

TOMMY CLAIMED HE was constantly praying about it all, asking God how he could love two women so completely, his wife and me. God had told him he had a plan, and Tommy knew for sure that God's plan was good. After all, "all things work together for good to them who love the Lord," he insisted, quoting Romans. When I voiced questions about *how* it could all be "for good," Tommy said my anxiety must be because I didn't love the Lord enough.

It mortified me to imagine that my love for the Lord might be faulty, so I tried to squelch my questions. Besides, I learned that if I pressed too hard, I might wind up getting the concubine lecture, and that one *really* bothered me. Tommy would talk about how God gave concubines to great godly men like King Solomon, suggesting that this was God's role for me as well. But I didn't want to be a concubine. Sure, concubines were in the Bible—including one who was cut up into twelve pieces—but I never could figure out exactly what a concubine actually was. A kept woman? A member of a harem? Tommy said a concubine was like a wife, but with less rank than the first wife.

Like so many of his explanations, I understood the words but I still didn't have a smidgen of comprehension. Since the thought that God might want me to serve as a concubine disturbed me so much—for reasons I couldn't explain—I learned not to push too hard for understanding and to simply accept his "all things work for good" answer.

Then there was his "I have come that they may have life and have it more abundantly" answer. He was big on that bit of scripture, proclaiming that everything we were doing was part of what it meant to have a more abundant life, and that the rules and limitations of "the world" were not ours, because we were true believers.

"God's ways are not our ways," he'd say, reciting Isaiah: "For as the heavens are higher than the earth, so are my ways higher than your ways . . . saith the Lord." As a girl for whom "saith the Lord" said everything, I accepted that as explanation for how I, too, could be Tommy's wife in God's eyes, even though he already had a wife. I also accepted that I could never tell anyone because, as he said, other people weren't mature enough believers and so they wouldn't understand.

Yeah. I bought that. If anything, I felt proud for being so mature in my faith that God would entrust me with such a special role.

It all became normal. Tommy could go straight from teaching our Training Union class, with plenty of scripture, to a quick session in his locked office with his hands under my bra, to walking out to take his place for the evening worship service, with hymns and hallelujahs flowing from his mouth. Over and over, he simply acted as though nothing had happened, and I followed his lead.

Yet, in truth, so much *did* happen in that office of his, and it also happened just about everywhere else at the church, even in the sanctuary. Not a single square foot of that church was safe or sacred. But of course, back then, I believed otherwise. Tommy told me otherwise. He said that since God had sanctioned his love of me, what he was doing to me was sanctified, which meant the sanctuary was the perfect place for us to be together.

Who was I to question it? God himself had told Tommy that this was what he wanted. It was God's will. And like scripture says: "He that doeth the will of God abideth forever."

It also happened at the parsonage. One of the worst times was when his wife, who was then about seven months pregnant, had gone out of town to visit her family, taking their toddler son with her. This meant Tommy had the house to himself. He pulled a couple beers from the fridge and insisted I drink. I was shocked. Because, of course, we were Baptists. Drinking alcohol was against our religion.

"Christa, I've told you before. The rules are for lesser believers. They're meant to protect them. Without rules, lesser believers might go down the wrong path. But for more mature believers like us, God's grace has opened up an infinite world of freedom. We don't have to worry about all those rules."

"I can do *all* things through Christ," he said, reciting from Philippians. Then followed the familiar soliloquy, one I'd heard so often I practically had it memorized.

"It doesn't say '*some*' things, Christa. It says '*all*' things. And *all* things means *all* things." I nodded as he continued, until finally, he ended it the way he always did, with an admonition: "Do not be anxious about anything."

If you weren't raised in the kind of church I was (and I hope you weren't), you might think those are just more words. But no, that's a Bible verse too, which is what makes it an admonition. That was the word of God telling me to "not be anxious." If I persisted in staying anxious anyway, then I would be rebelling against God.

Tommy shoved the beer in my hand. I didn't want it, but I took a sip. It tasted awful and I set it aside, but Tommy kept pushing it back at me, insisting I drink some more. Finally, he got so frustrated with me that he poured the beer into a glass, claiming it would taste better that way. It didn't. So I kept setting it aside and he kept putting it back in my hand. Back and forth we went, with me mostly just pretending to sip while he kept guzzling from the cans. At one point, I got up to walk around, and he yelled at me to get away from the window.

The next thing I remember is being naked on the bed on my stomach, and with that memory, the awful disjointed filmstrip in my mind starts running. *I'm crying and saying no and squirming. I can't move. His weight is on me and his beer-smelly voice is in my left ear. Afterwards, I'm standing naked in the bathroom with a washcloth while he yells at me to clean myself. I keep trying but he's upset with me and tells me I should "clean better down there." He's standing there, arms crossed, blocking the doorway. I'm crying. He hands me another washcloth and tells me to do a better job, but I can't figure out how I can possibly scrub myself any more thoroughly. Finally, he makes me stand in the shower and yells at me not to get my hair wet. It all seems strange, and I feel like I'm doing everything all wrong. It's a smallish shower stall, and I've never taken a shower before—only baths—so I focus my thoughts on trying to avoid getting my hair wet. I'm trying my best to do what he says, and yet he's clearly angry. Eventually, he lets me get out, and I dry off and put on my clothes. As we're going into the garage, his voice softens: "God loves you, Christa."*

In the garage, he directed me to get on the floorboard of the car. Obediently, I did. He didn't want anyone to see me as he drove to the shopping center where I had parked my bicycle.

In truth, I struggle to remember exactly what happened that day. In the surreal filmstrip that runs in my mind, there are gaps, which is probably just as well because the frames that are there are so awful I can scarcely bear to see them. I've always wondered whether he put something in the beer and drugged me. *Why else would he have been so infernally insistent that I had to drink?*

After that, he took to telling me what a terrible temptress I was. He said I had allowed Satan to enter into me, accused me of "harboring Satan," and berated me as "Satan's ally." The thought was terrifying.

How had Satan managed to take up residence inside me? I became obsessed with that question. Since I didn't know how Satan had gotten into me, I didn't know how to make Satan leave either. Nightmares began to plague me.

Finally, one day, Tommy took me into his office and made me kneel. Standing over me with one hand gripping my shoulder and the other hand raised, he prayed aloud, beseeching God to cast Satan from me and to cleanse my soul. My knees ached; my tears became a torrent; and still he kept praying for a hellish eternity. When he was done, far from feeling cleansed, I felt lower and more evil than ever.

I slithered away to go do my own praying. I did so desperately and without ceasing, but none of my prayers did any good. I begged God to keep me safe from Satan, but God was gone. He had left me utterly alone.

Before all this, God had been my constant companion, a presence as real to me as any physical being. But after Tommy's prayer, it felt as though even God turned away from me. Everything went dark inside me, and I didn't have a clue how to make the darkness leave me.

Convinced that I had harbored Satan, and perhaps still did, I grew more distraught. I was terrified that I would burn for all eternity in hell—the kind of literal hell that the pastor had so often pounded the pulpit about—the kind of hell where my thirst would never be quenched—the kind of hell where I would exist in excruciating unrelenting torture—the kind of hell where I would eternally hear only the sound of my own screams. My mind filled with the kind of hellfire images I'd visualized my whole life while sitting in church pews, except that this time, *I* was in those images.

Before, I had always assumed that hell didn't affect *me*, because I was saved. But the knowledge that I had harbored Satan changed everything. I became so distressed that, one day, I completely broke down during a piano lesson in the sanctuary, and I wound up telling the music minister—my piano teacher, Jimmy Moore—that I'd been having an "affair" with the youth pastor. "Will I go to hell?" I asked.

Moore stopped the lesson and took me into his office, the one right next to Tommy's, and demanded to know what I had done "exactly." I looked down at my lap. My mind flooded with images. I stayed quiet. How in the world could I answer that? How could I even muster the words to describe sexual acts—exactly—when I'd never even said such words to myself? I prayed for the earth to swallow me whole. I prayed for something—anything—that might remove me from that room. Yet there I sat, and Moore kept demanding I answer: "What exactly did you do?"

"Everything but . . ." I finally whispered, my voice trailing off.

"That's good," he said, and then—at last—he assured me that I wouldn't go to hell. I began to breathe again. "Have you told anyone else about this?" Moore asked, and reluctantly, I admitted that I'd told my friend Barb. Moore instructed me not to speak of it to anyone else. "It will be easier that way," he said. I didn't have a clue what "easier" even meant. But I was so fixated on avoiding the fires of hell that I readily promised I wouldn't tell anyone else.

"Just leave it in God's hands," said Moore. Then he pointed out that since Sue was pregnant, Tommy's marriage was probably suffering. From my perspective now, that seems a terrible explanation, but at the time, combined with everything Tommy had told me, it all made sense: Sue was pregnant, Tommy's marriage was going through a rough patch, and I had been a temptress who harbored Satan.

Obediently, I did exactly what Moore told me and didn't speak of it to anyone else. I didn't mention it to him again either, nor did he bring it up. The next week, I went to my piano lesson as usual and pretended as though nothing had ever happened. Moore pretended too.

Many years later, in my near-futile court case—futile because the statute of limitations had expired—I learned that nothing I said that day had come as a surprise to Moore. He had known about Tommy's abuse of me long before I broke down at that piano lesson, because Tommy himself had told him. Tommy was afraid a congregant had seen him "in a compromising position" with me and he had shared that worry with Moore, who then did absolutely nothing.

When I learned that Moore had known about the abuse even before I broke down at my piano lesson, I retched up everything in me. Some of the worst of what Tommy Gilmore did, along with the terror of his exorcism, happened *after* Moore knew. Moore could have prevented it, but he didn't. That knowledge nearly killed me. He was not only the church music minister but also my longtime piano teacher. He was someone I looked up to. Yet, my life and body had mattered so little that, even when Gilmore himself told of what he was doing to me, Moore still did nothing.

Others knew as well. The senior pastor pulled me aside one day and, out of the blue, told me I should rededicate my life to Christ. Desperately, I latched onto his advice, and the very next Sunday, I did exactly what he'd instructed—I rededicated my life to Christ. All the people said "Amen," and I didn't feel a bit different afterwards.

Meanwhile, in my high school English class, we were reading *The Scarlet Letter*. I felt kinship with Hester Prynne and saw myself as a scarlet letter wearer. It was the identity I had already absorbed from all that Tommy had said about how I'd harbored Satan. I wasn't a victim but an adulteress and seductress. And like Hester, alienated and alone, I resolved to make up for my sin by redoubling my efforts toward goodness.

3

Aftermath

I feared I might lose my faith. If you've never had a faith, you will not understand. . . . Everything is dying . . . everything that defined you is being burned away. . . . You feel exiled, as if you are lost in a dark wood. . . . The world was emptying itself of meaning. Everything was hollow.

—Witness 369A in *The Testaments* by Margaret Atwood

NOT LONG AFTER the music minister's humiliating "what exactly did you do" interrogation, Tommy left the church. As best I can figure, it wasn't what he'd done to me that prompted his departure; it was the fact that I had broken down and talked about it. After all, Tommy himself had spoken of it before that—had effectively confessed what he was doing—and neither Moore nor anyone else had thought any action was needed. They had apparently trusted that *they* could keep Tommy's conduct a secret, but after I broke down, they must have worried that they wouldn't be able to control *me*. So, it was only then that they concluded Tommy should move on, which he did, but only after he called me into his office one last time and insisted I apologize to his wife.

Obedient to the end, I blubbered and begged for Sue to forgive me for what I had done. She stood stone-faced and said, "I'll pray for you."

On the last Sunday Tommy was there, Brother Hayden preached from the pulpit about how blessed we'd all been to have such a great man of God in our church. Then, after the worship service, the church threw him a big potluck reception in the fellowship hall. The tables were laden with casseroles, Jello molds, potato salads, deviled eggs—*why were they called "deviled?"*—pies, pitchers of sweet tea, and more sticky banana pudding than even a whole church could possibly stomach.

I watched while my whole church family hugged Tommy, shook his hand, and wept tears for how much he had meant in their lives. As if I weren't already plenty brainwashed enough, that church reception furthered my incomprehension exponentially. The contrast was inescapable. The fault was unavoidable. He was a great man of God; I was a girl who had harbored Satan.

While I was left to worry feverishly and face the darkness alone, Tommy thrived. He moved on to become the children's minister at First Baptist Church of Tyler, which was a bigger and more prestigious church where, he told me, he would make more money. From there, he eventually became the children's minister at First Baptist Church of Atlanta, whose senior pastor was Charles Stanley, who became a Southern Baptist Convention president. And from there, he went to First Baptist Church of Oviedo, Florida, whose senior pastor, Dwayne Mercer, became a Florida Baptist Convention president.

Through Tommy Gilmore's entire career, there were always church leaders who knew what he had done, who knew that he had sexually abused a kid. But it simply never mattered. There was never any consequence. His ministerial career prospered.

MOSTLY, THROUGH ALL the months of abuse, I had simply pretended it wasn't happening. My family life had provided me with lots of practice in that mode of coping. It worked to get me through the worst of it and also to numb me to the madness that persisted even after the abuse had ended.

How could the person I was then have ever imagined putting a "rapist" label on a pastor? It wasn't within the realm of thinkability. He was a man of God. And how could the person I was then have ever imagined that all those Bible verses I'd memorized could become weapons? Everything got so twisted.

Strangely, it was the fact that Tommy was married that always worried me the most. Though he'd insisted that God would eventually bring us together in marriage on earth, I just couldn't imagine how *that* could possibly "work for good." *Wouldn't that mean his wife would have to die?* Somehow, it never occurred to me to labor over the fact that I was an underage kid. Or that he was my pastor. The wrongness of those facts—the criminality of them—eluded me until I was much older and had a kid of my own.

Meanwhile, I took on a label bestowed by my sister: "slut." One night, confused and distraught, and lying next to Judy in the darkness of our shared bedroom, I told her about what had happened with Tommy. "You slut," she hissed.

After that, I didn't speak of it again. Not for decades.

"BROTHER HAYDEN THINKS it would be good for you to stay busy." Mom said it matter-of-factly, as if that was all the explanation I should need for why I would be starting work at a job I'd never sought—a job at the Farmers Branch Public Library. She didn't explain *why* Brother Hayden thought the job would be good for me or how it had even come up in discussion. She'd arranged it without any input from me, and I would start work the next day. It was just a couple weeks after Tommy had left the church.

Working at the library meant I had to quit the Lionettes because I could no longer stay after school for practices. But I didn't fight Mom on it, because I had already concluded for myself that I should quit. I had convinced myself that everything had been my fault for parading around in that short Lionette skirt, and I was determined to be even more pure and holy than ever. That meant the short skirt had to go.

When I first started working at the library, it required that a married woman provide her husband's place of employment when she applied to get a library card. I listened to a few women argue about it with Joanne, who was in charge of circulation. "Why should I put down where my husband works when I'm working too and I'm the one who wants a card?" they'd ask. Joanne always stuck by her guns. She said the women probably wouldn't be working for very long anyway. But when Mrs. Honea got hired as a new head librarian, she put a stop to the policy. Never again did a married woman have to list her husband's employer to get a library card. Even as a teenager, I knew it was a small but important victory.

They differed vastly in their views of the world, but I loved both of those women. For all her talk about women being unlikely to stick with a job, Joanne herself worked at the library for well over a decade. And Mrs. Honea—a divorced woman raising a child on her own—had previously lived in Switzerland, a fact that made her, hands down, the most interesting person I'd ever met.

The library wound up being a natural fit. It became a sanctuary where I took solace in the quiet orderliness of its rows. Books had forever been my truest of safe places. I loved the very smell of them.

Also, I had learned a long time ago that books often gave better answers than people. In second grade, I tried to ask Mom what a "harelip" was. That was what some of the kids at school had been calling me. I had no idea what it meant, but since the kids who called me "harelip" were the same ones who taunted me about the heavy, clunky shoes I wore for my inward turning feet, I figured it wasn't anything good.

"I don't want to hear you whining," answered Mom harshly. "You should be grateful you're not in a wheelchair!"

It was an answer that made no sense. Of course, I was glad I wasn't in a wheelchair, but what did a wheelchair have to do with a "harelip"? I had no idea. The only thing I understood from Mom's answer was that it was something I shouldn't ask about again. So I didn't.

Instead, I determined that I would figure it out for myself. I surreptitiously took the dictionary off the shelf, waded through all the big words, and finally found "harelip." The definition said "cleft lip." I didn't know what a "cleft lip" was, so I looked that up too. But I still didn't understand. The dictionary said a "cleft" lip was "split." I thought that sounded like something bleeding, and I wasn't bleeding. My lip wasn't split. I just had a white line. I had asked Mom once before about the white line, and she said I was born that way. That meant there wasn't any split. I looked up "hare," too, and learned that a "hare" was a rabbit. But that didn't get me any closer to understanding why someone would call me a "harelip." And on and on it went, with seven-year-old me looking up all sorts of other words like "congenital" and "deformity," and I never did quite figure it out. It wasn't until the day I got braces on my teeth, when I was twelve, that I heard Mom tell Dr. Penley about the three surgeries I'd had as a baby and I finally understood that the white line was actually a scar.

But it was earlier, in second grade, when I was still trying to figure out what "harelip" meant, that I beat up a kid during recess at school. To this day, I can still call forth the memory of how good it felt. He'd been endlessly taunting me, and finally I went for him. I had him down in the dirt and was sitting on top of him, flailing away, when suddenly, out of the corner of my eye, I saw big shoes right next to me. I knew those big shoes meant big trouble, but I didn't care. I just kept on hitting him. Even when I heard the teacher's voice telling me to stop, I didn't.

Finally, the teacher pulled me off and told the boy to go inside and clean up. I waited for the inevitable punishment, but it never came. The teacher with the big shoes looked at me for a moment and walked away. All afternoon, I kept thinking I would get called to the principal's office, but I didn't. Then I thought the school had probably called my mom and that, for sure, I'd get a really bad spanking at home. But that didn't happen either. No one ever said a word. It was as though the whole thing had never occurred, except the boy never bothered me again.

NOT LONG AFTER Tommy moved on, Dad went to bat for Judy, which put him at odds with our pastor. The high school had offered a Bible history class, and it was taught by none other than our pastor, Glenn Hayden. Judy wound up getting a C, and Dad got pretty upset, not at Judy, but at Brother Hayden and the school. Judy had never gotten a C in anything, or even a B. I figured that she just hadn't given Brother Hayden the precise rote answers he wanted, or maybe she had dared to question him. Dad just couldn't imagine Judy legitimately making a C, so he petitioned to have the C removed from Judy's record so that it wouldn't calculate into her grade point average.

He and Mom went round and round about it. Mom thought he should just let it go, but Dad argued that the C shouldn't count because Brother Hayden wasn't a state-certified teacher. He said it was one thing if the school wanted to offer Bible history as something extracurricular, but it was another thing entirely for the church to claim that Brother Hayden could give out grades and that the school had to accept them. Besides, Judy didn't need the class to graduate.

Ultimately, Dad won the debate. His petition to the school district was granted, and the C was removed from Judy's transcript. With that blemish gone, Judy wound up being valedictorian of her graduating class, and so, like every other public high school valedictorian in Texas, she automatically got a four-year tuition scholarship for a state university.

AROUND THAT SAME time, Dad also got crossways with one of the deacons in the church. Mr. Adams was an insurance agent and almost every family in the congregation had given him their business, including us. But when he told Dad that our car had dented the car of another church member, Dad was furious. Mr. Adams claimed someone had seen our car drive off and that I had been behind the wheel. "You know how teenagers are," he told Dad, who questioned me about it and repeated to me what Mr. Adams had said.

I was horrified at being falsely accused by a deacon of the church, and I couldn't figure out why Mr. Adams would say such a thing. But from the get-go, Dad believed me. He knew that if I had hit another car, I would've told him. And our car bore no mark. Dad finally concluded that Mr. Adams had wanted to conjure an excuse for getting the insurance company to fix the other church member's car and decided the easiest way was to say the dent had been caused by a teenager whose family car was covered. Dad railed to Mom about how fraudulent it was.

The incident with Mr. Adams was the last straw for Dad, and I don't think he ever went back to church after that—not that he'd been going all that often before. Occasionally, Mr. Green or one of the other deacons would ask me about why my father wasn't in church, and I'd just shrug and say he had to work, which was mostly true. Then there were those times when Brother Hayden would start on a pulpit roll about how sinful it was to work on Sundays. It worried me, but whenever I asked Dad about it, he'd just say, "I figure God expects me to feed my family."

Many years later, I realized that Mr. Adams, Mr. Green, and all the other deacons had almost certainly known about what Tommy did to me. There they were criticizing my dad for working on Sundays when all the while they themselves were turning a blind eye to the youth pastor's sexual abuse of a child. I remembered, too, how just a few weeks after Tommy left, my friend Stuart told me that his dad wouldn't let him ride bikes with me anymore because he thought I might be a "bad influence." I was mystified and hurt. I'd known Stuart since I was ten years old, yet it suddenly seemed I'd acquired satanic cooties. Stuart's dad was a deacon.

So many people knew. I realize that now. The music minister, the senior pastor, the deacons, Tommy's wife, probably some of the others' wives, my friend Barb, my sister Judy, and even the pastor at another Baptist church in town. Almost certainly my mother knew as well. I didn't figure that last part out until decades later.

I did what everyone tells kids they should do. I told. But telling helped not one bit. It only made matters worse.

On the outside, I probably appeared normal to most people. I had a lot of crying jags at home, but still, I went to school and to work, and I mostly maintained my grades. They dropped just a little—from A-pluses to A-minuses—but not so much that anyone would take note. Normalcy was, however, a thin veneer. Inside I was dying.

I felt old, incredibly old. How could I be a normal adolescent, flirting with boys in the school hallway, when I had already experienced adult traumas? How could I engage with the giggling normalcy of other girls when what had happened to me couldn't even be spoken of, much less giggled about? I felt profoundly alone and alienated from my peers. It was as though I stood on the other side of a soundproof glass wall, always watching the ordinary lives of others, but always separated and disconnected.

Even God abandoned me. It wasn't a matter of unbelief, for unbelief would have been a mercy. Rather, it was as though God had become something monstrous—at least toward me—an uncaring and rejecting God who was prone to sadistic whims.

I started having nightmares combined with a sort of sleep paralysis. Night after night, I'd find myself terrified, but unable to move or make a sound. It felt like some heavy demon sitting on my chest and suffocating me. I grew afraid of sleep, and I drifted into a downward spiral. Mom took me to a doctor—an exceedingly rare event. He was a general practitioner whom I'd never seen before, and he talked to me for about two minutes.

"Your mom tells me you've been having some problems lately," he said. "Not acting like yourself. Is that right?"

"Well, yeah, I guess." That's what I said, though in truth, I had no clue what he was talking about or what Mom may have told him. But that's all it took for him to write me a prescription for Mellaril, a first-generation antipsychotic. The pills made me sleepy and dull, so I took them for only about a week. I never told Mom that I'd stopped, but she seemed to forget all about it anyway, never asking me whether I needed a refill.

Mom became convinced, though, that she could cure me of whatever affliction I was having by "laying on hands." It was a power she said her own mom had possessed, and she claimed to have it too. She'd place her hands on my head and then just sit there while I wondered what exactly she was healing me from. After one session, she gave me her cross necklace, and another time, her blue rosary beads—Mom had been raised Catholic. She said these things would protect me. From what, I wasn't sure.

4

German Fairy Tale

So we are a happy family and we have no
secrets from one another.
If we are unhappy,
we have to keep it a secret
and we are unhappy that we have to keep it a secret
and unhappy that we have to keep secret
the fact
that we have to keep it a secret
and that we are keeping all that secret.
But since we are a happy family you can see
this difficulty does not arise.

—R. D. Laing

MOM WAS SO depressed she could barely function. Nancy, in ninth grade, had already started coming home drunk. In my senior year, it was all I could do to rush home after school, get a fried egg sandwich packed into Dad's industrial metal lunchbox, char a couple wienies on the stovetop or open a can of Vienna sausages to shove down my own throat, and then get to my job at the library on time. When the library closed at 9 p.m., I'd rush home to try to clean the house a little. Mom had given up, and Nancy didn't care. Looking back on it, I can't imagine why I *did* care. It's not as if I ever had friends over. Mom's moods were too unpredictable. But the piles of dirty dishes kept building up, and the carpet of dog hair on the perpetually grungy linoleum floor disgusted me. So I'd try to do *something*, and then, when I was thoroughly exhausted, I'd stay up late to get schoolwork done. The next day, I'd do it all again.

During spring break, Judy came home from her freshman year of college and married Darrell. She was eighteen; Darrell was twenty-four. Dad never trusted him, Mom didn't like him, and I thought he was far too full of himself. Though he presented himself as an intellectual, I just thought he seemed patronizing and condescending. But Judy thought he was cool.

The day after Judy's wedding, Dad was in the same kind of over-the-top terror-dispensing rage that he'd entered after Rita's wedding. That time, it had lasted a solid month, and I think Mom could see that the same nightmare was unfolding again. Or maybe, since Mom, too, had been only eighteen when she married, Judy's wedding reminded her too much of her own forgotten dreams. While Dad was out in the yard, Mom took an overdose of sleeping pills.

She said she was just going to lie down and take a nap, and she gave me strict instructions not to bother her. "No matter what," she said.

Even though I was a pathologically obedient child, I sensed something was amiss, and after a while, I quietly turned the knob on the bedroom door, cracked it open, and peeked in on Mom. Then I pushed the door a little further. Tiptoeing closer, I whispered, "Mom?" But, though she was typically a light sleeper, she didn't move. I put my hand on her shoulder. "Mom?" She didn't respond. Finally, with fear mounting, I put both of my hands on both of her shoulders and shook them. She didn't even blink. I stood there looking at her, trying to figure it out. I saw the empty prescription bottle on the nightstand. I took in the silence. There was none of Mom's usual snoring, not even any sound of breathing that I could detect.

I tore out of the bedroom, ran down the hall and out into the yard. "Mom won't wake up," I yelled, but Dad had seen the look on my face and was already in motion. He took off toward the house, ran to the bedroom, gathered Mom in his arms, carried her to the car, put her on the back seat, and slammed the car in reverse.

A couple days later, when Mom came home from the hospital, she sat herself down on a bench at the back of the yard and stayed there until dark. I took food out to her, but she wouldn't have it. "I. Told. You. Not. To. Bother. Me." She emphasized each word in a hoarse and angry monotone. I tried to talk with her, but she just kept cutting me off with the exact same words over and over.

Each time, I felt the weight of Mom's rage and of my own guilt for having inter-rupted her "nap," and I wondered whether she would ever forgive me.

After all, I knew that Judy had never forgiven me for the time I told on *her*. She was four when she climbed up to open the medicine cabinet, pried open a bottle of aspirin, poured the pills in her mouth, and swallowed them with water, just like a grown-up would do. That was so like Judy. She always loved candy cigarettes too.

At age three, I dragged Mom into the bathroom to show her the empty bottle. Mom piled Judy and me into the car and rushed to the emergency room, where I sat, hands in my lap, and watched wide-eyed while they pumped Judy's stomach. It is my earliest memory, and it's something Judy never forgot either. She brought it up again and again, long into adulthood, always ending her reminiscence by calling me a "tattletale."

I didn't know how to help Mom and thought she might talk to Rita even though she wouldn't talk to me. So I called Rita, who was living in a neighbor-ing town with her husband, Richard. I begged her to come over and talk to Mom, but Rita said she had her own married life to worry about and that Mom would just have to sort things out for herself. So I was on my own.

I tried hard to hold things together those last few months of my senior year. Nancy, depressed and sometimes drunk, was no help. I begged her to straighten up, at least until Mom could recover, and I pleaded with her to stop back-talking Mom and to help out with chores. "And can't you please come home on time?" I seethed.

Nancy would hear none of it. "You aren't my mother," she'd slur.

At the time, she infuriated me. I felt like I was trying so hard and she was trying so little. But nowadays, I think Nancy, at age fourteen, may have been the first of us to realize how senseless it all was. Certainly, my strategy of trying to be Miss Perfectionist wasn't effective, and it made me ancient beyond my years. I learned to be un-sad, un-angry, and un-needy so I would be less of a bother, and in all that unconscious belief that perfectionism could protect me, I was wrong.

I've aged decades since those years in Farmers Branch, but though my numerical age has gotten larger, I think I was at my all-time oldest back then. Between Mom's depression, Dad's rage, and the cursed church of shame, by the time I entered adulthood, I was exhausted, as if I'd lived a whole life already. I've grown younger almost every year since leaving Farmers Branch, and every other thing I've ever done has been easy by comparison.

Ultimately, Dad's rage broke all of us during those worst years. Over and over, his eruptions transformed us into ash as we replayed our lunatic roles of trying to fend off the lava flow, only to be swallowed into searing darkness. Once, in desperation during one of Dad's rampages, Mom violated our code of silence and called Dad's sister, Opal. I asked Mom about it afterwards and she said she was just trying to do something—anything—to break the pattern. Of course, Dad immediately huffed off to work in the yard, so Opal didn't even talk to him. Instead, she asked Mom to put Nancy and me on the phone, and what Aunt Opal said was "Don't be fussin' any 'cause that's hard on your mom and dad"—as if we were somehow responsible for Dad's rage. I'm sure she meant well, but in those words, all I heard was the renewed hopelessness of trying to reach out for help. No one could save us. We were on our own.

I GOT A check from the Farmers Branch Women's Club for $200 for being the "outstanding girl graduate," a check from the PTA for $200 for graduating in the top ten—I was third—and a check for $500 from the Farmers Branch Rotary Club. With the money I'd saved from my library job and babysitting, and with the money Mom had promised as assistance for the first year of room and board expenses, I calculated that I could get through at least two years at North Texas State in Denton. I had tried to talk to Mom about the possibility of applying to some other schools, but she wouldn't hear of it. "You think you're gonna go to Radcliffe?" she'd cackled.

I'd mentioned Radcliffe and Vassar to Mom because Mrs. Holt, the school counselor, had talked with me about them. She'd been urging me to consider some private schools where she thought I'd be a good candidate for a scholarship. At first, I'd been so excited every time Mrs. Holt wanted to talk with me, but it got less exciting after I told Mom what Mrs. Holt had said and Mom just derided me.

After that, things just got awkward. Mrs. Holt kept calling me into her office to talk about things like grants, loans, scholarships, and work-study arrangements. She asked me over and over if my parents had filled out the financial aid forms. And over and over, I made excuses, telling her I lost them, or the dog chewed them, or I forgot them.

The truth was Dad just wouldn't do it. He refused to fill out the forms. "No daughter of mine is going to take government charity," he growled. "We work for what we get and we don't take money from others."

I tried to explain that, even though it was called a "financial aid" form, it was the same form they used for deciding about grants and scholarships. I wasn't asking for charity. "Why did I bother making such good grades if I can't even apply for scholarships?" I asked.

But Dad wouldn't hear of it. "If it's for a scholarship, then they don't need to know how much money I make," he said. "It's none of their goddamned business."

I argued and pleaded, but he said taking charity from the government was like taking money from other people. I begged Mom to talk to him, but she didn't want to risk sending him into a rage. "You'll go to North Texas and we'll help you for your first year. You don't need any of this other stuff anyway," she said.

Perhaps I should have told Mrs. Holt the truth, and maybe she would have talked to my parents, but that possibility never occurred to me. Talking to outsiders about family stuff was something we didn't do. Finally, Mrs. Holt gave up on me, and by then, it was a relief.

Back then, unless you were twenty-one or married or had lived on your own for a full year, you had to have your parents' signatures on the financial aid form. At least that's what I was told. So, unless I wanted to completely put off college and live on my own for a year, I wouldn't be getting any financial aid, and I sure as heck wouldn't be going anywhere other than North Texas State.

At the time, Dad's misplaced working-class pride seemed so limiting. But as an adult, I know that, in my whole life, I've never encountered another human being with such a strong work ethic. I benefited from that, not only from the hard-working example he set, but also from all his overtime pay that helped provide our family with a middle-class lifestyle. Lower middle class, for sure, but still middle-ish, and it was a much better life than what Dad had when he was young.

Once I asked Mom about some faint scars I'd glimpsed on Dad's back, and she told me about the time when his father had lashed him with a switch. Dad's offense? He'd been short a dime when he tried to buy a pair of shoes, and the merchant had told him to go ahead and take the shoes and pay the dime the next time he was in. A couple weeks later, Dad's father made the trip into town for supplies, and when he stopped at the general store, the merchant asked if he was going to pay the dime his son owed. His father paid it, but then went home and beat Dad brutally, because as Mom explained, "Browns don't ever make themselves beholden."

The story was hard for me to reconcile with the one encounter I'd had with Dad's father when I was about seven. He'd been a frail and gentle white-haired man with a cane, who had given me a silver dollar. That was the sum total of what I'd experienced of him. Nevertheless, I could see how the story might have something to do with why we were never allowed to borrow a cup of sugar or an egg from our neighbor. They borrowed from us all the time and seldom paid us back—Mom kept a mental tally—but we were strictly forbidden to borrow anything from them. We couldn't be "beholden."

Many years later, when Dad was frail, I got him talking one day about running because I wanted a subject that would take his mind off his pain. So I asked him about races he'd run in high school, and as he talked, his whole face grew less strained.

Then he began to tell me the story about the shoes. "I thought, with shoes like that, I'd be able to run like the wind." He beamed. He told me how he had saved some money from doing extra chores for neighbors—chores that were in addition to all the work he did on his own family's farm—and when he thought he'd saved enough, he went to buy the shoes. He was short a dime.

"A dime," he repeated, his voice starting to quiver. "A dime." His gaze journeyed off and his eyes filled with tears. "It was just a dime. I was gonna go back, but Dad got there before I did." He stopped then, staring out the window, and I didn't have the heart to try to push him into recounting the rest of it. We sat together in silence.

After a long wait, I said, "Those must've been *some* shoes, huh?"

He came back to himself and grinned from ear to ear. "Yes, they were. With those shoes on my feet, I could outrun all those smart-aleck city kids." I smiled, knowing that a lot of those "city kids" were really kids in a town that had a population of barely over one thousand.

The familial aversion to being "beholden" or to accepting any kind of charity was so deeply ingrained that some of Dad's siblings lit into him for using the

GI Bill to go to college and to get a low-interest, zero-down loan on a two-bed-room frame house in Denton. They called it "charity" and accused Dad of taking "unfair advantage," as if four years in the military, with much of it in combat, was somehow an "advantage." Mom told me Dad never got over their criticism; hard feelings lingered. He was the only one of his siblings who had served in the military, and this meant he was also the only one who had seen any part of the world outside of North Texas. And though he only managed to get about a semester's worth of college credits, none of his siblings had any college at all. These differences set him apart.

For example, I always thought it strange that Dad's siblings would readily use the "N-word" and Dad didn't. On trips to visit his relatives, I often sat around listening to the grown-ups talk and wondered why they kept saying the word my parents had insisted we should never ever say. Finally, one day when I was a teenager, I asked Dad how was it that his brothers and sisters all said the "N-word" and he didn't.

"They got shot at the same as me," he said. "And they bled the same. No difference."

That was it. Dad never was one to be long-winded.

AT THE END of my senior year, I wrote an essay that awarded me a trip to Germany as part of a summer exchange program sponsored by the Lions Club. It meant I would travel around Germany by bus for several weeks with other young Texans and then live with a family in Cologne for several weeks. I was thrilled. Not only was it a trip to Europe but it was a chance to finally get to meet my longtime Belgian pen pal in person. But Mom insisted on dragging me with her to talk to Brother Hayden about whether I should be allowed to go.

I knew that, after her suicide attempt, Mom had gone to several counseling sessions with Brother Hayden, but I couldn't imagine why she wanted me to talk to him about my trip, and I couldn't bear the thought that he might be able to veto it. But he gave his blessing, and with Brother Hayden's approval, Mom gave hers.

The trip meant I wouldn't be earning any income over the summer, which would cut into my finances for college. Even still, I calculated that I would have enough for the first couple years, particularly since Mom had promised that she and Dad would pay the cost of my room and board for the first year, just as they had for Rita and Judy. So I put up the deposit for a dorm room at North Texas State and made preparations for Germany.

Just before I was scheduled to leave, I arrived home after work to see one of my classmates sitting on the lime-green vinyl sofa in the den. She mumbled something about how she was just dropping by to wish me a good trip, but she was so obviously uncomfortable that I knew there had to be something more going on. Besides, though I'd known her since fifth grade, we'd never been close and the idea that she would suddenly drop by my house was bizarre.

The "something more" soon became apparent as the doorbell kept ringing and, one by one, more classmates and friends kept arriving. I was mortified. After not allowing me to attend any of the graduation parties at my friends' houses—because she feared there would be alcohol—Mom had asked me if I wanted to have a going-away party before my trip. I'd said no, and she'd given me her usual lecture on how I needed to be more "outgoing," but I'd still thought it was understood: no party.

Rita had asked about it too, and I'd told her the same thing: no party.

Yet there it was: a surprise party.

Mom had asked a friend from church to invite my church friends, and a friend from school to invite my school friends. The two worlds didn't mix. Most of my school friends lived in the well-to-do part of town, close to the country club. I'd been to their houses for weekend work sessions with the yearbook staff. They were the kind of houses that had real Kleenex boxes in the bathrooms, often inside color-coordinated containers. At my house, we all blew our noses on toilet paper.

It's not as if I'd ever pretended to be a rich kid, but I'd also been careful to never call attention to the differences in how we lived. Yet suddenly they were all in my house, with Mom serving up frozen cardboard-style pizza as if it were something special. At my friends' houses, they had always ordered pizza-parlor pizza, delivered.

While my school friends stayed in the house, my church friends separated out and went to the garage to play Ping-Pong, fetching errant balls from amid the paint cans. I tried to move back and forth between the two crowds—church friends and school friends—thinking that was what a good hostess should do.

But of course, I had no idea how to be a good hostess, particularly for a party I'd had no chance to plan, and besides, in my family, I had never seen any example. It wasn't as if Mom and Dad ever socialized.

I felt panicked with so many people in the house. Some of them were kids who had scarcely spoken to me in the school hallways, and now they were sizing up my home. My eyes kept seizing on the griminess of the vinyl floor and the dinginess of the old shag carpeting. Coming back in from the garage, I overheard Mark whispering to Shelly, "And have you seen the bathroom?" I was mortified. In that instant, I was filled with shame for the shabbiness of our home. It was why I'd gone all through high school without inviting friends to the house—that and the fear of what sort of mood Mom or Dad might be in. But in the end, all my efforts at fitting in had come crashing down.

I could tell by Mark and Shelly's faces that they too felt shame on realizing I'd overheard them. Then I felt even worse. I was ashamed of my shame, which had only served to make them feel shame. After all, why should they feel ashamed for noticing what I myself had noticed long ago—that their material lives were different from mine? Indeed, if I'd had someone to talk to, I might have said much the same thing on returning from one of their houses—"You should have seen the bathroom!"

Just about then, Mom shouted out a lively suggestion that we should all go in the living room to play pin-the-tail-on-the-donkey. I stood frozen, trying to convince my brain that she hadn't really said what I'd heard, but there she was, holding the donkey poster in her hands. Desperately, I tried to divert things by suggesting we play a spy-winking game. I tore strips of paper and marked one as the "spy." A dozen of us sat down and started playing, with whoever had drawn the "spy" trying to wink, unseen by others, so as to "kill" his target.

Mom and Rita came in to watch, and they sat laughing at us, which put a real damper on things. I saw the eyes rolling. I heard the sighs. People started making excuses to cut out. By nine o'clock, all my school friends had left. My church friends finished up a Ping-Pong game, and then they left too.

It was a disaster. I knew that the last memory most of my friends would have of me would be this memory of a fifth-grade style party on the tail of all their "we're almost adults" graduation parties—the parties I hadn't been allowed to attend. And though I'd managed to go all through high school without most of my friends ever seeing the inside of where I lived, the party showed it to all of them. At the last minute, just when I thought I was safe, I'd been exposed as a fraud. I wasn't like them and I never had been.

Even ninth-grader Nancy knew how awful it had been. "I'm sorry, Christa," she said as soon as everyone was gone.

The next day, Dad asked me about it. "I wasn't sure it was such a good idea," he said. "I told her she should ask you, but your mom said it had to be a surprise. So, was it okay?"

Mom was standing in the kitchen, wiping off some aluminum foil, but I knew she was in earshot. "Oh yeah. It was great," I answered. Mom smiled.

IN COLOGNE THAT summer, I experienced something new while living with my host family. With five children, their household had an air of cheerful chaos, but there was no undercurrent of anxiety. No fear lurking in the shadows. Although I didn't understand German, it seemed they were all polite and kind to one another. I never once heard anyone yell or even raise their voice. No one ever threw anything. No one hit anyone. They laughed together and seemed to enjoy one another's company.

True enough, they were a family far more affluent than mine, and that was part of what made their lives different. But it was something more. They were emotionally at ease. All of them seemed less stressed than members of my own family. The household was peaceful. On the one hand, it seemed a fairy tale, but on the other hand, it was a reality I saw day in and day out during my stay.

This was something I may have been incapable of even imagining if I had not seen it with that German family that summer. They gave me a vision of a different kind of life.

I CAME BACK from that summer trip to Germany to discover that Mom had stitched a new sunflower-print bedspread for me. It was the first thing I noticed when I set down my suitcase. Since Judy had gotten married before I went to Germany, I had the room to myself. But the new bedspread puzzled me because my plan was to move into the dorm in just a couple weeks. *Why would Mom*

make me a bedspread for a double bed when I'll be leaving soon and my dorm bed will be a twin? The answer revealed itself soon enough; the bedspread was a subterfuge.

It came time to pay the first month's rent for the dorm, and Mom informed me that they wouldn't be contributing anything toward my room and board. While I sat dazed, trying to absorb the impact of what she was saying, Mom rambled on and on about how living on campus was a way for girls to find a husband, and since that wasn't going to happen for me anyway, it didn't seem worth the cost. I could commute, she insisted. I tried to argue with her, saying I'd never imagined college as a husband-hunting venture, but in truth, I was so taken aback that my effort was weak. In any event, Mom had still another punch to deliver.

She set about berating me for being selfish and for thinking only of myself. After all, she explained, lots of families have one child who stays home and takes care of the parents. "In our family, you're the natural choice," she said, "since you're not likely to get married anyway." Again, I felt her words as a blow, but there was no fending her off. She was on a roll. "That's what's normal," she insisted. "When children grow up, one of them stays with the parents to take care of them. Look at Jack. That's what he did."

Mom's brother Jack had stayed a bachelor until his midforties, living at his parents' house and waiting to marry until they both died. Then he married an older, well-to-do woman, who wore gaudy jewelry, reeked of cloying perfume, and was always crabby. She and Jack had never seemed happy, and I always wondered why he married her. So I found it upsetting to imagine that my life could wind up like Jack's. Yet, that seemed to be exactly what Mom was contemplating for me.

In tears, I went to my room and pulled out my savings passbook. I ran the numbers every which way, but every calculation ended the same. If I went ahead and moved into the dorm, I would spend up all my savings in one year's time and would have nothing left for the second, third, and fourth years of college. It didn't seem likely that I would readily find a job in small-town Denton, competing against thousands of other college students, especially without a car. And I wasn't eligible for work-study jobs on campus since Dad had refused to fill out the financial aid forms. But if I stayed in Farmers Branch, I could continue working at the library, live at home, and save my money.

So, I did the practical thing. I watched as almost all my friends went off into the world, while I stayed behind in Farmers Branch and commuted to college.

～

AS TIME WENT by, I set aside the painfulness of what Mom had said and told myself that my parents had probably been going through a time when money was even tighter than usual. That was something I could understand, so I believed their practice of paying for their daughters' first year of college living expenses had simply come to a natural halt after Rita and Judy. But three years later, when they resumed the practice for Nancy's first year of college, it was hard to stomach.

I would be the only daughter who didn't get any help for the first year of college. It was something that occasionally weighed on my mind through the years, and so one day, after I was married with a kid of my own, I broached the topic with Mom and told her how I'd always wondered why they'd been willing to help Nancy with her first year of college but not me.

We were folding clothes on the dining table, and Dad was in the recliner watching a football game. "I made great grades," I said. "But it was just so hard to not have any help. I just never did understand it."

"Oh, but I always knew you'd make it no matter what," Mom responded breezily. "One way or another, I knew *you'd* find a way to finish and get your degree. But with Nancy, I wasn't so sure. She wasn't such a hard worker, and I was afraid that if we didn't help her, she'd drop out or maybe wouldn't even go to college at all. Nancy *needed* our help. You didn't."

While I was still pondering that, relieved to hear Mom at least allowing that what I was saying was true and not trying to convince me that things had been otherwise, Dad suddenly looked up from the TV. "We didn't help Christa?" he asked.

"No, Chuck, she didn't need it," Mom answered, sounding instantly exasperated.

"We agreed to help all four."

"But Christa didn't need it. She did fine."

Dad harrumphed, got up from his football game, and walked out to the yard. But Mom still had more to say to me. "You remember how things were back then—I needed you."

"What?"

"I needed you. Rita was gone. Judy was gone. And then you were gone to Germany for the summer, and I realized how much I needed to have you here. Nancy wasn't any help, and I knew that if we didn't pay your room and board, you'd probably keep your job at the library and live at home."

There it was. Something that finally had a ring of truth. And of course, she had guessed right: when she backed out of paying for my room and board, I had stayed home and commuted to college. Mom had known me well enough to accurately predict my behavior.

I looked out the sliding glass door at Dad, bent over and digging hard at something just beyond the patio, hitting the dirt over and over with his hand spade. I wanted to feel angry too, but all I felt was relief. Mom had given me the rock-bottom truth, which was something she ordinarily avoided. "Thanks for telling me, Mom."

5

Vomit-Cleaner

We honor our parents by not accepting as the final equation the most troubling characteristics of our relationship.

—Bruce Springsteen

THE FIRST TIME Mom slapped me, she connected. Full force. The second time, I dodged, and she, probably loaded on sleeping pills, fell to the floor.

Living at home that freshman year of college was a bad year from start to finish. Mom was flat-out crazy with crying jags, and fifteen-year-old Nancy was starting to double down on vodka and beer. Late at night, her friends would drop her off on the porch, ring the doorbell, and take off. I'd open the door to find Nancy barely able to stand or sitting on the step. Often, she would puke all over the living room carpet as soon as she stepped inside. I'd scream at her— "Not here, not here"—and try to push her toward the bathroom, but she would just stand there, glassy-eyed and wobbling, until what had to come up came up.

Then she would lurch away to her bedroom, leaving me to fight back my own nausea and clean up the mess. Mom was usually already in bed and oblivious, and I knew the mess had better not be there when Dad got home early in the morning from his night shift.

Once I tried waiting for Nancy with a bucket. But even though I held it right in front of her, Nancy still managed to turn her head and miss.

One night, when Mom stumbled out half-asleep, I'd had enough. "Why do I always have to clean up Nancy's mess?" I yelled. "You're her mother, not me."

The slap landed hard and sudden. That was the first time.

"Momma!" I cried out. Like a child. Instinctively. As though the mother who had slapped me would also be the mother to protect me.

"If you want to live in this house, you'll clean up after your sister," Mom screamed. "Now clean it up!"

"I'm sorry," I whimpered, but Mom had already turned and was shuffling back to her bedroom. Sobbing, I dropped to my knees and returned to the task of cleaning Nancy's vomit out of the carpet. Holding back my own retch, I frayed the carpet threads, trying futilely to rub out not just the vomit but the hatred in Mom's voice.

When I was finally ready to crawl into bed myself, I paused for a long stretch in front of the bathroom mirror. My face appeared so dead I hardly recognized myself. Like some animal on the side of the road, I looked barely alive and too weak to even cry. *Is this why Mom wanted me to stay home from college and commute? Is this who I am? My sister's vomit-cleaner?*

The next morning, it was always as though nothing had happened. Nancy never even seemed to remember—and maybe she didn't. Mom would say nothing at all to me or to Nancy. The next weekend, it would happen all over again.

Most of the time, I just quietly did what needed to be done, but eventually, there came another night when, exhausted and frustrated, I yelled at Nancy and woke up Mom. I'd been trying to steer Nancy to the bathroom and had almost gotten her onto the den's linoleum when she stalled and threw up all over the last two feet of carpet.

While Nancy stumbled off to bed, I stood there over the vomit and glared at Mom. "Why can't Nancy clean up her own mess? Why does it have to be me?"

That time, I saw the slap coming and took a half step backwards. Expecting to connect with my face, Mom lost her balance and fell to the floor.

"I'm sorry, Momma, I'm so sorry." I said it over and over as I helped her get on her feet. Once upright, she shuffled back to her bed without saying a word. I scrubbed out the vomit.

I wish I could tell you why I apologized. Was it because I hadn't stood still and let the slap connect?

I STARTED COMMUTING to college with two friends, Annie and Mike. On the way home from the very first day, Annie's car went off the road. The rain was coming down in sheets, and the car hydroplaned, hit a guardrail, and rolled down the embankment on the south side of the bridge over Lake Lewisville. We wound up in a wet ravine.

Stunned, we sat there for a while until Mike took charge. He'd been riding shotgun, and he turned to look at me in the back seat, asking if I was okay. I could see his face only a couple feet in front of me, yet his voice seemed far away. Miraculously, none of us were seriously hurt. We were lucky not to have gone into the lake.

Annie and Mike set off walking to find a payphone to call Annie's dad. (This was long before cell phones.) They asked me to stay with the car in case a tow truck got there before they could walk back, so I did. After a long stretch of time, a car pulled up on the shoulder above the embankment. It was Annie's dad, who had sped over after he got their call. He'd found Annie and Mike near a payphone under an awning, and then driven to find me with the car. He stood for a while sizing up the wrecked car, and then he drove the three of us back to Farmers Branch.

As soon as I stepped in the door, Mom started yelling at me. "Where have you been? You're late to work and Mrs. Honea's been calling."

"We had a wreck," I said, suddenly realizing that I was indeed late for my job at the library. I'd been so stunned from the crash that my job hadn't even crossed my mind.

Mom kept yelling at me even as I continued trying to explain. Over and over, she insisted I should have called, accused me of being with a boy, and berated me for being irresponsible and thoughtless. She wouldn't hear my excuse that I had stayed with the car, nor my explanation that we had been just past the lake and not near any phones.

"Where was I gonna call?" I asked.

"You could have found a phone if you'd wanted to!" she screamed back.

Finally, when I had sufficiently apologized and Mom was all screamed out, she let me walk away. I got into some dry clothes and hustled myself over to the library. I was three hours late, but the library ladies had a totally different reaction. I told them how sorry I was to be late, but when they learned I'd been in a wreck, they all gathered around to make sure I was okay. Mrs. Honea, Mrs.

Miller, Joanne, and Lucille all listened to me and questioned me about my neck and elbows. Then Mrs. Honea said that, after such a bad experience, I shouldn't worry about work, and she urged me to go home and go to bed early. But I told her I'd be happy just to shelve some books. The library felt safe, and I could disappear into the rows of books, far from the sound of Mom's yelling.

A WEEK OR so before Christmas, Mom went into the hospital for surgery. Convinced she had cancer, she was scared. So were we. While Mom was being operated on, Rita, Nancy, Dad, and I sat in the waiting room, with no sound but the ticking of the clock on the wall. Suddenly, I felt jolted from the solemnity of our vigil by a wave of relief washing over me, and I knew Mom was okay. I knew it with such electric certainty that I let out all my breath with a snort, and my face broke into a smile.

Glaring, Rita reached over and slammed her fist down on my thigh. "How dare you?" she hissed. "Your mother is on the operating table and you're laughing?"

Before I could answer, the surgeon walked in, still wearing his scrubs. He said that Mom didn't have cancer, the tumor was benign, and the surgery had gone smoothly—a hysterectomy. Mom went home a few days later.

Her recovery was slow, and her moods could shift with alarming speed. There was no way to ever know which version of Mom I'd find when I got home from school—the weepy version, the angry version, or the mean version. A week or so after Christmas, she lashed out not only at me but at my boyfriend, Kevin.

I had made a special dinner for the two of us, with beef stroganoff and a strawberry cream cheese tart. Mom had said she was fine with my plan to fix dinner for Kevin because she was going to bed early every night anyway and wouldn't be trying to watch anything on TV. So, since Dad always left for his night shift around six thirty and Nancy was staying the night with a friend, I had decided it was a chance to invite Kevin. All he had ever done before was step into the living room, and I wanted to show off my cooking skills. I had even bought canned mushrooms, imagining that such an exotic food would leave an impression.

"Hamburger meat?" he said when I served it up.

"It's a stroganoff. That's what the recipe called for. And it has mushrooms!"

Seeing my crestfallen face, he tried to backpedal and told me it was delicious. He had just been expecting something else, he said. "Like maybe a steak?"

I don't think I had ever even seen a steak—not like what he was talking about—and I wouldn't have had the slightest notion of how to cook one. In my family, the only kind of "steak" we ever ate was the Salisbury steak in Banquet TV dinners, and that was basically just a ground beef patty with onion soup sauce. So, the stroganoff wasn't half so impressive as I had anticipated, but at least there was the strawberry cream cheese tart. He ate three pieces, and I felt like a homemaking goddess.

After eating, we moved to the living room couch, where we sat listening to "Let It Be" on a boom box. We had a dim lamp on, and we were using shared headphones so as not to wake Mom. After a while, we started making out, which was the first time we had begun to get close. Though I was eighteen by then, I was so messed up that I couldn't let myself have a normal adolescent boyfriend-girlfriend relationship. Vaguely terrified of "sins of the flesh," I had been determined not to be ensnared. So, until that night, I had resisted all the moves of an ordinary teenage boy—a boy who actually cared about me.

Suddenly, Mom's voice bellowed from around the corner of the doorway.

"Christa, get out here! Now!"

I leaped up, stepped into the next room, and Mom started in. She was flat-out berserk with rage. Spitting through her teeth, she called me a "slut," and she accused Kevin of taking advantage of her post-surgical weakness to move in on me. She started screaming that she wanted him out of her house. Glancing over my shoulder, I saw Kevin quietly moving toward the door. He left without a word while Mom kept yelling.

When she'd exhausted herself, Mom stumbled back to bed, and I told myself that we would work it all out in the morning. I figured Mom was just messed up because she was taking pain pills, and I suspected she was taking sleeping pills again too. I knew she was wrong about Kevin because I hadn't even told him about Mom's hysterectomy—that would have been too embarrassing. All I'd told him was that Mom was planning to go to bed early.

The next morning, I tried to explain that to Mom, but she was still angry. She banned Kevin from ever again stepping foot into our house.

MOM BASICALLY HAD two modes in those days: a depressed sulk and angry outbursts. Either way, she wasn't emotionally available to either Nancy or me. To the contrary, day after day, our Sisyphean task was to try to prop her up. She managed to stick with her job teaching second grade at a nearby school, but beyond that, her energy was completely gone.

I pretty much lost myself in trying to keep the household together—always trying to maintain a calm and stress-free environment for Mom's sake—as if I could rein in the power of volcanic forces. I was chronically exhausted and vaguely realized that my own life had drifted to the sidelines. Sensing the unspoken truth that my mother's emotional health was somehow tied to how much of myself I depleted for her, I vowed that, once I left that house, I would never again allow myself to become so enmeshed in Mom's emotional emptiness.

When Mom was having a quiet bout, she would walk aimlessly around the house, weeping. But at other times, in fury, she flung dishes to the floor and launched plates at the wall. (Fortunately, I'd moved her good Franciscan plates—the ones we used only for holidays—to the back of the bottom cabinet, out of easy reach.) Then, after exhausting herself, she'd retreat to the bench in the back of the yard, and I would clean up the broken shards so that it would look as though nothing had happened when she came back in.

Nancy and I could do nothing right during those times. Mom's bouts just had to run their course. So we relished the rare calm moments, which typically centered around plates of spaghetti or bowls of Rocky Road ice cream. Food was how we comforted ourselves and bonded.

Depression was simply not acknowledged. *Pick yourself up. Try harder. Work harder. No whining.* These were the mantras of our house. So it never occurred to us to think that Mom was ill. Nor did it occur to any of us to take note of Nancy's early depression, which was masked by binge drinking.

For Mom, the mere thought of any kind of mental illness must have been terrifying. When she was ten years old, her mother had been committed to a thirty-day stay, and she had watched as her mother was taken away in a strait-jacket. I knew because, during my senior year of high school, when I'd been crying a lot, Mom suddenly told me that if I didn't shape up, they'd have to put me in a straitjacket like they did her mother.

"What's a straitjacket?" I asked.

"It's what they put people in when they act up," said Mom, and then she told me about how they'd forcibly removed her mother, limbs bound, when she caused trouble.

At the library, I'd gone straight to the dictionary and looked up "strait-jacket," and after that, I learned to cry invisibly. I knew I didn't want to get carted off like my grandmother. She had no doubt been unmoored by the death of her toddler son—Mom's younger brother, Georgie—and she had always been eccentric. Finally, she had her autonomy completely taken away.

Years later, after Mom died, while clearing out some old documents and letters, I learned that my grandmother had divorced my grandfather not long after being released from that thirty-day commitment. She had stayed in Illinois with her two daughters—my mom and her sister Ava—while my grandfather moved to California with their son Jack, who had dropped out of high school to go with him.

So often, I had heard Mom talk about that move to California and never once had I ever heard her say a word about her parents' divorce or about the fact that her father and brother had moved out a couple years ahead of them. "It was the Depression" was how she always explained the move, telling me how her family had lost their home and piled the last of their belongings onto the top of their car and headed west.

I looked at letters that Mom's father had written to his sister while he was in California. The divorce was already a done deal by then, but he was com-plaining about Virginia—my grandmother—and how he was "determined not to let her break up the family."

"I'm determined to do whatever it takes," he wrote.

Ultimately, he succeeded in convincing my grandmother to bring their daughters—my mom and Ava—to California to join him and Jack. There, the two of them remarried each other. But then, about seven years later, she was committed permanently to a psychiatric hospital, with her husband—my grandfather—named as her guardian. She lost her agency and never recovered it. When my grandfather died, my uncle Jack stepped into the role as guardian, and by the time my grandmother died, she'd spent nearly twenty years institutionalized.

With that kind of familial history, it didn't sit well whenever Mom tried to tell Dad that he needed "help," or that he had a "chemical imbalance." Dad never failed to point out that it wasn't *his* family who had the problem. He wasn't about to give anyone the chance to do to him what Mom's father and brother had done to her mother.

So, the thought of "mental illness" seemed more akin to a looming threat than any sort of medical problem. Seeking "help" was seen as the road to oblivion.

It wasn't only Mom who was depressed; Dad struggled as well. He had never fully recovered from the fusion back surgery he'd had a few years earlier, and he was in near-constant pain. Nowadays, there's a name for it: failed back surgery syndrome. But back then, we just knew he was hell to live with.

It was always an illusion to imagine that we could fend off one of Dad's rages. Yet we tried. We were obsessively careful to make sure the TV schedule was precisely in its place, and we never left a room without turning off the light. But it was an impossible task. Anything at any time could set him off. If Mom answered a random call from a telephone solicitor, Dad would seethe in some paranoid rage about who she was talking to or about how the call was from someone "out to get him" or "up to no good." If one of us answered and said "the lady of the house isn't available," Dad would yell at us that we should have just hung up. With a sneer, he'd say it wasn't anyone's business whether "the lady of the house" was available. Or, if he was already riled up, he'd say it was probably people spying on us. Then the next escalation would be to blame us for having answered the phone at all. But if we let it keep ringing, he'd rage about why we didn't answer the goddamned phone. Suffice it to say that I grew to hate hearing the phone ring. Nothing good would come from it. About the only thing worse was when some unknown soul would knock at our door. Then only heaven could help us.

I wrote a song about the craziness of things Dad blew up about, and though I can't remember all the verses, the chorus went like this:

It's always somethin'.
It's never nothin'.
We can't do nothin'
To keep from doin' somethin'.

When things were really berserk, I'd softly hum my song and even Mom would smile a little.

Dad's explosive rages were often followed by weeks of scowling glares. We were always left wondering whether the first eruption would be followed by a second, or whether the scowls would subside into a fraught normalcy. It was a normalcy so incomprehensible that I used to wish my dad were an alcoholic. I told myself that if he were a drinker, it could at least provide some explanation. But Dad never touched alcohol—he'd had too much of a Baptist upbringing for that—and of course it was lunacy of me to wish for it. But when you live in a crazy house, you sometimes grasp for crazy answers. Mom always explained it by saying that he was a "Dr. Jekyll and Mr. Hyde," but to me, that seemed more like a description than an explanation.

Growing up in such an unpredictable environment, with an explosive father and an often mentally unstable mother, I became hyper-attuned to every nuance of human gesture, always seeking to fend off the next apocalypse. It's a trait I still retain, though with less desperation behind it. I always knew that the smallest of things—the slight rise in a voice, the twitch of an eye, the flaring of Dad's nostrils, the curl of his lip, a wateriness in Mom's eyes, a drop of blood on a torn cuticle, a shift in body weight—could signal big things in the making. And big things could suddenly become breaking points when the whole house would implode with terror. So, pathologically, I'm prone to try to manage moods, read a room, smooth things over, and navigate the tiniest of clues for danger.

Mealtimes often seemed the worst. When the tension was mounting, sitting around the table felt too close. We'd all hover there quietly in the ominous lull, forks hovering over our TV dinners, stomachs roiling in angst, heads down, no eye contact. Even when all of us knew full well that an explosion was imminent, we'd stay frozen in our seats. I always hoped the explosion wouldn't come while we were still at the table because when it did, Dad's rage-fueled spittle would spray out laden with food bits.

The more frequent Dad's rages got, the more depressed Mom got, and the less frequent family mealtimes became, which all in all, seemed like a good thing. None of us wanted to sit at that table.

Since Rita and Judy were married and gone, Nancy and I were the only sisters left at home during the worst of those years, when the house was filled with seemingly endless yelling and cursing. "Two-legged bitch!" he'd snarl, mostly at Mom, but sometimes at us as well, his whole face contorting into that of a monster.

Hearing "two-legged bitch" was worse than hearing "good-for-nothing whore" or whatever else his creative curse-of-the-moment might be, because whenever he got to the point of calling us "two-legged bitches," I knew all hope was lost. It was a sure sign that he was too worked up for any turning back, and we would be in for several more days of rage until he finally depleted himself. Sometimes, his mouth would literally foam like a rabid dog's. And on the rare nights when he wasn't at work, the three of us—Mom, Nancy, and I—would all sleep together in the front bedroom.

Awake with his rage, he'd stalk the house in the middle of the night with a giant flashlight and eventually would come in the bedroom to shine it straight into our faces. It was terrifying, but less so with all three of us together. Years later, when I watched *The Shining* with Jack Nicholson, it brought back the horror of those nights. I knew Dad wasn't right in the head, and Mom knew it too, but none of us could figure out what to do about it. Besides, family stuff was kept in the family.

When one of his rages was mounting, there was nothing worse than being stuck in the car with him. While hurling cusses, he'd drive too fast, recklessly rounding corners, and all the while talking to himself, or to some invisible someone, or maybe to Mom in her absence. "Make a fool of me again, will you?"

Occasionally, he would threaten to bomb us. *Where would he get a bomb?* I always wondered. It was surreal. But he claimed he "knew guys who could do it." Having occasionally overheard stories about some of Dad's coworkers, I never doubted that Dad might indeed know some rough characters. So I was always on edge.

Mom said he just couldn't control it. Perhaps that was partly true and maybe even mostly true. But I noticed that, even when he was in a full-on rage, he still went to work. I didn't imagine he threatened the other men in the press-room the way he threatened us at home.

Sometimes, when he wasn't too crazy and when he was in lots of pain, Mom would urge him to call in sick and stay home from work. More than once, I heard him say that he'd "get some uppers from the boys on the dock."

"It'll keep me awake and I'll get through it," he'd tell her.

That was Dad. He often worked double shifts and sometimes even triple and quadruple shifts. But when he worked on too little sleep—which happened a lot—Mom worried about his getting a hand caught in the presses. She'd beg him not to take the extra shift. But Dad didn't know how *not* to work, so he always did.

For Dad, the answer to almost every problem was to work harder. So he pretty much wore his body out. Once he physically collapsed just as he was getting in the car to drive to work. I heard Mom yell, and I ran to help her, only to see Dad on the floor of the garage with the car door open. As it turned out, he had a raging kidney infection. I wondered what would have happened if the pain had hit him when he was driving down the highway.

6

Conditioner!

Cruelty is cheap, easy, and chickenshit.

—Brené Brown

FOR MY SECOND year of college, I moved into a dorm. *Nothing* could have deterred me. I was in Bruce Hall, one of the older dorms on campus, with concrete floors, no air conditioning, and communal bathrooms down the hall. Everyone complained about the food, but I thought it was great. The meals were hot and plentiful, and I could ask for white meat chicken without anyone insisting that I liked dark meat better. Truth be told, I didn't know which I liked better because, at home, whenever I asked to try the white meat, the response was always the same. Mom would put a thigh on my plate, remind me that Dad, Judy, and Nancy would eat only white, and say, "You know you like the dark meat better—you're like me."

Finally, in the cafeteria at the dorm, I got the chance to decide for myself what kind of chicken meat I liked better. All I had to do was tell the woman working the line, and with no questions, no lecture, no guilt, she'd put whatever piece I wanted on my plate.

I loved life in the dorm. Ironically, my new best friend was a girl who'd grown up just a couple blocks away in Farmers Branch, but she had always gone to Catholic schools, so our paths had never crossed. She'd been one of those kids that I'd always worried about when I saw them in their navy blue uniforms walking to Mary Immaculate.

Brother Hayden had always said that Catholics would burn in hell because they worshipped Mary and were a "pagan religion." So whenever I saw those kids walking to the Catholic school, I fretted about how unfair it was. Even then, I knew those kids didn't have any more of a choice about where they went to school than I did. *Why should they burn in hell for something they had no choice about?* When I told Madge how much I used to worry about the Mary Immaculate kids, she laughed and laughed. I loved her for it, and I also envied her. When I learned that she prayed to Mary, I wished that I, too, could pray to a woman. Madge said I could if I wanted. "I don't think she checks for Catholic credentials," Madge teased.

Dorm life was a relief, but the clouds of Farmers Branch still followed. There was no reprieve from Judy. After a year of living in Houston, she and Darrell had moved back to Denton where they lived in a small trailer not far from my college campus. Often, after classes, I'd arrive back at my dorm room only to hear Judy cackling in the room next door with my neighbors. They thought she was cool—Judy could ooze charm when she wanted—and I wondered why she so often poached my friends instead of making her own. But my closest friends wanted nothing to do with her.

"Your sister's a real piece of work," said my friend Myrna one day. I just laughed, not even bothering to ask why she'd said it.

JUDY AND DARRELL had already been through a couple dogs by then, an Irish setter and a bull terrier. Over the next couple years they acquired four more: a chow chow, a husky, a Samoyed, and a malamute. Given our superhot Texas summers, I never understood why they chose dogs more suited for cold weather. They seldom kept a dog for more than six months, and then suddenly, the dog would be gone. Judy would have some vague explanation that was typically just as dodgy as the story of how they'd acquired the dog.

Thinking it must be hard to lose so many dogs, I asked her once how she could handle it. But Judy just laughed it off and said she didn't get that attached to them because she knew from the start that they wouldn't have them for long.

"Darrell gets them from breeders," she divulged. As she then laid out their scheme, I gasped at understanding that Darrell would search ads for dogs, go to the location under cover of darkness, and take "just one pup."

"They probably don't even notice," Judy said.

As though they wouldn't miss "just one"? I was horrified by what I was hearing.

Then Darrell would wait several months, she said, and sell the dog for "good money." Judy seemed almost proud.

"Oh, don't be such a goody-goody," she said, seeing the shock on my face. "He takes them from people who have plenty of other dogs, and we make sure they get good homes. If anything, we're saving them some trouble."

It reminded me of the time when Judy told me about "lifting" jewelry and books from stores. "They charge way too much anyway. The whole capitalist system is unfair and we're making a statement against 'The Man.'"

"The man? What man?" It was the first time I'd heard the expression, and my ignorance set off gales of laughter.

Over the years, I'd grown to understand that Judy sometimes exaggerated her exploits, but that didn't stop me from worrying about the possibility that she could get caught. Judy just said I was "a baby."

When she gave me a beautifully illustrated fairy tale book for Christmas, I immediately wondered whether it was something she had shoplifted. While I folded the wrapping paper and set it aside, Mom launched in, railing at Judy: "Christa doesn't need fairy tale books! You're just encouraging her. She lives in a fantasy world as it is, and you aren't helping." As I sat there thinking how bizarre Mom's criticism was, I read Judy's inscription: "To the girl who makes fairy tales and princesses believable." I couldn't decide whether it was veiled ridicule or she was actually being nice. Judy had long made fun of me for liking the story of Cinderella, never realizing that, for me, it was more about the terror of the evil stepsisters and the magic of the gentle mice than the happily-ever-after transformation of a princess.

I FELT SORRY for Judy in those years. She seldom seemed happy, and though she had no trouble acquiring records, books, earrings, and cute clothes, she often had trouble coming up with money for tuition. At the start of each new semester, she would ask to borrow money. Sometimes she paid it back and sometimes she didn't. But even though money was always supertight for me as well, I had trouble turning Judy down, until one time, when she fed me a line of total bullshit. After a couple months of waiting for repayment, I had finally mustered up the courage to ask her.

"I paid you a month ago," she claimed.

I knew she hadn't, and I saw in her eyes that she knew it too.

After that, the next time she wanted to borrow money, I told her I couldn't because I needed the money to buy my textbooks, which was true. But Judy was furious. She told me I could wait to buy my books or could get them from the library. She claimed she would have to drop out of school if I didn't help her. She said I *had* to because she was family. I still refused. She must have gotten the money elsewhere because she didn't drop out of school.

Toward the end of my last semester on campus, I was working late in the pottery lab one night, trying to make three perfect straight-walled eight-inch cylinders. I'd been there for hours, wedging balls of clay, kicking the wheel, and throwing cylinders, one after another. With most of my efforts, I had immediately decided that they weren't good enough, and so had cut the cylinders down and re-wedged the clay. But finally, I had managed to place five cylinders on my rack, planning to choose the best three from among them. I would be graded on those after I had glazed and fired them.

That's when Judy suddenly appeared, my roommate having told her where I was. "Are all these yours?" she asked, eyeing my cylinders. When I told her they were, she began to ridicule me.

"Why do you even bother? You've never had a creative bone in your body. Just look at them. They're boring." As she spoke, she took a pencil and, much to my horror, began jabbing holes in the still-wet clay of my cylinders.

I yelled at her to stop. She didn't. Hours of work were destroyed by Judy's whim. I told her that "boring" was exactly what I was supposed to be making, that the assignment was for eight-inch straight-walled cylinders, and that she had just ruined my grade. "Oh well, you can make more," she said nonchalantly as she breezed out the door. I wondered why she had even come by. But in my already-exhausted state, I couldn't ponder it for long, because there was nothing to do but to set about throwing more cylinders.

I WAS RUNNING down the back stairs of the dorm, on my way to a final exam, when I fell. The stairs were concrete and it hurt like hell, but I finally got myself up and hobbled to class, where I took the exam with my leg throbbing. By the time I went home for Christmas, a few days later, my leg had turned every shade imaginable of black, blue, and purple. Mom just said, "Well, I guess that'll teach you not to run down the stairs."

After the holiday, when I showed up back on campus with my leg still discolored, my friends talked me into going to the student health center where an x-ray showed a hairline fracture that was partially healed. "No doubt you also tore some ligaments," the doctor said. By then, more than a month after the injury, there wasn't much point in putting the leg in a cast.

"Why didn't you come in sooner?" he asked. I didn't have an answer. My upbringing was so much about never being a bother that, even with a fractured leg, it hadn't occurred to me to care for myself. Many years later, I had reconstructive ankle surgery to reattach the ligaments and stabilize the joint, but until then, the injury left me prone to falling.

IN COLLEGE, I was always seeking to blend in with those from other social strata. Once when I'd gone to a group dinner at a friend's house, I was puzzled by something on my plate that looked like a miniature green tree. "What's this?" I asked, and every eye at the table suddenly stared at me. It was one of those times when I knew I should have kept my mouth shut. That's how class differences often are. They sneak out in small ways.

"Uhhh, broccoli?" someone finally ventured, as though he'd been trying to figure out whether I might be asking about something else since the answer was too obvious. But I honestly didn't know. I had never eaten a whole piece of broccoli. Beyond potatoes, carrots, onions, and iceberg lettuce, fresh vegetables hadn't been much of a menu item in my family. The mushy frozen broccoli I'd grown up with looked nothing at all like what was on my plate.

That wasn't the only time I showed my ignorance, though my dorm friends never made me feel bad about it. And they taught me a lot. Time after time, I'd come back from washing my hair in the showers down the hall, and my roommate, Gloria, would watch me spend the next half hour painstakingly combing out the tangles in my long, thick, curly hair. Finally, one day, she asked me why I didn't use a conditioner.

"Conditioner? What's that?" I asked.

So, Gloria let me try out her conditioner, and that wound up being one of the most life-altering bits of knowledge I gleaned from college life. Hair conditioner was just one of those things that, in my family, we had never bought. I didn't even know it existed.

THOUGH IT WAS never often enough to please Mom, I made frequent weekend trips home, where Mom constantly badgered me about choosing a major that would be "practical." After auditioning to take lessons from one of the university's finest pianists and getting accepted, I declared myself as a music major, and Mom had nothing but criticism.

"You need something to support yourself," she insisted. "You can't count on having a husband, you know."

"But I *like* playing the piano," I replied, ignoring the "husband" remark. "So why wouldn't a music major be a good thing for me?"

"And what are you imagining?" Mom laughed. "That you'll be a concert pianist? Get your head out of the clouds, Christa. Major in education. Then, if you really want to, you could make music your teaching field."

"But I don't *want* to teach school."

"Christa, you need something to fall back on because you probably aren't ever going to get married."

This conversation repeated itself at least a half-dozen times over the course of a couple years. But when I actually tried to be more practical and told her I thought I'd like to be a "stewardess" so I could travel, she derided that too. "Don't be silly. Stewardesses have to be pretty." So, finally, I declared myself as a French major with a minor in English, and though I got a teaching certificate on the side, I felt victorious for never having yielded to my mother's insistence that I should major in education. But I did forgo any further music instruction, so I guess Mom had a partial victory too.

FOR MY LAST eight weeks of college, I moved back home to be close to the high school where I did my student teaching. Dad was massively preoccupied. A bitter labor dispute was brewing between the pressmen's union and the *Dallas Morning News*, and Dad would come home from union meetings worked up and distraught. He could see where things were headed. "Those young guys think it's gonna be easy," he complained. "But they don't know. They're full of themselves, and it's gonna cost us. All of us. Management has all the cards."

I asked Dad if he didn't feel angry about how management was treating them. He did, but he wanted me to know that the union didn't always do the right thing either. "Both sides can be at fault," he said.

It surprised me to hear him say this because Dad was a union man through and through. But then he told me the story about our move to Wichita and how the union had let him down.

He had surreptitiously joined the pressmen's union while working at the *Denton Record-Chronicle*. Whenever I think about it, that fact alone amazes me. This was Texas, after all, a virulently anti-union state, and it was the tail of the "Red Scare" McCarthy era. But Dad always did have a mind of his own. "I wanted better training and better safety procedures," he explained.

The union had promised they wouldn't tell anyone he'd joined until he had a chance to quietly muster support among other pressmen. "And I was workin' on it," Dad said. But the "union honchos" got impatient, and they let it leak that he had joined.

People began calling him a "commie," and I could tell from the way he told it that there was surely more to the story. Dad sometimes talked about men who'd lost fingers and hands in the heavy machinery, and I got the impression he'd been worried about his odds for having an "accident" in such a hostile work environment. There were "threats," he said, without elaborating. As it turned out, Dad didn't work there much longer because a brick came flying through the window of our home one night. Then Dad worried not only about the safety of his fingers but the safety of his whole family. We skedaddled.

Almost overnight, our family picked up and moved to Wichita, where there was a union shop at the *Wichita Eagle*. Dad went straight to work, and the six of us settled into a cheap motel. Nancy was just a few months old.

"So you see," said Dad, "whether it's union or management, both can be wrong. Both can *do* wrong. What's important is that, wherever *you* wind up, you just try to do what's right and you keep your word."

I often think about how frightening that must have been for Dad and Mom to have a brick come through the window of their home, with four young children inside. We moved so suddenly that Uncle Jack, who was driving from California to come visit us, arrived in Denton to find our house empty. He had phoned before leaving Burbank, and by the time he got to Texas, we were gone. A neighbor told him we'd headed to Wichita, so he drove on up to Kansas and phoned motels until he found us.

I had heard the last part of that story—the part about Uncle Jack arriving to an empty house—at least a half-dozen times through the years. Uncle Jack loved to tell it. But I only heard the first part of that story the one time, and that was from Dad. Mom never once talked about how she'd felt when a brick came through the window in the nighttime.

Years later, back in Texas, the pressmen's union was never a good fit with the *Dallas Morning News*. After months of futile bargaining efforts, the union voted to strike. Management was ready and immediately began helicoptering in nonunion labor onto the roof of the building.

The strike dragged on, and every day, Dad would come home from the Union Hall talking about how many helicopters had come and gone. Once, he took me with him to the top floor of a parking garage where we stood looking out at the roof of the *Dallas Morning News*, watching the helicopters land. I think he wanted me to see it with my own eyes.

The paper barely missed a beat. Dad told me he had hoped only that the news might miss one day of getting the paper out, but even that didn't happen. They had helicoptered those workers in so fast that the paper was only a few hours late in hitting the stands.

The strike nearly killed Dad. At age fifty-four, and without work, he didn't know what to do with himself and descended into despondency, which exacerbated his PTSD. Of course, back then, we didn't have a name for it. It's only now, in looking backwards, that the fact of Dad's chronic PTSD seems so obvious. He was a man deeply damaged, not only by the violence of his father, but by the killing and dying of World War II. Like so many other families, we were ripped asunder by those dreadful war wounds, and, over and over, we just did the best we could to put ourselves back together.

Dad had fought in the Pacific Theater, including in the battles of Leyte and Luzon. He once told me that he credited his survival to the fact that he had hunted rabbits and squirrels in his childhood, because that made him a skilled sharpshooter. I thought at the time that it probably wasn't the faces of rabbits that were haunting his sleep.

I had heard the story of how Dad was wounded with shrapnel in his legs and back, and of how he survived by pretending to be dead while they bayonetted bodies around him. He waited for cover of darkness and crawled back through a field to Allied lines. Mom's brother Jack, who was also fighting in the Pacific, had visited Dad shortly afterwards in an army field hospital, and he'd gotten him to recount what he'd been through. Over the years, it was Jack who would occasionally relay the story.

Mom said it was why Dad had so many nightmares. But Dad himself never spoke of it, at least not in any detail. Only twice did he get close to it, and they were both when he was much older. The first time, I had tried to prod him into talking a bit about the war and asked about his injuries. Dad just told me how lucky he was and that if he hadn't been injured when he was, he would have been "dead for sure."

"How can you be so certain?" I asked.

"Because near everyone else died," he said. That was one of the few times I ever saw my Dad's eyes tear up. So I just held his hand and told him how glad I was that he hadn't died, that he had lived to come home, and that I got to be born. He just smiled and we sat quietly together, and that was enough.

The second time he spoke of it, Dad was only a few weeks short of dying, and I'd been asking him again to tell me about some of the track meets he'd run in high school. He started recalling the details of long-ago races, and then suddenly, he shifted into telling me about a different race.

"But the fastest I ever did run wasn't on any track," he said. "They told us to charge forward, and I was scared as all dickens, but I just kept tellin' myself that if I could get over that ridgeline that maybe I'd be okay. I never run so fast in my life. Heck, I flat-out flew." He paused then. "But I got too far ahead of the rest I guess."

A shadow crossed his face and he fell silent. I assumed he was remembering the rest of the story—the part about how he lay wounded in that field while they bayonetted bodies. We both stayed quiet for a while. I didn't want to press him. But suddenly, with a twinkle in his eyes, he laughed out loud. "Man, it sure felt good when I was flyin'!"

Every so often over the years, Mom would mention Dad's injury, but always with her own complaint. "He should've had a Purple Heart," she'd say. "They told him he would." At the time, I scarcely had any idea what a Purple Heart was, but Mom would sometimes nag Dad, telling him his commanding officer didn't do right and wanting him to write a letter to someone in the government to make it happen.

"I'm alive, ain't I?" That's what Dad would always say whenever Mom started down this track. For him, those four words said it all.

AFTER THE *Dallas Morning News* busted the Union, Dad was adrift. Even if he'd wanted to, he couldn't go back to work as a nonunion pressman, he said, because without the seniority he'd had in a union shop, he'd have to do too much heavy lifting, which his back couldn't tolerate.

Mom badgered him to take a job as a mall security guard. She had a teacher friend whose husband worked in management at the mall and her friend had said it could be "a sure thing." Dad refused. He was a man who had no concept of leisure, a man whose entire identity was bound to the constancy of work. Despite that, he didn't budge, telling Mom, plain and simple, that he would not do a job that required him to carry a gun.

"But you won't have to shoot it," Mom insisted. "No one ever does. It would be a job—an easy job—and it's something you could do."

Every time I was at the house, she'd bring it up again, and then she'd take me aside and try to talk me into working on Dad about it. But I wanted no part of Mom's effort; it was obvious Dad had made up his mind, and I figured he had his reasons. To Mom's mind though, it didn't make sense, and she was convinced he would surely be happier if he were working again.

But Dad would not yield.

"You don't carry a gun unless you're willing to shoot it," he'd growl each time Mom brought it up. Then he'd walk away, out into the yard, where he'd pick up his tools and prune some poor shrub nearly into the ground. Mom would wait for another day to replay the conversation yet again.

I imagined Dad knew all too well what guns could do. When I slept in the bedroom next to theirs, I often heard his night terrors for myself. For all the sacrifices that were made by Dad's generation of men, there was never much in the way of postwar counseling for them. There was just a "get over it and get back to it" sort of American muster. Families across the country were left to deal with the fallout on their own.

God knows he tried hard to pull himself back together, but the wounds of that war stayed with him. They did for one of our back neighbors as well. He also went into loud rages and sometimes lashed out with fists. After his kids were grown and his wife had left him, he deteriorated to the point that he became an isolated recluse who would occasionally shoot off a gun. Once, a bullet came through Mom and Dad's kitchen window.

Of course, none of this is to excuse or minimize my father's rage. I lived with it. I know how berserk he could become. But even though I'll never understand how it was that my father could seem like two separate human beings, the better understanding I've gained of PTSD as an adult has helped me to hold him in my heart with softness.

7

Libération

With each new language, you acquire a new soul.

—Slovakian proverb

JUST BEFORE I graduated from college, I managed to line up a job in Lyon, France. Deliberately, I had *not* sought a job in Paris because I feared I would encounter too many Americans there, and I wanted a total immersion experience so that I would be forced to speak only French. So, in exchange for room and board and a small stipend, I agreed to tend a French family's kids as an au pair—essentially a governess. I was scheduled to start right after graduation, and I bought my plane ticket before breathing a word of it to anyone in my family.

I was also looking for a way to put the brakes on my relationship with Brad, an engineering student who was working toward a degree after four years in the navy. We'd been dating for over a year, and he had asked me to marry him. Even though I'd stalled on giving an answer, he had talked to my parents about his intention, and I felt like I was suffocating. In my heart of hearts, I didn't think I really loved him, but it seemed easier to go off to France than to tell him that. Heck, I couldn't even manage to tell *myself* the truth of how I felt. I was too confused. But I thought a year in France would give me time to think.

I waited until just a couple weeks before my flight to tell Mom about my plan, and she was furious. Not only was I rejecting a marriage proposal, but much to my surprise, she claimed I was also rejecting a teaching job at the local high school. She attacked on both fronts.

"Mrs. Wilson has been waiting for you to finish college so that you could take her place when she retired, and now you're just going to go off to France?"

"But, Mom, no one's said anything to *me* about a teaching job."

"You aren't even appreciative? Mrs. Wilson postponed her retirement for you!"

"I didn't even *know* about it. How can I be appreciative of something I didn't know about?"

Mom said they had intended it to be a surprise for when I graduated. They all thought I would be thrilled, she said, as I surmised that she and other teachers must have been talking about it.

"But I don't want to teach French if I can't actually speak French," I explained, "and the only way I'm going to learn to speak French is if I live there for a while."

Mrs. Wilson had been my high school French teacher, and though she had taught me to love the French culture, she never spoke a word of French in the classroom. She didn't even start the class with "Bonjour." It was all in English and almost nothing but worksheets with grammar exercises. I knew that if I were going to teach French, I wanted to do it differently.

"Don't you realize what a chance this is?" Mom was practically screaming at me. "You can have a teaching job right here in Farmers Branch and instead you're going to go work as household help?"

I paused as my mind filled with doubt. I had debated the decision a hundred times in my head, but all that seemed for naught as I tried to fend off Mom's attacks. "I'm just going for a year," I finally mumbled. "Maybe the job will be here when I get back."

"Don't be silly. There's only one French teacher and Mrs. Wilson isn't going to wait another year. She's ready to retire and when she does, they'll find someone else to fill her spot. If you pass this up, you won't get another chance."

"Well, I guess that's a chance I'll have to take," I answered, pushing my doubts back into the corner where I wanted to keep them. "I've made my plans. I'm going to France."

"And what about Brad? You think he's just going to twiddle his thumbs and wait for you?"

"I don't know, Mom. I don't know what will happen with Brad." I should have stopped right there. It was almost always a mistake to share too much with

Mom, but on this, I was a slow learner. "I don't know if I really want to marry him anyway," I added.

"What do you mean you don't know? *Of course* you want to marry him!"

Mom's voice was rising again, and I was feeling worn down. "I don't know. I just don't know if it's what I want."

"You *aren't* going to turn him down! He'll be an engineer!"

"What's so great about being an engineer?" I don't know why I bothered asking. Mom had spent years envying her friend Rachel, who taught in the classroom across the hall from Mom's. Rachel's husband was an engineer, and Mom would often regale me with stories of the trips that Rachel and her husband had taken and the parties they'd been to. I would listen, but invariably, what I wound up hearing was Mom's disdain for my father and her longing for a different life.

"He'll make good money, and you'll have someone to support you," Mom said. "What's the *matter* with you?"

"I don't know, Mom. Maybe I'll just support myself."

"If you don't marry Brad, you'll *have* to support yourself, and *then* you'll be sorry."

By now, my legs were sticking to the vinyl lime-green couch, and I felt like any minute I'd be cooked. I stood and, with a couple steps, stared out the sliding glass door. In the abyss of silence, I watched the sparrows and listened to the hum of the old fridge. Mom began rummaging in the pantry for a used piece of foil to wrap some leftovers in.

"Why are you doing this?" she asked. "What's the matter with him?"

I paused, gazing at the yard. "Nothing's the matter with him," I finally said, my back still turned to her. "It's just that I don't really love him."

There it was. I said it not so much to Mom as to the trees and the birds. It was something I'd been turning over in my mind for weeks, yet I still felt stunned to hear myself saying the words out loud. But even as I stood shocked at hearing the words from my own mouth, wondering if they were really true, Mom moved in for the kill.

"What do you know about love?" she sneered. "You think it's going to be like one of your silly fairy tales? You'll *grow* to love him, you'll see."

"Mom, if I don't love him, I shouldn't marry him. It's just not right. I want to love the man I marry."

"Don't be an idiot. A girl like you won't get many chances, you know."

I paused. "What do you mean, a girl like me?"

"You know what I mean."

And of course, I *did* know. Mom had always made it plain that I wasn't pretty. Year after year, we used to all watch the Miss America pageant together, my three sisters and I joining in with Mom's imaginings, as though we could be contestants ourselves. We cheered for our favorites and chose the dresses we'd wear if we were in the pageant. Mom went along wholeheartedly with the imaginings of Rita, Judy, and Nancy, but she always rejected mine.

"You can't be Miss America," she'd proclaim. "But you could enter a talent competition."

I got the message. I wasn't pretty and I never would be.

"If you don't marry Brad, you'll wind up as a lonely old maid," she declared. "Is that what you want—to spend your life as an old maid? Alone and miserable?"

I sucked in my breath and felt myself drowning. It was the same desperate sensation I used to feel when Judy would hold me under water at the swimming pool. All I wanted was to fend her off and get to the surface. I realized I'd been holding my breath and consciously exhaled.

"Mom, I don't think that marrying someone I don't love is going to make me happy. Maybe I'll have a happy life *without* being married."

Then I made the mistake of trying to lighten things up by pointing out that Mary Richards wasn't married and *she* didn't seem miserable. After Mom figured out who I was talking about—the character on *The Mary Tyler Moore Show*—the disdain in her voice grew.

"Christa, that's fantasy. In the real world, you need a husband. You're lucky Brad wants you."

"Lucky." The word stuck like a burr in my mind as I stood, looking at her, hardly believing what she was saying.

"Mark my words," she continued, "you won't get another chance. You're almost twenty-two and you're about to finish college, and you haven't had any other offers. If you don't get married now, you'll regret it for the rest of your life, and you'll be nothing but a lonely old maid."

Even all these years later, I am swept away by the harshness of those words.

In hindsight, I have come to believe that Mom's insistence was really a reflection of the sad limitations of her own life. She herself had married at age eighteen, and my two older sisters had married at nineteen and eighteen. So, comparatively, I was indeed old. Most of my friends were married by then as well—young marriages are common in Baptistland. So Mom probably thought she was helping me to be realistic. But what I heard was the icy coldness in her voice, and something more. Maybe it was the edge of some sort of hatred, but whether it was hatred for me or hatred for herself, I couldn't say.

I shut down everything inside me, turned my face away, and made myself into steel. "Maybe there are worse things than being an old maid," I finally said, staring out the glass door and trying to muster as much ice in my own voice as I'd heard in hers. "Because if there's one thing you've taught me, Mom, it's that marriage doesn't save people from being lonely. Look at you, you're married, and you're one of the loneliest people I know."

Only after I spoke did I turn my head back to look at Mom's face, and I knew in an instant that my dagger had gone deep. It was perhaps the meanest thing I ever said to Mom, and I wished immediately that I could suck the words back into my mouth. But even with the hard knot of guilt in my gut, I couldn't bring myself to appease her. If I yielded an inch, I feared my life would be over.

We stared at one another as though sizing each other up for a duel. The silence was a palpable dark cloud, filling the room from floor to ceiling and choking even the thought of any conciliatory words. Mom glared at me through the fog and I glared right back.

"You don't know anything," she finally snarled. "Your father and I support one another. We're there for each other. You'll *never* have that."

I held my ground. "I'm not going to marry someone I don't love just so I won't be an old maid. I'll take my chances."

I'd been cruelly direct. But I was also right: Mom was a lonely woman who used her daughters to try to fill her own emptiness. Years later, after she died, I found myself reading a journal entry she'd written just a few months after that angry confrontation. It was her fiftieth birthday, and she was fearful that the rest of her life would continue to go "downhill."

> This last year has not been easy and maybe that's some expla-
> nation for the feeling of sadness—the realization that Chuck

and I really have little in common now that the girls are gone. It's a lonely feeling not to be able to talk to your husband and share things with him for fear he'll fly into a rage or at the least misinterpret what you say, or ridicule you. . . .
It's sad that we can't share and learn together, but we can't.

I realize now that this was probably why Mom reacted so harshly toward me: I had said what she knew was true.

A COUPLE WEEKS later, when I left for France, Dad took me to the airport. Mom was still mad, and I had refused Brad's insistence that he should take me.

Despite having stood my ground with Mom, I still couldn't find the sureness in my heart to tell Brad the truth of how I felt. All I'd told him was that my year in France was something I just had to do. It was chickenshit of me, and Brad deserved better, but it was all I could manage. We parted with a plan to marry when I returned.

During the first months in France, I missed my first couple periods—probably because total French immersion was so stressful—and I worried that I might have accidentally gotten pregnant right before leaving. In my fretful state of mind, I wrote in a letter to Judy about my fear. I asked her not to tell Mom, but of course, she did. She gave Mom my letter, and Mom read the whole thing, including the part where I specifically said "please don't tell Mom."

Mom wrote to tell me about it, saying that she hoped everything was okay and that I wasn't really pregnant. "But you should know," she said, "that you need to be wary of Judy because she did this to hurt you." The letter continued: "Judy will always try to find a way to hurt you whenever she can. I hate having to tell you this about your own sister, but you need to be on guard against her."

Just a couple days later, a letter arrived from Brad, telling me that Judy was acting strangely toward him. He had signed up to take a dance class, he said, because he wanted to know how to dance when I got back from France. He'd mentioned the class to Judy when he bumped into her at the store, and lo and behold, Judy showed up in the class. "She was all over me," wrote Brad.

"She's your sister, Christa, and I don't even hardly know what to say, but I just thought you should know."

Great, I thought. *Here I am all the way across the ocean, far from family and friends, living every minute in a language I don't yet fully understand, working as domestic help, and my mother is warning me against my own sister, who is putting the moves on my fiancé.* I felt exhausted by even the thought of what those letters had in them.

As fast as I could—to get it over with and out of my mind—I wrote reply letters. To Mom, I told her not to worry and that I wasn't pregnant after all. Deliberately, I didn't mention her warning about Judy because I couldn't figure out what to say about it. To Brad, I said not to worry and that Judy had *always* been weird. And to Judy, I decided to forgo any mention of Brad and instead focused on telling her how upset I was that she had given Mom my "I think I'm pregnant" letter when I had specifically asked her not to say anything.

Judy wrote back defensively, claiming that she "didn't actually *say* anything at all" and that showing it to Mom was just an accident. "I dropped by the house and your letter was in my purse and I just thought Mom might like to see it," she wrote.

Maybe I could have believed her if she'd stopped there, or if she'd apologized, but she didn't. "I don't know why you have to make such a big deal out of something that was nothing," she continued. "Mom didn't even react. It wasn't important, and I'm not going to walk on eggshells just because you're so sensitive. By the way, I've been taking a dance class with Brad and he's a really good dancer."

As soon as I saw that not-so-veiled taunt about Brad, I knew Mom was right: Judy had given Mom the letter on purpose. In my head, I'd been trying to cut her some slack since she was in the middle of getting divorced, but her conduct with Brad was a long-familiar pattern. For example, poor sweet Luke never knew what hit him. In seventh grade, after I told Judy how much I liked Luke—the first boy I'd ever had a crush on—Judy immediately made advances. Luke was in my class at school and a year younger than Judy, but he lived in the neighborhood. The next time I went to the swimming pool, I came upon Judy making out with Luke in the water.

Of course, she knew I would see her. That was the point. When she saw me looking, she pulled away from Luke and dunked me under the water, bearing down with her whole weight on my head and shoulders. I struggled frantically until Luke finally yanked her away. Then I came up spewing water out my nose and mouth, choking and gasping desperately for air. Humiliated, I left the pool. But at least I was accustomed to that kind of thing. For Luke, it must have been a mystery. Judy never showed him a lick of attention after that. He had served his purpose.

That's just how it was with Judy. Maybe she was just born mean or maybe she subconsciously blamed me for her maternal deprivation, since I was born so soon after her. In any event, she often found it easier to impress *my* friends, who were younger, than to make her own. She seldom kept any of them around for much longer than she did with Luke, just long enough to show me who held the power. But always, I had a few friends who weren't taken in by Judy's flash.

The summer I turned seventeen, Judy told some of my friends that I "liked girls." I knew what she was doing because, with a lot of hesitation and embarrassment, a couple of my friends mentioned it to me.

"Judy's being weird," said Bryan, a boy in my church youth group. "I just thought you should know what she's saying."

I didn't understand. "Well of course I like girls," I said breezily.

"That's not how she means it," he replied, looking as though he'd like to just sink into a hole. Finally, searching for the right words, Bryan managed to convey the gist of it into my thick skull. "She means you like girls the same way boys like girls."

I stood quiet for a long time, trying to mentally sort out exactly what he meant—what Judy meant—but Bryan didn't want to explain further. Finally, with my puzzlement not entirely abated, he let it go, saying, "Look, I just wanted you to know that I don't care what Judy says. You're my friend."

I'd known Bryan since fifth grade and he'd always been a natural jokester, but as I studied his face, it gave not the slightest sign of any withheld punchline. I wondered if maybe he'd misunderstood. But then, a week later, another friend Barb told me almost exactly the same thing: "Judy's telling people you like girls."

"I don't care what Judy says, and I don't care what anyone else thinks," said Barb.

As I stood there vaguely pondering who the "anyone else" might be, she added, "I'm *your* friend, not *hers*, and I just want you to know that." Something about the way Barb emphasized those words made me suddenly realize that

Judy's "Christa likes girls" gossip was probably the reason a couple friends had been so obviously avoiding me and sticking close to Judy instead. I hadn't been able to figure out why I had inexplicably become invisible, but I hadn't dwelled on it much because it was a pattern I'd seen before. Judy was the interesting sister; I was the book nerd.

Right after separating from Darrell, Judy moved in with my former room-mate Mary Kay, and a few months later, she imposed herself on my friend Cathy. Through all four years of college, in every French class I'd taken, I had sat next to Cathy, and we were both officers in the French honorary society. Later, when I asked Judy why she'd moved in with Cathy instead of with some friend of her own, she told me Cathy had said we were never friends anyway.

"She said you're way too square," Judy told me. "You're a drag. You always have been. So why are you making a big deal out of it when you weren't really friends anyway?"

It hurt, but I tried not to let it show. I knew that if I allowed even a few drops of my woundedness to scent the water, Judy would move in like a shark. So I kept my pain to myself. And though I never really believed Cathy had said that, it was hard to want to stay in contact with my friends once Judy had co-opted them as her own. I was always left wondering about what lies Judy may have told them.

IN LYON, I would lean far out my small bedroom window, and turning my head to the left, I could see the Rhône river, and to the right, the Saône. The family I worked for lived smack in the city center, on the narrow strip of land in between the two rivers. And though I was little more than a domestic servant, I felt freer than I'd ever imagined possible.

Ambling the sidewalks of Lyon, I began to quietly absorb the long tug of a traumatic history. On countless buildings, there were metal markers noting where French Resistance fighters had been slain by Nazis, and I was often aston-ished to see fresh flowers and handwritten notes set beneath the markers. In my young mind, I had viewed World War II as ancient history—a done deal that had ended long ago. Yet in Lyon, thirty years after the war's end, the past still breathed.

The past also breathed within the great Gothic cathedrals. I loved sitting in their empty stillness where I could almost feel the presence of countless others who had tread the stone slabs before me with their prayers and pleas. In the cathedrals, I could feel the mystery of life, and my spirit was always revived.

For several months, Brad wrote me almost daily. But finally, with time apart and more certainty in my heart, I mustered the courage to write him a long-distance "it's not you it's me" letter and said goodbye. I took comfort in recalling that Charlotte Brontë, the author of one of my favorite books, *Jane Eyre*, had also rejected a marriage proposal when she was twenty-two.

As an au pair, my position was one of low status. The monsieur and madame reinforced this reality with a fair amount of criticism—the roasted chicken wasn't just the way monsieur liked it or the kids' underwear wasn't ironed just right. (Who ever heard of ironing kids' underwear?) And when I struck up with a Moroccan boyfriend, Ahmed, I knew to keep my mouth shut whenever they referred to Maghrebian people pejoratively as "bougnoules." I had no place to speak my mind when my legal existence in France rested at their whim. Yet, despite the downsides, I was at least living in a household that was calm. There was no yelling, no cussing, no throwing things.

In those days, there was no such thing as FaceTime or email, and international phone calls were prohibitively expensive. Snail mail was the only practical option, which meant my family couldn't easily intrude on me when I was in France. They couldn't control me, judge me, criticize me, or berate me.

With a reprieve from family drama, I felt as though I were learning to breathe. A joie de vivre took hold in me.

I grew more confident and stopped habitually ducking my chin. My timid English-speaking mannerisms didn't follow me into French. Instead, I engaged shopkeepers with an air of assurance, and when some man on the street would harass me, rather than ignoring him, I'd sometimes reproach him: "Laissez-moi!"—"Leave me alone!" Best of all, whenever I could, I took the train to Paris, where I rode the Métro, spent precious coins on croissants, and went wherever I wanted all by myself.

In France, I learned that I had it in me to love life.

I CAN STILL see the knife in front of my eyes. As soon as the door shut behind me, the blade had appeared out of nowhere. It was a skinny thing. *Was it a switchblade?* I stood transfixed, unable to move, my eyes fixated on the blade as he toyed with it—toyed with me—turning it this way and that about five inches in front of my face.

It was Easter weekend, and with the family away for the holiday, I had gone to visit a friend who lived in a university residence hall in the suburb of Villeurbanne. It was just starting to rain, and I was waiting outside where we had agreed to meet. A guy I didn't know asked if he could help me, and when I told him who I was waiting for, he said that he lived in the same building and asked if I wanted to wait in his room.

I hesitated, but only for a moment. It was after all a student dormitory. So I followed him up the stairs to his room. The instant the door shut, I knew I'd made a terrible mistake.

He kept insisting that all he wanted to do was look at me. I said no. I pleaded. But with the knife in front of my face, I slowly undid the top button of my blouse. It wasn't enough. He touched the knife to the next button and then raised it back to my face. With my eyes fixated on the knife, I undid that one as well. And so it went, one button at a time.

With the knife still in my face, he began pushing me toward the bed. I yelled, but that only served to make the knife more visible. I kept thinking someone would hear me and arrive at the door. But no one did. Finally, he got me onto the bed and straddled me, all the while with the knife in my face. On *his* face, I glimpsed a sick, leering grin, but mostly all I saw was the knife.

When he started to struggle with unzipping his pants, he set the knife beside my ear. Suddenly, finding strength from somewhere primal, my whole body heaved upward. Without thought, I was in motion. Propelling myself with an absolute singularity of purpose, I saw only the door. As I fought to get it open, I heard his scuffling and cursing behind me. He started kicking at me, but by then, I had the door ajar, and as I pulled it wide, his last kick shoved me to the ground. But I was across the threshold.

I leaped to my feet, hesitating for only a split second: *elevator or stairs?* In the next fractional moment, I was charging down the stairs. At the bottom, I took in the emptiness of the lobby—*where was everyone?*

I ran out into the rain, my legs churning beneath me. At the first bus stop, I paused and threw up by the side. But afraid he might be following me, and terrified of seeing that knife again, I kept running.

At the second bus stop, I paused once again, frantically hoping for the miracle of a bus and the safety of strangers. But fear consumed me and I kept running.

I ran all the way from Villeurbanne to central Lyon, and only after I was inside the apartment with both of the locks bolted did I begin to mentally relive the nightmare of what had happened in that room. *What had become of the knife? Had it fallen to the floor in the ruckus? Was it knocked under the bed? Why hadn't he used it? And who was that wild creature who moved with animal instincts and made it out the door?*

I stayed up all night pondering these questions, and in the process, threw up my insides a couple times more. When it finally dawned on me that the reason the dorm was so empty was because almost all the students were away for the Easter holiday, I realized how alone and vulnerable I'd been. Later I learned that my friend had forgotten our plan and hadn't even been anywhere nearby. So, if I hadn't managed to save myself, no one else would have.

The wild creature who escaped from that room was me—a part of me I hadn't even known existed.

8

Return

The truth does not change according to our ability to stomach it.
—Flannery O'Connor

AFTER A YEAR in Lyon, my visa ran out and I returned to the profoundly unhappy household of my parents. They picked me up at the airport, and I sensed the combustible mood as soon as I got in the car. Of course, Mom was talking a mile a minute trying to cover for it. But sure enough, within a matter of days, Dad detonated, and within a couple weeks, Mom moved out. It wound up being the first of many separations to follow. That time, it lasted about six months. I went to stay with Mom in her small one-bedroom apartment.

Mrs. Honea had hired me back to do puppet shows at the library and to help with the kids' summer reading program. I started the day after my return, and in the midst of my culture-shock transition, it gave me work I loved. I got to make my own puppets, write my own scripts, and enlist another employee to help in the performances.

More than either my parents' house or my mom's apartment, the library felt like home. Among the rows of books, and nourished by the women who worked there, I felt calm. But in the evenings, there was nothing to do but listen to Mom bemoan her life and cry about Dad. It was as though nothing had changed . . . except me.

I missed French with every fiber of my body. I yearned for the sound of it and for the part of myself that had been living and dreaming in French. It felt as though a part of me had been hollowed out, but there was no one with whom to share my grief. Mom and Dad were wrapped up in their own misery, and other people, no doubt well intentioned, seemed only to want to tell me how wonderful it must feel to be back in the USA. But I felt nothing like that at all.

The end of my year in France brought a powerful sense of loss. I missed Ahmed, of course, but my misery was much more than that. I ached for the smells and splendors of France, and I missed my own French-speaking self—the person I had been when I was there.

The long-standing traumas that hid in the English-speaking parts of my brain had not followed me into French. So the French-speaking me had felt safer, and with my return to an English-speaking life in Farmers Branch, the darkness seemed to lurk much closer. Without even knowing how to name it, I missed that sense of safety within my own French-speaking brain.

After a couple weeks, Brad somehow found out I was back, and he stopped by the library, appearing suddenly just as I was getting ready to start a puppet show. More than a dozen toddlers were already gathered on the floor in the children's room, their parents standing against the walls, and there in the middle of the library, Brad started rambling on about how much he loved me and how he still wanted to marry me.

"Christa, I don't care about anything that might have happened in France," he declared. "That's behind us. That's in the past. You're back now. Just marry me."

I should have been giving him my full attention, but I was stunned and distracted. People were staring at us. Brad insisted I step outside to talk.

"I can't, Brad. I just can't," I whispered. "Not right now. I have to do a puppet show. The kids are waiting."

"I've waited a whole year!" he responded. "You have to decide! Right now!"

I heard the anger and frustration in his voice, and I tried to listen to him. But at the same time, I could hear the kids getting restless, and out of the corner of my eye, I saw the children's librarian looking at me with concern. I knew I had to go do the puppet show. You can't put a room of toddlers on hold for very long.

"Just give me thirty minutes," I pleaded. "I'll be done then and we can talk."

"No! I've waited long enough! Come with me. Now!"

"I can't, Brad. I've got to go do this. I'll be done soon." With that, I stepped away from him and began moving to go behind the puppet stage.

"I'm not waiting another minute," he called after me. And sure enough, when I was done with the show, Brad was gone.

THE ONLY NEGATIVE part of that library job was the fact that *The Total Woman* was on the *New York Times* bestseller list during that time. The book's author, Marabel Morgan, taught that women should take on an affirmative daily obligation to make sure their husbands felt like heroes and to be constantly available as smoldering sexpots. Its lessons were more than I could stomach, so with all the power afforded me in my barely-above-minimum-wage job, I undertook a clandestine campaign to keep it hidden. Even though the book was in high demand, I never shelved it with the display of "new books" and instead would deliberately misshelve it with car repair books or travel books. I figured I was saving dozens of Farmers Branch women from ingesting that crap.

At the end of the summer, I got hired to teach French and English at a high school, working as a long-term substitute for a teacher who'd been in a bad car wreck. Quickly, I moved into an apartment of my own. I also worked occasional evenings and Saturdays at a Sears store where I put a good wool coat on layaway. It was gold with a cinched waist, and it was the first coat I'd ever owned that wasn't a hand-me-down with moth holes.

I tried to build a life of my own, but Farmers Branch loomed too close. Mom had moved back with Dad, and it seemed that something was always on the verge of a boilover. When my friend Mike was home from law school for Christmas, I invited him to my apartment for dinner, imagining that maybe there could be something between us. I spent a couple hours in preparation, and if nothing else, I was looking forward to catching up and hearing about law school.

Mike was barely seated when there came a knock. Glassy-eyed and incoherent, Nancy was being held up by a friend, who told me that my dad was on a rampage and that Nancy had fled to his house. She'd begged him to take her to my apartment, and had also begged to stop by a bar on the way. So, despite my guest, Nancy came stumbling in and pretty much killed the evening. Even in my own apartment, there was no escape from the dark clouds of Farmers Branch.

MOM WANTED ME to take tennis lessons with my oldest sister, Rita. She said we needed "sister-bonding time," and she also thought Rita needed a night away from the demands of her husband and toddler. It was a class that met on one of the nights when I wasn't working at Sears, so I didn't have a good excuse not to. Reluctantly, I signed up, mostly just to please Mom.

I'd rush over to the tennis courts as soon as I got off from teaching school, take the class with Rita, and afterwards, we'd sit on a picnic table and chat a few minutes. But then there came a class when she wanted me to go get margaritas with her, and I just didn't want to. She insisted, but knowing I had to get up and teach school the next day, I declined. She even said she'd buy, but I still refused.

"I'm sorry, but I've still got to finish a lesson plan tonight," I said.

The next thing I knew, Rita was throwing a full-on, red-faced, foot-stomping tantrum right there on the sidewalk. "You never do anything I want to do!" she screamed. "You're never there for me!"

Shocked, I tried again to tell her I was sorry, but nothing I said made any difference.

"Rita, I'm trying. That's why I'm taking this tennis class. I'm trying to be with you."

She kept screaming. "You never support me! You aren't a real sister at all!"

If it weren't for the fact that she was five-foot-five and had a pretty fair cussing vocabulary, you might have thought she was a two-year-old having a meltdown. Finally, I just mumbled that I had to go, and I turned and left her there, still stomping her feet and yelling. I'm not exaggerating. She was literally stomping her feet.

The next week rolled around, and I went back to the tennis class. Rita showed up too, and we both just pretended nothing had happened. But even though we never spoke about the tantrum, I wasn't able to forget it. After a couple more classes, I took on another evening shift at Sears just to have an excuse to quit going to the class.

Then I decided to take a belly dance class. It was something I really wanted—the music reminded me of the kind Ahmed would listen to. But when I told Mom about it, she was livid. With some kind of carnal image fixed in her head, she railed against me for showing off my body. In actuality, with its long skirt and gauzy net draping around my middle, my belly-dancing costume covered more of me than my old school-approved Lionette uniform had. But there was no telling that to Mom. She wasn't interested in the reality of what I wore or how I felt about it.

When it came time for our class "recital"—a performance onstage at the rec center where the room would be filled with families and kids—I made the mistake of telling Mom about it, thinking she might want to come and see what I was doing. She didn't.

Yet, one day when I was at the house, she insisted out of the blue that I perform for Dad—they were back living together again. "If you can't perform for your father, then you shouldn't be performing for others," she railed, as she dragged Dad and me into the living room. Dad looked even more embarrassed than I was, but there was no deterring Mom.

"So, show him," she yelled. "Show him the kind of dance you're doing!" I protested that there wasn't any music, but Mom just kept screaming at me to "show him!" So finally, in silence, sitting on the edge of a chair, I did a five-second undulating arm movement that I was particularly proud of. Dad applauded and left the room. Mom glared.

Years later, when I decided to take hula lessons, I never told her.

DANCE CLASSES WERE one of the few things that gave me brief reprieve from my inner chaos. They took me outside of my messed-up head and at least gave me evenings when I was in the company of others rather than being left to my own solitary ruminations.

Alone, I would obsess over how meaningless and empty my life was, and I would ponder the possibility of simply ending the pain of it. I could see only a bleak void stretching into the future; my mind could conjure no reprieve. I grew fearful of my own self, of the darkness within me.

Apart from occasional phone calls with my old college friend Madge, I hid my despondency from everyone. Of course, that wasn't anything unusual. With my family, I was accustomed to concealing my thoughts.

I didn't manifest my inner turmoil in foot-stomping tantrums, like Rita; I guzzled alcohol instead. Having always been the one in the family to hold things together, on my own, I fell apart. Alone in my apartment, evenings would often descend into despair, and ruminations would descend into plans—exit plans.

Over the course of months, I grew determined to end my life, and once the decision was made, I felt peace about it.

So, finally, there came a morning when I woke up lying in my own vomit. I felt only revulsion at the stench, self-loathing for my ineptness, and rage at finding myself still alive. I had taken every pill I could gather, including some sleeping pills I'd filched from Mom's medicine cabinet, and had chased them with as much cheap vodka as I could pour down my throat.

Despite that, I had failed at doing away with myself. There was nothing to do but clean up the mess.

SAYING THAT SHE wanted her life to be completely independent of men, Judy told me she had "decided" to become lesbian as a "political act." She claimed her decision was driven by years of disgust with the men in our family: Dad, her ex-husband Darrell, and Rita's husband Richard.

"What good are they?" she asked. "Women don't need men, and if you were a true feminist, you'd realize that."

I never could see how Judy had any greater claim to being a "feminist" than I did. After all, I was the one who had ridden my bike across town to see Gloria Steinem and had shared the first issue of *Ms. Magazine*—the one with the eight-armed blue woman on the cover—all around the dorm. But of course, Judy never lost an opportunity to condescend. She relegated me to the role of rube.

Though I never believed Judy's "lesbianism as a political act" bunk, it was easy enough to see why she'd fallen for Charlotte, a young college student Judy had met after her divorce from Darrell. Years later, I felt only relief when Charlotte finally left Judy, because Charlotte deserved someone kinder. There had been too many times when I'd wanted to exhort her to "Run!" It was advice I probably should have heeded for myself.

But I'll give Judy credit. She made a bold move in announcing to Mom and Dad that she was a lesbian. She had asked me what I thought about her telling them, and naively, I'd predicted it wouldn't be a big deal. It was obvious that she and Charlotte were a couple; I couldn't imagine how Mom could have missed it. I'd seen them holding hands on the sofa while they talked with Mom in the kitchen. Surely, Mom had seen it too.

"She *has* to already know," I'd told Judy. But of course, I hadn't yet arrived at any understanding of how easily people can blind themselves to what is right in front of their eyes.

Mom pronounced Judy "dead," and declared that she could no longer set foot in the house.

Repeatedly, in visit after visit, I struggled to defend Judy. She was, after all, my sister. This was still two decades before Ellen DeGeneres would take the landmark step of coming out as gay on a television sitcom. So Judy didn't have any models to follow for how she did it, and Mom didn't have any models for how to handle it. I didn't have any either, so I just kept trying to talk to Mom about it. Over and over, in the face of Mom's clamped jaw, I kept bringing Judy up.

"She could choose to be normal, if she wanted," Mom insisted.

"But what if she can't, Mom? What if this is just the way she is?"

"She's just being stubborn. She's chosen this and she could choose *not* to be this way if she wanted to."

"No, Mom, I don't think so. This isn't something Judy can really choose." That's what I told Mom despite Judy's own insistence that she had indeed "decided" on it. I didn't figure it would help to share Judy's reasoning. It was enough to just keep working on mentioning Judy and not letting Mom pretend she'd never existed.

Since Judy wasn't welcome in the house, Mom spent more time railing at me about it than berating Judy. "But the Bible says . . ." Whenever Mom started down that track, I'd try to cut her short. So often it seemed she was just parroting something she'd heard from someone else, and I figured she'd probably been talking to Brother Hayden. Mom would read to me from Leviticus and scream that Judy was "rebelling against God" and was an "abomination"—almost certainly not her own words.

It became a sore spot between Mom and me, but stubbornly, every time I visited, I still kept trying to talk about it. I wasn't about to let Mom erase Judy without putting up a fight.

Meanwhile, Dad secretively tried to keep up a connection with Judy. Once when I was visiting, Mom left for the grocery store, and as soon as her car was out of the garage, Dad went straight to the phone on the kitchen wall and got Judy's number off the paper still taped to the back of the pantry door.

"Don't tell your mother," he said, winking as he pushed around the numbers on the rotary dial. "I just like to hear her voice."

I loved Dad for that. I imagine the whole notion of lesbianism remained a mystery to him until the day he died. But that wasn't what mattered. For him, it was simple and unconditional: Judy was his daughter and he loved her.

For a couple years, Judy completely disappeared from family life. She moved to Louisiana for a job with a big accounting firm—the first of many career moves—and Charlotte went with her. Eventually, Mom's hard-heartedness softened, or maybe she just finally realized that withholding her love wouldn't make Judy yield, wouldn't change her.

There was no big announcement, nor any dramatic scene. One day, Mom simply declared that Judy and Charlotte would be joining us for Thanksgiving. And we all acted as though nothing had ever happened.

9

My Face

She conquered her demons and wore her scars like wings.

—Atticus

AFTER A DAY of teaching school, I dropped by the house. With Dad in his chair and *Wheel of Fortune* blaring in the background, Mom started talking about Lizzie's nose job. Lizzie was the daughter of the teacher whose classroom was across the hall from Mom's, and she was about my same age. Ordinarily, I tended to tune out Mom's ramblings about Lizzie because Lizzie's family was so obviously well-to-do. Maybe Mom didn't see how she was playing the comparison game, but I sure did. It was like listening to someone extol the accomplishments of Susie on Saturn. It was a different world.

"And you'll never guess who her surgeon was!" said Mom. "It was the same doctor who assisted Dr. Mills with *your* third surgery when you were a baby."

My ears perked up. "Oh? What was his name?"

"Klein. Dr. Klein. I remember him," said Mom. "Back then, he was a young surgeon just getting started."

Mom continued, telling me how great Lizzie looked when she dropped by the school to pick up her mother. But I tuned all that out and stored the name: "Klein." For the first time ever, I had health insurance with my teaching job, and I'd been wondering whether it might be possible to make my face look a little more normal. Unwittingly, Mom had given me the nudge I needed to follow through.

A few weeks later, I stepped into Dr. Klein's office in the ritzy Turtle Creek part of Dallas. "We were expecting to see you seven years ago," said Dr. Klein, the first thing out of his mouth when he stepped into the examining room. Seeing my look of befuddlement, he explained that, ordinarily, they would have evaluated someone like me for a nose job at around age sixteen.

"A misshapen nose goes along with having a cleft lip," he said, "so that's a routine part of the treatment protocol. Ordinarily, we would do it a little sooner, but now is fine."

I kept trying to absorb what he was telling me—that most people with a cleft lip would have had their nose fixed sooner, and that he had told my parents to bring me back when I was sixteen. But they hadn't.

Many years later, I also learned that, in addition to surgical repairs of the soft tissues, most children with clefts also have bone graft surgery. But for me, that never happened either. I remember, just before I got braces, lying in a chair with a doctor and Dad on either side, talking over me, and the doctor was trying to convince Dad to let me have the surgery. The more the doctor tried to persuade him, the more irritated Dad got.

When I was in my fifties, a new young dentist insisted that I had some serious bone loss. He referred me to an endodontist who referred me to an oral surgeon, who in apparent frustration, said he suspected the dentist had simply never seen a cleft that was left unrepaired at the bone. "I don't know why this wasn't done for you as a child," he said, "but in this country, a bone graft is so routine for clefts that your dentist may have never seen an unrepaired one." He didn't recommend that I do anything at this point, explaining that the graft surgery would be much more complicated and disruptive for an adult than for a child.

The nose surgery Dr. Klein recommended was something else that, in this country, most kids with clefts would have had done earlier. It was considered reconstructive, not cosmetic, so it would be covered by my health insurance, and I went forward with scheduling it. Then I told Mom and Dad.

I started out by just saying that I'd been to see Dr. Klein for a consultation. "Oh, did he show you the pictures of what you looked like when you were born?" asked Mom.

"Uhh, yeah," I lied.

"Then you can imagine how shocked I was. I thought I'd given birth to a monster."

I looked at Mom's face and wondered if she had any inkling of how her words made me feel. "I'm sure it must have been upsetting, Mom."

"I couldn't even feed you like a normal baby," she continued. "You didn't have any sucking ability, so I had to use a giant eyedropper." I pondered that image for a second and saw the look on Mom's face as she conjured her own memory of it. Then, since I couldn't figure out what more to say, I surged onward with telling her I'd scheduled the nose surgery.

"Don't be silly," she said. "It won't make any difference."

"What do you mean? Dr. Klein says it's a surgery that could help me."

"It won't make any difference. You'll never be perfect."

"Well, sure, I know I'll never be perfect. But I don't think anyone's perfect anyway, so why shouldn't I try to be better?"

"You know what I mean. You'll still have a scar."

"I know that, Mom. I know that."

"Then you know it won't make any difference."

"But it might make a difference to *me*, Mom."

"It won't make any difference. You *think* you're going to be beautiful, but you won't."

In the chasm of a long silence, I stared down at the yellowed linoleum covered in dog hairs. "Maybe I won't be beautiful, but I can be better. Besides, *you* had a nose job."

That was stepping over a line and I knew it. Mom had mentioned it a few times, but it was one of those things that only *she* could talk about. Not that there was a rule written down somewhere, but like so many of the other unspoken rules of our house, I knew it instinctively. Still, Mom's nose job wasn't some secret.

As the story went, when Mom was around ten, her older brother, Jack, had punched her and broke her nose. Her mother tried to push it back into place without taking her to a doctor, which resulted in Mom being left with a lump on the bridge of her nose. So, when she finished high school, her parents gave her a nose job as a graduation present. It made a dramatic difference; I knew because I'd seen some of her old pre-surgery high school photos.

Mom glared at me, and I knew she was irritated that I would dare to draw any comparison between her and me. I thought about how awful it must have been for her to have a baby as freakish as me—a baby who had needed three surgeries before she even turned three. I wondered if some part of Mom thought it was her fault. Once, out of the blue, she told me that she'd taken "diet pills" when she was pregnant with me because she hadn't lost all the weight she'd gained when she was pregnant with Judy and didn't want to gain still more while carrying me. I thought about that glamour-shot portrait she kept in the cedar chest and realized she must have been trying to hang onto that beauty queen image of herself even when she was pregnant.

I wondered whether with each surgery I'd had, Mom had been disappointed. Had she imagined each time that, afterwards, I would look normal? Had she waited each time for the stitches to come out, for the bandages to be removed, for the swelling and redness to subside, only to still see the scar smack dab in the middle of my face?

Mom had always treated me like a mistake in need of correction. "Stand up straighter . . . Be friendlier . . . Smile more . . . Don't mumble." Constantly, there was something wrong about me that seemed to catch her attention. Did it start the moment I was born? When she first looked at my face? Or had it begun even sooner?

She'd flat-out told me that I wasn't planned—that I was "a mistake"—and that I'd come too soon after Judy. "Those things happened in those days," she'd said matter-of-factly, almost magnanimously. So maybe the feeling of "a mistake" had originated the instant she learned she was pregnant with me and had remained attached to me ever after. Maybe, even if I'd been born perfect, I would have still been "a mistake." As it was, she had to deal with the fact that I was *both* "a mistake" *and* defective. Strangely, whenever I contemplated this, I felt sorry for Mom.

But one day, I found myself wondering whether Mom had ever once tried to imagine what it was like for *me*. Had she ever considered what it was like for me to be made fun of at school? To have other kids call me names? To struggle up to age fourteen with trying to learn to talk well, in a way that wouldn't cause other kids to laugh?

I remembered a story Mom once told me about the time her brother Jack had sent her on an errand to the corner store, telling her that her mom wanted her to go get "three spools of silver thread." Mom recounted how grown up she had felt to be entrusted with an errand on her own, so she skipped off to the shop, holding the money Jack had given her. But when she arrived and tried to tell the shopkeeper that she needed "three spools of silver thread," the shop-keeper couldn't understand her. "Thee thpooth of thiva thed." Mom herself had imitated how she recollected sounding. As she repeated it over and over, seem-ingly transported back to age eight and trying all over again to tell the shop-keeper what her mother wanted, tears came to her eyes. She said that she ran home crying, and "Jack laughed and laughed."

That was when I first realized that, even though Mom wasn't born with a cleft lip, she'd still grown up with a serious enough speech impediment that people struggled to understand her. And her own brother had set her up to be humiliated. I began to understand that maybe the reason Mom had never been able to put herself in my shoes was because, with a severe speech impediment and a facial disfigurement, I reminded Mom too much of her own younger self, and it was a place in her memories that she didn't want to go.

Still glaring and obviously angry at me for bringing up *her* nose job, Mom finally answered me. "I wasn't like you. I could be fixed. You can't."

Unsure of exactly what she meant, I tried again to explain that the doctor thought the surgery could fix my nose just fine. But Mom only grew more frus-trated. "No," she insisted. "You can't be fixed. You'll still have a scar."

"Yeah, I know, Mom. I'll still have a scar, but he thinks the surgery might even help me breathe better. Afterwards, I should be able to breathe through my nose. So even if nothing else, that'll be an improvement."

"That's not why you're doing it and you know it. You're fooling yourself. It won't make you pretty."

I can't remember which of us had the last word. I remember only the feel-ing that nothing I could ever do would make it up to Mom for the horror she'd felt when I was born. She'd just never gotten over it.

But of course, Mom's aversion wasn't all that unusual. Plenty of studies have shown that, from an early age, humans are instinctually drawn to more attractive faces. Babies show a preference for more symmetrical faces. Jurors tend to side with better-looking defendants. Teachers give more attention to more attractive children. And children themselves prefer to have the handsom-est children as friends. Heck, some biblical literalists might argue that even God rejects those with a facial disfigurement. There it is in Leviticus 21: a person with a "marred face" is forbidden from going to the altar or making any offering to God.

And how could I forget the time when, in the midst of proudly prattling on about her new grandson, my regular hair stylist had suddenly blurted, "He ain't no harelip, that's for sure." At first, I thought I must have misheard her, but the awkward silence that followed told me I hadn't. I looked at her in the mirror and knew she realized her slipup. Finally, she broke the dead space and tried to smooth it. "Well, you know what I mean—he's just perfect in every way. There's nothing at all the matter with him. He's totally perfect." I knew what she meant, but I also knew that, even though she'd intended no harm, she'd revealed something true about her thoughts. I tried to help her move past the blunder by oohing and aahing over the baby's photo, but I knew I wouldn't go back to her salon again.

So I had the nose surgery. It was Dad who took me to the hospital, who stayed with me late into the night before surgery, and who came by each afternoon of my four-day stay as I was recovering. Weeks later, after the insurance company had processed the claim, Dad asked me how much I'd had to pay out of pocket and tried to reimburse me—about $300 as I recall. "We should have done this a long time ago," he said, "so let us help you with it now." I was so moved that I nearly started crying. But before he could actually put the bills in my hand, Mom stepped between us and told him to put his money away.

"She's the one who wanted to have the surgery, so she should be the one to pay for it."

Mom glared. Dad hesitated.

"Can you handle it?" he asked, still extending his hand.

Mom pushed Dad's hand back down in his lap and pronounced her firm conclusion. "She doesn't need it." But in Dad's eyes, I still saw the questioning look. He knew the truth: $300 was a huge sum for me back then. He felt bad about it.

"Don't worry about it, Daddy," I reassured him. "I can manage it."

Nine months after the surgery, I packed up my apartment and moved to Austin to start graduate school at the University of Texas. In deciding to get a Master's degree in anthropology, I again chose an impractical path, as Mom was quick to point out. But I received a generous fellowship, and most importantly, it gave me an excuse to move farther from Farmers Branch.

The Second Death

10

Married the Wrong Sister

The saddest thing about betrayal is that it never comes from your enemies;
it comes from those you trust the most.

—Author unknown

WHEN MY NO-GOOD scoundrel of a brother-in-law decided to make a move on me, my life ended again, then and there. But once again, I didn't realize it at the time. The sun kept right on rising and setting, and I just kept going from day to day, acting like nothing had happened. But now that I've been through a couple more lifetimes, I can look back and see those moments of death— moments when everything changed.

Those moments always take you by surprise. One second you're a flower, and the next you're a weed, and like a dandelion, all the seeds of your whole identity are being blown into kingdom come.

I was moving out of my apartment in Austin and was going to be in Farmers Branch for a few days before leaving the country to work on an archaeological dig and then to meet up with my Moroccan boyfriend, Ahmed, whom I'd stayed in touch with ever since leaving my au pair job in France. On my last day in Austin, Richard called, saying that Patty, my niece, would love to see me before I left. He asked if I could babysit her for a couple hours in the afternoon when I was in town.

"Sure." I said it without even thinking. I knew that Richard and Rita had gotten divorced a couple months earlier, and Rita had moved to an apartment. But it didn't even occur to me that their divorce would be a reason I shouldn't babysit three-year-old Patty, and the thought of seeing her before I left the country had seemed like something good. But when I told Mom that I was going to babysit Patty, she threw a tizzy.

"He's dead to us," she screamed. "You can't go over there."

"But he's still Patty's father," I protested, "and Patty's part of our family. So why shouldn't I babysit her?"

"Because Richard is *not* part of our family."

"But what about Patty, Mom? Richard's her dad. So how can we just pretend he doesn't exist?"

Mom and I went round and round; she was flat-out livid. Every time I said, "You can't just erase him," Mom responded with "only family is family." She repeated those four words as if they were some kind of mantra, and though she insisted "you know what I mean," I had no clue. In my twenty-four-year-old brain, Mom's rage wasn't reason enough for me to not go babysit like I'd said I would. So I got into my old Mustang and rolled down the window.

"Mark my words," yelled Mom, "if you go over there, you'll cause a permanent rift between you and your sister." I just started up the engine.

Richard was still living at their house, trying to get it ready for sale. It was a house I'd been to dozens of times, and strangely, despite the rupture of Rita and Richard's marriage, the house itself didn't look as though much had changed. Much of the furniture was still there and everything seemed almost normal . . . until suddenly it wasn't.

Patty was down for her afternoon nap when Richard returned from his errands and offered me a beer. "No thanks," I said as I started corralling Patty's toys. Richard guzzled his beer and launched into some rambling story about how what he had really wanted in life was to be a journalist. I was only half-listening, but it had something to do with him lamenting that, since he had to work during college, he couldn't put in the late hours to be on staff for the university newspaper. Mostly I was just ignoring him, but then, suddenly, he shifted.

"You know, Christa, I think the biggest mistake of my life was that I married the wrong sister."

That's what he said. Out of the blue. I froze.

Geezus. Mom was right. That's what I remember thinking. I had ignored Mom because I thought she was being overly dramatic about Rita and Richard's divorce, the same as she'd been when Judy announced she was a lesbian. Immediately, my mind replayed everything Mom had said.

"Richard is dead to us," she'd yelled. But it had felt as though she was lecturing me, and I hadn't wanted to listen.

"Married the wrong sister." Richard's words began to ricochet wildly in my brain, but I pretended I hadn't heard him and I moved to pick up my purse off the counter. Pretending: It was a longtime familial pattern. Whenever things went wrong, we just lapsed into pretending things were normal, as though pretending could make it so.

But then I felt his hand on my shoulder. He was standing right behind me—looming over me. My stomach lurched. My fists clenched shut.

"I got the right family, but I picked the wrong sister. I should have picked you, Christa. You're the one I want."

I took a step away from the hand and turned around, my arms crossed over my chest.

"Richard, you've been with Rita since I was ten. I was there at vacation Bible school when you washed Judy's bloody sock after she stepped on a nail. Remember?"

Even as I said it, I knew it was a stupid thing to say. *Vacation Bible school? Where did that come from?* I tried again.

"Look, all I'm saying is . . . you're like a brother to me."

Torn between wanting to be kind and wanting to run, I felt a faint frisson of fear—or maybe it was déjà vu—curling up the back of my neck. My mind froze. Stupidly, I remember worrying about whether I was hurting his feelings, but at the same time, all I wanted was to get out of there. Out of that house. Out of Farmers Branch. Out of the country.

He stepped forward. I stepped back.

"I'm not with Rita anymore," he said, reaching his upturned hands toward me. "I've felt this way a long time, Christa. And now, finally, I can be honest and tell you how I feel. I'm free."

"Free." That's what he said. I remember because my mind fixated on that word. There he was talking about being "free" while I was feeling stupid and afraid and trapped in his house. Finally, I just felt angry and wondered whether he had given even a moment's thought to the kind of predicament his confession would put *me* in.

"Look," I railed, "the whole reason you're not with Rita right now is because you cheated on her."

"That was a mistake."

"Yeah. And you're making another mistake right now."

"Christa, I just . . ."

"No. You made a huge mistake and that's the only thing you need to know."

"You're right. I made a mistake, and I'm sorry about it. But I couldn't keep living a lie. It's *always* been a lie. When will *I* be loved?"

Linda Ronstadt? That was my first thought. Of course, it's really an Everly Brothers line—"when will I be loved"—but at the time, my mind went to Linda Ronstadt. Then it went all over the place, trying to find some place to hide to avoid hearing what Richard was saying.

"Please, just think about it—give me a chance."

Oh God, I hate it when Mom is right. Over and over, that's where my mind kept going. *I should have listened.*

"No. I don't want to think about it. I'm leaving the country tomorrow, and that's the *only* thing I want to think about. This is bullshit."

I felt trapped. His hulking frame was between me and the door. And every side step I took, he shifted in the same direction. *Is it my imagination?* I began to feel frantic.

"Christa, I heard you were leaving and that's why I knew I had to say something. I didn't want you to go away and not know how I felt. Just promise me you'll think about it."

Geez. Don't I have enough to think about? Ahmed had invited me to go with him to the wedding of his sister in Marrakech. After two years apart, I was going to reunite with him and meet his family. I was nervous. It seemed like do-or-die time for our relationship, and I didn't know when or if I'd be coming back to the States.

I had managed to get a summer job working on an archaeological dig in Israel, which had gained me a trip across the Atlantic, along with eight weeks of room and board. After that, I was going to meet up with Ahmed in Belgium, and then take the train with him to Morocco. My mind was reeling. The logistics and emotional weight of it had overwhelmed me.

"No. I don't want to think about it," I told Richard. "I'm leaving the country, and I've got plenty of other things to think about. I'm leaving."

"Promise me you'll call me when you get back."

"No. Why would I call you? Besides, I don't know when I'm coming back. I don't even know *if* I'm coming back."

How can I get out that door? Why won't he step aside?

"I don't want you to leave when you're upset like this. Just promise me you'll call me. That's all I'm asking."

"Look, I need to finish packing. I've got a lot to do before I leave."

"Promise me you'll call. I'll buy you a cup of coffee, and we can talk about things."

"No. There's nothing to talk about."

"Just a cup of coffee. Come on, just call me."

"I don't drink coffee."

"Just call me, okay? That's all I'm asking." I stared at him and then stared past him to the door. In the gap of silence, he whispered, "Please."

That was when I saw the sadness in his eyes and wished I hadn't. "Okay, fine, I'll call."

"You have to promise. Promise you'll call me as soon as you get back."

"Look. This is stupid. I told you. I don't even know if I'm coming back. I don't know what's going to happen."

"Just promise me you'll call. Whenever it is. Promise you'll call me before you talk to anyone else. Promise me."

"All right. I promise. I'll call." With that, he shifted slightly to the side, and I stepped forward, brushing his arm as I passed. I didn't say goodbye. I went out the door, got in my car, and drove away.

The next morning, I got on a plane.

Should I have told Rita? Maybe. But didn't she have enough hurt already without knowing that her ex-husband had hit on her sister? That's what I thought at the time. Mom was the one who had given me the down-and-dirty on all the layers of deception wrapped up in Richard's affair—how he'd been carrying on even while he and Rita had been trying to adopt a second child. But I had also seen Rita for myself on an Easter break trip. She had a Judy Collins song stuck in the turntable of her brain, and every other sentence she spoke ended with "there ought to be clowns." I had driven the four hours back to Austin, haunted by the deadness of what I'd seen in Rita's eyes and vowing that I never wanted to hear that song again.

With that memory of my last visit with Rita, I couldn't imagine telling her what Richard had said.

Even if I had wanted to, how exactly could I have told her? By letter from across the ocean? That didn't seem right. And I sure as heck couldn't tell Mom. She was already on simmer, barely speaking to me, and it would not get better if I told her about Richard's pass. One way or another, I knew I'd be blamed.

Mostly I just didn't want to think about it. My whole life felt topsy-turvy, and all I wanted was to get out of there. It was Dad who took me to the airport the next day. Mom was still mad.

ON THE ARCHAEOLOGICAL dig in Israel, I did daily battle with scorpions, sun, dehydration, exhaustion, and endless dirt. It was hard physical labor, and I lost all illusions about the glamour of archaeology. But mentally, I was enmeshed with the religious imagery that surrounded me, not only near the Sea of Galilee where I was working, but also on weekends when I would hop on a bus to travel the small country.

When the dig-time was done, I flew to Paris, met up with Ahmed in Belgium, and then together, we traveled southward on trains following the coast of Spain, ferried across the Strait of Gibraltar, and finally arrived in Marrakech. After stopping by a traditional hammam, where in a sparsely lit subterranean room I was surrounded by naked women and children and given two wooden buckets of water for washing myself, we went to his uncle's house, a traditional *riad* in the ancient, maze-like medina of the city. Never in my life have I encountered more hospitable people. They gave me a *takchita* to wear to the wedding festivities.

It was a Berber celebration with three days of feasting and dancing, unlike anything I had ever seen. Because we'd missed one of our train connections, we arrived just after the nuptials, with the post-wedding event in full swing in the central courtyard. It was a sensory overload of spice and sweat and music and drums, with heaping platters of couscous abounding. *Djellaba*-clad men were singing while women with hennaed hands ululated. Around them twirled dancers dressed in white. According to tradition, all of this was going on while the bride and groom consummated the marriage in a room off the courtyard.

The bride was fifteen years old. The groom was in his late twenties.

Late into the night, as I watched from the rooftop, a roar went up from the crowd in the courtyard, and I glimpsed a wave of something white. I was told that it was the bloody sheet.

The next afternoon, we went back over to the house of the wedding party, and I sat down on a cushion in the women's room. The men gathered in a separate room. In turns, the women danced for one another, old and young, moving their hips, swaying and laughing. I couldn't understand their chattering because the women didn't speak French or English, and I didn't speak Berber or Arabic. But I joined them in the universal language of giggles and grins. Ahmed told me that this was when women shared with the bride "the secrets of marriage."

The bride sat huddled at the end of the room underneath her bloody sheet. I glimpsed her hennaed hand when other women lifted the sheet's corner to pass her a morsel of food, and occasionally, I heard a low moan from the amorphous mass beneath the sheet.

The blood was spread and splattered. It was a lot, more than just a spot. I tried not to look at it. In my mind, I kept hoping that maybe it was the blood of a goat because I had heard that brides sometimes ensured the display of virginity by carrying a vial of goat's blood into the bridal chamber.

But in one brief moment, when the sheet was lifted, I found myself looking straight into the girl's kohl-lined eyes. What I saw in them was fear.

In that moment, I lost all sense of anthropological detachment. I was overcome with the sense that I was witnessing something wrong, and I couldn't intellectualize it. Though I told myself I was being ethnocentric—and perhaps I was—I couldn't shake what I had seen in those eyes.

When the days of celebrating were done, I left Ahmed behind and got on a train alone, intending to make it to Luxembourg for a discount flight back to the United States. The last of my money had been stolen in a street-grab, and I didn't even own a credit card. I had only my train tickets, my plane ticket, my passport, and seven stashed-away one-dollar bills. But I wasn't too worried. I figured my tickets would eventually get me home.

On the train, I conversed with two young girls sitting across the compartment from me. They were engaging and inquisitive, eagerly practicing their French by politely barraging me with questions about myself and America. I was duly impressed because I knew it was unusual for Moroccan girls to be taught French, and because the two girls were charming. But somewhere between Marrakech and Tangier, the conductor came by. He became irate, but since his tirade was in Arabic, I couldn't understand. Still, there was no mistaking his tone, and the two young girls grew eyes as big as saucers. After the conductor left, they fell totally silent.

The girls' *djellaba*-dressed dad told me that the conductor was upset because of the Israeli visa in my passport and because I was on the wrong train. It was a train that went to the same destination, the ferry port of Tangier, but it was a faster, more expensive train than the one allowed by my ticket. The conductor was going to put me off at the next station.

Sure enough, when the train started slowing down, the conductor appeared again, waiting in the corridor. I looked out the window and knew I was in serious trouble. The station was little more than a stop in the middle of the desert. *Without money, how would I ever get out of there?*

I think the girls' dad must have seen the fear in my face. He stood, pulled out his wallet, and pressed some bills into the conductor's palm. I wept with relief and thanked him, but he simply shrugged. "*J'ai deux filles*," he said—"I have two daughters."

WHEN I ARRIVED back in Farmers Branch, I did what I had promised—I called Richard. I did it almost immediately because I wanted to get it over with before I headed back to Austin.

Right away, he told me that he and Rita were back together. I gushed my congratulations and told him how happy I was to hear the news. "So, I guess I'll just see you around at some family thing or other," I said, and that was the end of it. Relieved that no awkward discussion would be necessary, I imagined everything would go back to normal. But of course, I underestimated the weight of such a secret.

For decades, I didn't tell anyone other than my therapist about that "married the wrong sister" conversation with Richard. But for the next twenty-five years, I spent every family gathering trying to make sure I didn't wind up in a room alone with him. If everyone else left the room, then so did I.

Still, despite my vigilance, there were a few times when I got stuck. Not long after Rita and Richard remarried, I was sitting on the patio when Rita and Mom got up to go in the kitchen. Dad, who was half deaf by then, was tending a pear tree to the side of the patio, so my instinct failed me. I didn't sense myself as being alone with Richard, so I didn't hop right up. Sure enough, that was a mistake.

"Christa, I want to show you something," he said. "It's something I bought for Rita."

He pulled from his pocket a small metal disc and held it out in his open palm. I looked but didn't take it. "What is it?" I asked.

"It's an antique Roman coin. It's the same kind of coin that was paid to Judas Iscariot for his betrayal of Jesus. It's like one of the 'thirty pieces.'"

"Really?" I was skeptical, but Richard continued.

"It's symbolic," he explained. "It's to show I've bought back my betrayal of Rita. Now, it'll be as though it never happened."

"I see," I said. But, of course, I didn't. I just couldn't figure out why he was telling *me* about it. Besides, even if he thought he had "bought back" the betrayal of his affair with the secretary, I didn't imagine for one second that he had ever told Rita about what he'd said to me. That was a betrayal that couldn't be remedied with a coin from an antique shop. Nor did I imagine that he had ever given a moment's thought to what his "married the wrong sister" confession did to *me*. He left me holding a dark secret that alienated me, put me at risk of unmerited blame, and undid my identity within the family.

11

Mad Dog & Beans

Love. It was the beginning and the end of everything, the foundation and the ceiling and the air in between.

—Kristin Hannah

IN AUSTIN, AT a hole-in-the-wall called Mad Dog & Beans, I watched him saunter across the parking lot with a grin that said "I'm trouble." He wore a faded red flannel shirt that was torn at one elbow, and when he sat down, I saw that his aviator glasses were held together with duct tape. But when he said hello, I saw behind those mangled glasses the steadiest clear blue eyes I'd ever encountered. I was smitten.

When I met Jim, I was at a place in my life where I didn't really want to be in a relationship. I was twenty-five and at ease with being on my own. And though I wouldn't have acknowledged it at the time, I was terrified of trusting someone. With prior boyfriends, I had remained more emotionally detached. So they hadn't been so scary. But with Jim, I felt something powerful, and on some level, I think I knew that he could be life-altering. So I told him that I couldn't possibly be serious about someone who hadn't read *Anna Karenina*.

Yeah. I kid you not. That's what I did.

I loved *Anna Karenina*, but given its weight, most people view it as a bear of a book, and I didn't figure Jim would actually read it. But he surprised me. Of course, he didn't love the book as much as I did, but he talked about it enough that I knew he wasn't lying. He had read it. So, what was I to do?

I moved into his tiny garage apartment overlooking Stacy Park, and in that dingy, musty, roach-infested place, Jim gave me his heart and I gave him mine.

We were both hardheaded loners by nature, and living together didn't come easily. The close quarters and lack of air conditioning didn't help. We fought long, hard, and often. But whenever our battles became too bitter, one of us would storm out to the solace of Stacy Park. If we hadn't had the park as a release valve, I don't think we ever would have lasted.

Sometimes my crazed skittishness got the best of me. Feelings of trust triggered breathtaking terror, and the closer I grew to Jim, the more fearful I became. In recent years, I've learned this is common for survivors of long-term childhood sexual abuse. It's why many of us have such enormous difficulty in building strong relationships. It's one more way in which the abuse robs us.

Whenever the inexplicable fear overwhelmed me—when I couldn't manage to tamp it down—I would run out of the apartment in the middle of the night, go down to the park, and wander along the creek. I'd whisper to the ancient oaks and listen to the response of their rustling leaves. Finally, when I tired of walking, I would crawl under one of the bridges where I'd sit in the dark with my knees folded up against my chest and wait for the waves of terror to subside.

Jim would sometimes awaken and go out in the dark to search the park for me. I could hear him calling my name, but I seldom answered. It didn't matter. Jim knew every nook and cranny, so he usually found me. He would sit down beside me and try to soothe me, talking softly as though I were a wounded wild animal, which I guess wasn't far from the truth. Jim didn't know what was wrong with me, and neither did I, but in the dark of the park, the only thing that mattered was the steady sound of his voice. That sound carried the power to return me to my own self—the self that existed in the world that Jim and I were making.

THE FIRST CHRISTMAS after meeting Jim, I drove to Farmers Branch alone. Jim hadn't yet met my family, and as a respiratory therapist, he was working the holiday shift at the hospital so that coworkers with families wouldn't have to.

I knew Mom and Dad's problems had again intensified, but by then, I was numb to the random and repetitive cycles of escalation and de-escalation. On a visit a few weeks earlier, I'd arrived home to find Mom with a black eye. We'd all just ignored the obvious question until, finally, while helping Mom with some laundry, I'd managed to have some time alone with her.

"He didn't really hit me," she'd insisted. "He just pinned me against the doorframe and *pressed* his fist there. But it wasn't a hit."

In my mind's eye, I could visualize the scene—Dad spewing curses, his face inches from Mom's, his balled-up fist pressing into her temple, and Mom whimpering "Chuck, Chuck," calling him by his nickname and pleading with him. I'd also noticed a piece of patched drywall—more evidence of Dad's rage—and had tried then and there to get Mom to leave. But she'd said I was being "silly," that he hadn't realized how hard he was pressing, that I was making too much of it, and that it was "just a one-time thing."

Not long after that, Mom had called me, frantically repeating, "He got the gun." I knew right away she was talking about the shotgun Dad kept in the back of their bedroom closet. It was one of those things we never talked about, but somehow I'd always known it was there. I had tried to talk Mom into leaving the house, but she'd insisted it would all blow over and then proceeded to tell me in more detail about how Dad had stalked around the house carrying the gun. Mom said she had moved into the front bedroom, barricaded the door, and opened the window so she could get out fast if she needed to.

"But Mom," I'd begged, "he could shoot through the door! Or he could just get it open a crack. You've got to leave!"

Mom wouldn't budge. "How will you go to the bathroom?" I'd asked, try-ing to make her see how impossible it was. But she'd insisted she could just hold it until he was asleep or out in the yard or gone on some errand. I visualized Mom sneaking to the bathroom in the middle of the night with Dad hearing her and terrorizing her, but no amount of trying to reason with Mom made a bit of difference. When she told me she kept a bucket in the room just in case she really *couldn't* hold it, I agonized over whether I should drop everything and drive straight to Farmers Branch. But it was the end of the semester and I had papers that needed finishing, and I told myself that if I couldn't talk Mom into leaving on the phone, there was no reason to think she'd change her mind just because I was there in person. So, I decided to wait the couple weeks until Christmas to make the trip. Meanwhile, the next time I talked to her on the phone, it seemed the storm had indeed blown by.

With Christmas presents in the back seat, I drove the four hours north to Farmers Branch and arrived at their house just after dusk. I knocked at the kitchen door, and, puzzled by the lack of any greeting, I stepped inside, set my suitcase down, and walked the six steps into the den to flip the light switch. Suddenly, just about the time I made out his shadowy form in the chair, Dad let loose a string of expletives, yelling that I'd better not turn on that light and cussing about how I could go to hell with all the other two-legged bitches. His rage took me by surprise. I'd had no chance to see it building.

"Where's Mom?" I asked, trying to keep my voice free from the terror I felt inside.

He didn't answer. I could scarcely make out his face, but the sound of his breathing was ragged and wild. "I'm just going to get something from my car," I said, still trying to act normal even as all my nerve endings were buzzing with fear and every cell in my body was screaming, "Get out!" So, with my purse still over my shoulder, and with no plan other than to flee, I moved back toward the kitchen door. Leaving my suitcase where it sat on the kitchen floor, I stepped back into the garage. My car was at the curb, but before I could get to it, I heard the front door open and saw my suitcase flying through the air. It landed hard, split open, and scattered my clothes in the yard.

I gathered everything up as fast as I could, threw it all into the back seat of my car, fumbled my keys a couple times, and finally managed to pull away. I drove straight to Rita's house, and sure enough, that's where Mom was. Immediately, I used Rita's phone to call Nancy because I knew she'd be driving in too, and I wanted to warn her. Judy was no worry; her visits were rare—only about once a year—and she wasn't expected.

Much to my surprise, Nancy already knew that Mom was at Rita's house. Mom had called Nancy a day earlier. I felt betrayed.

"Why didn't you call and warn *me*?" I asked. "He was just sitting there. Stewing. In the dark. I was terrified."

"I wanted you to see how bad he's gotten," said Mom. "It's why I need you to move home."

"But I'm in school," I protested. "I can't just move home."

"But he's always better when you're around. If you lived with us, he wouldn't get like this."

"He threw my suitcase in the yard!" I screamed. "How is that better?"

"But he wouldn't have ever gotten to that point if you'd been here."

Mom's insistence that I should move back home didn't let up for the two nights that I stayed there at Rita's house. I felt afraid for Mom—*very* afraid—but I didn't want to stop my own life to live in my parents' house and try to protect her. To even contemplate it felt like dying. I swore to myself that I would stand firm against Mom's entreaties and would build a different kind of life than what Farmers Branch offered. *That* was my Christmas present to myself.

DURING THOSE YEARS in graduate school, I began seeing a psychiatrist at the student health center who put me through a smorgasbord of psychotropic medications. Though I was a long way from understanding why, I knew I needed help and was willing to try almost anything. My relationship with Jim was a powerful motivator. I loved him but I was depressed, anxious, and volatile. I was constantly pushing him away. The closer he got, the more I wanted to run. The thought of marriage was a no-way-no-how nonstarter. Even thinking about it took my breath away. Literally. My whole chest would tighten up.

In one of my first visits with Dr. Grey, I asked him if he could just hypnotize me to forget some things. "Sort of like a partial lobotomy," I said, laughing nervously, "with some memories just wiped out of existence?"

Strangely, I can't even remember exactly what it was that I wanted wiped away. Was I referring to family memories? Things Mom had said? I don't know. What I *do* know is that I never told Dr. Grey about having been sexually abused as a kid. I couldn't have because, even though it was wreaking havoc in my psyche, I didn't yet consciously view what happened as abuse. To the extent I thought about it at all—rarely and fleetingly—I still regarded it as some kind of affair.

Of course, my inability to understand the reality of what had been done to me wasn't at all unusual. Inherent to the trauma of childhood sexual abuse is a silencing effect. Like me, many survivors don't even recognize that what was done to them was abuse, and even if they show up in therapy, it can still take a long time before they talk about it, if at all. This is normal.

I was so uncomprehending that, when the psychiatrist told me my psychological manifestations were consistent with incest victims, I adamantly rejected his analysis. "Well maybe I'm messed up in the head, but that doesn't mean I'm an incest victim. Nothing like that ever happened to me."

Yet, despite my protest, he wasn't far off the mark. Clergy sexual abuse and incest give rise to similar traumas.

WHEN I FINALLY took Jim to meet my parents, Mom cast a long side-eye at his unkempt beard and then began interrogating him about his religion and his "intentions." I was aghast and protested meekly, but Jim took it in stride. Dad sat in the room with us, looking as if he'd been ordered to do so, but he stayed quiet, seemingly fixated on using a fingernail to scrape at some bit of dirt on his palm. With every one of Mom's questions, Jim answered truthfully and diplomatically. He was choosing his words with care, and I kept hoping Mom would be satisfied and stop. But she kept pressing.

Asked about his religion, Jim answered that he'd been raised Southern Baptist but that he didn't see himself that way anymore. Then he shifted amiably to talking about his uncle, who was a Southern Baptist missionary, and about how his mother and both grandmothers still went to Southern Baptist churches.

Mom interrupted. "But what about *you*?" she asked. "If you aren't a Baptist anymore, what *are* you? Are you a Methodist?"

Jim said no, that he wasn't a Methodist, but since he didn't volunteer anything else, Mom persisted, demanding to know what religion he was. "None," said Jim. Finally, Mom boiled her interrogation down to a single question: "Well, are you an atheist?"

Jim responded that some might call him that, but that he really didn't like labels. "Sometimes I think I'm an atheist and sometimes an agnostic," he said, "but mostly, I just don't think any of us really *know*, and I've never seen the need to put myself in a box."

But "in a box" was exactly where Mom was determined to put him, the box of an "unbeliever." She looked at me. "You're going to yoke yourself with an unbeliever?"

"Mom, we aren't 'yoked.' We're just together." I'm embarrassed to recall my own feebleness. Jim deserved better. But in the moment, I was pretty much irrelevant. Mom ignored me and went straight back to Jim.

"And what about your children? Have you thought about that? Will you raise your children as atheists?"

I was horrified. Jim and I hadn't even discussed marriage, let alone children. But by then, I had entered that numb state that my mother's presence so often induced. I could feel myself as a girl, lying in a snowdrift, hearing Mom calling me and choosing instead the coldness that surrounded me. But while I remained mute, incapable of mustering any coherent challenge to Mom's inquisition, Jim held steady. With an ever-so-slightly increased firmness in his voice—I may have been the only one to notice it—he said, "Well, if that day ever comes, I imagine Christa and I would talk about it a lot, and it would be up to the two of us to decide how we would raise our children."

I felt so proud of him—and so in love with him. Gently, but firmly, he had stood up to my mother even when I had failed to. Out of the corner of my eye, I caught a glimmer of a smile on Dad's face, and I swear, from that day forward, Dad took a liking to Jim. It always seemed a bit strange to me because, while they occasionally talked about running, it wasn't as if they sat around bonding over beers and football or anything like that. But though he was a man who liked few people and trusted even fewer, Dad took an unshakable liking to Jim. I think it was because he saw something true and honest in him, and Dad respected that.

Years later, I remembered Mom's inquisition when Jim and I were buying a teardrop camping trailer, and suddenly, out of the blue, before he put the key in our hands, the seller said, "We'd like to pray with you. Would that be okay?" Jim and I both hesitated.

"You're believers aren't you? People of faith?" He and his wife were holding out their hands, as if to take ours.

I cringed, but Jim said yes and took the man's hand. So I followed suit, and the four of us stood there on the sidewalk, holding hands in a circle, while the man prayed that God would use the trailer to strengthen our family bonds and that we would have safe travels. "Amen," he said, and I echoed with a soft "Amen" of my own.

"Do you feel like you lied to him?" I asked Jim later as we drove down the highway.

"No. I'm a person of faith too. It wasn't a lie."

"How do you figure?"

"I have faith in lots of things. I have faith in you. I have faith in us. I have faith in science. I have faith in the future. I have faith in humankind. I have faith the sun will come up. Christians don't have some monopoly on getting to define what faith is and isn't. I'm a person of faith too. It's just different."

I realized Jim was right. He was indeed a person of faith, and he had lived his faith day in and day out the whole time I'd known him. Meanwhile, I was the one still floundering in the paradox of being a person of faith who wished not to be. How many times had I prayed that God would please cease my belief? Too many.

At least Jim had a faith that made some sense.

I'D BEEN WITH Jim a couple of years when, one day, I made the mistake of saying something honest about my feelings in a conversation with Mom and Rita. Sitting on the patio, I told them how unsure I was about getting married and how I didn't think I really wanted to. I didn't give them the details of all that went on in my mind—probably because I feared it would sound too crazy—but for me to even imagine a wedding made my whole body shift into fight or flight mode. It filled me with a sense that death was imminent. It conjured inchoate memories of finding Mom unconscious in her bed after Judy's wedding and bodily memories of the horror of what had happened at First Baptist Church of Farmers Branch, where Rita and Judy and several of my friends had married. Even the faintest thoughts of church were *always* fraught, and in my mind church and weddings went together. I just couldn't let my mind go there.

At best, the prospect of a wedding made me want to hop on a bus to Alaska and disappear. Every time Jim tried to bring up the topic of marriage, that's exactly what I would start planning in my mind. So, as Jim grew to realize how unrelentingly skittish I was, he brought it up less and less. But even though we were happy the way we were, I knew there was something not quite normal about my reflexive urge to bolt.

I had hoped that if I talked about it, I might be able to sort things out. But immediately, Mom and Rita launched into berating Jim. They said I should give him an ultimatum: marry me or else.

I tried to clarify. "But I'm not talking about Jim. I'm talking about *me*. I don't know what *I* want."

"Oh, don't be silly," said Mom. "Of course, you want to get married."

Rita chimed in, "You're just afraid to admit that he doesn't really love you enough to marry you. It's your own little fantasy world, Christa, and all he's doing is using you."

"No. It's not like that. Jim would marry me tomorrow if I wanted. I don't doubt his commitment. It's *me*. I don't know what *I* want."

It was as though they hadn't heard me.

"Christa, if you give him the milk for free, he'll never buy the cow."

I stared at Mom, hardly believing what I'd heard. *Did she really say that?*

"Mom, I'm not a cow, and I'm not for sale."

"You know what I mean."

"Yeah, but it's not like that. I don't doubt Jim's commitment. That's not what I'm talking about."

"You're naive, Christa. *All* men are like that. They think below the belt. If you ever want to get married, you need to quit giving him what he wants."

Rita sat there, nodding her head in agreement, and I saw there was no point in continuing. So I tried to end it.

"Look, I'm sorry I brought it up." I picked up my iced tea and turned to go inside. But Mom couldn't let it go.

"Mark my words," she shouted after me, "if you keep giving him the milk for free, you're going to wind up an old maid."

Not long after that, on my next trip to Farmers Branch, Mom started in again with insisting I should move home to live with her and Dad.

Sensing the yawning chasm of Mom's neediness, I protested. "But I live in Austin now, Mom. I live with Jim. I can't just up and move back here with the two of you."

"That's not real. You know it's not. We're your family. You belong here."

"But it *is* real, Mom. It's real to me. I belong with Jim."

THE NEXT TIME Mom and Rita started in on me about why Jim and I weren't getting married, I told them what I often told other people: that we had decided to wait until *everyone* had the right to marry—gay people included.

They both looked at me uncomprehendingly, so I tried to explain that I was thinking of people like Judy and Charlotte. "Shouldn't they be able to get married too?" I asked.

Mom and Rita broke out in gales of laughter. "Don't be silly," said Mom when she recovered her breath.

"That'll *never* happen," said Rita. Then they looked at each other as if they might high-five one another, apparently content to have put me in my place.

For a couple of years, that remained my standard response to the "why aren't you getting married" question. It had a rough truthiness about it since I was deeply aware of the economic and cultural unfairness that the prohibition against same-sex marriage placed on my two lesbian sisters. By then, Nancy too had entered a relationship with a woman. And though their relationship was obvious, Nancy simply didn't take the risk of making an announcement about it, like Judy had. That way, Mom never had to talk about it.

Of course, my long reluctance to wed was far more complicated and deeply embedded. I was incapable of even imagining a happy marriage; I didn't want to curse what Jim and I already had; and I felt that we were already mated for life anyway, like snow geese.

And yet we did get married—with a wedding on our own terms. Nowadays, people have friends who get quick credentials so they can preside at weddings, but back then, most people still used pastors. And though I couldn't have said why, I was incapable of even imagining the possibility of allowing any clergyman the authority to declare us married. Jim and I would declare it for ourselves. We would be our own authority.

Ultimately, Jim and I had our own private ceremony in Stacy Park, and we declared ourselves married under common law. In Texas, this has been a valid way to marry ever since the frontier days.

Everything was soggy after Memorial Day floods, but with the trees and squirrels as witnesses, I wore an embroidered white cotton dress that I got for $17.99 at Manju's Boutique on the Drag, and Jim wore a brand-new white cotton shirt with his blue jeans. I picked flowers to put in my hair, and we stood under our favorite Stacy Park tree to exchange the plain ten-karat gold bands we'd bought at JCPenney and recite our vows. I chose an Emily Dickinson poem:

It's all I have to bring today—
This, and my heart beside—
This, and my heart, and all the fields—
And all the meadows wide—
Be sure you count—should I forget
Some one the sum could tell—
This, and my heart, and all the Bees
Which in the Clover dwell.

Afterwards, we went to Taco Village for a celebratory breakfast. Then we stopped by Whole Foods—the original, first-ever Whole Foods—and bought a crate of oranges at its post-flood clearance sale. Feeling rich, we reveled in drinking all the fresh-squeezed juice we could.

It was just the two of us. By that time, Mom had become so critical of Jim and so relentless in her push for me to move back to Farmers Branch that, even for a small common-law ceremony, I couldn't imagine having her there. If I'd revealed what I was doing, she would have likely told me yet again that my relationship wasn't real. And even in the best scenario I could imagine, she would have at least tried to talk me into having a ceremony *her* way. If I'd had to listen to all that, I almost certainly would have gotten so anxious that I would have bolted.

So, I kept my mouth shut and didn't tell *anyone* about what Jim and I were doing. It was the only way. On the one hand, in risking Mom's disapproval by not having a "real" wedding, it felt as though I was risking my family. On the other hand, I was risking it all precisely for the sake of the "real"—for the real of what Jim and I had together.

AT THE TIME, in addition to my weekday job in the University of Texas library system, I was working part-time cleaning a dentist's office on Wednesday and Saturday nights, and Jim always went along to help. So that we wouldn't have to work the weekend of our wedding, we decided to clean the office Friday night, instead of Saturday, assuming it would be okay since the office wasn't open on Saturdays anyway. But on Monday morning, the office manager— a bleach-blond, big-haired young woman with ultra-long vampire-red nails—called to ream me out. She had gone in on Saturday morning to do some work in the lab, and on Monday, she was furious to see that the lab area remained uncleaned. I tried to explain that I had gotten married over the weekend and had cleaned on Friday night instead, but she just ranted about how she wound up having to clean things herself. "I'm going to dock you a week's pay," she announced.

I protested. "But I came in. I cleaned." And finally, trying futilely to have a conversation, I said, "You know, I didn't think it would matter to come in on Friday instead, but I guess it did. I'm sorry. I should have checked with you, but even if you dock me for Saturday's cleaning, I don't understand why you're docking me for the whole week."

"You didn't clean Saturday, and I had to clean for you this morning. That's two cleanings. That's a week's worth. You're docked."

I told her how unfair I thought it was to dock me a whole week, but she didn't budge. So, even though every dollar mattered in those days, I told her I was quitting. Right then on the spot. "I'll just drop by and pick up my paycheck for the prior week," I said.

"Well, if you're going to quit without notice, then I'll have to clean several more times while we find someone else, so I'll dock you for those as well. There's no point in your dropping by. There won't be any check."

By then, I'd had plenty of crummy just-trying-to-get-by jobs—the kind of low-level waitressing and secretarial work where someone was always hitting on you—but that janitorial job was the worst of all. Wholly apart from the big-haired, small-time tyrant, the place was unhygienic. The dentist had a practice of just dumping his used needles, loose, into small plastic-bagged bins, and I was always terrified of getting pricked by one. This was before the big AIDS scare, but it still seemed gross and germy.

Jim and I would often make up the gap between income and expenses by selling blood plasma and flowers. The first was initially unpleasant but quickly became routine. Twice a week, we'd meet up at the plasma center for donation "dates." These "dates" not only gave us extra dollars, but we also got to fill up on orange juice and cookies each time when we were done.

The second—selling flowers from plastic buckets on a street corner—seemed almost a community service in the Austin of that day. It was a trade rendered iconic by Max Nofziger who later became a popular member of the

Austin City Council. Once when Max was away, Jim got lucky enough to be assigned to Max's corner. He got a lot of Max's regulars, so it was a good day. My own best shift was a Valentine's Day when the vendor assigned me the corner across from Bergstrom Air Force Base. Every airman leaving the base to go see his sweetheart stopped to buy flowers. I made $200 that day, which seemed like a small fortune. My favorite times, though, were when Jim and I worked a corner together. We didn't make as much money as when we worked separately, but at least we got to spend the day together.

I SUSPECT THAT, for many people, nothing about how Jim and I married would sound very romantic. There was no engagement ring, no long white dress, no fancy invitations, and no honeymoon. After our private Stacy Park ceremony, we sent short handwritten announcements to family, informing them that we had married in a common-law ceremony and signing the announcements as "Christa Brown and Jim Hill." I thought it would be obvious that I was keeping my own name, but with some of Jim's family, it apparently never was. Over the course of decades, and even with a few gentle reminders from Jim, they still sent Christmas cards addressed to Mr. and Mrs. Jim Hill. In my own family, it was as though nothing had happened, but at least they began addressing Christmas cards to both of us.

To my surprise, Mom kept her mouth shut about our wedding. I was waiting for her condemnation, but it never arrived. Neither did any congratulations, cards, or celebratory gifts, but of course, I hadn't imagined such a possibility anyway. In any event, I no longer much cared. Whether Mom approved or disapproved, it was the same to me: Jim was my mate.

Ultimately, our love withstood all the toxic residue of Farmers Branch and all the brutality of Baptistland. It outlasted eleven moves and survived a couple dozen just-getting-by jobs as well as several cars that failed us in the worst of circumstances. It endured years when our cobbled-together paychecks barely stretched to the end of the month and when sometimes the month stretched longer. It persisted amid the travails of law school, first for me and then for Jim, and through a year of living apart because Jim's law school was in Houston. It thrived through parenthood, secondary infertility, and my cancer. With all of it—wrenching heartbreak and unimaginable joy—we loved each other fiercely and relentlessly. And over the course of so many years, I learned through Jim to live from a position of love instead of lack.

Always, he pulled me in a direction of faith—faith in goodness, faith in something more, faith in human integrity. Jim had then—and still does—the kind of rock solid ethical core that no wrecking ball could dent. He was stable, strong, and steady, with a love that was constant. And unlike the "what happened didn't happen" world of my family and my childhood church, with Jim, all was as it seemed. There was never ever any hidden agenda.

Little by little, I learned to feel viscerally safe with Jim, and day in and day out, I grew habituated to being treated lovingly. Over time, that helped me get better at recognizing the familial cruelty for what it was, because cruelty no longer seemed normal. From these small seeds of safety, love, kindness, and consistency grew my own sacred defiance, founded in an inchoate belief that I was worthy of a life that didn't degrade me.

12

Becoming a Lawyer

Justice, justice you shall pursue.

—Deuteronomy 16:20

I WISH I could say I became a lawyer for noble reasons—for the pursuit of truth and justice for all, or some such lofty ideal. But it wouldn't be true. Though I did spend most of my career working on underdog cases and trying to do good with my law degree, in the very beginning, those were not my primary motivations. Instead, I was driven by the pragmatics of how to make a living in Austin, Texas.

Jim and I had spent a year in Portland, Texas, with me commuting thirty miles north to teach school and Jim commuting twenty-five miles south to work as a respiratory therapist. For reasons we couldn't quite get a handle on, we were miserable, constantly carping at each other and pulling apart. So, on the last day of school, Jim loaded up a U-Haul and picked me up at the school-house steps. With only a vague sense of saving ourselves as a couple, and with little rationality, much less any jobs, we headed back to Austin.

With a mattress on the floor, we settled into a roach-infested apartment near our beloved Stacy Park, and even the trees seemed to speak "Welcome back!" We celebrated our return by dancing like wood nymphs under the park's historic moonlight tower. For better or worse, we decided to stick with Austin.

Mom once again railed against me, saying we were "reckless and irresponsible" for moving without jobs. But though our reasons may have sounded feeble, Jim and I had made the decision that was best for us. Austin nurtured us and allowed us to grow in ways that might not have been as possible elsewhere. Through the years that followed, there were times when it would have made more sense financially to move to Houston or San Antonio, but we always chose to stay in Austin. We built our lives and forged our bonds there—in swims at Barton Springs, bike rides around Lady Bird Lake, and sunsets on Mount Bonnell. Over time, the city rewarded us a thousandfold.

But all that came later. In those early days, we were just trying to get by. On my last attempt to get a teaching job, I had clenched the steering wheel for thirty miles through the notorious traffic of Highway 183, where every third car had a bumper sticker saying "Pray for me. I drive 183." I'd sat for a two-hour interview, feeling more confident with each passing minute because I couldn't imagine that the superintendent would talk to me so long unless he was planning to hire me. Then, at the end, I felt my heart sink.

"Well, Miss Brown," he drawled, "there's something you gotta understand. I've still got four coaches I've gotta hire in this district, and before I can hire anyone else, I have to wait and see what their wives need to teach."

As I drove back toward Austin, grinding my teeth against the harrowing traffic, it occurred to me that maybe I was trying too hard to teach, that maybe I could do something else. Then, as I drove through the central part of the city, I looked around and saw all the state office buildings, and suddenly I knew: Austin held jobs for lawyers. That's what I would do.

I took the LSAT and applied at the University of Texas. It was the only law school I applied to. Jim and I were determined to stay in Austin.

BARRELING UP THE interstate toward Farmers Branch, with the windows down and the fourteen-wheelers blasting past, I planned what I would say, rehearsing my words and trying to anticipate Mom's reaction. I hadn't informed her I was applying to law school, so telling her I'd been admitted would come as a surprise. Classes were set to start in just a few weeks, but I was still feeling tentative and I feared Mom might say something that would prod me to back out. So I was nervous, and when I got there, sitting on that lime-green vinyl couch with a glass of iced tea, I blurted it out.

"I've decided to go to law school."

Mom laughed—a long rolling guffaw. "Oh, don't be silly," she finally said, looking as though she expected me to laugh too, as if I were making a joke. When I didn't laugh along, she paused and seemed to assess the seriousness of my face.

"I'm going to law school," I repeated.

"Oh, Christa, you're such a dreamer. You know how you are. You've *always* lived in a fairy-tale world. People like us don't go to law school."

People like us? I pondered that for a moment, then soldiered on. "I've already been admitted. I've been accepted. I'm going."

Mom's face showed a flash of surprise, but she quickly recovered.

"Well, just because you managed to get yourself admitted doesn't mean you can actually *do* it," she retorted. "You'll never finish. You won't last even one semester."

"Why not?" I stammered, suddenly reeling.

"Because you don't have the emotional stability for it."

Ouch. It was a hard punch that landed, probably because I myself wasn't sure about my emotional stamina. Though my suicide attempt had been nearly five years earlier, and Mom had never even known about it, the realization of my own fragility had remained as a presence in my consciousness.

I felt a slow sob building in the back of my throat. Worthless, incapable, weak: all those old feelings began to well up in me. But as I let myself go numb—it was the only way to protect myself—I considered what exactly Mom knew about law school. She had watched the grillings inflicted on law students by the stony Professor Kingsfield on the TV show *The Paper Chase*. That was it. I didn't know much more than that myself, but I'd had one friend who'd gone to law school. He was from a blue-collar family too, and though he was plenty smart, I didn't figure he was all that much smarter than me. He was, however, far more assertive. *Would I be able to stand up to a law professor's questioning?*

I felt all my old foolishness for being hopeful. Hopeful for what? That Mom might be proud of me? I wondered whether there had ever been any other University of Texas law student whose mother had responded so negatively. Wouldn't most parents swell with pride on learning their child had gained admission to a top-ranked law school?

I felt like one of those dogs that someone has kicked and kicked, but the dog keeps skulking back, cowering and wagging its tail, hoping the master will love him. And every now and then, the master does indeed dish out a pat on the head, so it all stays confusing.

But even as I felt the pain of Mom's words, I was simultaneously proud of myself for having had the good sense not to tell her about my plans for law school until I was actually admitted. Intellectually, I knew Mom didn't have a clue about law school, but emotionally, her words still held power, and I harbored some of that same narrow vision within myself. If I had heard Mom's words earlier in the process, before I was admitted and before I had scholarships and loans in place, I might have fallen back on my own limited imagining.

Dad had sat silent through the whole conversation, but I caught a glimpse of a slight smile on his face. After Mom walked out of the room, he finally spoke. "That's really somethin', Christa. I'll be pullin' for ya."

IT WAS MY last week of working in cataloging at the University of Texas's rare books collection, and three coworkers—Melanie, Darla Sue, and Kaylie— wanted to take me to lunch to celebrate my starting law school. All three were single moms, barely scraping by. I'd listened to the tension in their voices whenever they talked about the cost of day care or even just the cost of kids' shoes. So I protested. But they insisted.

They were proud of me, they said. And though I had always felt myself an outsider to their group—I tended to keep to myself—they told me I was one of them and that, if I went on to "something bigger," they could live vicariously and imagine it for their children. I had "broken free," they said.

I couldn't remember having ever said a word about my family to any of them. Yet, instinctively, they recognized that I too had blue-collar roots like them.

"Don't forget where you came from when you're a big fancy lawyer in a suit," said Melanie, laughing.

"Yeah, remember us," chimed Darla Sue, with Kaylie adding, "If things get rough, just know we're cheering for you."

I started crying. Their generosity and camaraderie overwhelmed me. These were super-smart women whose own ambitions had been stymied by bad marriages, abusive husbands, early motherhood, deadbeat dads, and lack of money. Up until that lunch, I'd been parroting the voice of Mom in my head, thinking I must be crazy to try to go to law school and that I should just forget the whole thing. *Who did I think I was?* But how could I reconcile my doubt-filled urge to turn tail with the fact that these three women were cheering for me? Envious of the fact that I even had such a possibility, they were using their hard-earned money to celebrate my "escape."

So, I promised myself that I wouldn't bail before I even started—that I would commit to giving law school my best effort for at least one semester and then see how I felt after that. I owed these women nothing less.

IT DIDN'T TAKE long at the University of Texas School of Law to realize that I was different from many of the other students, who seemed to come from vantages of ease. They were the sons and daughters of doctors, bankers, attorneys, and businessmen, and they carried an almost visible weight of entitlement on their shoulders, striding through the halls as though they already knew they were destined for entrance into the ruling elite.

Day after day, as I ate my peanut butter sandwich in a central gathering room, I pondered banana peels. Though the trash bins were mere steps away, students left banana peels, sandwich wrappers, and Coke cans on the tables. *Who did they think was going to clean up after them?* One day, in disgust, I started picking up the trash myself, but my friend Diana immediately put her hand on my arm.

"Christa, you're in law school now. You can clean up your own stuff, but you can't go around cleaning up after others. If people see you acting like a janitor, you'll get treated like a janitor. You don't want that."

I knew she was right. Diana, an extrovert who never failed to say hello to everyone, including the janitor, was a daughter of affluence, a graduate of private schools, and someone who knew the unspoken rules of this social world. Gently and subtly, she nudged my consciousness, and I began to observe my classmates as closely as an anthropologist might.

Professor Hamilton started every Corporations Law class with ten minutes of reviewing something in the *Wall Street Journal*. I felt the amazement of encountering an alternate universe—stocks and bonds and P/E ratios. But many of my classmates spent those minutes looking at something else behind the shield of the open newspaper—the day's assignment or the campus rag. They were obviously bored—already familiar with the domain of business—while, for me, the world was expanding at light speed.

All of law school was liberating. Though I listened to other students grouse about how hard it was, to me it seemed the easiest academic experience I'd ever had. As far back as eighth grade, I'd been babysitting every chance I got, plus dealing with the constant chaos at home. Then in high school and college, I'd had more regular jobs, which I'd supplemented with more babysitting, tutoring, and janitoring, while still also dealing with the chaos at home. But with law school, I took every dime of financial aid that was offered, and with the security of student loans and scholarships, I was finally freed from always worrying about money. I wasn't trudging around campus gathering up Coke bottles to cash in for a nickel apiece. I wasn't schlepping pitchers of beer at a cheap bar where drunken frat boys seemed to think a twenty-five-cent tip entitled them to act obnoxious. I wasn't working a cash register on weekends at Sears and rehanging all the clothes that sloppy shoppers left on the dressing room floors. I wasn't stocking the shelves after-hours at the local five-and-dime, or putting on an ugly orange uniform and driving across town to wolf down a free meal before a waitressing shift. I wasn't cleaning up a dentist's office in the middle of the night, and I wasn't hauling myself to the blood plasma center twice a week.

My lifestyle was spartan, but I had enough to get by, and with freedom from money worries came the ability to fully focus on school—something that was new to me. For the first time ever, I found myself doing more than just the required assignments. I had time to follow the rabbit trails of my curiosity and to do additional reading if I wanted. It was a luxury the likes of which I had never previously imagined.

I held a part-time job as a law professor's research assistant, but he was lenient, and the research was relevant, so the job contributed to my studies instead of taking away from them. He would frequently engage me in dialogue, peppering me with questions and actually listening to my answers, as though my thoughts and opinions mattered. Best of all, at the end of each day, I rode my bicycle home to Jim, and there was never any crisis to manage. No weeping mother, raging father, or drunken sister. Life was stable.

Until the first exams, I was fearful that Mom would be proven right—that people like me weren't meant to go to law school. I worried that my good grades in college and graduate school were no measure of whether I could hack it in law school. But wearing a locust encased in plastic amber as a good luck amulet, I aced the first exams.

When I tried to get my first job as a summer law clerk, I spent precious dollars I didn't have on a suit to wear for interviews. It was more of an Easter Sunday suit than a law firm suit, but at the time, I knew nothing at all about business attire. It felt unnatural—my usual uniform was a blue jean skirt with a T-shirt—and I'm sure I lacked the polish and poise of most law firm applicants. So, despite my great grades, not a single firm hired me. One prominent firm told me that it appeared I'd be better suited as a legal secretary and asked if that would be of interest to me. I declined, and instead, took an anonymous low-paying job working once again in the bowels of the University of Texas library system, and I spent the summer deciding whether to go back to law school or give it up.

When fall rolled around, I went back.

THROUGH ALL THREE years of law school, Mom never asked a single question about what classes I was taking or how I was doing. Dad did, but never Mom. Instead, at the start of every semester, she'd ask me why I was buying my books instead of checking them out from the library. I'd try to explain that the amount of reading was formidable, and that I needed to be able to highlight pages and make margin notes so I could participate in class and review things quicker for exams, but that answer was never acceptable. She would invariably berate me for my extravagance. I'd tell her that, at the end of the semester, I could usually sell the books back and recoup part of the cost, but that never satisfied her either. She'd always end by telling me how her brother Jack had known someone who went to law school, and *he* had done it by using books in the library.

Typically, Dad would hang back from these conversations, but each time after Mom was done and had turned her attention elsewhere, he would come right up next to me. "We're just so proud of you," he'd whisper, beaming. Then, with a sly wink, he'd add, "I reckon you know a lot more about law school than we do, Christa. You do what you need to do." A couple times, he pressed a hundred-dollar bill into my palm. "Maybe this can help," he said, "but your mother doesn't need to know about it." So grateful was I for the extra cash that I welled up in tears. But of course, I had to quickly squelch them so as not to draw Mom's attention. That was a frequent dynamic in interactions with my parents during those years: Mom would find ways to berate me while Dad would quietly support me.

ULTIMATELY, I GRADUATED from law school with honors and took an immediate job as a briefing attorney to the Supreme Court of Texas. In preparation for *that* interview—an interrogation by nine men around a table bigger than any I'd ever seen in my life—a kindly clerk at an upscale store on Austin's Congress Avenue took me under his wing and outfitted me in just the right professional attire. That time, I got the job.

Every year, the court chose eighteen new law school graduates to work as briefing attorneys. For decades, every group of briefing attorneys had been all men, but slowly, women had been infiltrating the ranks until, finally, with my own group in 1984, it was the first year in history when there were as many women as men.

In the judges' conference room, we sat just behind the nine judges—all male—and we spoke only when one of the judges afforded us the floor.

Another briefing attorney that year was a guy I called Jacobson—I couldn't bring myself to use his first name. One day, at the tail end of a case presentation, he segued into an underhanded remark with one of the female briefing attorneys as the punchline—something about how everyone knew where to go for a piece of action. I sat there like a stone, cringing at the crudeness. Drunk on the derivative power of being a briefing attorney, he had trampled a woman's dignity in a juvenile attempt to cultivate a locker-room camaraderie with the judges.

I took my gaze around the conference table, looking squarely at the face of every judge there. Fortunately, not a single one cracked the faintest hint of a smile at Jacobson's remark, but none said any word of reprimand either, at least not right then. In that moment, I would have sold my soul for the sake of seeing a single female judge at that table. But that day didn't come until seven years later when a woman finally won election to the Texas Supreme Court. Meanwhile, I needed only to amble through the hallways to see decades' worth of historical photos, documenting the court's all-white, all-male membership.

Jacobson presented other problems. He took to sneaking up behind me to startle me when I worked late. "Don't do that!" I told him clearly, directly, and repeatedly, but it made not a bit of difference. He had no respect for boundaries. Finally, I started taking work home rather than staying in the building.

Despite the male-dominated environment, I relished my time of working for the court. When my year as a briefing attorney ended, I went to work for a law firm, but a year later, when a court staff attorney position came open, I returned to the court and stayed five more years, advising the judges on the cases before them. It was a task of at least *trying* to further the pursuit of justice, and it was a job I loved.

Though the judges welcomed my views on cases and afforded me respect, it was nevertheless a job that rightly demanded a significant measure of discretion and deference. Ordinarily, that was no problem—I was temperamentally well suited for the job—but once I overstepped.

Judge Oscar Mauzy changed his vote on a particularly difficult case, and I was pissed. I had worked on the case for months, arguing it not only in the judges' conferences but also sitting with individual judges in their chambers—rehashing the points, detailing the facts, answering their questions, and lining up the votes, one by one, to push the case through. Mauzy had been on board in every prior vote count. Then suddenly, on motion for rehearing, in the final-final vote, he reversed himself. And he'd given me no advance warning.

With a 5-4 vote, the case went out, but not the way I'd pushed for, not the way I'd lobbied for. Wrongly, I took it personally.

Right after the vote was taken, the judges took a break, and in all my righteous fury, I stormed down the hall straight into Mauzy's office and launched in with guns blazing. I demanded to know what had happened. To say I was out of line would be an understatement, but I was too angry to notice or care.

Finally, having spewed forth everything I could think to say, I stopped to catch my breath, and the horror of what I'd done began to dawn on me. With an ever-so-slight smile, Mauzy looked me square in the eyes.

"Christa," he drawled, "this is why I trust you so much. I know you aren't gonna be going up and down the hall, bad-mouthing me to anyone who'll listen. You'll just march right in and tell me to my face. I trust that. Someday, I'll tell you what happened. But not today."

I walked out of his office, feeling lucky I hadn't been fired. I'd learned a lesson. While I knew that I could never again let my temper run away with me, I also saw that some people in power valued straight talk. Mauzy was known for being cantankerous. Other staff attorneys would cower at the thought of having to talk to him, and some even avoided walking by his door for fear he might see them in the corridor and bark at them. But I had talked to him straight—albeit with anger—and he valued that.

From that day forward, whenever Mauzy was having a rough day, his administrative assistant would call me up. "Christa, could you just come and talk to him?" she'd plead. "It's one of those kinda days, and I can't stand him, and you always seem to do him some good." So I'd stop my work, head to his office, and stick my head in his door. Invariably, no matter the time of day, he'd invite me to have a cup of coffee. We'd sit a bit and talk about anything and everything, but mostly mundanities, and when I left, he'd be in a better mood. I grew to love the man.

Once when my parents were in town, I took them to a popular breakfast diner and, lo and behold, Oscar Mauzy walked in. I smiled and gave a small wave, but he, leaving his wife at their table, walked straight over to where we were sitting and extended his hand. I introduced him to Mom and Dad, and they beamed as though they were meeting royalty. For Dad, I think it was even more than that. He was meeting one of his heroes. He had often talked about "LBJ, Sam Rayburn, and Oscar Mauzy"—always saying the three names together—as "the only Texas politicians ever worth trusting"—the only ones who really understood "us working people."

Mauzy chatted amiably with my parents, putting them at ease, drawing on the commonality he had with Dad from service in the Pacific Theater, and making both of them feel like they were the most important people on the planet. I realized that I was seeing the Mauzy who had been such a successful long-term politician. In my own career, I'd known him only as a justice of the Texas Supreme Court, but before that, Mauzy had spent twenty years as a titan of the Texas Senate. Intellectually, I'd known about his career in the senate, but as he chatted with my parents that day, I saw the emotional component up close—the reason so many Texans had loved him for so long.

The last phone call I ever got from Oscar Mauzy was five days before he died. By then, I'd had my own solo law practice for a number of years—an appellate practice—and Mauzy would often call me up. Sometimes he wanted to run something by me—he had a law practice of his own—and other times he just wanted to ramble about political "war stories." But that last phone call was different, and I was too wrapped up in my own head to pick up on it. Though I'd talked with him several times since his lung cancer diagnosis, I had no inkling of how fast the cancer had progressed. That day, which seemed like any other, I failed to give him my full attention and instead found myself thinking about the deadline for the brief I was working on and wondering when he would get to his point. He never did. He asked about my husband, Jim, and he chatted about seemingly nothing. Then he said how much he'd always appreciated me and told me to keep fighting "the good fights." He pronounced me "a good American"—always his highest compliment. The conversation ended with me still wondering why he'd called.

Days later, I got the news of his death and only then, belatedly, did I understand that he'd been saying goodbye.

THROUGH THE EARLY years of being a lawyer, as I struggled to find my footing in the culture of the professional class, Mom seemed all the more intent on criticizing me. She picked at everything. My hair was too long or too short. My body was too big or too small. My gifts were too expensive or too cheap. My clothes were too frumpy or too extravagant. My accomplishments were too ordinary or too uppity. It was always something.

Though she invariably claimed that she was telling me things for my own good and that she didn't want me to get "a big head," slowly I began to understand that her criticism was a reflection of her own insecurity. She was trying to hang onto me—to keep me from moving too far beyond the realm of what she was comfortable with. I broke through the boundaries of my mother's limited expectations, but it came at a cost.

Our country prides itself on the dream of social mobility for all who want it, but for most, such mobility remains a myth. We seldom talk about that. We also ignore the fact that, even for those who manage to change their social station, there are unspoken costs. Social mobility not only means moving *toward* something—a more financially secure and stable life—but moving *away* from something. Having moved from working class to professional class, I am a cultural emigrant, and particularly in my early years as an attorney, I often felt alienated and culturally adrift. From the big things—having a reliable car and a checking account with a bit of ease—to the small things—fresh broccoli, cloth napkins, and salon haircuts—I was often acutely aware of being in unfamiliar terrain.

13

Motherhood

Every flutter of the wing,
Every note of song we sing,
Every murmur, every tone,
Is of love and love alone.

—Henry Wadsworth Longfellow

AFTER A LONG and fretful time of trying, I finally got pregnant at the age of thirty-four. When I made the announcement at Thanksgiving, my tears of happiness overtook me, and I could scarcely choke out the words. Mom and Dad teared up too, but Judy had a different reaction: "You don't get any awards for that, you know."

I looked at her, uncomprehending.

"I mean, really, why are you making such a big deal of it?" she continued. "It's not as if you accomplished something. Anyone can get pregnant."

I started to explain to her that, actually, it hadn't been such an easy thing for me, but fortunately, Mom cut me off with "time for dessert."

After dinner, Mom busied herself with making sure Jim and I would be comfortable in their guest room. My parents had just bought an old two-bed-room fixer-upper in the stagnant West Texas town where Rita and Richard had moved. Mom had convinced Dad to buy it as a second home, so they could spend more time helping Rita with her children. The town held little more than a courthouse, a Baptist church, and a Methodist church, but it was where we wound up spending a lot of Thanksgivings. And that particular Thanksgiving, when I was pregnant, was when I sensed a vague shift in my relationship with Mom; she was trying to take care of me.

With my daughter Stacy's birth, my world was upended in so many ways I never could have imagined. Sure, the work of parenting an infant was exhausting and disruptive of all routines, but it was also true that, suddenly, anything seemed possible. Together, Jim and I had taken one plus one and made it into three. The mystery of love's transformational power became an in-the-flesh presence in our lives as we constantly inhaled the sweet-sour smell of Stacy's soft baby head and sealed the bond between us. It was magic.

From Stacy's birth onward, the siren call of the past had a powerful challenger. Jim and I gave ourselves over to the world of parenthood, and it was to that new world—*our* family—that we pledged our fealty. Whatever the future would hold for me, it would be a future with Jim and Stacy. Everything else—*everything*—was ancillary.

EIGHT WEEKS AFTER Stacy's birth, going back to work was a challenge. I had a mostly supportive workplace, an all-in committed partner, and reliable high-quality childcare, yet it was *still* incredibly hard. All of it. So, several months later, when I sat listening to Judy rail about how lazy her secretary had become since having a baby, I felt a sense of solidarity with the secretary. When Judy said she was going to fire her, I spoke up.

"But she's been with you a long time," I said, noticing a spot of spit-up on my shirt. "You've liked her for years. Maybe she just needs a little more time."

"Time for what?" Judy demanded.

"Time to learn to balance things? It's hard to be a new mom."

"Balance what?" she sneered. "How hard can it be? You give them a bottle and you change their diapers."

I could see that Judy was utterly oblivious to the unrelenting exhaustion of a newborn, but I couldn't bear the thought of her secretary getting fired. "Well, it's a big adjustment," I said. "Stacy still doesn't even sleep through the night."

"Oh please. I've stayed awake with puppies, and I still managed to go to work and do my job."

"Babies aren't puppies," I countered futilely.

"No, puppies are harder because there's more of them," she insisted, but I was already turning my attention back to Stacy, thankful for the distraction.

BECOMING A MOTHER meant confronting the legacy of my own mother. I knew I had to reckon with what had gone wrong if I were to have any hope of leaving my own daughter with a different legacy. And although I was consciously determined to do just that, I quickly realized that mere determination would not be enough.

Mom wasn't a villain and neither was Dad. But together, they'd had enough psychological dynamite to blow us apart. They were profoundly wounded people who had lacked the tools and support to do better as parents. So the four of us kids suffered. I wanted things to be different for Stacy, and that meant I would need to be fearless in interrogating the past.

People talk about "breaking the cycle," but it's not like breaking a chicken wishbone. You can't just pull it apart with a lovely little wish and expect it to come true. "Breaking the cycle" means breaking it again and again, with endless small decisions that seem insignificant at the time but that all add up to something more than their sum. There's not one heroic decision to do things differently, but instead a daily tedium of striving always to remain mindful.

Day in and day out, mothering Stacy awakened me to the traumas that had been transmitted intergenerationally in our family, to the avoidant patterns of coping, and to the necessity for change. How could I make sure the same patterns didn't manifest in me, when mental illness, violence, and familial dysfunctions ran rampant through my bloodlines? (And at that point, I didn't know the half of it.) As the product of those generations, I knew I had to transform what had been transmitted.

More and more, I could see that the wounded child I held within me was also the inner child of Mom and Dad. They, too, had been vulnerable as children and had suffered greatly. Yet, as adults, neither had known how to handle the childhood suffering they held within, so they wound up making their own children suffer such that we, too, were victimized by *their* childhoods. These realizations, albeit vague, were present enough in my mind to further my motivation to be a different kind of parent. Without some kind of transformation, I knew that I would pass on suffering to Stacy just as surely as Mom and Dad had given theirs to me.

I knew then, as I know now, that my parents probably did the best they could, and yet, their best was severely lacking. *But how to do better?* How to lessen the odds that, forty years down the road, my own daughter would be feeling the ache of her mother's failures and saying the same thing about me: "I know she did the best she could"?

It was a massively humbling task, and constantly, I realized how lucky I was to have a parenting partner like Jim. Even as I watched in wonder at Stacy's every development, I also beheld Jim growing as a father. He held Stacy for hours when she couldn't sleep, tended her cuts and bruises, cleaned her vomit and diarrhea. He was commuting three hundred miles round trip several times a week to finish law school. Yet, even when he was dead tired, with an exam the next morning, he would still dance around the room with Stacy in his arms, singing along with the Traveling Wilburys. Jim had strengths and skills and patience I had never imagined, and I grew to love him all the more.

In those early days, time seemed like an endless ocean of exhaustion. But it was precisely when I was beyond the limits of my own endurance that I felt more bonded with humanity than I ever had before. I knew in my bones that I shared some commonality with almost every parent on the planet.

Neither Jim nor I had a clue what we were doing, yet everything we did or said seemed to matter. Even what went on in my mind could spill into Stacy's. For example, I quickly learned that I had to shut down whatever had gone on at work and calm myself before picking Stacy up from daycare. If I gathered her in my arms when my mind was secretly agitated—even if I tried to conceal it—Stacy would pick up on it the instant her skin touched mine, and she would begin to cry, as though my agitation had transmitted wordlessly through the skin. But when I honestly packed away my anxieties before seeing her, she was always happy. I had to teach myself that—to find the calm within so that Stacy too could be calm.

In the beginning, there were some days when I managed it and other days when I didn't. In particular, I struggled with the "slow the heck down" lesson. I had a habit of always trying to check off one more thing on the to-do list. In my head, I knew what was needed—to slow down—but in the day-to-day reality of my life, what I too often said and did was "hurry up."

Often, I was overwhelmed, not only by the usual challenges of new motherhood, but by the difficulty of mothering without a role model. Following the rutted roads of my own mother's ways did not feel safe. I couldn't assuredly ask myself "What would Mom do?" because the answers couldn't be trusted. Imagining what Mom would do could just as likely show me what I *didn't* want. So, I had to learn to trust myself and my own instincts, which meant evicting the voice of Mom in my head. It was a constant, unending process.

Once, when I was driving up to Farmers Branch with Stacy strapped into her car seat, I suddenly realized that I was white-knuckling the steering wheel. Worse, I was talking out loud, and Stacy was staring at me. Who was I talking to? My absent mother. Immediately, I pulled off at a McDonald's, and even though I'd sworn I wouldn't be the kind of mom who went to McDonald's, I bought Stacy some animal crackers and took a break to reset myself. That was what trying too hard to please Mom could do; it left me detached and snappy with the people I loved most, Jim and Stacy. It was a hard lesson to learn.

I wanted so badly for Stacy to have a normal childhood, to take it completely for granted that she was safe and that her world was stable. Yet, I realized that I didn't truly know much about what normal looked like. I recalled how puzzled I'd been when I saw the movie *Mommie Dearest*. I couldn't figure out what the fuss was about. Joan Crawford had some tantrums, but surely they weren't so extreme as to be movie-worthy. The "no wire hangers" scene seemed only marginally worse than an episode in my own memory of Mom repeatedly screaming "only six sheets."

I was probably about four years old, and Mom had been in the bathroom with me when I accidentally rolled off more than the mandated six squares of toilet paper. She began shouting in my face, "Six sheets! Six sheets! How many times have I told you? ONLY SIX SHEETS! I know you know how to count, so why didn't you?"

Sitting there on the toilet, trapped in that tiny room, I quaked, promising I'd do better and try harder. "I'm sorry, Mommy, I'm sorry," I pleaded, until finally, she huffed off.

Mommie Dearest had conjured that "six sheets" memory, but it had also left me feeling numb. I thought I must have missed something and decided to read the book. Yet, even with the book, my emotional reaction was flat. Intellectually, with all the hype the movie had garnered, I knew I wasn't seeing it the way other people did. It was supposed to be shocking, yet to me it seemed only marginally beyond a routine bad day.

Abuse, neglect, violence, rage, and untreated mental illness had all been part of the lens through which I'd experienced childhood. This meant that if I tried to shape my parenting patterns by looking to my own family, I was drawing from a polluted well. So, to a large degree, I did what I had always done—I relied on books. And Stacy, too, became my teacher. I could see how she absorbed every word I said, and daily, that realization reconnected me to my own determination to be the change and to break the intergenerational patterns.

It was hard. Even as I tried to give Stacy the love, attention, safety, and stability that I had lacked, I was simultaneously picking open the scabs of my own wounds. But the repetitive emotional housecleaning was self-altering. For that, I thank Stacy. So often, in the process of mothering her, I had to also mother myself, and ultimately, I became the person I am because I was Stacy's mother. I gave birth to Stacy, but it is equally true that Stacy gave birth to me.

Stacy also became a bridge for me to my own mother, who dished out love and only love toward Stacy. In Mom's unbounded love for my daughter, I felt the expression of her love for me as well. And, much to my relief, after Stacy's birth, Mom finally gave up her demands that I should move back to live with her and Dad.

Mom often sang an Irish lullaby to Stacy—"Too-ra-loo-ra-loo-ral." It was "just a simple little ditty," but every time she sang it, I felt I could hear all the mothers of all time singing to their babies. Mom told me she could remember her own mother singing it to her younger brother, Georgie, and no doubt her mother had sung it to her as well. Mom taught it to me, and I sang it to Stacy. Years later, when Stacy herself became a mother, I taught it to her, and she sang it to her babies, so the circle is unbroken.

The happiest I ever saw my parents as a couple was when they were with Stacy. Even though they were both stiff with age, they'd get down on the floor to play with her, talking and cooing, and then looking back and forth at each other in obvious delight. As I watched this scene play out on countless visits, I could imagine how they must have been as a young couple, still filled with love for one another and wonder at the life they were building. In the glances they exchanged, I wondered if that was exactly what they themselves were remembering. Each time, as they struggled to help one another up from the floor,

Dad's whole face alit with joy, he would invariably look at Stacy and say, "She's got a smile that would melt butter."

IN THE EARLY days, I lacked confidence and struggled to assert myself as a mother, particularly against the dominant duo of Rita and Mom. Rita had three children: Patty, who was twelve when Stacy was born, and Bobby and Molly, who were close in age to Stacy. So Rita carried the voice of a mom with experience.

At one year old, Stacy still wasn't sleeping through the night, and Jim and I were exhausted. Mom urged me to let Stacy cry it out in her crib. "She just needs to learn," she said. "You have to let her know who's in charge."

Rita joined in. "You have to break her or she'll have you wrapped around her little finger."

"Break her? I don't think it's like that," I started, intending to talk about Stacy's ear problems but also wondering whether maybe I really was a wuss of a mother. Rita cut me off.

"Put her in her crib and just let her cry. She'll cry herself back to sleep and eventually she'll learn. It's only hard for the first week or so. You just have to steel yourself. If you don't, she'll control you."

Still, I just couldn't do it, and it didn't feel right to Jim either. So, night after night, we took turns with one of us getting up to sit in the rocking chair so that Stacy could sleep upright on our chest.

Finally, her pediatrician sent us to an ear, nose, and throat specialist who recommended that she have tubes surgically implanted into her ears. He said that her natural ear tubes were so small that, when she would lie flat, fluids would accumulate without draining and put pressure on the eardrum, causing her pain. So, that was why she couldn't sleep.

On the one hand, I felt validated. It had always seemed like a genuine cry of pain, and the fact that she slept perfectly when we held her upright substantiated the doctor's theory. In that position, the fluids drained down her throat. Nevertheless, even though it was a common, minor surgery, I resisted.

I was afraid of the anesthesia for her and fearful that the hospital would traumatize her. I worried the surgery would hurt her. And beneath it all was a dread of something inchoate, something that was more than all of that together.

While visiting with Mom one day, my anxiety spilled forth. I told her what the doctor had recommended and how afraid I was.

"Don't be silly," she said. "Just do it. Babies don't feel pain."

"What? What do you mean? Stacy feels pain."

"No. Sometimes it might look that way, but babies don't feel pain the way adults do. That's why doctors don't use anesthesia on them."

Suddenly, my fear grew tenfold. I could scarcely get words out of my mouth. "What do you mean—they don't use anesthesia? They give them *something* don't they?"

"No. Babies don't need it. They didn't use any anesthesia with you for your first two surgeries, and you were just fine."

As the horror of what Mom was saying began to sink in, I felt aghast. Not only did it give me some urgent questions for Stacy's doctor, but it also made me wonder about what I myself had experienced.

I was six weeks old for the first of my facial surgeries, six months old for the second, and not quite three years old for the third. Through the years, I had occasionally pondered what it might have been like to be born with a face like mine in a time before such surgeries were common. But it had never occurred to me to wonder about what the actual experience of the surgeries had been like.

When I looked into it, I learned that, in all likelihood, I had been given a paralytic drug that rendered me immobile but left me awake and without pain control, while the skin and tissues of my face were cut and rearranged. I was surrounded by strange people, voices, lights, and smells while enduring what must have been extremely painful and frightening things being done to my face. I was unable to cry, unable to protest, and unable to move away from the pain.

According to Mom's recollection, this is what was done to me—twice.

The brutality of it is hard to fathom. I am incredulous to imagine that this sort of medical practice could have ever been commonplace, yet my research confirmed what Mom told me. It was long believed that a baby's nervous system wasn't developed enough to feel pain—and anesthesia for babies was a concern—so babies routinely had surgery without anesthesia until about the mid-1980s.

I don't hold conscious memories of those two no-anesthesia surgeries. But I believe my body remembers them. And yet . . . how could I not be grateful? What would my life have been without those surgeries?

When Stacy was eighteen months old, we finally went forward with her first ear-tube surgery—with anesthesia. She did fine and so did I. The first night after the surgery, she slept through the night lying flat in her crib. It seemed a miracle.

"WHATEVER HAPPENS, YOU have your own family now," said Mom, "and you can't let anything else interfere with that."

It came out of the blue, and it was the most important advice she ever gave me. I was distracted and hardly paid any attention at first. But Mom was making a point, and she was determined to make sure I got it.

"Christa, now that you're a mother, you have to always put your own family first. No matter what."

"I know, Mom."

"No, you *don't* know. Not yet. That's why I want to make sure you hear it from me. Remember this. Your *own* family has to come first. No matter what. Do you understand? No matter what anyone else might want—not even me and not even Dad. Your own family comes first. Ahead of all the rest of us. Sometimes it will be hard, but you owe it to Stacy."

"Mom, I don't think there's anything that's gonna make me have to choose between you and Stacy," I said, still not really honoring the earnestness in her voice.

"You don't know what the future holds," she persisted. "So I want you to remember this. Promise me you'll remember."

Finally, I slowed myself down. "Well sure, Mom."

"No, you have to *promise*. Look at me. It's what I had to do. I had to live apart from my family. I hardly ever saw them. But I don't regret it. It was the way it had to be. And if that's the way it has to be for you, then I want you to remember this. So, promise me you will."

"All right, Mom. I promise."

"Say it back to me," she insisted. "You promise, no matter what, you'll put your own family first."

So I said it back to her out loud. "I promise I'll put my own family first no matter what." Finally, Mom was satisfied.

Nowadays, I look back and see that episode as Mom at her very best. Maybe she gave me that lecture purely out of her boundless love for Stacy. But I think it was more than that. It was a mother's love for the generations that stretch beyond a lifetime. She was granting me the freedom to forge a new family and let go the weight of the old.

It was a powerful gift, and it's a memory I hold close to my heart.

"GRANDDAD!" SHE YELLED out the window as soon as we pulled in the driveway in Farmers Branch. Dad dropped his rake and, with a look of pure adoration, scooped three-year-old Stacy up in his arms and told her he loved her "a bushel and a peck." Stacy had no idea what that meant, but she knew she was loved and she commenced to chattering, reveling in Dad's rapt attention. After a while, and after Mom, too, had gotten in some hugs, Dad put Stacy down, held her hand, and walked all around the backyard with her.

I looked at them side by side and could see my father in Stacy's eyes, as well as his mother, his grandmother, and no doubt other ancestors even earlier. Dad's sisters called them "the Sullivan eyes." For as far back as I could remember, relatives had always said that I had them—"the Sullivan eyes"—and now Stacy had them too.

As Stacy continued to chatter, Dad listened attentively as though she was expounding on the meaning of the universe. Eventually, she let go of his hand and came running over to where I sat on the patio. "Granddad said I could pick pears!" She grabbed a basket and ran back out to the yard, where Dad scooped her up again and held her up to reach the highest fruits.

For a long while, it was this way with every visit. Stacy would run toward Granddad as though electrocuted with joy at seeing him, and Granddad would show her everything that was happening in the yard. That was Dad's turf, and whatever the season, there was always something to see. Each spring, a vibrant riot of blooming bulbs would turn the yard into a festival ground, and he'd always be so proud of whatever new bulbs came up—the ones he'd planted the preceding fall just so Mom would be surprised by them in the spring.

The inside was Mom's domain. Plastic apples sat in the fruit bowl and plastic flowers in a vase, but in the yard, the only plastic things were the owls hanging in the pear trees to scare the grackles . . . which they never did. But though the grackles were voracious, there were always enough pears to make preserves, and year after year, I looked forward to helping Mom fill her pantry with jars of spiced pear preserves and fig jam. With all the cinnamon she used, it brought forth good memories of helping her make snickerdoodles and molasses crinkles when I was a kid. The kitchen was where Mom made sweetness in a house that often held bitterness.

EARLY ON, I saw that Judy couldn't be trusted with Stacy—she wasn't a safe person. While Nancy was sitting on the couch, with Stacy in her arms, Judy sat down next to her and yanked the pacifier out of Stacy's mouth. In those days, Stacy's "bobo" was like an extension of her body, and she became immediately distraught. Judy proceeded to taunt her, holding the "bobo" just out of Stacy's reach, as Stacy stretched out her arms and cried for it. Every time she almost touched it, Judy would move it away. *What kind of person bullies a one-year-old?* I wondered. As fast as I could, I went for my bag, pulled forth another pacifier, and even though it was dirty, I handed it straight to Stacy and then lifted her from Nancy's lap.

Judy never outgrew her need for cruelty. When Stacy was about five, Judy came to Austin for a visit. Nancy, who was also living in Austin, came over, and we all three sat around chatting at my kitchen table while Stacy built a Lego tower in the living room. Eventually, Judy shifted from chatting to ridiculing.

She poked at Nancy, mocking how Nancy used to repeatedly call out "I love you, Mommy!" when she walked off to school in first grade. Of course, from Judy's mouth, it sounded snarly and twisted. Remembering how Nancy would always hold my hand when we walked to school, I still felt protective of her. "Geezus, she was six years old," I blurted.

That only spurred Judy to dig in harder on *me*. She launched in with her story of what a tattletale I'd been that time when she climbed up in the medicine cabinet and took out the bottles that Mom had always told us not to touch.

"Judy, I was three," I protested, uncomprehending of how she could still hold something against me that I'd done as a toddler.

Even Nancy came to my defense that day, telling Judy that, as a three-year-old, I might have saved her life, because Mom had rushed Judy to the emergency room where she got her stomach pumped. But as always, when Judy was in the mood to get in some blows, nothing made any difference. She launched in with all her remembrances of beating up on me and siccing the dog on me, reveling in her own brutality. It was story after story, sitting there at my own kitchen table.

I sat mute, pondering the glee that Judy took in her stories of besting me, and I realized that my humiliation was the source of her pleasure, the crux of her delight. My pain wasn't merely an incidental side effect of her bullying; it was precisely the point. I was like the bugs she used to turn on their backs for no reason other than to watch them squirm. I saw the sickness of it, but still I sat there.

Jim saw the sickness of it too. He came back from the grocery store, and as he put things away, the anger in his face grew and grew. With lips pressed tight, he jammed items into the freezer and then left the rest of the sacks on the counter. He walked into the living room and took Stacy by the hand. "We're going out," he tersely announced as he walked past the table where we sat.

Jim returned only after Judy and Nancy had left, and then, only after Stacy was in bed did he let loose his anger. "How could you let her talk like that? And in front of Stacy to boot!"

"It's just the way Judy is. I'm used to it."

"Yeah, Judy's a bully all right, I get that. But what I don't get is *you*. I couldn't believe you just sat there. I kept waiting for you to say something but you didn't! You're a lawyer, for God's sake, and a damn good one. You're more than capable of defending yourself. You could have shoved it right back at her, but you didn't. You just sat there! Why?"

"I don't know. What good would it have done?"

"You should have shown her the door. That's what you should have done."

"But she was a guest."

"What are you saying?"

"She was a guest. It would have been rude."

"Rude? You're worried about being rude to someone who ridicules you in your own home? Guests have obligations too, you know. I nearly threw her out. That's what I wanted to do, but then I thought, no, she's your family, not mine, and I was afraid you'd be angry if I kicked her out. So I couldn't figure out what to do, and I couldn't figure out why *you* weren't doing anything."

I couldn't figure it out either. It was a visit that had rendered me completely numb, but Jim was still going on about it.

"I can't believe you even let her talk that way in front of Stacy!" he exclaimed. "Your daughter shouldn't have to listen to someone ridiculing her mother. She was hearing every word and you just sat there! I wasn't going to have Stacy hearing that crap."

"You're right. I'm sorry."

"No. I don't give a shit about you being sorry. I don't want you to be sorry. I just want to know *why*. Why would you let her sit there and make fun of you that way? Why?"

"I don't know."

"Well, I'm not going to tell you what to do. She's *your* family, not mine. But as far as I'm concerned, she's not welcome in our house anymore. I know you'll probably still let her in anyway, but I want you to know, I'll be civil if I have to but not one bit more. That's it. Don't expect anything more from me. And if she ever goes on like that in front of Stacy again, I *will* throw her out."

"Yeah, sure. But really. If she doesn't leave on her own, what are you gonna do?"

Jim stared at me in frustration. "What part of this don't you understand? This is our home. *Our* home. If she doesn't leave, then I will make her leave. One way or another."

"DON'T YOU DARE give Patty that dollhouse!"

Mom's response was swift and sure. I had asked her about our family dollhouse because Rita's now-grown daughter, Patty, had come to Austin for a concert and dropped by our house to visit. It was the first time she'd been to our house on her own as an adult, and I'd served dinner for her and her friend. A week later, I got a letter from Rita asking me to give Patty the dollhouse because Patty had memories of playing with it on Grandma's porch.

I'd noticed that Patty had taken an interest in the dollhouse, but even though she'd commented on her memories, I was still shocked to get Rita's letter bluntly asking for it. Mom had given the dollhouse to Stacy, who also had plenty of memories connected to it and who was still young enough to play with it. In fact, I myself had memories connected to the dollhouse because Mom had furnished it with the same miniature toy furniture I'd played with as a kid—the two-inch refrigerator, tiny pink dining table, and itty-bitty dishes. Mom had found them in the attic in a shoebox with my name on it.

The more I pondered it, the more I couldn't figure out what to do. Rita seemed to think I would surely understand and "do the right thing," but Stacy loved the dollhouse. Besides, I thought it would be rude to just give away Mom's gift to Stacy, and I knew Mom would find out about it. Unable to extricate myself from the conundrum, and worried of Rita's wrath, I decided to make a trip to Farmers Branch—four hundred miles round trip—just so I could talk with Mom in person.

She didn't hesitate for a second. "I gave that dollhouse to Stacy and I wanted her to have it," she insisted. "Besides, I asked Patty years ago if she wanted it and she said no. She didn't care about it. The only reason she wants it now is because she sees it in *your* house and so she wants it for herself. But that's Stacy's! Don't you dare give it to Patty!"

There was no mistaking how Mom felt. So I wrote a short note to Rita, apologizing and telling her that I just couldn't do it since the dollhouse was something Mom had given to Stacy. I promised that if the time came when Stacy no longer cared about the dollhouse, I wouldn't discard it but would then give it to Patty, which I did a decade later.

FROM TIME TO time, Jim and I toyed with the thought of dropping Stacy off at a Sunday school somewhere so that she might learn moral lessons in catchy kids' songs and absorb some of the cultural referents of Christianity. But we never did. I chose instead to simply read stories to her from an illustrated children's Bible, and it was in that "story time" context that she absorbed some of what Christianity had to offer, but without indoctrination, proselytizing, fear-mongering, or guilt-tripping.

My own hyper-religious childhood had been built around fear—especially of sin and of being cast aside and doomed to hell. I grew up worrying about that nasty-tempered God who'd sent a flood to wipe everyone out. *Would he send another one?* Constantly, I fretted over whether I was being good enough so that, when the time came, God would spare me and my family. But it seemed near-impossible to be so perfect. After all, God had turned Lot's wife into a pillar of salt when all she did wrong was to glance backwards at her home.

I didn't want anything close to that kind of fear for Stacy.

Years later, when we were playing Trivial Pursuit, Stacy answered "six" on a trivia question asking how many books were in the Old Testament. She had no clue, and indeed, hardly understood the question. "Isn't it all the same book?" she asked, as I nearly jumped for joy. It was one of those moments when I realized that Stacy had been spared—released from all the religious fear that had dominated my own childhood. I felt proud of myself as a mother and proud of her as an engaged citizen of the world. She hadn't needed fear of damnation to learn morality. She had grown up wholly unchurched, yet she was filled with empathy and kindness. She was and is goodness incarnate—original sin be damned.

I TRY TO honor my parents by carrying forward the best of what was in them. I believe I do that by looking squarely at the darkness in our familial history— and in my own self—and by constantly working to tame the demons that often laid them low and that now reside in my sisters and me.

The family I built with Jim and Stacy has never suffered the discord and chaos of the family I grew up in. Nevertheless, I know the seeds of that chaos are within me. But in Stacy's generation, it appears those seeds will not bear fruit. For that, I give thanks.

Nothing I've ever done or ever will do can hold a candle to the importance of the work I did as a mother. Forget lawyering on multimillion-dollar lawsuits, writing a couple books, or graduating law school with honors. Forget learning to talk without an impediment and learning to speak French. All of it is nothing by comparison. To be a good mother, I had to learn to matter to myself, both for Stacy's sake and for my sake. That sounds simple in words, but it never was.

Yet, for all the difficulties of building this life, the very normalcy of it brought my greatest joys: ordinary days of waking next to Jim, drinking coffee at the kitchen table, remarking on birds at the feeder, seeing Stacy's smiling wave as I dropped her off at school, listening to her tales of the day, eating a quiet dinner—or a pizza on Fridays—and curling up next to Jim at night to start the cycle again. These were days of ordinary paradise.

14

My Law Practice

The arc of the moral universe is long,
but it bends toward justice.

—Martin Luther King Jr.

WHEN LONGTIME TEXAS Supreme Court justice Franklin Spears retired from the court, he hired me to help him build an appellate law practice. He was a mercurial man—I knew that—and he had become even more so after some serious health issues. Still, his name carried heft, so it seemed like a good arrangement. As a practical matter, it meant I'd be the one to do most of the legal work while he'd be the one to bring in the business. But I would be well compensated—at least that was the plan.

The arrangement was short-lived. When a major case settled shortly after I filed our briefs, he made excuses for why a deal wasn't a deal. He claimed the settlement had happened solely because of the power of his name and that it had nothing to do with my briefing. When I protested, he called me a "nobody."

It felt like an existential crisis. If I didn't walk out, I'd be transmogrified into a doormat. So, I quit with no notice.

Convinced that I had ruined my appellate career, I feared no trial lawyer would ever again hire me once word circulated that I'd walked out on the great Franklin Spears. I had little in savings and no clue what I was going to do. But a prominent trial lawyer named Pat Maloney—I'd previously worked on just one of his cases—heard about what I'd done, and he FedExed me a retainer check for $10,000, with a note saying he would have a lot more work for me if

I wanted it. So, with fear and trepidation, and without any plan, I hung my shingle and started up my own appellate law practice.

At the time, Maloney and I didn't talk about what had happened; I just set to work. But a couple months later, when I was at his San Antonio office, out of the blue, he said, "Christa, I want you to know something. I grew up with Franklin . . . known him my whole life. He was *always* an arrogant little bully. Always thought he was better than everyone. Even as a twelve-year-old." I just laughed and laughed. Somehow, without us ever even discussing it, Maloney had intuited the gist of what had happened.

Like many others, I called Pat Maloney "PM," and oh, how I grew to love him, both as a lawyer and a human being. Years later, when he died, the *Washington Post* described him as "combative and controversial," but I knew him as so much more than that. True to his word, he hired me on case after case—for appeals, for summary judgment motions, and sometimes for strategizing at the very inception of a case. An Irishman who signed everything in green ink, he was a lion of a lawyer and juries loved him. On cross-exam, he could ever-so-gently grip the throat of a lying corporate executive and rip the truth right out of him, sometimes with the executive scarcely realizing what had happened. It was something to see. Consistently, he took on high-risk cases, saying modestly that, since he'd achieved a measure of success, it was his duty to take cases most other lawyers wouldn't or couldn't. "How will the law ever get better if we don't try to push it some?" he'd ask.

I got the joy of helping him "push it."

"WHY DID YOU buy all these books?" asked Mom when I showed her the office condo I'd rented just a couple blocks from Stacy's school. I was excited to give my parents a tour of my new workspace. It was a huge step for me professionally, and a big risk, but things were going well.

"I do civil appeals," I answered, thinking Mom was asking a real question. "So reading cases is a big part of what I do."

"But why did you *buy* them? Why don't you just go to the library to read them?"

I saw then that it was really a criticism, not a question, yet I plowed ahead anyway as though there might be some answer that would satisfy her.

"Well, sometimes the lawyers I work for want answers fast, and it saves me time to have the books right here. In fact, sometimes, they're in the middle of trial, and it helps when I can give them a case on something almost immediately without having to get in the car and drive to the law library downtown."

"I don't know how you think you're going to build a business if you just haul off and buy things like that. It's extravagant."

Suddenly, all the pride I'd felt in my new office seemed to be slipping away. Juggling lawyering and mothering had always been a struggle, but it helped that my new space was close enough that fourth grader Stacy could walk to it after school in five minutes. No matter what I was doing, when she walked in and plopped herself on my couch, I would stop everything and listen as she told me about her day. Then she'd get a snack from the kitchen and go in the library where she'd do homework or watch TV until it was time to leave. It was a good routine.

I wish I could have explained that to Mom, but she didn't seem interested. Her criticism played into my own insecurities. The financial roller coaster of self-employment could still be unsettling. It had been a huge leap of faith for me to go out on my own, and that was only the first of many leaps: moving to my own office, buying my own law library, extending my credit line, and taking my first contingency fee case. I was proud of what I was doing, but sometimes, the risks seemed overwhelming. I had to learn to trust myself—my own instincts and my own choices—and I had to cultivate an "in it for the long haul" perspective, because the cases I worked on often dragged out for years.

Finally, I gave Mom a simple answer. "This is what I needed to do to build my practice."

"No, it's what you *wanted* to do," she replied. "If you would just work a little harder, you could take the time and trouble to go to the library, and you wouldn't need all this."

"Well, anyway, that biggest set of books belonged to Ralph Yarborough," I said, trying hard to let Mom's criticism roll off my shoulders. "He's who I bought them from, so I think they're kind of special—a good legacy."

Mom was pursing her lips by now. I knew that if I failed miserably in my solo law practice—always a possibility—Mom would no doubt kick dirt in my face. But meanwhile, I could swear I saw Dad grinning.

Former US Senator Ralph Yarborough was the only Southern senator to vote for all five major civil rights bills between 1957 and 1970. "Put the jam on the bottom shelf where the little guy can reach it," he often said. Yarborough had a long, storied history of fighting to make government do better for veterans and working people, and that meant something to my dad, who had voted for Yarborough in multiple elections.

Though prices came down for online law libraries only a few years later, such that law books became less essential, I never regretted buying Yarborough's library. To the contrary, I grew to believe that Yarborough's books carried good juju, and since I worked primarily on underdog cases, I needed all the good juju I could get.

DAD WOULD SOMETIMES ask me about the kinds of cases I was working on, and I'd do my best to tell him. He always listened attentively, and sometimes when I was done, he'd quietly say, "I'm so proud of you." Every single time, it was all I could do to keep from weeping. I could feel Dad's pride in my bones.

But once, when Mom overheard his "proud of you" remark, she stepped in from the kitchen and, with her arms crossed, planted herself right in front of Dad as he sat in his recliner.

"You don't need to be tellin' her any more about how proud you are. She knows it already."

Dad looked at Mom, a long steady gaze, and then slowly responded. "Maybe I don't *need* to. Maybe I just *want* to."

I waited for Mom's rejoinder, worried that Dad's simple pride might spark a confrontation, because it often seemed as though the more I rose in Dad's regard, the more I triggered Mom's anger. The factions of our family were always somehow in play. But that time, Mom just walked away.

ONCE, WHEN MOM asked what I did as an appellate attorney, I tried to explain. "Well, mostly, I think of myself as a writer," I said. "That's what I actually spend most of my time doing."

Strangely, Mom seemed to take offense. "Oh, don't be silly. You aren't a writer and you shouldn't say that."

"Why not? It's what I do. I research things and I write about them."

"You're a lawyer, not a writer. You go to court."

"Sure, I go to court sometimes, but the way I spend *most* of my time is sitting at my desk and writing. And I get paid amazingly well for what I write."

"That doesn't make you a writer," she retorted. "Writers are creative. You just write about the law."

"Well, not exactly. Every case I work on has a story that goes with it, and I always think the most important part of what I do is how I tell the story. Sometimes, I have boxes and boxes of testimony and evidence, and I have to condense it all down to ten or so pages to tell the story in a brief. I think that takes some creativity."

"You aren't a writer," she repeated, glaring at me with her arms crossed. I looked back at her and wondered why she had bothered asking me what I did if she didn't want to hear the answer. Then I thought about how Mom wrote poems and, each year, picked her best ones to include in a spiral-bound book put out by the Farmers Branch Poetry Society. So, Mom saw *herself* as a writer and, apparently, that meant I *couldn't* be. It reminded me of how Judy had gotten so angry, and endlessly ridiculed me, when I started making pottery. She was the artist, not me, and I couldn't intrude on her turf.

"Okay, fine, Mom," I finally conceded. "I'm a lawyer. I'm an appellate lawyer, and I'm a good one, and what that means is that, day in and day out, I write a heckuva lot. That's what I do. That's how I get paid. Call it whatever you want."

This pattern made me cringe whenever Mom would brag to someone about me as her lawyer-daughter. It was similar to how she used to boast about my piano playing and then criticize me for it in private. It never felt as though she was genuinely proud of *me*. Instead, it felt as though she simply wanted something to brag about for *herself*.

AFTER A COUPLE years of renting that office condo, I was able to buy it, and not long after, Judy came to visit. She stayed with Nancy but spent a Saturday with me and insisted on seeing where I worked. "There's not much to see," I said. "It's just a small thing." But she wouldn't be deterred. So I drove her over around noon, and with her third beer in hand, she trudged up the single flight of stairs.

"No elevator?" she asked.

"No, but you know, I don't see many clients here."

"Yeah, I can see why."

Ignoring her, I unlocked the door. I was proud of the place: two attorney offices, a reception and administrative area, a small kitchen, a bathroom, and a large library with a nook for the copier and a space for Stacy to do her homework. There was a wooded area out the back windows where I could watch the cedar waxwings, and I had even managed to put in new carpeting.

Judy wasn't impressed. "Kinda shabby, isn't it?"

I felt the sting, but I tried to be breezy. "Well, maybe a little," I said, "but it's a great part of town and I *own* it. I'll fix it up more eventually."

"Meanwhile, as soon as your clients see your office, they'll find another attorney."

"My clients don't actually come here much," I explained again. "They're mostly other lawyers with practices in San Antonio and Houston. When they need to see me in person, I go to them."

I don't know why I kept trying to justify my office to Judy. I was proud of having built my own solo appellate practice, and I was honored to have some of Texas's best trial lawyers as clients. I *knew* how fortunate I was: I got paid well to do work I loved on causes I found meaningful with people I revered. But of course, I didn't say any of that to Judy. What would have been the point? Her aim wasn't to inquire about my law practice, or even to offer unsolicited sisterly advice, but rather to denigrate what I had built. I knew that, yet I still tried to pretend we were having a conversation.

"It's really a perfect place for me to work," I continued, "just a block from Stacy's school, and she's able to walk straight here after school and then we go home together."

"And that's exactly why you'll never be a success," she retorted. "You've arranged your office for your child instead of your clients."

By then, I was struggling to stay cordial. I knew Judy didn't know diddly-squat about what it took to run a small business, much less a law practice, much less a solo appellate practice as a woman with male trial lawyers for clients. But her words still hurt. She was plenty successful and made good money working as an accountant for a large corporation, but she'd never built a small business on her own. I was seething, but "let's go" was all I said.

With the simulacrum of a smile on her face, Judy seemed content in the realization that she'd gotten under my skin. With a flourish, she deposited her beer can on the middle of the reception desk just before going out the front door. She didn't even bother to put it in the trash.

SOMETIME LATER, I shattered my wrist, but with my family, there was no reprieve from my expected role as a caretaker.

"Comminuted . . . complex . . . displaced." I didn't know exactly what all the words meant, but I understood it wasn't good. I'd taken a fall onto concrete from off a stepladder, and the consequences were severe. The surgeon finally put it in layman's terms: "Basically crushed."

To realign the pieces and put them back together, he drilled four large screws into the bones of my hand and arm. He called them "pins," but they were *not* thin little sewing pins, as I'd imagined when he called them that, and instead were something far more industrial-looking. He used the implanted screws to hold in place an external fixator—a long metal rod which ran the length of my arm like a bionic contraption. It hurt like heck, and twice a day, Jim had to swab the screw holes with peroxide.

My fingers were completely immobile—not even so much as a twitch—as though there were no longer any nerve pathways between brain and hand. Since it was my dominant right hand, this was alarming, but the doctor just kept saying it was too soon to tell. He offered no assurance that I would regain mobility.

With me in that state of uncertainty, Mom and Dad arrived at our Austin home for a visit, and Nancy dropped by. She was on a women's soccer team in Austin and had just played a game at a nearby park. She arrived with a cast on her arm—an injury she'd gotten in the preceding week's match—but it hadn't stopped her from playing.

Our circumstances were vastly different. Nancy's injury was a hairline fracture of a single carpal bone with no displacement, no tiny pieces, and no need for surgery. Nevertheless, Mom focused on how "cute" we looked with our simultaneous injuries. "So sisterly," she said as she snapped a photo of us—Nancy with her cast and me with my metal rod. Then, after Nancy got in her car to drive herself home, Mom started scolding me on how I should be a better sister and help Nancy out more. "Didn't you hear her talk about how frustrating it was when she tried to button her shirt?" she asked.

"Uh, Mom, I'm pretty incapacitated myself right now," I responded, wondering if she'd even noticed the screws sticking out of my body. Sure, I'd heard Nancy talk about how awkward her cast made it to get dressed, but in my frame of mind, I'd felt only envy for all that Nancy could still manage. I could scarcely even feed myself.

"But you have Jim to help you," Mom continued. "Nancy doesn't have anyone."

Of course, that wasn't true. Nancy was living with her partner, Tina. But when I pointed that out—as if it weren't obvious—Mom said Tina didn't count. She wasn't "family."

"Couldn't you just go over there and at least help her with laundry?" Mom asked.

"But Mom, I can't even drive. I can't do much of anything. Anywhere I go, Jim has to take me, and he's already working double time. He's doing all the cooking and laundry and pretty much everything."

"You could if you wanted to," she answered, effectively ending the conversation. With that, I felt guilty enough that I called Nancy and invited her to stay with us, but of course, she wanted to be in her own home.

As the weeks went by, my hand stayed frozen, and I wanted only one thing: to touch my index finger to my thumb. Every morning, as soon as I opened my eyes, I'd lie quietly and focus all my mental energy on my hand, trying to will my index finger to move. Morning after morning, it wouldn't, and I fretted that I'd lost the use of my hand. But finally, one morning, with enormous concentration, I exhaled while simultaneously pushing every bit of energy within me into my index finger, and I saw the tiniest twitch. It was a bare millimeter of movement, but I was elated and woke Jim to show him. Each morning, I continued the practice, focusing my mind to enlarge the range of motion, and millimeter by millimeter, I did. It took weeks, but finally there came a morning when I exhaled that finger all the way to the thumb.

Few accomplishments in my life have ever felt so satisfying. Though it still took well over a year of physical therapy to regain full functioning of my right hand and arm, that simple willed touching of finger to thumb was the moment I knew I had hope.

EVEN AS AN adult, Farmers Branch held the capacity to unravel me. Every time I would visit there, the sunshine of my heart would turn to a fog of dread and doubt. Before trips, I'd be filled with anxiety; when I was there, my adrenaline would be firing at full blast; and afterwards, I'd be left sleepless and snapping for weeks. In countless ways, the past would revisit me in Farmers Branch, reminding me of the lessons I had learned there: no one will protect you; keep low and stay alert; don't let your guard down. So, though I often felt the pull of "home," it was a pull that felt like teetering on the edge of a black hole.

The stakes were high, not only for my own preservation but also for the good of Stacy. So often, Farmers Branch left me struggling to separate my own inner voice from Mom's carping. Knowing that the way parents talk to their children often becomes the way children talk to themselves—and seeing that reality in my own life—I was determined not to allow my own inner critic to devolve into criticism of Stacy. I wanted her to have an inner voice filled only with kindness and self-acceptance. To hold hope for that, I had to guard myself against Mom and the black hole of Farmers Branch.

Thanksgivings were particularly problematic. Even its anticipation filled me with dread, as year after year, my insomnia would worsen starting in September. I'd gain weight, shoveling in the calories in vain efforts to soothe myself, and by mid-October, my whole chest would start clenching up with anxiety. Then when the holiday had passed, invariably, my body would collapse and I'd fall sick.

Year after year, it was the same. The group dynamics brought out the worst in all of us. And my contributions to the potluck feast were never good enough.

One year, I took a fabulous chocolate cake, but Mom chided me. "Stop trying to make something fancy and just bring something ordinary. Bring a pumpkin pie next time."

The next year, I took two pumpkin pies. Mom scolded that I should have known better, that pumpkin pie was what Rita made. "But that's what you *told* me to bring," I protested, but she just denied it.

The following year, I emailed that I was planning to bring an apple pie unless they wanted something else. No one said a word. But after the meal, Mom complained. "Everyone ate your apple pie instead of Rita's pumpkin pie. How do you think that makes *her* feel? Can't you for once just try to imagine how *she* feels?"

Then there was the year I gave up on desserts and made a sweet potato and leek torte. I'd made it for other gatherings and people always loved it. But not Mom and Rita. They said it interfered with the traditional sweet potato and marshmallow dish, which was what the kids wanted.

The next year, I overcompensated and prepared a half-dozen different dishes. Surely there would be something Mom would approve of, I thought. My yearning to please was ridiculous. And I was still just as depressed when Thanksgiving was over.

15

Rita Won't Like It

Presumptions of a lifetime are perilous things to overturn.

—Barbara Kingsolver

"SHE JUST NEEDS to learn."

That's what Rita kept saying when I didn't accept her invitation for Stacy to live with them over the summer. Rita and her husband, Richard, wanted to have Stacy stay with them so that all the cousins could be together, but I explained that Stacy still had trouble doing sleepovers at her best friend's house, just two doors down the block. She would do fine until around midnight, and then, when the neighbor's house got quiet, she would get upset and want to go home. Her friend's mom would call us and we'd walk down to pick her up. If Stacy stayed at Rita and Richard's house, two hundred miles away, we wouldn't be able to go get her.

"She's just not ready for it," I said.

But Rita insisted. "You shouldn't let her wrap you around her little finger like that."

It took me by surprise, her complete dismissal of Stacy's feelings. Foolishly, I had thought a child's difficulty with sleepovers might be something we could commiserate over as moms. I was wrong. I tried to rebound.

"I don't think she's got me wrapped around her finger—it's just that she's not quite ready," I said, feeling simultaneously defensive and also guilty for having shared Stacy's weakness. Her extreme homesickness embarrassed her, and she probably wouldn't like the fact that I had talked about it.

"If you keep giving in to her, she'll go right on thinking you're at her beck and call," Rita snapped back.

I bit my tongue as I realized that what had initially appeared as a simple invitation had become something Rita was trying to dictate. She went on and on about how great it would be for the cousins to spend the summer together and how much her daughter, Molly, wanted it. Over and over, she kept coming back to her "she just needs to learn" refrain.

But the more she talked, the more I knew for sure that my answer was no. Rita's reaction only served to solidify my decision. In my mind, I had reached the "no way in hell" point, but all I said to Rita was "It's just not the right timing."

My refusal had been instinctive—I knew it wouldn't be good for Stacy—but after Rita's reaction, I began to consciously catalog the reasons that had likely fueled my instinct. I remembered the summer before when we'd taken Stacy out to West Texas to celebrate her birthday with her cousins, Bobby and Molly. Rita had made caps for all three of them with "Cousins!" written in glitter glue-stick, and the kids had a great time together. But I held some additional memories from that trip.

While I sat across the table from Bobby and Molly, talking over their heads to Rita in the kitchen, I saw how Molly kept reaching out to pinch Bobby. Even as he pulled away and told her to stop, she just stuck her tongue out at him and kept on. Richard was just a few feet away, but he said nothing, and Rita had her back turned. Finally, in a sharp whisper I said, "Molly!" and gave her a good hard look, shaking my head. She smiled, folded her hands in her lap, and waited until I turned my attention back to Rita's conversation. Then she went right back to tormenting Bobby.

When Bobby couldn't take it anymore, he shoved Molly on the arm. It wasn't a hard blow, but Molly immediately began crying, "Bobby hit me, Bobby hit me." Only then did Richard pay attention. He stood up, put a hand on Bobby's shoulder and said, "Go get the paddle and wait for me in the garage."

Bobby's lower lip started to quiver. I could hardly bear to look at the fear in his face. It didn't seem fair.

"You know, she was really egging him on," I said, looking then at Molly who stuck her tongue out at me. "He stayed still and took it for a long time."

"Boys can't hit girls. No exceptions," replied Richard. "Bobby, go on. I told you to get the paddle and wait for me."

Bobby walked away whimpering, and after a while, Richard followed. It put a real damper on the birthday party—at least it did for Stacy, who appeared puzzled and confused. But Molly looked victorious. Bobby stayed gone about an hour, and when he came back, his face was swollen and red.

As I watched the smirk grow on Molly's face, it reminded me of the time Judy wrote *my* name—"Christa"—in the living room picture window right after Mom had cleaned it. We'd been playing a card game on the floor and Mom had just finished her task. "Don't either of you dare touch that window," she'd warned.

As soon as Mom was out of sight, Judy looked at me, grinned, and went straight to the window. I watched in horror as she fogged the glass with her breath and wrote my name. I was learning cursive at school and had been obsessively practicing on my Big Chief tablet, so I knew Mom would think it was me. Judy knew it too. Sure enough, when Mom returned and saw my name on her otherwise spotless picture window, she pretty near went berserk.

"But I didn't do it. I didn't do it," I cried.

Mom didn't believe me. She threw me over her knees, pulled down my pants, and kept on and on, hitting her palm onto my bare bottom.

"Stop lying to me," she screamed.

I pleaded, "I'm not lying—I didn't do it." But my wails had no effect.

"I'm not stopping 'til you tell me the truth," she yelled. With swat after swat, she screamed, "Admit it. Tell me the truth."

"But Momma, I *am*," I whimpered. "I *am* telling the truth. I didn't do it." She kept on.

I couldn't figure out what to do. If I admitted to it, she'd stop spanking me, but that would be a lie, and telling a lie would be breaking one of God's Ten Commandments. Which was worse, I wondered, to risk God's wrath by lying or to endure the endless swats that came from telling the truth? Being stuck between the God-god and the Mom-god was an awful dilemma for a hyper-religious eight-year-old. Ultimately, I decided it would be worse to lie, and I imagined that God was testing me.

I guess I must have finally passed out because I woke up lying in my bed. Judy was sitting cross-legged on the floor right in front of me, smirking, her face no more than a foot from mine, her eyes lit with some kind of sick delight.

These memories were forefront in my mind as I wondered whether Rita and Richard would feel free to spank Stacy if she spent the summer with them.

Mom would also be there for the summer, and I worried about her too. I knew she was still paddling kids in her second-grade classroom.

I couldn't imagine how traumatized Stacy would be if her aunt, her uncle, or her grandmother decided to spank her. It was unthinkable. Stacy had never been spanked in her life. But like many in Baptistland, my family members thought it was appropriate punishment for the most innocuous of childish behaviors.

For instance, Stacy had a friend who would sometimes let loose with an ear-splitting shriek when they were playing. I happened to tell Mom and Rita about it one day, just making conversation. But Rita said, "Those parents need to teach her a lesson. One good spanking and she'd learn not to shriek like that."

Horrified by such a harsh response to what I thought was just a "kids do the darndest things" story, I tried to clarify. "Oh, but it's like her way of laughing. She doesn't mean anything by it. She just gets excited."

Rita held her ground. "Well, if it's hurting people's ears, then she needs to be taught not to do it. She needs a lesson." I knew I could not put Stacy at risk of reaping any of Rita's "lessons."

With Mom, too, spanking hadn't been employed only for rare occasions; it had been routine. Even when we were in public, she'd never hesitated, particularly with Judy and me—we always seemed to reap more of Mom's frustration than Nancy and Rita. Whether we were at the five-and-dime or the grocery store, Mom would yank down our panties in a split second and go after it. Church was particularly precarious. If we squirmed in the pews, Mom would spank us in the car before she even pulled out of the parking lot, while other churchgoers just walked by. Since I usually sat next to Judy in the pew, I had to learn to bite my tongue when she pinched me; otherwise, if I made a sound, I'd be sure to get one of those parking lot spankings.

Sometimes, after a particularly hard spanking, Mom would wrap her arms around me and squeeze me so tight I could hardly breathe. "Oh, I don't know what got into me," she'd say. "You know how much I love you, don't you?" I'd always stop crying then, smile and nod. I never wanted Mom to feel bad.

But for Stacy, spanking remained such an unknown that, one day in first grade, she came home telling us that one of her friends had said she "got a spanking," and Stacy wanted to know exactly what her friend had gotten. We explained that "a spanking" was when a grown-up—usually a mom or dad—would hit a kid on the bottom to try to teach the kid not to do something. Stacy broke out laughing. She thought we were joking. In her mind, it must have seemed like something out of a Wile E. Coyote cartoon. She couldn't imagine grown-ups hitting kids. But when she saw that we were serious, she started to cry. She was imagining her friend and how much it must have hurt to be hit by her mom.

With memories like these, there was no way I could take a chance on leaving Stacy with Rita and Richard and Mom.

Then there was the bitter, backbiting nature of Rita and Richard's relationship. Anger and resentment seemed the principal emotions that bound them, and with so much mindlessly vicious bickering, they were stressful to be around. I couldn't imagine how it would be for Stacy if she were trapped there.

Finally, there was the fact that Mom refused to have Stacy wear a seat belt despite my repeated requests. The first time I knew about it was when Stacy came back from a trip to the grocery store proclaiming, "I don't have to wear a seat belt in Grandma's car." Naturally, I'd asked Mom about it.

"Oh, the van's safe," she said. "It's so big that if anyone hit us, *they'd* be the ones hurt, not us."

I explained that this was something important to us. "We want it to be a consistent rule for Stacy," I said, "so she automatically knows that, when she gets in a car, she puts on a seat belt."

Mom resisted, insisting that she should be able to make the rules in her own car. I told her about the defective seat belt case I'd been working on for several years—a case in which the client may as well have not had any seat belt at all. "Maybe it's because of the work I do," I said, "but this is something I feel really fanatical about. I've spent the past five years reading every case in the country that involves a seat belt failure. Day in and day out, I read about people's injuries. I look at medical records, coroners' reports, and photos of accident scenes. It's always awful. So, can you just indulge me? I need to know that if Stacy rides with you, she'll wear a seat belt."

I thought that blaming my own fanaticism would give Mom an easy way to save face, but instead she grew more defensive. "Oh, don't be silly, Christa. I raised four daughters and none of you ever wore seat belts, and you're all just fine."

I always cringed whenever Mom labeled me "silly," but I knew this issue was too important to get sidetracked by my own irritation. "Mom, I know nothing ever happened to the four of us, but it only takes one time. I'm sorry, but I really have to insist. Stacy has to wear a seat belt if she's going to ride with you. Okay?" Mom just looked at me and put up her hands. I took that gesture as a yes since I didn't want to keep arguing.

But I was wrong. On the next visit, I again let Stacy go to the store with Mom. Stacy didn't tell me right away, but later, on the drive back to Austin, she spilled it. "I wore my seat belt on the way," she confessed, "but Grandma said I didn't have to on the way back."

Jim glanced at me as he was driving, and I turned around and looked at Stacy. "Well, I'm glad you told us, but just so we're clear, you know you're supposed to *always* wear your seat belt, don't you?"

"Grandma said it could be a secret."

I saw then the bind that my mom had put Stacy in. Stacy knew the rule, but Grandma herself, someone Stacy loved with all her heart, had told her it was okay to break the rule and to ignore what her parents had taught her. Then she had told her to keep it a secret. I knew I could never again allow Stacy to ride alone with Mom. That, too, seemed a good reason not to let Stacy spend the summer with her cousins. The decision was final.

A MONTH LATER, Rita and Richard brought Bobby and Molly to our house for Easter. After watching the kids run wild as they hunted for eggs in the backyard, I went inside to mix up some lemonade. Richard followed me. Since I tried never to be alone with him, I cursed under my breath, but I ignored him, thinking maybe he was on his way to the bathroom.

"Must be nice not to have a real job," he said out of the blue, leaning against the kitchen counter.

I looked up. "What do you mean? I have a job."

"Naahhh. You can just work whenever you want to. You don't have a boss."

"It's not like that. I can't just work whenever I want. I have to work when the work is there. My clients are my boss—I work when they need me. And I have deadlines from the court. So that's like having a boss too." I couldn't figure out what Richard was driving at.

"Yeah, right. But you don't have a *real* boss. It's not the same. You can work whenever you want. You could come *too* for the summer if you're so afraid of Stacy coming by herself."

I saw then why he was denigrating my work: this was another attempt to talk me into letting Stacy spend the summer with them, and he was extending their beat-you-over-the-head-with-it invitation to me too.

"Thanks," I said, "but there's no way I could take a whole summer off."

"Why not?" he pushed. "You don't have a boss. Who's going to stop you?"

"Just because I don't have a boss doesn't mean I don't have deadlines. Sure, I've got some flexibility, but that also means that, sometimes, I have to work around the clock because there's no one else to get the job done. I don't get sick leave or vacation time. I'm the one who has to get it done."

"You could do this if you really wanted to," he said, not listening to me.

"Well, sure. But I like being self-employed, and if I just took off whenever I wanted, I wouldn't stay self-employed for very long. People expect me to get the job done."

"Jim's a lawyer—he could do your work."

"No, he couldn't. My work is specialized, and anyway, Jim's got his own work. Besides, I wouldn't want us to be apart all summer."

Again, Richard kept on as though he hadn't heard me. "You could hire some other attorney to do your work over the summer. You're the boss, right?"

"No. I can't just hire someone else to do what I do. My clients are all lawyers themselves—they're trial lawyers. If they thought just any lawyer could do the job, they'd turn it over to some young associate in their office. But they don't. They hire *me* because they want *me*. Besides, I've got cases I've been working on for years. There's a history and they're complicated. I can't just farm out an ongoing case to someone else."

"Oh. I see. It's *complicated*," he sneered. Feeling my blood pressure on the rise, I bit my tongue. *Who does he think he is to tell me how to do my work?* Inside I was screaming, but I reminded myself that he was a guest in my home. I didn't want to make a stink. So I pulled glasses out of the cupboard and started pouring the lemonade.

"Look, this just isn't something I can do," I said, consciously forcing myself to keep an even tone. "I've got briefs that are due and I've got deadlines and I just can't."

"But you could get extensions of time, right? Lawyers do that all the time, don't they?"

I couldn't believe it. He wouldn't let it go.

"Well, sure," I said, "but I'm not gonna tell the court I need an extension of time so I can have a three-month vacation. I'm just not gonna do that. Besides, Stacy has a pottery class that she's excited about this summer."

"Oh. So you'd rather let strangers take care of Stacy instead of your own family?"

"No. That's not what I'm saying. It's not like that. I'm just saying it's a class she's looking forward to. It's a day class. She'll be with us in the evenings."

By then, I was so fed up I could hardly see straight, but Richard still had one more guilt trip to try. "Maybe you need to think about something more than just whatever Stacy wants," he said. "Think about what's good for the rest of the family. Think about how happy it would make your mother."

In my mind, I hit pause, but only for a moment. Mom hadn't said a word about any of this. So either Richard was just trying one more angle, or he and Rita had been talking about it with Mom. If the latter, then good for Mom. She was plenty capable of guilt-tripping me on all manner of things, but she'd kept her mouth shut on this one.

I picked up my tray with the glasses of lemonade and headed for the door. "Richard, the answer is no. I'm sorry, but I'm doing what I think is best for Stacy, and that's that."

"Rita won't like it," he rumbled, but I was already walking out the door.

Not until many years later would I learn how wrong I had been in thinking "that's that," and how right Richard had been with his last words: "Rita won't like it."

WHEN DAD CALLED to tell me that Mom had left him again, for what was by then the third or fourth time, I could hardly bring myself to listen to the sorrow in his voice, the ache of it, his incomprehension. I resented being mentally dragged into the misery of my parents' marriage. But Dad had no one—no counselor, no friends. He was totally alone, and I wound up being the daughter he called when he was despondent.

It was rare for Dad to talk about Mom, and it typically happened only when they were separated. So it was hard to fault him, given that Mom had always talked about Dad freely and frequently. I could be having a perfectly lovely day, and a phone call from Mom would suddenly yank me back into the hell of Farmers Branch. Since I always tolerated it with Mom, I felt like I should at least listen on the rare occasions when Dad needed to talk. But it was always painful.

After I'd already sat through several phone calls from both of them, I made a trip to Dallas for a legal conference. Deliberately, I chose not to stay with either of them, but at the conference hotel. Still, I stopped by to spend a few hours with Dad, and the conversation turned to why Mom had left him. He was fixated on trying to understand how things could have gotten so bad and what he could do to get her to move back home.

At first, I told him he needed to ask Mom about that, but as he continued, I finally pushed back. "But Daddy, really, you know, don't you? You get so angry. I think that's a big part of it, don't you?"

"But she *makes* me angry, don't you see?" he responded. "She eggs me on. She *makes* me that way."

"No, Daddy. I know Mom can be infuriating, and she's wrong about a lot of things, but nothing she does can justify the anger you sometimes unleash. Yeah, she pushes your buttons. I get it. But, Daddy, you can be terrifying, do you *know* that?"

He protested. "You've been listening to your mother too much. I don't know what she tells you."

I wished we were having the conversation in the den where, if needed, I could make a fast move for the door. Instead, I was trapped in the hallway where it was too narrow to get by him. I felt in my bones that I should back off, but I just couldn't. I let loose.

"Daddy, I grew up in this house. I *know* how you can get. I've seen it. I've lived with it. You threatened to bomb us! Do you even remember that?"

I saw the incomprehension in his face. Still, I kept on.

"No one should have to live with the kind of anger issues you've got. You've been terrifying for *all* of us. You've called me really ugly names, more times than I can count. Do you even remember? Sometimes, I've been afraid you might actually kill us. Even now, I'm afraid. I'm talking to you, but I'm afraid. Are you going to blow up if you don't like what I say?"

Dad looked at me, and suddenly his eyes filled with tears. I could count on one hand the number of times I'd seen Dad cry, and yet, there he was, weeping, the anguish visible in his face.

"Oh, Christa, I would never hurt you. I would never hurt any of you. I love you. You must know that." His voice held such pleading. And though I knew what I'd told him was true, I felt such enormous sorrow.

"I love you too, Daddy, but it doesn't change what I know about you. You can be really scary. And even if you don't hit us, all the vile names and threats, all of it, it still hurts. A lot."

"I'm sorry, Christa."

I stared at him, uncomprehending. I had never before heard my father apologize. I saw the grief in his face, and I, too, began to weep. I wish I could say that we hugged one another and that everything was better after that, but Dad simply turned and walked away, his shoulders slumped. He went out into the yard, and I, emotionally spent, yelled a quick goodbye, and got in the car to drive back to Austin. I cried all the way. That day remained the only time I ever heard my Dad apologize, but on that day, I felt as though he meant it.

He and Mom got back together a few weeks later, and the cycle started anew.

WITH MY DESIRE for a second child came more of Mom's reprobation. "You shouldn't push your luck," she said as she picked a small stone out from the dried beans. "Be happy with what you've got."

"What do you mean?" I asked. "I *am* happy with what I've got, but we'd love to have a second child too."

"Stacy turned out beautiful, but you might not be so lucky the second time. One should be enough for you."

"What do you mean?" I asked again, still not accepting what I was hearing.

"You know. Another child might be like you. What would you do then?"

Silence filled the space between us as I studied the dried beans under Mom's fingers and pondered the fact that she seemed to think having a kid like me would be something so terrible. I understood what she was saying—there was no mistaking it. She was afraid that if I had another child, my cleft lip might be passed down to another generation.

"Well, I don't know," I finally replied. "I don't think it would be the end of the world. I guess we would just deal with it. And maybe it would be easier for them because I would know what it was like."

"You *don't* know what it was like," she insisted sternly, standing to take the beans into the kitchen.

"Yeah, Mom, I sorta *do* know," I answered, dumbstruck by her bizarre insistence that I didn't.

"No. You were a child. You can't possibly know how hard it was. Your face . . ." Mom's voice trailed off as she slowly shook her head and pressed her lips. "I didn't think you'd ever be able to find a husband."

"A husband? Is that what you were worried about?" But by then, I was really just talking to myself because I was already halfway out the patio door, unable to bear any more of what she might say and, as always, wishing I'd just kept my mouth shut instead of sharing a cherished hope.

For a full year, Jim and I had been using medical interventions to try for another pregnancy, and for four months, Jim had been giving me expensive fertility drug injections. Like liquid gold, every cycle cost around $1,500 out of pocket, and I had to be closely monitored. I'd had the last ultrasound two days before Thanksgiving, and the doctor was optimistic because I had so many ovarian follicles maturing at once.

I asked about leaving town for Thanksgiving—because I couldn't say no to Mom—and the doc said, "It should be fine." He made an appointment for me to come in on Saturday afternoon and said the follicles on my ovaries would probably be at the "perfect-peach" level of ripeness by then. He would ultrasound them again to be sure and then I could get the final shot that would cause them to burst. "This will have to be your last time," he warned.

Sadly, my ovaries didn't wait for doctor's orders. Something about being there in Farmers Branch. In that house. With my sisters. With my mom.

All day long on Thursday, I felt a growing heaviness. I couldn't eat and could scarcely walk. That night, the pain was intense—the follicles were rupturing. Jim wanted to take me to an emergency room, but I preferred to pretend it wasn't happening. It was how I had survived so much else in Farmers Branch, by leaving my body behind and rendering myself into oblivion.

Friday morning, just after sunup, we started gathering our stuff to leave, and Mom was irritated. I told her I was feeling pretty awful, but she insisted it would pass and said I should stay.

Jim had to hold me up as I walked to the car.

The next week, Mom called. When I couldn't bear to listen to all her goings-on about how ideal Thanksgiving had been, I finally told her. "Mom, I shouldn't have come. I was taking fertility drugs, and things went wrong. I lost my last chance for another pregnancy."

"Oh, don't be silly. We had a wonderful Thanksgiving and I don't want to hear anything else."

"But it wasn't so wonderful for *me*, Mom."

"Of course it was. We were all together and that's all that matters. We had a perfect Thanksgiving."

There it was, the official and only acceptable version of events: "We had a perfect Thanksgiving." No negative emotions allowed. Positivity imposed. Denial demanded.

I just couldn't. The more words I spoke, the more of myself I felt seeping away. The insistence on positivity felt poisonous. If I kept talking, I would lose myself. So I stopped, just stopped, with trying to say anything true about how I felt. I didn't even attempt to tell Mom how months of infertility treatments had left me battling constant waves of grief or how the storm of Thanksgiving had transformed those waves into a tsunami, rendering me bereft. There was nothing left but to echo her from across the great chasm. "It was a great Thanksgiving, Mom."

Years later, whenever I thought back on that Thanksgiving, I not only relived the grief of it, but also began pondering the many times when I'd asked Mom some question about her own family only to get her vague answer of, "Oh, I had a perfect family." I figured that if Mom's family was "perfect" in the same way that Thanksgiving had been "perfect," there was some serious denial going on. I had learned enough about her origins to have a different picture: her younger brother died under clouded circumstances when she was eight; her mother was first institutionalized when she was ten; her older brother mocked her speech impediment, broke her nose, and "tried things"; her parents divorced when she was eleven; her family lost everything in the Depression; her brother was accused of molesting her niece; and her mother was eventually institutionalized permanently. But according to Mom, she had a "perfect family."

LEARNING THAT JACK had "tried things" with Mom was a long process, and I struggled with seeing the picture that the pieces finally formed. The first peg in the process came not long after Mom's sister Ava died. Mom called me up, rambling about how Ava's death had actually been a suicide.

My mind went to all the letters Aunt Ava had sent me, almost always filled with lists of what she had salvaged from her walks in the alley behind the room she rented. I imagined her shuffling along with her cane, her legs unable to support her weight, pausing every so often to scrutinize the contents of a trash can. Her son had died at age nineteen after driving a car straight into a tree. Mom said that was a suicide too.

I tried to probe Mom for why she felt so certain that Ava's death had been a suicide even though Jack said it had been a stroke.

"I think she took some pills or something," said Mom. "She just didn't want to live anymore."

"Did she say something? Why do you think that?"

"We talked the day before," she explained. "Ava was so mad at Jack. And she still wanted me to join her in a lawsuit against Jack."

"A lawsuit? Why? Why would she want you to sue Jack?"

"She thought Jack should have shared the money when he sold our parents' house. That, and . . . and . . . she was still upset about what Jack did to Beatrice and thought Jack should have done something to help her. But Beatrice was messed up, and Jack didn't think it would ever end."

Beatrice was Aunt Ava's youngest daughter—my cousin—but I held no memory of ever meeting her.

I asked, "What are you talking about, Mom? What did Jack do to Beatrice?"

"Oh, it wasn't nearly as big a deal as she made it. Jack just got carried away a little, and Beatrice couldn't let it go."

"Carried away how, Mom?"

Mom shut down and didn't want to talk anymore. Every query I posed irritated her and she insisted I should "let it go." So, on that day, I did. But I never forgot the hint of that story, and I tried to get Mom to tell it to me straight on several subsequent occasions.

Each time I asked about it—"What happened between Jack and Beatrice?"—Mom would give me some vague version of how Beatrice claimed Jack had "messed with her" when she was a kid, but Jack said she was just being "opportunistic" and wanted to blackmail him for money. A couple of times, Mom simply said that Beatrice was mentally unstable. With each of Mom's tellings, I took what Mom said at face value, stored it in the back of my mind, and let it go. But one day, I pressed a bit more.

"Well, was it true?" I asked. "Did he? Did he mess with her?"

"Oh, I'm sure he did something," said Mom. "He messed with me too. But I don't think it was all that she said."

"What do you mean, Mom? What did he do to *you?*"

"Oh, boys are boys, that's just how they are. No need to make a big deal out of it."

I tried to pursue it further, but Mom shut down. She just kept saying that Beatrice had "exaggerated," that it wasn't as bad as she said, and that it "wasn't really a big deal."

Mom's words burned a spot in my brain: "He messed with me too." I could never quite put them out of my mind.

When I reflect on it now, I think Mom was having a classic trauma response. She had tried to tell me what happened, and almost did, but then she retreated before divulging too much could make it too real. Mom spent a lifetime warding off her feelings about how Jack had "messed with" her, and she'd never had any opportunity to work at healing from it.

I don't know whether Ava's death was a suicide or not, but if it was, it wasn't the only suicide in our family. One of Dad's brothers also died by suicide. He went out in the backyard, laid out a sheet on the grass, and then shot a bullet through his head. Everyone talked about the sheet and how he hadn't wanted to leave a mess for his daughter. He'd wanted to make it "easy for her," they said.

AFTER 9/11, MOM grew fixated on wanting to keep us safe. She not only compared 9/11 with Pearl Harbor and reflected on how much that singular event had transformed her world, but she also fixed her internal gaze on some unknown future event that I could never nail down. In every visit, she'd tell me that if anything happened, we should just run. "Don't wait," she'd insist. "Get out right away. You and Jim and Stacy." Every time, I'd try to figure out exactly what kind of catastrophe she was envisioning, so I could reassure her. But she would have none of it. "Leave your house. Leave everything. Just get in your car and go. Find a safe place. Stay together, the three of you. Don't worry about any of the rest of us. The three of you, that's all that matters."

Though Mom never specifically said so, I presumed she was imagining something like a nuclear attack and thinking that the three of us could just drive north to the Yukon.

Nowadays, I look back and wonder whether her fear was more nebulous than that. Maybe she had some sense of a future catastrophe, but had no idea what kind it would be. Maybe on a gut level she intuited that, someday, in order to find a "safe place," I would have to separate from them all—from everything connected to Farmers Branch. Maybe on some deep level she understood that I would have to leave them behind in order to keep my own family healthy. I'd like to think so.

16

And Charlie Was a Happy Man

The silence of a falling star
lights up a purple sky.

—Hank Williams

WHEN I OPENED the door to Dad's hospital room, I could tell in two seconds that something was wrong. Mom had told me he would be going home that day, so I'd driven up to help get him back to the house and settled in. Instantly, I saw the look on his face and felt the barometric pressure of the room, but still, I tried to act like things were normal. It was a longtime habit.

"So, you get to go home today," I said cheerily.

"Hmmmph. I guess that's up to her."

"But Mom told me you were going home today," I said, simply assuming that the "her" he was talking about was Mom. The oxygen canister that Dad was supposed to bring home was sitting right there in the room, so I thought it must just be some misunderstanding. I told Dad I'd find Mom and figure out what was going on.

Mom and Rita were holed up in a waiting room at the end of the hall. They told me that, the day before, Mom had hired someone to fix the garage door at their house, and when she'd told Dad about it that morning—and about how much it cost—he'd cussed at her and told her she'd paid too much. Upset by Dad's cussing, Rita then convinced Mom that she shouldn't let Dad go home, and Mom went along. So, thanks to a broken garage door, combined with a long, sad familial history, and a trauma-triggered and possibly vengeful daughter, Dad never lived at home again.

For several years, he'd done well at controlling his temper. Mom and he had seemed almost content. But after his outburst in the hospital, Mom and Rita told the doctor that Dad wasn't himself. They said something had gone wrong with him mentally after his last heart attack and that he needed to be in a nursing home. They told me this as though they were proud of it, as a scheme they'd concocted to prevent the doctor from discharging Dad.

"But he's *always* had anger issues!" I protested.

"But now Mom doesn't have to put up with it anymore," declared Rita.

So, the hospital transferred Dad to a nursing home.

"He has to learn," said Mom. "And until he does, he's not coming home."

Dad was declining fast, and the only thing he wanted was to be in his own home. He was miserable at the nursing home, but the more he gave voice to his misery, the more Mom dug in on keeping him there. In trip after trip, I tried to talk to her about arranging for Dad to go home. But like a puppet, she always replied with some version of "Rita says"—*Rita says he'll just blow up again* or *Rita says he shouldn't come home until he's learned his lesson* or *Rita says he needs to figure out how to take care of himself.* It didn't matter if I pointed out that Dad was too weak to be dangerous or that he didn't have much time left. I offered to help with arranging hospice care and home health aides, but everything was to no avail.

Repeatedly, when I told Mom that Dad was dying, she'd just brush it off. "Oh, don't be silly," she'd say. "He's just being stubborn, and he's not going to get his way just because he's sick."

Those conversations tore me apart, and conversations with Dad were no better. He pleaded with me to somehow get him home. "She thinks they're all so nice here," he said. "But she don't know. She's not here." I felt trapped in the middle between Dad's desperation and Mom's determined refusal.

One day, I noticed his long nails, got out some clippers, and took Dad's hand in mine. I paused, looked at him, waited for him to nod, and then began. Mom looked on in astonishment. "He won't let anyone clip his nails!" she shouted. "Not even me!"

Then she started in on Dad. It seemed that every time I visited, she railed at him about something, always wanting him to be more "extroverted" and "upbeat." She even carped at him about how he needed to make friends with the man in the next bed . . . who was dead a week later. It was as though she thought that, in his last few weeks of life, she could finally change him into the sociable husband she'd always wanted.

"Why do you let Christa clip your nails when you won't let anyone else?" she scolded. "Why won't you let Rita clip your nails? Why are you so stubborn?"

Dad didn't answer. He just kept quiet the whole time. To me, it seemed obvious: though he had control over almost nothing else at that point, he could still exercise control over his own fingernails—and so he did. When I finished, he said a soft "thank you."

Dad wanted me to find him a lawyer. He felt "imprisoned," he said. So I gave him the name of an elder law attorney I knew and told Dad he could call anytime. I didn't think Dad actually needed an attorney, but I wanted him to be able to talk with someone who was objective and outside the family. Dad never called him.

I told Dad I would drive him home if he wanted. But I also said that he'd have to have some help at home, that Mom couldn't take care of him by herself, and that he needed to work something out with her. I promised I'd help find some good people and assist Mom with getting things set up.

With eyes lost in sorrow, he looked at me as though I were imagining something beyond the realm of possibility. His words have haunted me: "She only listens to your sister, Christa. She only listens to your sister."

FOR THANKSGIVING THAT year, Jim and Stacy and I drove to Farmers Branch. Mom had told me Dad would come home just for the day, and I wanted to spend it with him. I was the only daughter there for dinner; Nancy arrived later. After our no-fuss meal, Jim helped Dad get his walker out to the patio. I wrapped a blanket around him, and we all sat there, almost like old times, and watched the birds for a while. Then we went inside, pulled the red dominoes out of the cabinet, and played 42. Dad grinned and bluffed and teased, and still as sharp as ever, he remembered every domino played.

Finally, the time came for us to drive back. Jim and Stacy gave handshakes and hugs and said their goodbyes, but I lingered. After a long hug, Dad kept holding my hand. Time stood still as he gazed at me, smiling. I couldn't let go and, with tears, continued to smile back at him. I saw so much love in his face, and I knew it might be the last time I would see him. I think Dad knew it too.

Jim came back to retrieve me, and I realized that Dad would hold my hand for as long as I would let him. It would have to be me who would let go. So finally, I did.

Dad died a week later, alone in the nursing home.

I WANTED SOME time apart from the scheduled viewing, to spend alone with Dad and to say goodbye. So I phoned the funeral home before we left Austin, and by the time we got to Farmers Branch, they had Dad's coffin open in a room for me. I needed the quiet and the solitude, so I didn't tell any of my sisters what I was doing.

Later, when we arrived at the house, Judy greeted me with a challenge. "I bet you don't know how Mom and Dad met."

"Well, I think I do," I said. "Just after Pearl Harbor, they met on a packed cross-country bus. Afterwards, they wrote to each other for six weeks, and then got married while Dad was on leave and before he shipped out in the war."

All three of my sisters looked at me in astonishment. "How did you know that?" demanded Judy. "We all learned it just this morning. Jack told us."

"I don't know. I've known it a long time."

"Dad must have told her," surmised Rita, speaking as though I wasn't there. "Mom would never have told Christa without telling us too."

"Well, I don't know," I said, "but I did get a lot of *other* stories from Dad. You know, we had all that time going back and forth to my orthodontist every month." I was choosing my words carefully because I couldn't figure out why they cared so much about who had told me.

"Oh, yeah. You had all those car rides with Dad," said Judy. "That must be how you knew."

With Judy's pronouncement, Rita and Nancy nodded their heads, and they all three seemed satisfied.

"Don't you think that just explains everything?" interjected Judy.

I paused. "Everything?"

"Yeah. Everything. How they met. It explains everything, doesn't it?"

"Well . . . no . . . I think it was a lot more complicated than that. After all, they stayed married for over fifty years." But Judy hardly heard me. She was off and running with a rant about how Mom never would have married him if she'd had time to get to know him better. Rita and Nancy were nodding, and once again, I saw the collective familial agreement about what was real. The accepted story had always been that Dad was the sole and whole cause of all our family's problems; it was a narrative that, for me, had always seemed too facile, but on that day, I kept my mouth shut.

I also didn't tell my sisters that I knew *why* Mom had been on that bus—or that I knew it straight from Mom. That part of the story was something she had made me promise never to talk about. She had journeyed from Los Angeles to New York to prevail upon her boyfriend to marry her before he shipped out in World War II. He wouldn't, and on the bus ride back to Los Angeles, Mom met Dad, an "impossibly handsome soldier in uniform," as she described him. Afterwards, they wrote for six weeks and then got married just before Dad shipped out. Mom was eighteen years old.

The story had allowed me to better see Mom as she was back then—a young woman with the moxie to travel cross-country on a bus by herself. Then, she had married a Texas farm boy and committed to "follow after him," which was a common Christian convention. Our family Bible had been a wedding present from Mom's best friend, and she'd inscribed it with the verse that was Ruth's vow to her mother-in-law Naomi:

> Whither thou goest, I will go; and where thou lodgest, I will
> lodge: thy people shall be my people, and thy God my God.
> Where thou diest, I will die, and there will I be buried.

I asked Mom about it once, and she said the inscription was because she, too, was leaving everything behind. I often pondered that. At a time when distances seemed greater—when air travel was a luxury for only the wealthy, and long-distance phone calls were exorbitant—her move to Texas must have seemed almost like relocating to another country. And in a time when interfaith marriages were far less common, Mom had crossed that boundary too, leaving behind her Catholic upbringing to become a good Southern Baptist convert.

FOR THE FUNERAL, I suggested playing instrumental versions of some of Dad's favorite songs, but my sisters stared at me as though I'd proposed holding the funeral on Mars.

"What are you talking about? Dad didn't even like music," insisted Judy.

Hoping to trigger some memory, I started singing "That Lucky Old Sun."

> Up in the mornin'
> Out on the job . . .

It was a song I'd heard Dad sing on countless occasions. As a man whose life had been defined by long hours of physical labor, it was a song that suited him.

"Don't you see?" I said. "It was Dad's song." But they didn't see, insisting they'd never even heard him hum it. As I kept singing, I could feel in my bones all the reasons why Dad had loved that song. It told the story of his life and of his yearning for some little bit of peace. But my sisters tuned me out.

Of course, I knew these weren't traditional funeral songs—if that had been their objection, I may have understood—but how was it possible that I could have such clear memories of Dad's singing while they apparently had none? How could they not remember all the times Dad had tuned the radio to the country station and sung along with Hank Williams? Or hear in their heads the low rumble of Dad's voice on "Old Man River" and his mimicking of Tennessee Ernie Ford on "Sixteen Tons"? And how was it possible they'd never heard the anguish in Dad's voice when he sang "Cold, Cold Heart"?

There and then I began to realize that I was the luckiest of all my sisters, because I'd been able to get to know Dad as a person apart from all his rage. Sure, I held terrifying memories of his blow-ups, just as my sisters did, but I also had good memories, many of which were wrapped up in the ordinary routine of Dad taking me to my monthly orthodontist appointments.

On my twelfth birthday, I got braces on my teeth, and for the next four years, Dad drove me once a month to an orthodontist in Denton. He said the orthodontist there cost less than the ones in Dallas, but I also think Dad simply liked Denton. Dad's mother was a Sullivan, and the Sullivans were some of the original pioneer settlers of Denton County. The land was in his blood.

The drive took forty minutes each way, and of course, Dad always insisted we get there early. I doubt he was ever in his whole life late for anything. So, one day each month, he'd give up sleep after working a night shift, check me out of school, and take me barreling down I-35 singing along to the crackling car radio. Then we'd sit in the waiting room together, finding the hidden pictures in *Highlights* magazine.

For four years' worth of appointments—probably at least forty-eight visits—I saw a different man there in small-town Denton. Dad would get me a fudgesicle to soothe my sore gums, and we'd walk around the square, admiring the old courthouse and looking in shop windows. Every so often, he'd step into a store to say hello to someone, and then he'd put his hand on my shoulder and introduce me. He always seemed to swell with pride. Sometimes, he'd pull a couple ice-cold "pops" out of a case—that's what he called Coca-Colas—and we'd sit on a bench to drink them. We never had Cokes at home—they were too expensive—so it always seemed like a treat. Sometimes we'd even stop in at Tom and Jo's Café where he'd order me a bowl of post-orthodontist ice cream and give me a couple quarters to plug into the tabletop jukebox player. He'd debate me a bit on what songs to pick, but ultimately, he always left the choice up to me. Of course, I tried to choose the ones I knew he liked, just to make him smile.

Remembering that Mom and Dad had lived in Denton at the start of their marriage, I once asked him why we hadn't moved back to Denton when we left Wichita. "Farmers Branch has better schools," he'd said, "and I can pull more money in Dallas." I realized even then that, for the sake of giving his kids a better education and a suburban lifestyle, Dad had consciously chosen to forgo the small-town life where he himself might have felt more at ease.

I got through his funeral singing "That Lucky Old Sun" in my head, praying that Dad had finally arrived someplace where all his troubles would be washed away. I imagined him as a young man running through the open fields, with the big Texas sun on his face, feeling the engine of his heart.

MOM ASKED THE preacher from Valwood Baptist Church to do the funeral. She and Dad had long ago withdrawn their memberships from First Baptist—Mom never said why—and she had eventually started going to Valwood. The preacher spoke about my dad as though he'd known him. Clearly, he hadn't.

"And Charlie was a happy man," he said in the homily. My sisters and I— all four of us—broke into spontaneous laughter. We each squelched it as fast as we could, but this remains as one of my favorite memories of my sisters. Reflexively, we had all four guffawed at something false about our family, and in doing so, we had momentarily united in honoring the truth.

My dad was a lot of things: a man who was beholden to no one, a man who kept dollar bills folded in a rubber band, a man who always carried a clean cotton handkerchief, a man who worked almost every waking hour, a man with unrelenting back pain, a man who grew gorgeous flowers to surprise his wife. But a happy man? No. That he was not.

WANDERING THROUGH THE house after the funeral, I saw one of my pieces of pottery sitting on a shelf behind a bunch of other stuff. It was a near-perfect straight-walled cylinder that I'd finished with a turquoise glaze dripping down the sides. I hadn't seen it in years.

As I held the piece in my hands, Judy spotted me. "Oh, you're so proud of it, aren't you?" she sneered. "Maybe the next time I'm here, I'll just take it and throw it in a dumpster somewhere."

I looked at her, uncomprehending. "Why would you do that?" I asked.

"Because I can," she hissed, smirking at my befuddlement. "Mom won't even miss it."

I put the cylinder back on the shelf and walked away, but the bizarre look of glee on Judy's face stayed with me. She was fifty-one years old and apparently hadn't matured a bit. She was still the same bullying eight-year-old who had broken the leg on my Betsy McCall doll and destroyed my Woody Woodpecker coloring book for no reason other than the delight she took in seeing my sadness.

In my childhood, and for many years even in adulthood, I spent far too much energy trying to appease Judy, anticipating how to head off her anger, and seeking explanations for her meanness. But by the time of Dad's funeral, I had grown to understand that, for Judy, cruelty was its own end, with no rhyme or reason needed.

On my next trip to see Mom, I saw the turquoise cylinder still there on the shelf. I took it down and told Mom I couldn't remember whether I had just left it in the house or had given it to her, but that, if she wouldn't mind, I'd like to take it to show to Stacy. I explained that Stacy was taking a pottery class and might be interested to see some of my own early work.

"Of course, take it!" she said. "You made it; you should have it." So I managed to keep at least that one piece of pottery safe from Judy. It felt like a small victory.

When Mom told me to take some of Dad's clothes for Jim, I picked an old chambray work shirt that was frayed at the bottom and had newspaper ink stains. Mom had already tossed it in the throw-away pile. "Why in the world would you want that old shirt?" she asked. I couldn't explain it, but something about its softness reminded me of how thrifty Dad had been, never replacing anything until it was completely worn out, and the ink stains reminded me of how hard Dad had worked.

Later that same weekend, Mom told me I should take her engagement ring and wedding band and hold onto them for Stacy. I hesitated. Mom was still wearing the rings.

"I don't know, Mom. It's awfully soon. Maybe you'll want to keep them a while longer for yourself?"

"I don't want to be buried with them," she said. "There's no sense in putting them in the ground. So if you don't take them now, then you be sure to take them off when I die and give them to Stacy. I want her to have them."

"Sure, Mom," I promised. "I know that would mean a lot for Stacy to have them someday, but I imagine that's going to be a long ways in the future."

I don't know why I was so hesitant to take Mom's rings when she offered them. For Stacy's sake, I wish I had, because nine years later, when Mom died, Rita had no hesitation in grabbing the rings and a whole lot more. She just did it. But what stymied me at the time may have been the memory of how upset Mom had once been about her cookbook.

During one of the many times when she was separated from Dad, she suddenly, out of the blue, handed me her Betty Crocker cookbook, insisting that she didn't even want it around and didn't want to ever cook again. She all but demanded I take it, so I did. Then, a year or so later, when she and Dad were back together, I pulled out the cookbook one day and asked if she'd like to have it back, and she blew up. "You stole my cookbook!" she screamed.

"No, Mom, I didn't—you gave it to me."

"Don't you lie to me. Rita asked me where my cookbook was and I couldn't find it. We looked all over. She wanted a recipe, and I couldn't even give my own daughter a recipe."

"Mom, I didn't take your cookbook."

"And you didn't even take care of it. Look at this!" She was pointing to the torn binding, which of course had been that way for years, long before she'd placed the book in my hands. But there was no way to win. My mother was convinced I had stolen her cookbook. It hurt.

I suspect that memory—whether consciously in my mind or not—had something to do with why I was so reluctant to take Mom's rings. I couldn't bear any risk that Mom might again accuse me of thievery.

Years later, after she died, and when none of my sisters wanted it, I *did* take the cookbook. It was exactly the same as I remembered it—the binding torn and mended with two kinds of tape, the pages splattered with grease spots and filled with handwritten notes. It was a book marinated in Mom's love for her family.

17

Caulbearer

If you don't name what's happening,
everyone can pretend it's not happening.

—Claudia Rankine

AFTER DAD'S DEATH, Mom's grief was compounded by guilt. "I wish I'd gotten hospice care for Chuck," she wept. "But I didn't know he was dying. If only I'd known. If only someone had told me, I could have brought him home."

Dumbfounded, I struggled with what to say. How could she not have known? Over and over, I had pleaded with her to bring Dad home. I had been so blunt and direct that I cringed at my own words. But whenever I'd told her that Dad was dying and just wanted to be at home, she dismissed me. Yet, now she was talking as though she'd never had any inkling that Dad was dying. I was mystified but tried to be supportive.

"Well, it was a really difficult time. You shouldn't be too hard on yourself." Over and over, that's what I told her.

After a few months, Mom's guilt took a turn. She kept wanting me to tell her that Dad had forgiven her. She said that she and Dad had promised each other they would always take care of one another in their old age so that neither would wind up in a nursing home. But of course, Dad *did* wind up in a nursing home. So, again and again, I listened to Mom's weeping refrain of "We promised each other . . . will he ever forgive me?" And in her grief-stricken, guilt-riddled brain, she arrived at the conviction that I could somehow talk to Dad beyond the grave.

"If he was going to talk to anyone, he'd talk to you," she insisted. "So why can't you just tell me what he says? Does he forgive me?"

No matter how much I tried to explain that Dad wasn't communicating with me, Mom wouldn't let it go. She begged and berated me. "You could if you wanted to," she argued.

"Mom, what I know for sure is that Dad always loved you." That was the best I could do. And though I offered that assurance many times, it wasn't enough. I couldn't deliver on her paranormal expectation, so she stayed angry.

The root problem was that I had been born with a caul—part of the amniotic membrane still on my head—and Mom thought it meant something. She believed I had some kind of psychic powers, just as many had believed about her mother, who had also been born with a caul.

The story was that, when boys went off to World War II, they'd stop by and ask my grandmother to lay her hands on them, apparently believing it would keep them safe. According to Mom, Grandma herself always denied that she had any power to give them protection; she only claimed that she could foresee which ones would come back and which ones wouldn't. So she would linger with her laying on of hands for the ones she divined would return and cut it short for the ones who wouldn't. Mom said it took a toll on my grandmother, foreseeing the deaths of so many boys who wouldn't come back. My grandmother even kept records, so I was told, and wound up being right about every single one.

Mom kept insisting that I had the same "gift." All I ever thought was: who in their right mind would want such a "gift"? It conjured the memory of when Uncle Jack had first told me the same thing when I was only eight: "You're like my mom. You've got the gift." At the time, I had no idea what he meant and was terrified at the thought of being like my grandmother. I had only been around her a few times during our family's rare visits to California, but from all I'd ever seen of her, she was always and only weird. She had wild unkempt hair and earlobes that stretched halfway down her neck with long gaping holes. She was obviously strange, yet everyone acted as though she were normal.

Mom said she had long earlobe holes because she'd worn heavy earrings for too long.

"Why didn't she stop before they got so big?" I'd asked. "Didn't it hurt?"

"Maybe it did," Mom said, "but she just wouldn't give up her earrings, and the hospital let her keep wearing them because she got upset when they took them away. Now, they've finally made her stop."

"Hospital?"

"That's where Grandma lives. She got to come home for a few days so she could see us while we're visiting."

I didn't understand when Mom explained it to me as an eight-year-old, but I knew it didn't sound like the kind of hospital where someone went to get better.

Grandma was weird in other ways too. Some days she wore an askew hairpiece that didn't match with her real hair, and worst of all, she always had a wild look in her eyes while her body shuffled around with a deadness to it. "It's the Thorazine," said Mom.

This was who Uncle Jack told me I was like. "Why? How?" I asked him.

"You'll understand when you get older," he said. "You've got special powers."

Later, when I asked Mom about it, she explained about the caul, confirming that because of it, I was "special."

Of course, a grandma with long-holed earlobes was just one of the many oddities of Mom's relatives in California. Once when we were visiting at her Aunt Kate's house, Judy and I encountered a Chihuahua apparently asleep in a chair. Judy wanted to sit down, so she began poking it. The dog didn't even blink. We tried to budge it, but the dog was stiff. We both broke out laughing. "It's a dead Chihuahua!" we whispered, giggling to one another about this curiosity. Mistakenly, we thought it was a decorative item, like a stuffed deer head.

There were a half-dozen other Chihuahuas and Pomeranians roaming around the house, and we wondered whether they would wind up as decoration too. With all the funny smells in the house—another thing the grown-ups seemed to ignore—and all the talk about ghosts and spirits, which everyone treated as normal, it didn't occur to me to think that a dead Chihuahua in a chair was anything other than ordinary for that house. Finally, when Mom came to see why Judy and I were laughing, we showed her the dead Chihuahua, fearful that she would be angry at us for making fun at her aunt's house after she'd given us strict instructions to be on our best behavior. But Mom just looked at the Chihuahua and went to get Jack, who carried the animal out to the trash.

"A dead dog doesn't belong in a house," said Mom sternly. "Why didn't you come get us?" I didn't have an answer. What could I say? It was the house of a grown woman, and I had just assumed that grown-ups knew what they were doing.

As the years went by, Mom occasionally brought up the caul of my birth, but I always brushed it off. Occasionally, she'd ask me to talk to the spirits of her mother and her sister, and was disappointed when I turned down her requests. The more she pleaded with me to try, the more certain I was that I didn't want to. So it became a sore spot, and one that festered still more after Dad's death.

But even long before, it had been clear that nothing good ever came of it when Mom talked about the caul. It was a curse. Even as I failed at meeting her paranormal expectations, the caul also made me the recipient of too much information. Of course, Mom tended to treat each of her daughters as a sort of surrogate spouse—a means to fill the void of her own loneliness—but for me, the caul factor seemed to exacerbate that tendency. I assumed it was because she'd been raised Catholic and missed having someone to confess to. In the Baptist tradition, there isn't any ritual of confession. So she made confessions to me, as though I could grant her some sort of cosmic absolution because I was a caulbearer.

Though this confessor role allowed me to sometimes hear stories of Mom's past, it was also a burden. I became a repository for Mom's dark side, and over decades, a repository can become an unwelcome reflection. I think my face became a reminder to Mom of things she didn't want to remember, of things she had told me, uniting me in association with the bleakness in her life.

Some of Mom's confessional revelations were not only unsought but deeply unwanted. Most especially, I didn't want to hear about her sex life or lack thereof. "I don't feel anything anymore," she told me. "Too many times of him calling me a bitch, and I'm just numb now. I don't want to have relations with him anymore."

"Uhh, I'm sorry, Mom." That was about all I could ever muster on that line of confession. And mostly, I just felt irritated, not only because I didn't want to be hearing it, but also because, invariably, Mom seemed oblivious to the fact that Stacy was sometimes nearby during these confessions. And if there was one thing I knew for sure, it was that kids hear almost everything.

Then there was the time Mom rambled on about some professor at Wichita State University. "We met up several times," she said. "It was innocent, just kissing. Nothing came of it. But Chuck couldn't stand it."

I wanted to plug my ears. It felt as though I were betraying my father by even listening. Mom kept insisting it was no big deal, but how could it *not* have been?

I wondered whether that "just kissing" relationship had something to do with why we'd moved away from Wichita. Then I wondered about all the times when, in one of his rages, Dad had called Mom a "two-timin' whore." But it wasn't until many years later when it occurred to me to also wonder whether Mom's relationship with the professor had been abusive, because a professor holds power over a student, even an adult student.

AFTER DAD DIED, Mom started volunteering one morning a week at the Shriners pediatric hospital, and she donated small amounts of money to a charity that provided free cleft surgeries. When she told me about this—and told me and told me and told me—I felt only numbness. Maybe it was her way of trying, after so many years, to connect with me, to finally open a door to discuss a topic that had always been forbidden to me. But I didn't feel any greater connection. It seemed only as though she were trying to assuage some guilt of hers.

She never asked what I thought about the particular charity. If she had, I might have told her that every time I saw one of their ads—always with a prominent picture of a child with an open, unreconstructed cleft—I felt gut-punched. To me, it felt exploitative, as though the shock value of the child's presurgical face was fair game if it got people to dig into their wallets. It was the same shock my mother had apparently experienced on the day I was born, and had transmitted to me again and again because she never got over it.

Rationally, I know this is a complex dynamic. I myself was a charity patient; my childhood surgeries were provided by the Shriners, and I can't even imagine what my life would have been without them. So how could I possibly fault the fundraising strategies of a charity that was providing surgeries for children with clefts? I couldn't explain it, but I also couldn't muster any great gratitude when Mom bragged about her volunteer work.

"Whenever I see someone who has a baby with a cleft lip, I'm able to reassure them," she said proudly. "I tell them I know exactly how they feel because of my own daughter, but that it's really no big deal—that it never bothered you a bit. And I tell them how you grew up to become a lawyer and you got married and you speak perfectly."

I ached with the pain of Mom's words. Mom had never once reassured me when kids made fun of me, and had in fact shamed me for even asking what a "harelip" was. She had never helped me deal with the social impact of it, yet she wanted to brag about me as though I should serve as the embodiment of proof that it was really "no big deal." I couldn't go there.

True enough, as an adult, it didn't seem like a big deal. Most of the time, I just didn't think about it. Nevertheless, the years of stares and taunts in childhood had taught me that I was different and that it mattered. Some adults would talk to me slowly and simply, as if my speech impediment rendered me mentally slow. People turned away when I opened my mouth, as though fearful they might not understand me and perhaps thinking it would be better not to engage with me at all. In the hallways of junior high and high school, boys would whisper "harelip" as I walked by—just loud enough for me to hear—and then watch to see my reaction. Through it all, I learned to duck my chin, keep my eyes downcast, and deal with it on my own.

From the moment of my birth, I had been different, and the difference was right there on my face, impossible to hide. I had learned to gauge other people's uneasiness with my difference, and much of the time, that meant keeping my mouth shut. I didn't talk a lot. The upside was that I became a keen listener and observer. Dealing with my difference had also given me an innate empathy for others who found themselves outside the narrow constraints of "normal." And it made me a fanatic for Halloween, the one day of the year when I could wear a mask.

The more Mom bragged, the more I felt my own ambivalence. I had always been the star student she could boast about to friends, the model of a good daughter, the accomplished pianist she could show off to relatives even while ridiculing me as soon as they were out the door. My achievements enhanced her own sense of social position, but they never seemed to earn her genuine pride for *me*. I remained as an incidental accoutrement to her own needs.

With so much history swirling in my head, I finally said, "I don't know if telling them it's no big deal is really true, Mom. I mean, there are plenty of things that are bigger deals, sure, but when I was young—and well into my twenties—if a fairy godmother could have given me one wish, I would have wished to not have this scar in the middle of my face. To not have all the heartache and difficulty that went along with it. That would have been my wish. Not a million dollars. Not a bunch of other stuff. Just that. So really, it *was* a big deal, at least for *me*."

Mom looked at me in silence, but only for a moment.

"Oh, don't be silly," she said, suddenly looking away. "It never bothered you. If it had, you would've talked about it. It wasn't a big deal."

There it was, Mom's edict on how I felt about something she had never even allowed me to talk about. With her "don't be silly" words, I heard the hiss of oxygen leaving the room. I felt the void between us and the beginning of that dreaded sense of suffocating. But Mom kept talking, apparently oblivious to the chasm that loomed. She wanted me to come to town on a weekday so she could introduce me to people at the hospital. "I can show you off," she said.

"Mom, I don't know if I really want to meet people like that—with people looking at me that way. I think it might feel more like I'm a show-and-tell piece or something."

"Oh, why do you always have to be so sensitive," she said, exasperated. "It wouldn't be like that."

There it was again. With Mom, so many disagreements were explained by the fact of there being something wrong with *me*, with *my* feelings about *my* experiences. Still, even as I felt myself being erased into oblivion, I tried to smooth things over.

"You know I work during the week, so it just wouldn't be possible, Mom."

"You could if you wanted to."

"Well, I'll try," I finally lied. "I'll let you know." Of course, I never did.

MOM WAS RIGHT about the fact that I'd grown up almost never talking about my lip. I'd tried in second grade, when her "you should be grateful you're not in a wheelchair" response had shamed and silenced me. I didn't try much after that.

In any event, I never imagined that anyone in my family would care to listen to my feelings about it or to my accounts of kids making fun of me. That just never even occurred to me.

One of the rare times when I talked about my lip with anyone in the family was when I used it as a tool to cajole Dad into getting a hearing aid. I was in law school at the time, and I did it deliberately. It was during one of my parents' separations, and I'd made a trip to Farmers Branch for that sole purpose—to persuade Dad to get a hearing aid. I was terrified because I knew I'd be alone in the house with him, and I feared the conversation would make him angry. But I thought it might make a difference, so I'd decided to try.

By then, it was apparent that Dad's hearing loss was compounding his paranoia issues. When he couldn't understand something, he'd accuse us of deliberately whispering about him. Sometimes, his misperception of a slight would then go off the rails into rage. Mom had tried several times to get him to have his hearing tested, but at best, he would deny he had any problem, and at worst, it would set him off for days.

So I launched in. The conversation was vinegary, both literally and figuratively. Dad had just washed his hair and it was still wet with the apple cider vinegar he often rinsed with. His eyes were bloodshot, a sign that he hadn't been sleeping since Mom was gone. As his voice rose and his face turned purplish, he said he didn't need a hearing aid and accused me of trying to make him look weak. I yelled right back and told him he was being stubborn. As I watched the saliva foaming at the corners of his mouth and the vein pulsing in his neck, I grew fearful. But I held my ground, almost nose to nose with him, and finally, I said something that got to him.

"Oh, so you're afraid you'll look funny? Is that it? You're afraid people will make fun of you? So instead of getting a hearing aid, you'd rather make all of *our* lives miserable because *you* don't want to be embarrassed? Oh, God forbid that Charlie Brown should have to be embarrassed," I sneered sarcastically. "Daddy, I've spent my whole life with a big scar right on the front of my face. You think I was never embarrassed? Never made fun of? Hell, I had to get over that kind of stuff when I was in kindergarten."

Suddenly, Dad's whole body seemed to slump and the shadow on his face shifted. His eyes, which had looked so scary a moment earlier, seemed only sad. For a moment, I thought he might cry, but instead he just walked away. Neither of us talked the whole rest of the afternoon. Dad watched TV and I stayed in the bedroom. When nighttime came, I jammed a small chest in front of the bedroom door, and mostly, I didn't sleep.

The next morning, when I heard Dad bumbling around in the kitchen, I got up, pulled the chest back from the door, and went out into the den. Without looking at me, he gave a chipper "good morning" and handed me a cup of coffee. Then, almost nonchalantly, he said he'd made an appointment for a hearing test. He'd managed to get in that very afternoon, he said, as he walked out into the yard to fill the bird feeders where the chickadees were waiting for him. I took my coffee cup and sat with him on the patio, and neither of us ever said a word more about it.

I felt as though our relationship turned a corner that day. I had stood up to him and hadn't backed down. I had told him the truth. The next time I went to Farmers Branch, Dad was wearing a hearing aid.

MOM GREW MORE demanding of my attention in those years after Dad's death, which was hard. Stacy was in high school and had so many activities that our schedules were constrained. Then, when she went away to college and was working on campus, Jim and I tended to use most of our vacation days to visit her. Keeping connection with Stacy became our top priority. And even though I also made occasional trips to Farmers Branch, it was never enough to satisfy Mom.

In the months leading up to the death of Jim's mother, when she was rapidly declining from pancreatic cancer, Jim and I made multiple trips to El Paso. When I told Mom about the condition of Jim's mother, her cold, clipped response was, "You have a mother too, you know." I cringed.

Over the course of a quarter century, Jim and I had made at least ten times as many trips to visit my parents as we had to visit Jim's family. Yet even with Jim's mother at death's door, my mom still felt the need to be the center of attention.

The reason for such lopsided familial visits wasn't entirely about Mom's neediness or my sense of obligation; it was also a matter of geographic distance. El Paso was a full day's drive. And as a good Southern Baptist woman, Jim's mother wouldn't let the two of us sleep together under her roof because we'd never had a church wedding, which meant our visits bore the added cost of a hotel. In the early years when money was tight, that was often a preclusive factor. So there was always a sad distancing there. Particularly after Stacy was born, it seemed tragic to me that she would choose such a rigid religious posture rather than welcoming her grandchild into her home. On her rare visits to see us in Austin—only four times over a quarter century—she never wanted to stay overnight in our house either.

Nevertheless, she was Jim's mother, and she had raised a good son. After she died, I ruminated for months about the hellfire damnation sermon the pastor preached at her gravesite. It was complete with an altar call. With my knees just inches from her casket, I listened to that pastor rant about the need to get right with God so as to avoid the fiery pits of hell, which he conjured in the traditional searing imagery.

To illustrate his message that it was never too late, he bragged about "winning" a lost soul "with only seconds to spare before Satan would've had him." As he recounted the story in all its self-aggrandizing glory, he told of visiting a man who was near death in his hospital bed.

"Preacher, I'm okay, I've had a good life," whispered the dying man.

Leaping on the man's theological error, the pastor launched into a last-ditch effort to save him from hell. "A good life isn't enough," he insisted. "It doesn't matter how good you've lived or whatever good you've done. The only thing that matters is salvation through Jesus Christ our Lord."

I was cringing, imagining the poor man, lying there at peace, accepting of his imminent death and recalling his "good life," only to have this preacher walk in who couldn't leave well enough alone.

"Do you believe in the Lord Jesus Christ and that he died on the cross to save you from your sins?" the preacher queried him.

Then, to all of us at my mother-in-law's gravesite, he said, "The man was never able to answer with words, but I could tell looking at his face that he was saying 'yes.' And he died in the very next few seconds."

"So, you see," continued the preacher, "it's never too late. I snatched victory from Satan at the very last minute. Why, if I hadn't been there, that man would have spent all eternity burning in the fires of hell. But because in his last breath, he believed on the Lord Jesus Christ, he was saved, and Satan did not have the victory. Hallelujah."

Hallelujah? I was furious at his hubris in using my mother-in-law's funeral to narcissistically brag about his soul-saving prowess. The dying man had probably been so annoyed by this full-of-himself preacher that he decided to just go ahead and die so he wouldn't have to listen to him anymore.

Jim didn't like it either, but he wasn't still recollecting it months later like I was. It rolled off his shoulders. Though Jim had been raised Southern Baptist, he would say it just "never took." As a high school athlete, he had been a prized player for his church's baseball team, but for Jim, it was just good fun. And though he spent several summers living in Louisiana with his Grandma Hill—the most God-fearing, Bible-reading, scripture-quoting woman I ever met—his memories of her were more about the love she showered on him and all the fish they caught.

From the very first time Jim took me to visit her in that tiny two-bedroom house, Grandma Hill extended only exuberant warmth and welcome. Of course, I knew we had something in common as soon as I saw the Folgers can of bacon grease on her stovetop. She was a solid Southern Baptist woman and had even raised one of her sons—Jim's uncle—to be a Southern Baptist missionary. But Grandma Hill's faith didn't carry the judgmental rejection that Jim's mom's did. Instead, I saw only the extraordinary love she held for Jim, which she extended to me by grace. Grandma Hill died before our daughter was born, but I always imagine her sending love from beyond to Stacy.

The Third Death

18

The Do-Nothing Denomination

When the truth is spoken and it don't make no difference
Something in your heart goes cold.

—Bruce Springsteen

ONCE UPON A time, I believed that if only I told my childhood church—again—about the abuse their pastor inflicted on me as a kid, the good people there would surely want to do something. They would care. They would want to protect others. They would feel remorse. They would want to do better in the present than they'd done in the past. I believed all that.

It was a fairy tale I told myself because believing the alternative would have been too awful. But the awful was what was true. Just as my childhood family had insisted on a "happy family" pretense, so too my childhood church insisted that what had happened was no big deal.

Then, once upon a time, I believed that if only Southern Baptist denominational leaders knew, they would surely want to do something. I thought that if I showed them the scope of the problem, they would take action. They would care. They would want to protect others and plug the safety gaps in their system. They would feel remorse.

Yeah, even after my childhood church kicked me with steel-toed boots, I still believed that *other* Southern Baptist leaders would care.

That, too, was a fairy tale.

It was a torturous death by a thousand cuts to reach the end of those fairy tales. It was a process that required enduring the awful responses of scores of church and denominational leaders—men who not only did nothing to help me, but who sought to silence me. They employed multiple tactics, from threatening to sue me, to calling me ugly names, to publicly smearing me, to impugning me on social media, to "stalking" me with anonymous phone calls and messages. Again and again, in earnest naivete, I held forth an open hand only to pull back a bloody stump. Finally, I bled out.

The Christa who resurrected no longer believes in those fairy tales. What I know now is that a recalcitrant institution like the Southern Baptist Convention—an institution marinated in lies, deception, image, and illusion—will not reform itself voluntarily based on mere appeals to reform itself. It will not do so for the sake of goodness. It will not do so for the safety of kids. It will not do so for the love of God. Rather, it will do so only if prodded by unrelenting outside pressure—from media, lawsuits, prosecutions, and independent investigations. Even then, it will do so with only bare minimum baby steps.

My prior book, *This Little Light*, is subtitled *Beyond a Baptist Preacher Predator and His Gang*. Lots of people seemed to overlook the "and His Gang" part, but I have always considered it the most important part of my story. This was *always* about way more than an individual predatory pastor; it was then, and still is, about the countless others in Southern Baptist life who enable these crimes, both directly and indirectly, and who maintain a system that fosters impunity and unaccountability. It is "the Gang" that inflicts the thousand cuts unto death.

THEY FIRST CAME at me with their many knives when I was still grappling with what was done to me—with understanding that I had been a victim. To admit, even just to myself, that I had been sexually abused, repeatedly and severely, by a trusted minister, I had to reinterpret my whole reality. Yet, as a mother, the one thing I knew for sure was that if any trusted teacher or coach were to do to my own daughter what was done to me, I would not call it an "affair." And I would not blame my daughter. From that singular truth—a truth I knew in my very bones—everything else followed. But it was a daunting process.

My mind put up walls to avoid seeing the reality of Pastor Tommy Gilmore's sexual assaults. He groped, mauled, and probed me. He used me as a sex toy. He slobbered all over me with his foul-smelling mouth. He asked me questions about how it felt and demanded I answer. He railed against me because, being frozen, I didn't respond the way he wanted. He took pleasure in my degradation. And because these are all merely words, they cannot begin to convey the full horror of what he did to me—of what I had to finally make myself see.

Going back in my mind to the time of Gilmore's abuse was so overwhelming that, for a while, I dealt with what I called my Jules Verne vision. I kept being struck by the sense that, at any moment, the ground would crack open and suck me straight down to the center of the earth—to hell, I supposed. It was wholly irrational, but knowing that didn't keep my body from reacting to it as, again and again, I found myself unable to breathe, immobilized with full-bodied fear.

I didn't know it then, but what I was going through wasn't unusual. Inherent to the trauma of childhood sexual abuse is a silencing effect that, consciously and unconsciously, causes many victims to delay in disclosing. According to Child USA, a leading think tank for the rights of children, fifty-two is the average age of a person bringing forward a report of childhood sexual abuse. I was fifty-one.

The mental hurdles are huge. Many child sex abuse victims wait until after the perpetrator has died, and many *never* disclose their childhood abuse. Many never even recognize that what they experienced was abuse.

While I was still in the throes of reliving the horror, I approached my childhood church. The same music minister was still there: Jimmy Moore, the guy who had known about the abuse when I was a kid and told me not to speak of it. I thought the years would have brought him more wisdom. I thought he and others in the church would want to help me in protecting others. I was terribly wrong.

Moore wanted nothing to do with me. He insisted my "relationship" with Gilmore had been "consensual"—even though I'd been an underage minor at the time.

The church then made a preemptive strike and threatened to seek "legal recourse" against me. In other words, they threatened to sue me. Simultaneously, they suggested that whatever "distress" I felt was likely caused by my home life at the time—as if the pastor's rapes caused no greater harm since I was already damaged by my troubled family. I received this response like a stab to the chest. It left me gasping. I had hoped for kindness, but instead my childhood church had doubled down and dished out still more cruelty.

When I realized that the church's attorney was also the longtime attorney for the Baptist General Convention of Texas—the largest statewide Baptist organization in the country—I saw the bigger picture. This wasn't just some rogue attorney who happened to work for my childhood church; it was an attorney who almost certainly had been referred to the church by the state convention. That made me wonder how many other churches he'd been referred to and how many times he'd used such hardball tactics with clergy sex abuse survivors.

As painful as it was, I eventually came to view the church's threat of a lawsuit as a saving grace. Combined with their other shaming tactics, it was unequivocally a scorched-earth strategy. They had shown their hand, and that clarity left no room for my wishful thinking.

In many ways, the church did to me the same as Gilmore had done. It dehumanized me. Just as Gilmore had treated me as a nonhuman to serve his own ends, so too the church treated me as a troublesome *thing*—an object to be controlled.

To be degraded by sexual assaults is one thing. But Gilmore had inculcated in me the belief that the assaults were God's will and that I harbored Satan. My whole childhood church had betrayed me not once, but twice, both as a child and as an adult. And then with the shaming and betrayal replicated at all levels of the denomination, it was beyond devastating. It was soul-murder.

I wanted to run as far and as fast as possible from everything that Gilmore and his gang of enablers represented—from the church, from Baptists, from all things religious, from the South, and at times from my own family. But in my bones, I felt compelled to do exactly the opposite—to fight back. So, I determined to speak the truth no matter what.

In the beginning, I just wanted to tell the truth about my own small story. But truth-telling has a way of snowballing. And truth-telling by one person begets truth-telling by others.

When Christa Brown opened her mouth about the exploitation she endured in the church, pastors began to fall one by one. It ended with the exposure of no less than 700 clerics involved in sexual abuse.

IN 2023, WHEN a reporter offered that summary of my history of advocacy, I pondered the weight of those two sparse sentences. They were true in a way that made me feel proud, but in the space between them, there was so much history, so much duplicity, and so much pain.

Ultimately, from Jimmy Moore, the music minister who had told me to never speak of it, I obtained a sworn statement in which he admitted to knowing about Gilmore's abuse of me as a kid. He said he knew about it not only because I had told him at a piano lesson, but also because, even sooner than that, Gilmore himself had discussed it with Moore.

From my childhood church—First Baptist of Farmers Branch—I obtained a court-filed apology for the "very serious sexual abuse" that their prior pastor Tommy Gilmore inflicted on me when I was a girl. The process of getting to that apology was a nightmare, described in my prior book, and by the time I finally pulled the apology forth from them, it had lost all meaning as a genuine statement of contrition. Instead, it functioned solely as a document of substantiation—proof of the truth of my story.

From the Baptist General Convention of Texas, an official wrote that they had placed Tommy Gilmore's name in their confidential file of "known offenders." By "confidential," what they really meant was "secret," because they weren't about to proactively share the names in that file with anyone—not with Baptist churches and not with the general public. Still, their letter constituted proof that they, too, knew about Gilmore. Under their published policy at the time, a minister's name could be placed in that file only if it was submitted *by a church*, not by a mere individual, and only if the minister had confessed to or been convicted of sexual abuse or if there was "substantial evidence that the abuse took place."

I managed to get the apology letter from the church even though I refused to sign the "confidentiality" agreement that the church's attorney presented. It was in effect a nondisclosure agreement that would have barred me from talking about the pastor's abuse or the church's response. At the time, I still held so much internalized shame that I had no intention of ever publicly talking about any of it, but as an attorney, I knew what the agreement meant and I took offense. I didn't want them to have one ounce of control over me, so purely as a matter of principle, I rejected it. As it turned out, that decision was critical. So much of what I wound up doing in the years that followed would have been stymied if I had signed that agreement.

I felt as though I'd walked through hell to get documentation of Gilmore's abuse; yet even *with* the documentation, no one in Baptistland gave a flip. I started out by informing eighteen Southern Baptist leaders about Gilmore—always in writing, with substantiation, and often via certified letters that they had to sign for. They were men in churches where Gilmore had worked, men in state and national denominational offices, men in Texas, Georgia, Tennessee, and Florida. None of them gave me a bit of help. National headquarters wrote back that they had no record Gilmore was still in ministry—even though he actually was, as I eventually learned.

Those eighteen were only the beginning; as time went by, I informed still more Southern Baptist leaders about Gilmore, including the late televangelist Charles Stanley, who was a former SBC president and, in Baptist life, a near demigod. Gilmore had worked for nineteen years as children's minister at Stanley's First Baptist Church of Atlanta, and I wanted Stanley to let congregants know about Gilmore so they could talk with their kids. Stanley ignored me, and the church called the police on me when, together with three other women, I handed out flyers to people exiting the church's parking lot. The police didn't care—we were on a public sidewalk—but I couldn't help but ponder the irony: Baptist leaders called the police on *me* but they never did diddly-squat about Gilmore.

In the whole of Baptistland, no one thought Gilmore's sexual abuse of a kid was consequential enough to do anything about it. As a mother, that was a reality I couldn't accept.

What I realized was that if Southern Baptist leaders wouldn't take action to oust the minister who had abused *me*—despite another minister's sworn corroborating statement, a church's written acknowledgment of the abuse, and a state convention's admission that his name was in a file of "known offenders"—there was little hope they would treat other clergy sex abuse survivors any better.

Finally, when I learned that, despite everything I'd done and all the people I'd told, Gilmore was still working in children's ministry at a Florida church, I had to run to the bathroom to vomit. In an effort to warn and protect others, I had tried everything possible within the Southern Baptist system, and everything had failed me. I knew that if I were a mother in his Florida church, I would want to know. So I contacted a reporter at the *Orlando Sentinel.*

That was something that finally made a difference, something outside the closed Southern Baptist system. Going public impacted their all-important image. Media attention brought about Gilmore's resignation from ministry. Or so I believed at the time.

I FEAR MY prior book, *This Little Light*, may have inadvertently left an erroneous impression. When I was writing it, I thought that I had gone through a hellish ordeal, but that at least, at the end of it, I had succeeded in getting Gilmore out of ministry.

I was wrong.

After the book was published, I learned that Gilmore had left employment only as a *staff* minister—so his name and photo didn't appear on any church staff directory. But for several more years, he continued to work in children's ministry on an independent contractor basis. Plenty of people knew he had sexually abused a kid in Texas, but nobody in Baptistland thought it mattered. Eventually, he simply retired, and even then, he traded on his "forty-five years in the ministry" to build his credibility as a realtor. It was how he marketed himself. A Southern Baptist megachurch in Orlando was even listed as a "church partner" for his real estate business. Despite all the information I had brought to light about Gilmore, Southern Baptists still promoted him.

Similarly, there was never any consequence for that music minister, Jimmy Moore—the man who could have stopped Gilmore's abuse of me so much sooner but instead let it escalate and then instructed me not to speak of it. Plenty of people knew that Moore had covered up Gilmore's sexual abuse of a child, yet Moore's career continued to prosper. He remained a music minister in a Southern Baptist church, became choral director for a Southern Baptist university, and had a church concert series named in his honor.

IN EARLY 2006, I wrote an op-ed column for the *Dallas Morning News*, calling on the Baptist General Convention of Texas to make public its secret file of what they called "known offenders." After a BGCT official wrote to tell me that Gilmore's name was in the file, I had begun to wonder how many other abusive pastors' names were in it and whether the pastors were still standing in pulpits.

At the time I wrote the op-ed, I thought that if I could just publish that little piece of my mind, I'd be able to put it all behind me and move on. I was wrong about that. In the aftermath of the op-ed, my inbox was flooded with emails from people with stories much like my own—of pastors who committed horrific sexual abuse, churches that covered it up, and denominational leaders who did nothing. It was my first glimpse of the pervasiveness of the Southern Baptist sexual abuse problem. So many lives had been decimated. With all their hard stories I wept.

With some forty-seven thousand churches, the Southern Baptist Convention was—and still is—the largest non-Catholic faith group in the country. In that fact, I saw the reality that a whole lot of kids and congregants were being left at increased risk for sexual violation by predatory pastors.

So, I launched myself into public advocacy work. In large measure, my efforts emanated from the impact of other survivors' stories and from my sense that *somebody* had to break the spell of the status quo and set an example that speaking out was possible. I figured that the somebody might as well be me. From the beginning, I engaged a three-pronged approach: 1) reaching out to other survivors, 2) documenting the stories and patterns, and 3) proposing specific solutions.

Together with SNAP—the Survivors Network of those Abused by Priests—I started writing letters to top Southern Baptist officials, urging them to use the example of my own case as a launchpad for change and asking for dialogue to make churches safer. Right away, I realized that we had to move beyond generalities and abstractions. It was far too easy for them to spew nice-sounding words—"abuse is bad . . . children are precious . . . church should be the safest place"—while doing absolutely nothing.

In the abstract, almost everyone imagines they will do the right thing. "I would NEVER cover up for a child molester," people say. But in the real world, what I've seen is that when child sex abuse allegations hit on the home turf, most churches do exactly that—they keep things quiet. They find ways to convince themselves that they don't really *know* what happened, or that it really wasn't so bad, or that it's not *their* responsibility.

So I wrote to top Southern Baptist officials, urging specific reforms, including the creation of an independent review panel and a system for recordkeeping on credibly accused clergy—i.e., a denominational database. I also requested that denominational officials publicly disavow the use of nondisclosure agreements in the context of clergy sex abuse allegations.

People told me "They'll never do it!" as though it were absurd for me to even propose these things. But from the get-go, I took a long-haul perspective—a trait that came naturally from years of working as an appellate attorney. I decided that the first step toward prodding Southern Baptist officials to move beyond generalities would be to force them to reject specific, reasonable tools for confronting abuse, and thereby to bring the reality of their recalcitrance into the public arena.

Around the same time, I flew to Nashville for my first sidewalk press conference outside Southern Baptist Convention headquarters—the Baptist Vatican—where I talked about the need for denominational recordkeeping on clergy sex abusers. As I stood there, my feet felt a rumbling of the earth, as though it might split and swallow me whole. But with trepidation, I spoke out anyway.

It was the mustering of media attention that made them angry. On behalf of three of the SBC's top offices—the Executive Committee, the president, and the ethics commission—SBC official Augie Boto wrote a brush-off letter saying "discourse between us will not be positive or fruitful."

So, my efforts were met with overt hostility, and mostly that didn't change for years and years. But the requests for specific reforms succeeded in garnering media, and to this day, some eighteen years later, those essential elements of reform, first proposed in 2006, are what people are continuing to advocate for in the Southern Baptist Convention.

Nowadays, it seems obvious that this is what's needed: independent review of clergy abuse reports and a centralized system for recordkeeping and information sharing. But back then, I was swimming hard against the tide, and many Southern Baptists treated my proposals as something radical. Repeatedly, they insisted they could never do such a thing because, they claimed, it would interfere with local church autonomy. The denomination would not exercise any authority over a local church, they said, even if a pastor were known to have sexually abused a child.

From the start, I viewed their use of "local church autonomy" as a phony excuse for inaction. Even as they proclaimed themselves unable to do anything about sex offenders, I knew that if a Southern Baptist church were to put an openly gay man in the pulpit, state and national officials would take action. Besides, I never could see how the mere keeping of a denominational database would interfere with churches' autonomy. I urged, instead, that it would be a resource to help churches exercise their autonomy more responsibly.

When I had my first opportunity to speak to members of the SBC's Executive Committee, I tried to think of how to appeal to them. Guessing that most of them were probably fathers, I settled on the commonality of parenthood and began by talking about my mother-bear instinct for wanting to protect children—*all* children. I hoped this motivation would be relatable, but everything I said fell on ears that were not only unhearing but hostile. As I continued, speaking more personally about the rapes I endured in my childhood church, one man literally chortled and another physically rotated his body in his chair so as to turn his back to me.

It was bizarre and hurtful. Yet, in that room filled with men in positions of power in the country's largest Protestant faith group, not one person said a word of reproach for their colleagues' incivility. But even as they treated me terribly, I told them plainly, "I won't be the last person to stand before you. There are countless others."

I wondered how so many Baptist fathers could so completely detach from their feelings to avoid any sense of urgency about protecting kids from sexual predators. And how could some of them ridicule a person recounting the rapes she endured as a child? Their detachment seemed inhuman. Yet, they justified it with a "Bible tells me so" excuse, as though the Bible somehow specified the precise parameters of their man-made notion of "local church autonomy" and declared it even more important than protecting "the least of these." The dark-heartedness of that immoral morass remains fundamentally unfathomable to me.

I couldn't help but ponder whether I was seeing nothing more than a cold calculus of profits over people—something I'd seen as an attorney with irresponsible corporations. It seemed to me that Southern Baptist officials had twisted "local church autonomy" into functioning as a tactical construct, not a theological construct. It was an approach that essentially said "the safety of kids be damned" and instead geared *everything* toward minimizing institutional liability risks and protecting denominational dollars.

YEARS WENT BY, with Southern Baptist leaders consistently sticking by their legless stance that keeping records on credibly accused clergy would violate their belief in local church autonomy. They continued to two-step around the horror of child rapes and church-hopping predators, and all the people said "Amen." Meanwhile, I worked at documenting the extent of the problem, deciding that if the Southern Baptist Convention wouldn't keep a database on their abusive clergy, then I would keep one for them—to at least show that it could be done and to get past the incessant deflections of those who insisted that Baptist cases were "just isolated incidents."

With an online website at StopBaptistPredators.org, I accumulated the names of Southern Baptist clergy who had been publicly reported for sexual abuse and linked their names to news articles. It was work I did in my spare time, without funding or staff, while also lawyering, mothering, and managing a household. So it was never a comprehensive effort, but it was more than anyone else had previously done.

Even though I took a lot of care with the database, I was still threatened with defamation lawsuits several times. They never materialized, but I figured it was only because I was indeed so cautious. Necessarily, this meant that I disappointed some survivors. I couldn't put every pastor I was told about onto the database.

Most of the entries were pastors for whom there was some public record, which usually meant a news article about a criminal conviction, because those were the kinds of cases that reporters tended to write about. This, too, was a limitation on what I was accumulating. Like my own case, countless clergy sex abuse cases are never criminally prosecuted, often because of church cover-ups that allow time limits for prosecution to expire. I knew I was documenting just the tip of the iceberg. But even knowing how inherently limited my efforts were, I wanted to at least begin archiving Southern Baptist clergy sex abuse stories in a single place.

In six years' time, I gathered the names of 170 Southern Baptist pastors in my database. Many had multiple victims. With every case I logged, I kept thinking there would eventually arrive a tipping point, and I wondered, *Will this one finally be enough that Southern Baptist officials will see the horror of the problem and realize they need to do something?*

It never was enough. Despite the mounting cases, and even in the face of significant media exposure, year after year, Baptist officials did nothing.

Simultaneous with keeping the database, I wrote a blog, exposing the patterns of clergy sex abuse, church cover-ups, and institutional recalcitrance in the Southern Baptist Convention. It was not only a way to further document the problem but also an early effort to build community among abuse survivors. This was before the widespread use of social media and long before the momentum of the #MeToo movement. My blog was an early place where Baptist clergy sex abuse survivors could see the awful commonalities in their stories, feel safe in making small comments, and begin to find their voices.

I always believed that one voice could give rise to another and another, because whenever one person speaks aloud in defiance of an unjust status quo, it helps others to do likewise. So, even though I felt like a lone voice in the wilderness in those early years, I also saw myself as gathering other voices. That part of my early advocacy effort bore fruit because, nowadays, there's a whole choir of survivors speaking out, as well as many others writing about abuse in churches.

Dee Parsons, author of the much-read *Wartburg Watch* blog, once called me "the mother of all abuse bloggers," which made me feel proud. By the time I quit blogging, I had written 572 posts.

SCORES OF BAPTIST clergy sex abuse survivors continued to tell me their stories, often beginning with "I've never told this to anyone else." I felt the weight of that responsibility. Sometimes, they'd say they had seen some quote of mine in a news story and believed I was someone who might be safe. So I tried to be exactly that—safe—because for people sexually abused by clergy, a sense of safety can be as rare as a desert rain.

When the sacred is transformed into sacrilege, trust is shattered. When rapes are committed in the name of God, then sexual abuse not only inflicts the trust-busting trauma of a bodily violation, but simultaneously, it yanks a primary resource for healing. Faith and its accoutrements become neurologically networked with rape. So rather than being a source of comfort, faith can become a trigger to flee.

When survivors seek to report abusive pastors within the faith community, that already-shattered trust often gets pulverized into dust. In story after story of faith-based cruelty, clergy sex abuse survivors told me that how the church mistreated them caused even more trauma than the abuse itself. That was my own experience as well, with religious leaders circling the wagons around the good-old-boy network rather than rendering aid.

Most people can scarcely bear to even contemplate child sexual abuse, and yet those who have actually *lived* that reality—as horrific as it is—almost always say that the church's mistreatment of them was something even worse. That mistreatment is what, for many, annihilates any last remaining possibility of feeling safe in faith.

One person at a time, with survivors who contacted me, I tried to acknowledge their pain, give encouragement for their efforts, and direct them toward resources. Always, I steered them toward understanding that they were never at fault and that much of what the church had told them was gaslighting. Some survivors eventually moved forward in various ways toward exposing their perpetrators and speaking the truth of their own lives, which was gratifying. But my inbox was frequently overwhelming. Often, the best I could do was simply bear witness. It wasn't enough.

As more survivors contacted me, I was plunged into darkness by the savageries inflicted on so many church kids and vulnerable congregants. My body became a knot of grief. Some survivors would call me up on the phone, and I was flat-out lousy at asserting boundaries. Always it seemed they simply wanted to spill the pain of their story to a human being who would understand. I couldn't say no, and it took a toll. Their voices haunted me. I would lie awake at night hearing their weeping.

Sometimes, I was awake anyway because a few took to calling me at night, as though I were a crisis line. The unpredictability of when the calls would come left me feeling out of control. I could be in the middle of a perfectly peaceful day when a survivor's phone call would wrench me back into the hellhole of Baptistland. Often, something in another person's story would trigger my own bodily memories, and I would relive my own assaults again and again.

Ultimately, although I felt privileged and honored that so many survivors trusted me, I wound up being crushed by the weight of their stories. I couldn't metabolize so much unrelieved suffering, and slowly, I grew to realize that I couldn't handle survivors' phone calls. Today, I communicate with other clergy sex abuse survivors almost exclusively by email or by social media. It's a way of putting a little space between my own porous self and the pain of what people are telling me.

ADVOCACY WORK ENTAILED talking to the media, and it didn't come naturally. Once, when a reporter was interviewing me in person, she asked, "What exactly did he do to you?" I fell silent. I had been rambling on about my database and advocacy efforts, and the bluntness of her more personal question took me by surprise. As I struggled with how to answer her, my voice stayed caged inside my throat. My mind began flipping through its file of lurid snapshots, wondering which event I should recount. There were too many of them, and I couldn't focus.

"Did he rape you?" she queried, trying to prod me out of my long silence. But no sound would leave my mouth.

Incongruously, I suddenly felt Gilmore's breath in my ear. "Don't worry, you'll still be a virgin," he'd whispered. The knot of anxiety pulled tighter. *How can I tell the reporter I was raped when, technically, I stayed a virgin?* I think Gilmore believed that so long as he didn't take my virginity, he wasn't really having "sex" with me; everything else was okay so long as my hymen stayed intact. So if I answered yes and divulged that Gilmore had raped me, then I'd feel like I had to explain further. Then what? Was I going to parse the meaning of "rape"? My mind flooded with unsought images, and I felt myself dying.

In her groundbreaking book, *Trauma and Recovery*, Judith Herman writes: "Certain violations of the social compact are too terrible to utter aloud; this is the meaning of the word *unspeakable*." On that day, with that reporter, I experienced the literal, nonmetaphorical truth of Herman's insight. I could not bring myself to speak. Sound froze in my throat.

With the reporter still sitting there, waiting, I finally managed to push out five words: "He did whatever he wanted." They came out as a bare whisper, so quiet I wasn't sure whether I'd spoken them aloud or only in my head. So I said them again. "He did whatever he wanted."

The reporter looked at me blankly. My answer wasn't good enough. She wanted details, and I just couldn't. She didn't wind up writing anything at all about me or about him or even about my advocacy work. The entire effort had been futile.

"IT'S A CATHOLIC problem" was the dominant narrative for so very long. Over and over, people told me that what I was encountering in Baptistland were "just isolated incidents," while in the Catholic Church, abuse was systemic. Even well-known experts would explain that clergy sex abuse was predominantly a Catholic problem caused by priestly celibacy.

Sometimes, I felt as though I were battling this narrative on all fronts. Even in the Survivors Network of those Abused by Priests, some made clear their view that SNAP should keep its focus on Catholic abuse and not divert resources to abuse among Baptists. One Catholic survivor, who had converted to become a Southern Baptist, was determined to prove me wrong about his new faith group. "Trust me, Baptists aren't like Catholics," he repeatedly insisted. Finally, in a week when we obtained more press coverage for the Baptist clergy sex abuse problem than ever before—a week when we had something to celebrate—I wound up on the receiving end of his over-the-top tirade, prodded perhaps by the pain of having his adopted faith group turn out to be just as unsafe as his childhood one.

This is the flip side of survivor solidarity. Even as I worked to reach out to Baptist survivors and build community, I sometimes felt the sting of that community. People who have suffered serious interpersonal traumas often have trouble with interpersonal interactions. The very nature of the wounds can work against solidarity. And because I've been such a highly visible survivor, sometimes other survivors' displaced anger gets tossed my way.

I understand it, but that has never lessened the hurt of it. Again and again, nothing has been as morale-busting as grenades tossed by presumed allies in the survivor community.

TEN YEARS AFTER the 2006 *Dallas Morning News* op-ed that launched my public advocacy efforts, the Baptist General Convention of Texas stopped keeping its file of clergy sex abusers. At that point, it had maintained the file for fifteen years, accumulating information submitted *by churches* about pastors for whom there was a conviction, a confession, or substantial evidence of sexual abuse. Rather than revealing the information in the file as I had requested, they destroyed it—at least that's what they said. The BGCT reported this in their own press arm, *The Baptist Standard*, almost as if they were proud of having destroyed what was in the file—as if it were a righteous deed.

Even with as much awfulness as I'd seen by then in Baptistland, I was shocked by this apparent destruction of evidence. My own perpetrator's name was in that file. *How much evidence on how many other abusive pastors had been destroyed?* I thought about survivors who had gone head-to-head with church leadership—no doubt at enormous personal cost—to get churches to submit pastors' names to that file. And for what? The files were destroyed. I thought about churches that had tried to do the right thing by submitting pastors' names to that file—probably a contentious decision in many congregations. Yet, their efforts had been undone by denominational leaders sitting in an office. It was infuriating.

Dealing with the Baptist General Convention of Texas made me wary of almost *everyone* in Baptistland, because, supposedly, they were "the good guys." That's what dozens of people told me. But for all I could ever see, there was never more than a hair's breadth between "the good guys" and "the bad guys." If anything, I found "the bad guys" less disorienting. At least with them, you could readily see what you were dealing with—the meanness was overt. By contrast, the BGCT people had smiles that hid daggers.

At times, BGCT officials tried to downplay the Baptist abuse problem with an "at least we aren't as bad as the Catholics" schtick. They claimed that while the Catholic abuse problem involved children—and usually boys—the Baptist problem was more about clergy "misconduct" with adult women. "Most of ours are heterosexual relationships with adults," they said.

It was an offensive and minimizing claim, supported by no evidence. To the contrary, the Associated Press had gathered insurance data showing that the abuse of children in Baptist churches was likely just as pervasive as in Catholic churches. As I saw it, Texas Baptists were effectively *using* the sexual abuse of women to divert attention from the sexual abuse of kids, thereby exploiting adult victims to further their public relations strategy of rendering the other epidemic invisible.

The good-guy/bad-guy dynamic also played out in Southern Baptist Convention presidential elections. I saw it as far back as 2006, when people assured me that newly elected SBC president Frank Page was a "good guy." As it turned out, he was the kind of guy who perpetuated a rotten system. In the years that followed, people told me I should root for SBC presidential candidate J.D. Greear, then Ed Litton, then Bart Barber. All were said to be "good guys"—men who would address the clergy sex abuse problem. But mostly, they were just good at crocodile tears and talking the talk.

IN 2007, AFTER an ABC *20/20* episode on "Preacher-Predators"—one in which I invested heavily with energy, time, angst, and a personal interview—there seemed a flicker of hope. I showed up outside the SBC annual meeting in San Antonio that year, and together with other survivors, handed out over two thousand flyers urging Southern Baptists to create a database of convicted, admitted, and credibly accused clergy sex abusers. A pastor named Wade Burleson put a motion onto the floor of the convention, and delegates—called messengers in Baptistland—voted to instruct the SBC Executive Committee to conduct a study on the feasibility of creating such a database.

The SBC garnered a heap of press for that, but once the vote passed, no one bothered to bird-dog what the Executive Committee actually did. So it was left to me to try to push the committee to conduct a legitimate study, and my efforts were to no avail. Under the leadership of Executive Committee President Morris Chapman, there was never even a budget allocated for the study, much less any process resembling what most ordinary people would call a "study." Yet, no one in Baptistland questioned it.

In 2008, when the time came to report back on the results of the purported "study" about creating a database, Chapman stood before thousands of Southern Baptists and preached a powerful sermon:

> We shall not turn a blind eye ... We shall protect the weak and vulnerable ... We shall provide safe havens ... We shall not allow

predators to infiltrate our ministries . . . We shall not allow fear of reprisal to stifle the stories of those who have been abused.

Then, in the next breath, he declared the SBC couldn't possibly keep a database of clergy sex abusers because it would violate Baptists' belief in local church autonomy. Shrouded in religious rhetoric, Chapman's sermon was effectively a declaration that the denomination would do nothing. The throng of Baptist believers applauded.

Even Burleson, the pastor who had put forward the motion, reacted as though hypnotized by the hive, telling the press that SBC leadership had taken the abuse issue "very seriously" and that their response was "adequate."

As it turned out, their response wasn't even honest, much less adequate. SBC attorneys had specifically told SBC officials that they could indeed establish a clergy abuser database without violating their beliefs. And even as Chapman was declaring they *couldn't* keep a database, the Executive Committee was *already* keeping a list of clergy sex abusers but holding it secret. This deception was something we didn't learn about until years later, after hundreds more kids and congregants had been sexually abused.

MY OLD COLLEGE friend Madge saw a news article about my advocacy work, found my website, and emailed me. I hadn't heard from her in decades, but I could still feel the friendship in her words. After praising my work, she recalled her memories about some of my worst times.

> I will always remember the bravado in your voice (probably
> due to our over consumption of homemade Kahlua) and the
> pain on your face the night we sat on the floor of your Bruce
> Hall dorm room and you first told me about what you then
> referred to as "your affair." I know I was a naive little twit
> and my jaw fell open, but I was still shocked and sickened
> that you blamed yourself and not the married minister and
> that there was no one who could or would counsel or sup-
> port you. I ached for you as you described how you felt you

were unworthy of love and respect and were so distressed that you had lost your connection to God. Despite all of your academic achievements and global travels, you buried your victimization so deep, but I always felt this abuse was the reason for your despondent and sometimes suicidal phone calls. For years I was haunted by the loneliness that was revealed in those phone calls and prayed that you would never give up hope.

Reading her words, I felt the anguish of that girl I used to be—a girl so tainted that even God had turned away from her.

Though I didn't remember the specifics of the dorm-room conversation, the suicidal phone calls a few years later were another matter. Those were seared into my brain, as was the morning I woke up lying on the floor in a sludge of vomit. I would have likely tried to kill myself more often—and maybe gotten better at it—if Madge hadn't been on the other end of some of those phone calls.

I'm lucky to be alive.

SPEAKING OUT ABOUT Baptist clergy sex abuse began to feel like an endless Whac-a-Mole exercise in some sadistic, surreal circus. Hundreds of names began to blur in my mind. As soon as one predatory pastor was knocked down, another would pop up. The problem was systemic, but it seemed people in Baptistland simply didn't believe in systemic issues. With a theology oriented toward individual sin and individual piety, their lens was limited, which in turn constrained any notions of institutional accountability. So the cycle continued, again and again, with survivors mustering media attention, only to have SBC leaders say or do some tiny something to momentarily give the illusion of caring before they showed the institution's true recalcitrant colors.

As I continued to speak out, I realized that I could not allow myself to focus on whether the SBC was implementing meaningful reforms. Because they weren't. I decided to continue raising my voice anyway for the simple reason that truth matters.

Someday, perhaps far in the future, I imagine people will look back in wonder, and ask, "Really? Did a powerful multibillion-dollar faith institution really use 'local church autonomy' as an excuse for doing nothing about reported clergy child molesters?" It will seem so lame and horrific as to be almost inconceivable. I hope the spreading of truth may eventually bring that day to pass.

19

Hateful Faith

Nothing draws fire like drawing attention to
sexual abuse and cover-ups in white evangelical churches.
Nothing even comes close.

—Kristin Kobes Du Mez

WITH HATE-FILLED SCREEDS and obscenity-laced curses, the Baptist bullies came after me, and I was wholly unprepared for their fury.

I'd encountered so many levels of hell in the Dante's *Inferno* of Baptistland. There was the hell of the many who denied and minimized the horror, and the hell of the pseudo-pious who, with buttery pastoral voices, pontificated on forgiveness while heaping shame and blame on victims. There was also the hell of the double-faced denominational leaders who, from one side of their mouths, publicly proclaimed how much they cared, while from the other side, worked at shooing and silencing victims—all while simultaneously leaving perpetrators in their pulpits. But even having traversed all that, I was still unprepared for the even lower level of hell filled with those who felt it was their right to deliver vile name-calling, vitriol, and even threats, publicly, privately, and anonymously. It was a hellscape with no end.

Month after month, as I continued speaking out about clergy sex abuse and posting cases on my database, hateful messages arrived in my inbox. Many of them began with "I'm a Christian and . . ." or "I'm a Baptist and . . ." before descending into a vomitous gush. The writers led with their faith and then spewed hate. Each one, standing alone, might not have amounted to much, but added together, they took a toll.

It was hard to fathom how so many people who had never met me could hate me so much. Just as Gilmore had raped me in the name of God, so too they wielded their verbal viciousness in the name of God. I imagined them sitting in church pews in their Easter best with smiles on their faces, which only made them all the scarier: they looked so normal. Yet, given that they harbored so much evident wrath, I wondered whether they beat their wives, hit their children, or kicked their dogs.

They called me just about everything you could imagine, often in all caps: slanderer, Jezebel, bitch, temptress, seductress, opportunist, truth-twister, attention-seeker, evildoer, harlot, heretic, anti-Christian, anti-church, anti-Christ, spawn of Satan (my personal favorite), and whore of Babylon. They said I was bitter, dramatic, kooky, hysterical, unforgiving, witchy, broken, spiteful, wayward, nasty, desperate, destructive, shameful, untrustworthy, unloved, and fake.

Those were the mundane missives. Some were more ominous.

"What do you want, you little f*cker? We're gonna cut off your head." Instantly, I deleted the anonymous comment from my blog site, hoping to spare other survivors from seeing it. But I marveled at how the sender apparently saw no obscenity in threatening to cut off my head—that was within the bounds of the acceptable—but saying "fucker" without an asterisk would have been a step too far.

Another anonymous comment said, "My holy mission is to see you destroyed." I quaked a bit over that one too.

Then there was the day a twenty-five-page diatribe arrived on my doorstep in a thick brown envelope. The anonymous sender included a printout of a page from my blog and mentioned that he was "dead serious." It was all the more unnerving because I had moved not long before, so the sender must have tracked me.

Once, I got a phone call from a guy who immediately threatened, "I'll get you fired; you'll be done by the end of the week."

"Well, good luck with that," I said, hanging up. Since I was self-employed, I laughed, but I also thought about other survivors. I'd seen the pattern of religious leaders so accustomed to silencing dissent that they thought nothing of threatening someone's employment or professional standing. A denominational attorney had once threatened to haul me before a state bar disciplinary board, for no good reason except as another intimidation tool in his arsenal. And days earlier, a city manager had told me how terrified he was of losing his job if he publicly disclosed a pastor's abuse of him as a child. "They'll destroy me," he said. "Baptists run the whole town."

Occasionally, Jim took to answering unknown calls on my cell phone. He was good at quickly dispatching the hate-mongers and he tried to protect me. Once, after I'd already hung up twice on a guy who refused to identify himself and yet labeled me as a "hussy" who needed "to learn some politeness," I stood by Jim's side as he dealt with the third call. Jim undertook to explain common courtesies, as though the caller were a six-year-old.

"It's simple: you say your name, you tell the name of the organization you're with, and you state the purpose of your call. You think you can do that?" Jim asked.

But the man wouldn't. "I'm a Baptist pastor," he said, insisting that he was accustomed to being treated with more respect. Finally, Jim said, "Look, I've got your number and I can track you down. So don't ever call here again. Do you understand?"

The guy began to verbally squirm. "It's not even my phone. I borrowed it from a friend." At that, Jim flat-out laughed at him, but then reiterated, "Don't call here again."

It's not normal to answer your phone to hear someone you don't even know spewing vitriol. Or to open your computer to messages saying you should be destroyed. Yet, abnormal as it was, it became a regular occurrence in my life. Some days I could laugh it off—like when a pastor who was describing my flesh forever burning said, "Not even aloe vera gel will help you." Other days, it paralyzed me. I learned to never look at emails or blog comments in the evening, because the graphic messages about my peril—both earthly and eternal—would preclude all possibility of sleep.

At least on my own blog, I could exercise some control to keep the space safe. As fast as I saw them, I would delete victim-blaming comments like "If girls dress like they're asking for it, they shouldn't be surprised when they get it"—that was a common one. But the awful things men would say on some Baptist pastors' blogs were so seldom challenged, or moderated, that they were effectively normalized.

People working in denominational offices launched smears and innuendos in apparent efforts to discredit me. A public relations staffer for the Baptist

General Convention of Texas tagged me as "That Woman"—the slur made famous by former president Bill Clinton. Others said I was "just a kooky woman," and perhaps most bizarre, "someone who wants a statue." When reporters relayed these comments to me, I wondered how many more such insults I never heard about.

I even got messages that said I should be crucified. How was it possible that people of faith didn't recognize the hatred in those words—didn't feel themselves as part of a mob? Even the more mundane messages—"you should be ashamed of yourself" and "it will hurt the cause of Christ" and "stop being so bitter"—were admonitions edged with anger. Other messages came from those who merely wanted to give "advice." They told me I needed to be "nicer," that I had too much of a "hard edge," that I was "too strident," and that I needed to "listen more." I also received lots of mini-sermons on forgiveness.

What I saw in the Southern Baptist Convention was that if you dared to speak up and urge concrete action—as opposed to simply talking pabulum about awareness—and if you dared to name your clergy perpetrator and ask that he be removed from the pulpit, then all pretense of civility would fade.

Friends said that if I were going to persist, I'd have to grow a thicker skin. So I did. I hardened myself. I took an attitude that I would fight until hell froze over, and then I'd lace up my skates and fight on the ice. It felt like psychological warfare, and I was determined not to let the bullies win. But ultimately, the sheer volume of vitriol overwhelmed me. I was being pulled under by the waves of meanness.

With so many disturbing messages, it was impossible to view them as the product of a few "bad apples." Rather, they were the predictable consequence of a mob mentality that was fomented at the highest levels. After all, it was Paige Patterson, a seminary president and former SBC president, who called me an "evildoer" and said that I and other child rape victims in SNAP were "just as reprehensible as sex criminals." (Patterson was angry because we had written to the seminary's trustees urging that he be suspended and investigated for his handling of rape and abuse reports. The trustees did nothing, but ten years later, we were proven right. With the momentum of the #MeToo movement, the trustees finally fired Patterson, citing his "mishandling" of a rape allegation.)

Another SBC president, Frank Page, used Baptist-controlled media to publicly castigate me and other survivors as "nothing more than opportunistic persons." Apart from the bewilderment of a religious leader who apparently imagined that being raped as a kid was an opportunity, I felt in his "nothing more" words the dehumanizing erasure of every other part of my identity— mother, wife, lawyer, daughter, friend, runner, neighbor. (Later, it came to light that Page himself had what was described as a "morally inappropriate relationship" that "reportedly involved a female congregant under his care." But of course, like so many hidden wrongs in Baptistland, even when it came to light, nobody seemed to think it mattered much. Page went on to pastor another Southern Baptist church.)

Still another former SBC president, Jerry Vines, used a national Christian news network to accuse me and other survivors of making "false charges." And the *Baptist Press*, a publication controlled by the SBC Executive Committee, smeared me as making "false accusations"—the article was written under an anonymous "Staff" byline. Then, in a public meeting with media present, an SBC Executive Committee member maligned me as "a person of no integrity." In the face of all this and more, one reporter described me as the survivor who has "received the most aggressive public scorn from SBC leaders."

No doubt they said worse things privately. In later years, a letter from an SBC insider described how top SBC officials and staff called survivors like me "crazy" and referred to us with "spurious biblical analogies." And an internal email from Executive Committee president Augie Boto came to light in which he described me as being part of a "satanic scheme." It seemed a painful echo of what Gilmore himself had done years earlier in insisting I harbored Satan.

When the highest leaders of a powerful religious institution set this kind of example—castigating a survivor with poisonous rhetoric—it has an insidious trickle-down effect. It's not a far stretch for others to then conclude that it's acceptable to take the brutishness even further and behave like thugs. I carry the brunt of this reality in my body. Not only do the months of sexual abuse reside in my cells but so too do the endless slurs from so many others who sought to dehumanize me.

With the hate came panic attacks. As I worried about the religiously engendered rage of so many men determined to send me to hell, I grew anxious in the extreme, always looking around for danger. Traveling solo became impossible—a loss I felt as a narrowing of my life. There were days when even stepping outside my front door could make my breath grow short. My nightmares returned with a vengeance: constantly, I was either fighting an attacker or running across an empty tundra chased by wolves.

This was not harm from the sexual abuse I suffered, nor even from the cover-up and bullying of my childhood church. Rather, it emanated from the dehumanizing rhetoric spewed by the highest leaders of the Southern Baptist Convention and from the virulent pestilence of hate that they unleashed.

Again and again, the task of bringing me out of the nightmares fell to Jim. With his hand on my shoulder, he would say my name. "You're safe, Christa. You're here with me. Stacy is safe too. Everything's okay." He would speak to me like this—gently but firmly—until he could see in my eyes that I was surfacing. I would home in on his voice as though it were a life buoy, and I would cling to that sound until, finally, I was awake and in the present.

20

You Did Not Choose to Seek Help

If you are silent about your pain, they'll kill you and say you enjoyed it.

—Zora Neale Hurston

WHEN I REALIZED that Dallas media were probably going to do a story about me, I knew I had to tell Mom. I didn't want her to be surprised by seeing my face on the TV or by hearing about it from someone at the senior center. So, when she came to Austin for a visit, I sat at Nancy's kitchen table and told Mom there was something we needed to talk about.

"Remember that time when the police came to our house?" I asked.

She nodded.

"Well, Tommy Gilmore . . ." I saw her vacant stare. "The youth minister at the church. He used our family dysfunction against me. After that, he began sexually abusing me."

"Family dysfunction? What do you mean?"

"Mom, we had a dysfunctional family. We just did. And he used that."

She turned defensive. "I don't know what you mean. We had a happy family. What are you talking about?"

Realizing that I had started the conversation all wrong, I took a deep breath and tried to get back on track.

"Mom, we had a dysfunctional family, and I'm not going to debate that. But that's not my point. I'm trying to tell you how things began. How he used that to isolate me and start pretending to counsel me, and all the while he was setting me up to sexually abuse me."

She didn't seem surprised. Her reaction was flat. I paused, trying to register what I was seeing on her face.

She took my hands. "Tell me what he did," she said.

I started in but cut myself short. I knew I didn't want to go into details. "He did whatever he wanted, Mom. I was just a piece of meat. He raped me. Repeatedly. And he did it all while reciting Bible verses."

Mom held fast to my hands, looking at me.

"You're so strong," she finally said, breaking the silence. "You always have been. You'll be fine. I know you will."

I pulled my hands away. *Would I be fine?* I was a long way from being sure about that, but I knew I had done what I needed to do with Mom. So I wrapped things up by telling her there might be some press coverage. "I just didn't want you to be surprised," I said.

I left Nancy's house thinking I'd done the right thing and that it was good to have done it while Mom was staying with Nancy. That way, if Mom had questions, she'd have Nancy to discuss them with. But a few days later, when I asked Nancy whether Mom had asked her about it, Nancy said no.

"It seemed as though she already knew," said Nancy. "She wasn't surprised."

"MOTHER TOLD ME what happened to you in Farmers Branch such a long time ago," wrote Rita on a notecard with a pink flower on the front. "It's too bad that you did not choose to seek help from family members and/or professionals at the time or sooner throughout the years."

Sucking in my breath, I stared at her note. It was so deceptive: the innocuous-looking flower that spewed poisonous nectar.

"And/or? And/or?" I fixated on those words, as I handed the note off to Jim. "Who *says* that?"

"Christa, she's always been a cold bitch. You *know* that."

Jim was right, of course, but it didn't provide any comfort. I thought back to when Rita taught me to read. She had sat with me while I pointed to every "look" and "see" in a *Dick and Jane* book. They were the first printed words I learned to recognize and associate with meaning, and Rita was the one who taught me. True, she had a temper and an insatiable need for control, but I had a long history of keeping my mouth zipped—of not talking back to her. This time, I wasn't sure I could.

The next morning, I met my friend Elaine for our weekly walk around Lady Bird Lake. At first, when I told her how disappointed I was in my sister's reaction, she softly pointed out that, sometimes, it takes people a while to absorb new information and they don't always know the right thing to say. But then she asked, "Well, what exactly *did* she say?"

I had been awake all night turning Rita's note over in my mind, so I spilled forth the words by rote: "It's too bad that you did not choose to seek help from family members and/or professionals at the time or sooner throughout the years."

Elaine's face visibly hardened. Her body stiffened. "Christa, sometimes people have to make their own families. I think that might be how it needs to be with you. There's no talking with that kind of cruelty."

I wish I had heeded Elaine's wisdom then and there. But I didn't. Instead, I decided to write Rita and tell her the truth of how her note had made me feel.

> Rita,
>
> I know you as a person who chooses her words carefully, so I don't take them lightly.
>
> I can readily see that you are completely ignorant on matters relating to clergy sexual abuse. Most people are, and I don't presume to think that people should have the kind of understanding I have. However, what I cannot accept is that, even in your ignorance, you would nevertheless make a little jab. I suppose you just couldn't help yourself.
>
> Your statement . . . sends a chastising message and seems essentially victim-blaming in nature. I can't believe that, in a note of just a few lines, this was what you deemed important to say. What in the world makes you think you're in a position to tell me what I "chose" when it's obvious you haven't a clue about any of this?

Probably, I should have stopped there, but I went on at length, trying to explain that I'd had no choice in any part of what was done to me—"neither the happening nor the harm."

> My long silence was perfectly normal. If I could have chosen to understand and speak of this sooner, I surely would have in order to try to prevent it from happening to others. It is why I speak of it now—because I finally can—because I understand better than most the horrific nature of the harm—and because I am determined to do all that I can so that young church girls today can be safer than I was . . . I look at three girls running and playing in the yard across the street. I also see them when they're getting into the car on Sundays to go to church. I cannot look at them without thinking that I must do all I can with my own experience and my own voice to try to make churches a little safer for kids in the future.
>
> I had a knife held to my throat when I was twenty-three. I imagine there would be many who would simply assume that such an event as that would be more traumatic. But what I know for sure is that having God himself used as a weapon against me when I was just a dumb naive sixteen-year-old church girl was a thousand times more traumatic and far more damaging. Such utter blasphemy—all done in the name of God, in the house of God, with words of God, and by a man of God.

Even now, it makes me sad to see how hard I worked at trying to defend myself to my own sister.

Rita's terse reply came a week later: "I'm sorry that I did not choose my words as you would have liked. I will expect your own apology in return."

"'*Your own apology?*' For exactly what?" I wondered aloud to Jim. And I couldn't help but notice that Rita had expressed not one word of sympathy for my story of being attacked with a knife. It was the first I had ever mentioned it to anyone in the family.

As I pondered what to do about Rita's expectation of an apology in return, I kept reliving the forced apology I'd made to Gilmore's wife when I was a church girl in Farmers Branch, begging forgiveness for something that was never my fault. Ultimately, I chose to ignore Rita's expectation and didn't respond further. It would be years before I understood the full measure of her wrath. I had violated the rules by talking back to her. I had spoken the truth and called out her cruelty. She would make me pay.

AS THE MONTHS went by after my initial disclosure—and after Rita's poisonous note—Mom began to rail at me about it. She insisted I should "leave it in the past," "get over it," and stop "making a mountain out of a molehill." Again and again, I floundered.

"You act like it was something terrible," she hammered. "But you didn't act like that then!"

"Mom, it *was* terrible. And I can't just gloss over it. I can't pretend it didn't happen."

"But why do you have to make such a big deal out of it? It's not as if you were hurt. Rita was dating Richard when she was the same age as you were, and it didn't hurt her any."

"What?" I couldn't make sense of it. "Mom, it's not the same. Tommy wasn't a boyfriend. He was way older than me."

"Well, Richard was older than Rita," she countered, "and I *know* they were out necking in the car sometimes."

"Mom, it's not the same," I said redundantly. "Richard went to school with Rita. He was just a year older. But Tommy was a preacher. He was married. It wasn't some kind of normal boy-girl thing."

"I don't see how it's any different. You were doing the same thing Rita did at that age, and you don't hear *her* whining about it, do you?"

These conversations left me reeling. By then, I'd had enough counseling to understand that I'd been blameless in the sexual assaults inflicted on me as a kid, but I was still struggling with moving that cognitive knowledge from my head to my heart. Talking to Mom never helped.

"You need to own your part in it," she insisted. Her words landed like a slap across the face. I gripped the doorframe for support. The whole house seemed to lose solidity.

"Mom, no. I was a kid. He was a grown-up. He was a pastor."

"You were old enough to know better. You had a part in it and you have to take responsibility for your own part."

"No, Mom, no." It was all I could muster; my every effort was in trying to hold myself upright and stay on my feet.

Again and again, these death-dealing conversations replayed themselves, both in person and on the phone. Occasionally, when Mom would call and leave a message, Jim would plead with me. "Put down the phone. You don't have to call her back right this second." Too often, he'd seen the emotional cost of Mom's calls. But still, only once did I fail to call her back. My hand reached for the phone but before I could punch the number, my breath grew short. Struggling for oxygen, I sank into a morass. *How to talk to Mom without succumbing? How to survive as a person? As me?*

I would have been content to never again talk to Mom about anything connected to my abuse, but she invariably brought it up, always wanting me to assure her that it was really "no big deal." It was what she wanted to hear, and it was the one thing I couldn't give her. I could not participate in minimizing my own abuse.

"SOMETIMES SECRETS ARE supposed to stay that way," said Mom. "No one meant to hurt you, but what *you're* doing—talking about it—that's different. You're doing it deliberately and you're hurting people."

"Who, Mom?" I asked. "Who am I hurting?"

"You know."

But of course, I didn't know, and the more I pressed her, the more evasive she became. First she complained that I was hurting her. "I'm the one who has to live in this town," she said, "and I'm the one who has to hear what people say." But trying to find out exactly who was saying what was impossible.

Then she told me how much I'd hurt Rita by calling her "ignorant." Clearly, Rita had told Mom about my response to her toxic note.

I tried to explain. "Mom, I didn't call her 'ignorant.' I said she was 'ignorant about clergy sex abuse.' And she is."

"Don't you mince words with me!" Mom retorted. "It's time you started thinking about someone other than yourself!"

Is that what this is about? I wondered. *Me being selfish? Me thinking only of myself?* It was the same old pattern of self-doubt that Mom's words so often instilled. Even as every bone in my body screamed "don't listen," I could be overwhelmed by a desire to just go along with whatever Mom wanted. The only defense was to walk away.

"HE SAID YOU would forget." It came out of the blue in a conversation while I was helping Mom peel potatoes.

"Who, Mom? What are you talking about?"

"Brother Hayden. He said you would forget about it." I heard the words, but though they lodged within me somewhere deep, I couldn't process them.

"What do you mean?" I finally asked.

"Oh, you know."

"No, I *don't* know. Forget what?"

"All of it. You were supposed to forget. That's what Brother Hayden said. So why didn't you?"

By then, I was feeling the edge of nausea. I didn't put my hands over my ears, but I may as well have. Whatever Mom was saying, I couldn't go there—so I immediately sidelined it from my consciousness.

In another conversation, Mom blurted, "Can you imagine what your father would have done if he'd known? We would have had to move."

Again, I let it go. But now I wonder: *Was that what had been going through Mom's mind back then—worrying about what Dad would do?*

Then in yet another phone call, things took a turn. "Are you over it now?" she began.

"Over it? What does that even mean, Mom?"

"All I'm saying is let the past be the past. Don't dwell on it. Nobody meant to hurt you, and we all did the best we could at the time."

"We?" That was the only word I could muster. As I felt my breath coming shorter, it seemed there was something just beyond my reach—something shadowy and dark—but I couldn't grasp it.

"You know what I mean," she said.

"No, I don't know, Mom, but I know I've got to go."

"Christa, mark my words, you aren't doing any good with this. It happened a long time ago. It doesn't matter anymore. You need to let it go."

"Anymore? What about then, Mom? Did it matter *then*? Did it *ever* matter? Did it matter to *anyone*?"

Suddenly feeling some fissure in my brain, I knew I had to save myself. I said goodbye and hung up.

"YOU KNOW YOU do this kind of thing. You always have. You're a crab," said Mom.

I sucked in my breath, knowing that yet another painful conversation was about to proceed.

When I didn't respond, Mom pressed on. "You've *always* been too sensitive. That's your problem. Why can't you just get over it?"

I didn't want her to see the pain in my face, so I started digging around in the pantry for some used foil. On some level, I sensed that Mom felt guilty, which I thought was the pain that any mom might feel on realizing something bad had happened to her child.

"Mom, I know this has hurt you too," I finally said, "and I think it might help if you could get some counseling about it. But I can't be the one to keep trying to explain it—to help you with it. I just can't."

"I'm not the one who needs help," she replied. "You are. Why don't *you* get counseling? *You're* the one who has a problem."

Taking a deep breath, I unfolded a piece of foil, heard the fluorescent lights buzzing, and made a mental note to ask Jim to check the ballasts. Finally, I answered, "I *do* get counseling, Mom. I see a counselor almost every week. It's something I'm really working on."

"Maybe you need to find a different counselor, because it's obviously not working."

Still not looking at her—I couldn't bear it—I began to slowly wrap the foil around some potatoes. "Mom, I've tried out several different counselors and finally found a really good one—someone I like. She's had lots of experience with this kind of thing."

"Well, she can't be any good because, whatever she's doing, it's not working."

"How can you know that?" I asked.

"If it was working, you'd be over it by now. It happened a long time ago."

"What do you think that would look like, Mom? If I were 'over it'?"

"You wouldn't keep talking about it!"

"But, Mom, *you're* the one who always brings it up, not me."

"That's because I want to know when you're going to get over it. I just want what's best for you, and I know you'll be so much happier if you just let this go and apologize to Rita."

There it was: "apologize to Rita." That infernal demand. I put the wrapped potatoes in the oven and walked out into the yard.

I could see that Mom wanted a version of me that didn't exist any-more. She wanted me to go back to being her quiet, compliant girl—the one who never caused trouble. I couldn't. Mom's script for me was the same one that had been used by my pastor-rapist and my childhood church. It was the same script that had led me down the long path of a deluded belief that I held blame. It was a script I could no longer accept, not even for the sake of Mom.

WITH NO ABATEMENT of Mom's criticism, and with my advocacy work in full swing, I grew to dread trips to Farmers Branch even more. Mom was living alone in the house and seemed needier than ever. The tightness in my chest would arrive with even the thought of a trip, and once there, the house itself would frighten me: its darkness, its smells, its smallness, its memories. With every visit, I would dust everything with lemon oil and clean out the mothballs Mom had piled into drawers. Still, my anxiety would intensify.

To hold myself steady, I would press my fingers into the sides of my hands and mentally recite the things I knew to be true:

My name is Christa Brown. I am born from a tenacious line of Sullivans. I am beloved of Jim. I am mother to a strong and beloved daughter. I am a lawyer and a good one. I am greatly loved and cared for. I am safe.

Yet, even with my mantras, every visit felt like an emotional mugging. Afterwards, I'd invariably drop into a wormhole of self-loathing that could take weeks to crawl out from. But I could not—would not—apologize to Rita. I could not—would not—go along with Mom's "no big deal" narrative. It wasn't mere stubbornness; it was survival. I could not swim free of the abuse trauma if I kept the anchor of Mom's criticism attached to my foot.

The bottom dropped out of our relationship, but I don't know if Mom even noticed. I kept hoping she might talk with Nancy about things, since Nancy had an undergraduate degree in psychology, or get some counseling, or somehow shift her perspective. I imagined things would smooth out with time, just as they had after Judy announced she was a lesbian. But what I finally knew for sure was that I could not work on healing myself while constantly having my experience invalidated and belittled by my own mother. It wasn't possible.

I had to choose. I chose me.

THE MOVERS HAD loaded up the last of our stuff, and Jim and I were driving north to Colorado. I had felt the mountains calling, but it was more than that. I also wanted to move out of the South—far from the strongholds of Baptistland where the cultural influences were so pervasive. Since our route would take us through Farmers Branch, I called Mom from the road, asking if we could take her to lunch at Marshall's Bar-B-Q.

"Ohhh Christa . . . I was just, uh, saying goodbye to . . . Clarine," said Mom, hesitating over the name. "Can you call me back in a few minutes?"

"Sure," I said. But I instantly sensed something was weird because Mom's friend Clarine had died a couple years earlier.

When I called back, Mom readily agreed to lunch but said, "I'm going to ask Rita to meet us there. It'll be good for the two of you to talk."

Intuiting that, between my first and second calls, Mom had already talked with Rita, I tried to be direct. "I was really hoping that it could just be us, Mom—that maybe you and I could have a chance to talk. It's been a long time."

She grew defensive. "What are you saying? You don't want to talk to your sister? You *need* to talk to her. You hurt her feelings, and this will give you a chance to apologize."

"Mom, I don't feel like I owe Rita any apology."

Mom's voice turned to ice. "Well, if you don't even want to talk to your own sister, then you don't need to talk to me either."

The air left my lungs. Silence lingered on the line.

"Mom . . ." I heard the word come from my mouth with such longing, as though I were hearing it spoken by every child who ever lived. I heard my love and yearning in it; I heard my daughter's voice in it; I heard the eternal bond of the utterance. Finally, choking back everything within me, I said, "You know, we've got a long drive ahead. So I think we'll just go on and try to get a little farther down the road. Maybe next time, Mom."

I cried for the next two hundred miles.

It had been my plan to give Mom a copy of my first book, *This Little Light*, and talk with her directly about the one place where I had written something about our family—where I recounted calling the police on Dad. I knew it would upset her, and I had hoped to soften it by talking in person. But it wasn't to be.

Later, after Jim and I got settled in Colorado, I asked Nancy whether Mom had said anything about my book. But each time Nancy had tried to talk to Mom about it, Mom had replied, "Rita says I shouldn't read it." Nancy also informed me that Rita had been ranting about how I brought shame on the family. So that was it: not only had I violated the rules by talking back to Rita and refusing to apologize, but I had also broken the family code of omertà and soiled the "happy family" image that we had all presumedly protected for so long.

21

Cancer

In the depth of winter, I finally learned
that there was in me an invincible summer.

—Albert Camus

WHEN HE DIAGNOSED the first tumor, my surgeon said it had probably been growing, hidden from imaging, for six or seven years. Immediately, I counted backwards and realized that the cancer had started during the time when, having resurrected the horror of the pastor's sexual abuse, I was trying desperately to get church and denominational leaders to do something. That time had been so stressful that the very cells of my body had mutated in rebellion.

A couple weeks later, on the day when I got news that the diagnosis was even worse than the doctors first thought, I also received this missive from a self-identified Southern Baptist: "When life goes sour for you, YOU WILL KNOW WHY!" It arrived with the usual slew of "you're going to hell" and "God will have judgment on you" sorts of messages.

There was no doubt about it; my life had gone very "sour." But not for an instant did I imagine it was because I had offended God by writing about sexually abusive pastors. Everyone's life goes sour at some point. Besides, from the first time I began speaking out about clergy sex abuse, I had reaped reams of Baptist wrath; if it hadn't been for my cancer diagnosis, his vitriol would have been just another day in Baptistland.

IT WAS ACTUALLY a double cancer diagnosis, and it arrived not long after I had retired from twenty-five years of practicing law. I had left behind our longtime home in Austin to move to Colorado, and almost everything familiar was gone. Moving into the cancer kingdom eradicated the last remaining roots of normalcy.

Though it had been my choice, shuttering my law practice was still a loss deeply felt. My work, my business, my colleagues, and my professional identity had all been cast off. Along with my career, I'd left behind my household in Austin—the yard, birds, and trees, longstanding neighbors, and daily routines. All of this I had said goodbye to voluntarily—in part, to get away from Baptist-land—and with the anticipation that Jim and I would create a new life. We had moved to a place where I had no acquaintances, no colleagues, no comrades-in-arms, and not even a friendly barista who knew my name.

Then came cancer. At first, I felt a resigned calm, as if I'd just been waiting for cancer to find me. *Let's get on with it*, I thought, defiantly. But then, before I could even process the implications of my first cancer diagnosis, I got the news that there was a *second* invasive tumor. This brought with it the even more devastating news that, because I had multiple independent invasive tumors at the same time, the medically recommended surgery was mastectomy. That was when the last bit of my identity that held true—my own body—became an alien form.

If anyone had asked, I never would have said that any part of my identity rested in my boobs. Sure, I liked them, but in the abstract, I would have said they weren't all that important. Yet, confronted with the disfigurement of a mastectomy, and with all the life-threatening terror that went along with it, I felt that every last shred of my selfhood had been lost.

I was still in a state of shock, having only begun to process the harsh reality of everything my many doctors were telling me, when Nancy happened to call. She sensed the stress in my voice and asked if I was okay. Like a fool, I answered honestly that I wasn't. I relayed the news of my double-cancer and told her I was scheduled to have a mastectomy in a few days.

Nancy immediately insisted I should tell Rita and Judy, but I didn't want to—not right then. Telling them would be one more thing to have to deal with, and I needed every bit of my energy for me. So I told Nancy that I just wanted to get through the surgery first, and promised I would inform our sisters later.

A week after my mastectomy, when I was debilitated and dealing with drains, when I was still facing massive unknowns and the need for high-stakes decision-making with inadequate information, Nancy phoned, insisting again that I had to tell Rita and Judy. I knew I would tell them eventually—I felt an obligation to give them family medical history—but I also knew I wasn't ready. In the margins of my consciousness, I suspected that Rita and Judy wouldn't care one whit, and I didn't want to face that. I also wanted to protect myself from the need to assure Mom that everything was okay. With two cancers at once, I knew I couldn't bear it if Mom tried to tell me that, really, there was no need to make a fuss.

I didn't want to put on a smile and pretend everything would be fine when I still didn't have any idea how things would turn out. I didn't want to shove my fears under the rug or feel guilty for being weak and self-centered. Instead, I wanted to wail and gnash my teeth. I wanted to honor everything I was feeling without discounting any of it, and then to go deep inside myself and muster every bit of my strength to squarely face the reality of whatever would come next. I was simply too exhausted for pretending.

But Nancy would not be deterred. "If you wait any longer, I'll have to tell them myself," she said.

So, I wrote a short email, giving Rita and Judy the bare bones and letting them know that, if they had questions, I had given Nancy more details. I knew I couldn't risk talking with them. Like Psyche in her visit to Hades, I couldn't afford to give away any of my resources if I had any hope of escaping the cancer underworld. I would not make it out alive if I let the demands of Mom and my sisters deplete me.

Rita emailed back a terse "Best wishes." Judy said nothing. There were no Hallmark cards, no flowers, no fruit baskets.

Two months later, Nancy told me, "They never asked a thing. Not one single question about how you were doing. It was as though they weren't even interested." Nancy was surprised, but not me. She was accustomed to receiving support from family members and, wrongly, had assumed that I would too.

In breast cancer support groups, I listened as others talked about how their siblings came through for them. One woman spoke of a sister who stayed with her a month and did all the shopping and cooking. Another's sister had stood with her in the shower to hold her up. Still another recalled a sister who sent poetry and playlists. I felt envious, but I also felt they were educating me on what true sibling care might look like. Rita's two-word email presented a stark contrast. When I was at my all-time weakest, I had to face full-on the reality that two of my sisters didn't care even one tiny bit.

A veil had been lifted on my relationships with Rita and Judy. Cancer offers few gifts, but one of them is the ability to see who you matter to. Even as it forced me to confront a hard truth about my sisters, it also brought to my eyes more clearly the precious life of love that I had created apart from my family of origin. My sisters were gone and, in truth, they'd been gone a long time. Like old dead stars, their light was still visible, but it came from a place of nothingness.

AS I STRUGGLED with recovering from multiple surgeries and keeping my head above water in the maelstrom of cancer, I began to realize that if I were to have any hope of wellness, I had to release every belief and habit that blocked me from living in peace. In addition to the two invasive cancers, doctors also discovered two types of in situ cancers, a squamous skin cancer, a large precancerous colon polyp, and a bizarre but benign growth inside my mouth. If one of these other aberrations had arrived on its own, I might have worried about it, but coming on the tail of the far more serious invasive cancers, they seemed of little consequence. Yet, I felt them as additional evidence of my body's cellular rebellion, and I knew I had to get to the root of it. So, with a sense of life-or-death urgency, I started into therapy yet again. The process was excruciating, like slowly self-extracting thousands of shards of shrapnel.

Cancer is a multifactorial process. Intellectually, I know that. But emotionally, I experienced it as the cumulative manifestation of all the evil that had been done to me in Baptistland. Done to my body. Done to my selfhood. Done to my soul.

Week in and week out, as I worked to inventory my life, I grew to understand how so much early-life trauma had left a trail of bodily ruination. When I first learned about ACEs—adverse childhood experiences—I felt doomed. Data from a large-scale epidemiological study showed a strong correlation between ACEs and a host of chronic health issues in adulthood. Among other things, people with four or more ACEs were twice as likely to get cancer and those with six or more ACEs had a lifespan twenty years shorter on average.

I saw myself in that data. If I wanted to live long enough to see Stacy build her own life, I needed to alter the biochemical environment of my body. That meant learning to say no to everything that depleted me. It also meant saying yes to things like yoga, counseling, and self-care. The anything-to-appease girl had to go, as did anything untrue. I wanted only what was real; everything else was rotten.

SHORTLY AFTER I was diagnosed, I took medical leave from the PhD program I'd entered at Iliff School of Theology at the University of Denver. The school had been generous, giving me ample time off and letting me retain my fellowship. When the time came to return, I was scheduled as a teaching assistant for a class on religion and sexuality, so I went to campus to make a video introducing myself to prospective students. It was a perfectly fine video, but as I played it back for editing, I flinched when I saw myself exclaiming, "I'm so excited about this class and looking forward to working with all of you!" Watching my face, I realized it wasn't true. I could hear the falsity in my own voice. That was when I knew: I didn't want to go back. With whatever days my life might still hold, I didn't want to spend them trying to gather more knowledge about clergy sex abuse just so I could try to convince uncaring men to care.

At the time I'd entered the program, I had imagined that a PhD might help me better explain how religion could foster such systemic abuses and cover-ups, and that it might help me comprehend the mass-scale denial, the failure to protect kids, and the victim-blaming vitriol. Post-cancer, I realized I'd been wrong in imagining that I could study my way to understanding such dark-heartedness. I'd been stuck in the "if only they understood" mode of thinking, and cancer cut that illusion out of me. The problem wasn't that Southern Baptist leaders lacked understanding or awareness; it was that they possessed a surfeit of arrogance and a fixation on institutional protection. I doubted that putting more academic credentials after my name would make any difference.

So, I dropped out of the PhD program and instead began training as a yoga teacher, eventually earning specialty certification in yoga for cancer survivors. During the worst of my cancer journey, yoga had been a lifeline, a thread that held me to hope and helped me attune to what was within. My body desperately needed that.

Cancer shares a commonality with sexual violence: it seizes bodily control. In the process of using yoga to help in dealing with cancer, I realized that yoga could also help me work at recovering a primal sense of safety within my own embodiment—something that the desecration of childhood sexual abuse had stolen. Yoga helped me learn to be in stillness with that desecration rather than running from it.

On my hardest days with cancer, I had done nothing more than to stand in Mountain Pose. Living in Colorado, the mountains held presence in my consciousness, and when headlines told of wildfires, I pondered how even when everything on a mountain is burned to ash, the mountain itself remains. That thought, combined with a simple yoga practice, sustained me.

Through everything cancer dished out, I also spent time in my mind at a babbling creek in Missoula, Montana, where we had once vacationed. Stacy, age seven then, wore her favorite blue dress with her red "happy-shoes"—the ones she said would always take her home, like Dorothy's in the *Wizard of Oz*. Her laughter merged with the sound of the water as she hopped from rock to rock, occasionally looking back over her shoulder to Jim and me. The steady warmth of Jim's arm rested on my shoulder as, together, we watched her in the dappled sunlight.

This was my personal portable paradise. It was where I placed myself mentally every time I lay on a pre-op table, every time they wheeled me into an operating room, and every time I lay in an MRI tube. It was Jim and Stacy and the loveliness of a Missoula creek-side that kept me steady.

CANCER IS HARD. It takes and takes and takes. My chronic insomnia grew exponentially worse, and in the midst of it all, Nancy took to calling me late at night. Invariably she was drunk, and though she'd start with the pretense of wanting to know how I was doing, the calls quickly devolved into ramblings about her memories of our family. "Did that really happen?" she'd ask repeatedly, as each resurrected memory seemed too terrible to be true—and yet it always was. Sometimes she'd bring her ramblings into the present, recounting some recent interaction with Judy or Rita. "Can you believe she said that?" she'd ask, venting her alcohol-fueled frustration to me instead of to them.

As Nancy's speech grew incoherent, I could visualize her tossing back shots as she talked. Worst of all was whenever she would go off on some self-loathing ramble about how her life wasn't worth anything. Eventually, she'd slur a sudden "bye" and hang up, leaving me to hope that she had merely collapsed into a stupor. Inevitably, her calls would leave me awake all night.

A couple of times, she emailed me the next day, saying that her friend had told her she'd called me, but that she couldn't remember anything she'd said. She'd apologize and tell me how they'd "polished off a fifth of espresso-flavored vodka," as if I needed to understand the precise type of alcohol that had caused her memory loss.

Several times, when she was sober, I begged her not to call me late at night anymore and explained that rehashing family history right before bedtime kept me awake. I was working to get healthy, and sleep deprivation didn't help. Nancy would promise not to do it again, but of course, another weekend would roll around and she would. Over and over, she told me she just didn't know what she'd do if she didn't have me to talk to about the "crazy family stuff." So week after week, the pattern repeated.

NEARLY TWO YEARS after my cancer nightmare began, I got a large, vivid-blue tree-of-life tattoo to celebrate what was, if not the certainty of an end, at least the taming of a beast. Stacy designed the tattoo and sat with me for every inking session, as the tree grew up my side, reaching from my waist and extending branches onto my reconstructed breast. It was my way of reclaiming my body—of choosing for myself what I would do with my body after enduring so much that had been *un*chosen. And Stacy, my beloved daughter, was the one who helped me make something beautiful of all the bodily awfulness—something that transformed it.

She had moved back in with us for a few months as she was changing jobs, and we were all living in a small bungalow of a house. Jim and I typically awoke earlier than Stacy. One morning, aware of how noises carried, I apologized for "clattering around making coffee" and waking her up.

"Oh no. I like it," Stacy laughed, standing in her pajamas. "I hear you making coffee and it feels all cozy. It reminds me of when I used to lie in bed as a kid and hear the two of you whispering out in the kitchen. I could never hear what you said, but it always felt so good. I *like* hearing you make coffee."

Her response so overwhelmed me that I nearly started crying. I was dumb-struck with gratitude for the realization of how dramatically different Stacy's upbringing had been from mine. When I was a kid, I was always listening for whether the house was safe or not. But Stacy had grown up habituated to the sounds of a house that felt cozy, and safety was a given.

The Fourth Death

22

Mom's Hospital Room

I don't know why the tears still flow,
Only that memories are deep,
And the ones I chose not to keep
Are still there.
My tears know.

—Nell Brown (Mom), "Autumn Thoughts"

STACY AND I hopped on the first flight we could get after Nancy's phone call, but it was evening by the time we arrived at the hospital. I pushed open the door to Mom's room, and we tiptoed slowly in.

"Mom, look who's here!" said Nancy as she got up from her chair by the bedside and motioned us over.

I stepped to Mom's side while Stacy stayed a few feet behind me. As soon as Mom's eyes focused, her whole face lit up. She was radiant. Tears began rolling down her cheeks.

"Oh, Christa! Christa." She reached out her arms and I bent down to kiss her cheek. Weeping, she held me there.

"They said I'd never see you again," she whispered in my ear, continuing to cry.

I pulled my face back just enough to look at her. "Who, Mom? Who said that?"

I watched as her eyes darted around the room, but she stayed silent, gripping tight to my hands.

"Well, you know you can't get rid of me," I laughed. "I'm here, and look who I brought with me."

"Oh, Stacy!" Again, her face lit up as Stacy said "Hi, Grandma" and bent to give her a kiss.

As we sat by her side, I told her that Stacy would be starting law school in just a few days. Mom beamed. We told her, too, about Stacy's boyfriend, Joe. Mom glowed.

After a while, I could see that she was weakening. Her words began to slur.

". . . so beautiful," she murmured.

"I know. She's really gorgeous, isn't she?" I babbled on, assuming Mom was talking about Stacy. "I think it's those big blue eyes she's got."

". . . you too," she whispered.

In the days that followed, whatever anger I'd ever felt for Mom—or that she had felt for me—did not seem to be part of us anymore. Her love was there in that hospital room.

THE NEXT MORNING when Rita came by, I could tell she was surprised to see me. Before she could flatten her expression, her face flashed anger, and as she said hello, her voice sounded high and tight. She extended her arms to hug me, but I just couldn't. I knew it was phony. I blocked the hug with my left arm and extended my right to shake hands. Flustered, she shook my hand, and then, as I stepped back to Mom's bedside, Rita motioned to Judy and Nancy, and they all three stepped out.

Eventually, they came back, all smiling, but later, Nancy told me how enraged Rita had been. "Who told her about Mom being in the hospital?" she'd demanded. Nancy had reluctantly acknowledged that she'd been the one, saying she thought I had a right to know. Then, according to Nancy, Rita had ranted about "how dare she not hug me" and launched into a diatribe about how I'd called her "ignorant" and never apologized.

"Can you believe it—she acts like she's the victim!" exclaimed Nancy, telling me how Rita was still "consumed with rage" because I had talked back to her.

Even long before Mom was in the hospital, said Nancy, Rita had been "bad-mouthing" me and "putting little bugs in Mom's ear" about how I was never there. And once, when Nancy had been telling Mom the latest news of Stacy's life, Mom was glowing with pride until the instant Rita pulled up at the curb. Then Mom had hushed Nancy and told her not to talk about Stacy anymore. "It will upset Rita too much," she'd said.

There in the hospital room, Rita had a hard time hiding her antipathy. She kept glaring at Stacy, and it wasn't an "it's been so long since I've seen you" sort of gaze. Later, Stacy asked about it. "Why was Aunt Rita staring at me the whole time? It was creepy."

It wasn't Stacy's imagination because I'd noticed it too. But for me, Rita had *always* had a creepy component. If you want an idea of what she's like, just watch *The Thing About Pam* with Renée Zellweger. The physical gestures. The facial tightness. The controlled voice. That character, Pam Hupp, reminded me so much of Rita that, when I watched the show, I couldn't help but transpose Rita's face straight onto Pam.

IN MOM'S HOSPITAL room, I tried to make small talk with Judy. Her arms were covered in crescent moon scars from her fingernails, and her face was pocked. Seeing her scars, I recalled all the times in high school when she'd stood in front of the bathroom mirror puncturing pimples and blackheads with her fingernails until she bled. I knew the old habit must have renewed itself even though zits were no longer a problem. I read somewhere that self-injury represents an attempt by people with low coping skills to try to "mother" themselves and wondered if that was what was going on with Judy. Was she still trying to make up for Mom's detachment? Then I considered the fact that all three of my sisters were obese, two of them quite seriously, and I saw reflected in their bodies the daily traumas of our childhoods.

As children, we had all responded differently, but together, we had exhibited all the classic trauma responses: fight, flight, freeze, and fawn. And I had labored to be impossibly perfect, believing subconsciously that if only I were good enough, everything might be okay. As adults, all of us, in our own ways, continued to manifest our traumatic histories.

As I silently pondered all this, Judy suddenly asked, "How many nights did you stay in the hospital when you had cancer?"

"Just a few nights," I answered, momentarily imagining she might actually be interested.

"So that was it? Just a few nights?"

"Well, that was for the first surgery. The others were day surgeries."

"What does that mean?"

By now, her tone had informed me that she wasn't interested, but was interrogating. Still, I carried on as though it were a normal conversation and answered her question, wondering quietly how Judy had been so fortunate as to reach sixty without needing any surgeries.

"So, even though you were only in the hospital a few days," she continued, "you went all that time without coming to visit Mom?"

There it was: Judy's real point. She'd just wanted to chastise me. Judy, who'd spent thirty years making one trip per year to Farmers Branch—and had only recently moved back to town—was criticizing me for not visiting Mom while I was dealing with cancer. I should have let it roll off my shoulders, but instead I tried to explain. *Maybe she truly doesn't have a clue*, I thought.

"There's a lot more to it than just time in a hospital," I said. "For starters, I had about four dozen medical appointments in the first couple months, and that was just the beginning." I told her how exhausted I'd been. "It was like a full-time job, and really, it was more than that. I didn't have the energy to be traveling *anywhere*."

All of it was true, of course, and I didn't even attempt to tell her about the emotional discombobulation of it. But Judy just looked at me, as though she hadn't heard a word, and pronounced her conclusion: "You could have if you'd wanted to."

Why do I bother to tell her anything at all? I wondered. She cared only about criticizing me.

That became all the more apparent a week later when I flew to Farmers Branch a second time. Mom's heart was failing. With repetitive blood clots, she'd had a couple small strokes, and she'd had a below-knee amputation of her leg that needed to be re-amputated above the knee. She was deteriorating. Again, I found myself with Judy in Mom's hospital room. Out of the blue, she suddenly asked, "Do you regret it?"

"Regret what?"

"You know," she said, "not being there for Mom. Not doing what she wanted."

"I *was* there," I replied, and sensing the attack she was trying to make, I continued. "I was there for a whole lot of years while you were living all over the country."

"You know what I mean. You didn't do what she wanted. Do you regret it?"

Immediately, my mind shifted to French as Edith Piaf began singing her great ballad in my head: "Non, je ne regrette rien"—"No, I regret nothing." As I paused, mentally listening to Piaf, I decided not to engage with Judy, particularly not there, where Mom might be able to hear. "No," I said simply. "I built a separate life with Stacy and Jim, and I think that's exactly what Mom would have wanted for me."

Afterwards, I kept mentally replaying Judy's question and still couldn't figure out what the "it" was. What exactly was "it" that she thought I should regret? If I were to regret not being there every time Mom had wanted me and not doing everything Mom had wanted, I'd have to regret my whole life. Because if I spooled the film of my life backwards to doing what Mom had wanted, I would have never left Farmers Branch. I wouldn't have married Jim, and Stacy would never have been born. I would have never become a lawyer, or built my own law practice, or spoken French, or learned yoga. It was an alternate reality that I couldn't bear to create even in my own mind—a scenario in which the person I'd become wouldn't exist and neither would all that I loved. So many life-altering decisions had been things Mom didn't want me to do and didn't think I was capable of doing, and all of them had contributed to making me the person I was. Not only did I not regret "it," I felt enormous gratitude for whatever source of strength had allowed me to stand up to Mom and find my own way.

I DIDN'T GO to the funeral. Mom died the day before Jim and I were set to leave for a month in Paris. It was what I had promised myself during all the long months of dealing with cancer, constantly visualizing myself strolling along the Seine. With every piece of bad news, I'd said a quiet prayer, imagining myself inside the Cathedral of Notre Dame, and with every physical therapy visit, I'd seen myself lining up under the Eiffel Tower for the start of La Grande Classique, the ten-mile race from Paris to Versailles. I had gotten through everything cancer had thrown at me and had worked hard to rehab myself. I was ready for this trip. We had our nonrefundable flights and we'd paid a hefty deposit on a tiny apartment.

Also, I was due for another scan shortly after our scheduled return. Fearful of what it might show, I heard cancer's siren cry: "Don't put things off!" In addition, I was expecting yet another surgery, which would again mean months of rebuilding my stamina. So I got on that plane. I think Mom would have likely done the same thing. Her last words to Nancy were, "Be happy."

On the first full day in Paris, I stepped into Notre Dame early in the morning when it was nearly empty. Immediately, I smelled Mom's heady Tabu cologne, but told myself it was just some incense. An organist was practicing, and the strains of "Ave Maria" filled the nave, the lower notes reverberating roundly and the higher ones soaring into the arches. It was the song that had been played at Mom's wedding.

Mom had always laughed about it whenever she told the story. "I didn't know any better," she'd say as she recounted standing in her suit at the front of a Baptist church in California, with a pastor neither of them knew and a handful of witnesses. When the organist asked what music she'd like, Mom, raised Catholic and only eighteen years old, said "Ave Maria." The organist hesitated and conferred with the pastor, but then found the music and played it.

For decades after, whenever Mom happened to hear "Ave Maria," she would weep and retell the story. There, sitting in the great Cathedral of Notre Dame, I felt as if I was crying along with her. Mom's presence was palpable, as though her shoulder were brushing mine, and I felt such peace. Finally, after sitting for most of the morning, I stopped at the Joan of Arc statue on my way out and lit a candle for Mom.

A couple of days later, while we waited in a line outside the Musée d'Orsay, street musicians started playing "Ave Maria," and I wept all over again. In the days that followed, I heard it several more times—a soprano's voice streaming from a boat going through the locks on the Canal Saint-Martin, a violinist outside a café across the Place de la République, and a recording wafting from a barge on the Seine. It seemed surreal that I should hear it so often. Every time, I felt Mom's presence, wept, and wondered whether she had managed to tag along to Paris for one last adventure.

23

Erased

*When we love rightly, we know that the healthy,
loving response to cruelty and abuse is putting
ourselves out of harm's way.*

—bell hooks

AS SOON AS I got back from France, I knew something was wrong. Nancy and Judy had told me I was a beneficiary on Mom's Chase Bank account, but Rita sent out an email saying she'd closed all the accounts. When I emailed back, asking about the Chase account, her reply was terse and vague. "The account was directed elsewhere. It is properly closed and distributed according to Mother's wishes."

When I pressed for more information, she said the money had gone "to charities" and named a nonprofit that provides cleft surgeries. I didn't believe it. For decades, my parents' Chase account had named all four of us sisters as beneficiaries. A sense of betrayal seeped into my consciousness. I went to talk with a banker at my own Chase branch, who told me Mom's account had named Rita and Richard as the two beneficiaries—no charities—and that the beneficiaries had been changed within the preceding year.

When I told this to Nancy and Judy, they asked Rita about it—twice. Both times, Rita insisted the account had been distributed to charities and then changed the subject. Nancy was livid, believing that Rita was lying to their faces. So Judy talked to Rita privately, telling her what the Chase banker had said. Only then, when she knew she'd been caught, did Rita finally admit that the account had actually been distributed to herself and her husband. It was "just a quick, erroneous answer," she wrote in an email. But to me, it carried the scent of self-dealing, with a "charities" lie as a cover-up. After that, things went downhill.

RITA SEIZED CONTROL and would reveal nothing voluntarily. I made a trip to Farmers Branch to look through boxes and papers that had been moved to Judy's garage, but I didn't expect to find much. Nancy had already told me that two days after Mom's death, Rita and Richard had used a dolly to wheel Mom's two file cabinets out of her apartment and back to their own garage. Nancy had protested, insisting we should all four see what was in the file cabinets, but they just ignored her. Nancy also said she'd seen Rita pocket something, but when she asked what it was, Rita refused to disclose it. "What was I gonna do?" asked Nancy. "The only way I was gonna learn what she'd pocketed was if I tackled her and took it. And I couldn't see myself doing that."

In Judy's garage, I found a box with all the cards Stacy had made for Mom through the years—birthday cards, Mother's Day cards, Grandparents' Day cards, get well cards, and valentines. Mom had kept them all. Then I saw the red and green sequined earrings I had made for Mom when I was seven. Year after year, she'd worn them on Christmas Day. I picked them up gingerly. How had they held together through decades of getting shoved around in Mom's jewelry boxes?

As I pondered all the memories—and love—in the things Mom kept, I also found a copy of a document in which Mom had granted power of attorney to Rita. It meant Rita could have made changes in Mom's accounts. But of course, any changes should have still been according to Mom's wishes. Rita claimed she knew nothing about the power of attorney—something I didn't believe for one second. By then, the lies were arriving in a blinding flurry.

When Rita filed a court case to get herself named as estate administrator— because a couple of Mom's accounts had no named beneficiaries—I intervened in the case to compel the production of bank records. I wanted to know the truth of what had happened.

Over the course of months, as I sorted through reams of documents— Mom had a jumble of twenty-four accounts—I saw that during the last eighteen months of Mom's life, there had been more changes in her accounts than in the preceding twenty years. Beneficiaries had been changed, rechanged, and changed back again, and money had been shifted from one account to another and another—repeatedly and chaotically.

I thought back on how angry Rita had been when I hadn't hugged her in Mom's hospital room. It had felt phony, but at the time, I'd had no idea of just how artificial it really was. The maneuvers in Mom's accounts—maneuvers that effectively cut me out—had begun months before that. They'd begun almost immediately after the death of Mom's brother Jack, who had left Mom a couple hundred thousand dollars, which she'd promptly deposited into an account at the credit union.

A year before her death, when Mom sold the house she'd lived in for nearly fifty years, she also deposited that chunk of money into the credit union. Nancy had told me about it when it happened, because she was pissed. Mom had sold the house to Judy for a mere $75,000, which Nancy said was about $50,000 below market price—and Zillow confirmed it. According to Nancy, Mom had been adamant about wanting to immediately split the $75,000 between her other three daughters—Rita, Nancy, and me—with $25,000 to each of us, so that all four of her daughters would benefit from the sale of the house. But Rita and Judy had "pressured Mom" to simply deposit the money into her account. Then, that $75,000 became part of a pool of money that was split without me, and Judy benefited from *both* the below-market sale price *and* from a share of the proceeds.

After Nancy spilled her anger about Judy's double-share a half-dozen times, I decided to talk to Judy. I tried to explain that, for someone who's elderly and frail, it can be particularly easy to fall under someone's influence. "I think that's what happened," I said. "Rita—and maybe you too—and maybe even inadvertently—convinced Mom not to share the proceeds from the family home the way she'd really wanted to."

Judy's response was hard and swift. "You can't prove that."

THOUGH I TOOK some comfort in knowing that Mom herself had wanted to include me, the fact that my sisters cut me out from the proceeds of the house hurt. A lot. It seemed they had erased me—as though I'd never grown up under that roof, never been part of the family, never made countless trips to be there.

Judy berated me. "If you're gonna be angry, you should be angry at all three of us. Why aren't you angry at Nancy? She was part of it too. But that just goes to show how stupid you are."

I should have paid more attention. Judy had an overconfident way of sticking her foot in her mouth and occasionally leaking clues. But at the time, since so much of what she said was bullshit, I had trouble sorting the clues from the caca.

Instead, I thought about all the times Jim had done some bit of work on that house. With nearly every trip to Farmers Branch, particularly after Dad died, Jim had done basic chores—changing light bulbs, ballasts, and fixtures, putting batteries in smoke detectors, caulking windows, pruning trees, dragging things down from the attic, and fixing faucets and toilets. Mom had only to name it and Jim would do it. His maintenance efforts would now accrue to Judy.

IN PHONE CALL after phone call, Judy would begin with her affected talk of "I just know Mother would want us to work this out," and then, when I didn't go along with whatever she said, she'd swiftly revert to her lifelong baseline of bullying. The pattern played out so many times that I learned to recognize the shifting tones in her voice. I could tell when she was moving from manipulation to maximum infliction of pain.

"Is money the only thing you care about?" she suddenly shouted, when just a moment earlier, she'd been oozing her smarmy charm, trying to get me to give up looking at bank records. "What kind of person cares more about money than they do their own mother?"

I tried to keep my voice steady. "Judy, I'm not the one who took the money."

It was then that I could have sworn I heard that sly little "heehee" of Judy's that had always been her tell for when she knew she was getting away with something. But she recovered quickly enough and launched in with a new attack, hammering me yet again for my failures while dealing with cancer.

"You didn't even call Mom when you had cancer!" she hissed. "*I* was the one who had to tell her!"

With one more surgery and another scan on the horizon, cancer still occupied an ominous space in my consciousness, but of course, with Judy there was no reprieve. "Even after you knew she knew, you *still* didn't call her!" she seethed. "Didn't you think she might worry? But nooo, you couldn't be bothered to even tell her you were okay, which you obviously were because you certainly aren't dead."

Wondering momentarily whether Judy was disappointed that I wasn't dead, I finally responded. "I told Nancy I didn't see any good reason Mom needed to know since she would just worry about it, and I didn't see how it could help her."

"Ohhh, that's just so like you. *You* didn't see a good reason," Judy sneered. "All the time all about *you*. Even when you had cancer, you just wanted to focus all your little thoughts on your own little self. It's no wonder Mom cut you out. You were never part of the family anyway."

Judy's words landed as a gut-punch, but I knew better than to fight back. She was a vacuous hole of parasitic cruelty.

On other calls, she hammered the line "you never gave Mom any joy"—an attack so ruthless that it stirred the bottom of the ocean, causing memories to rise from the deep: Mom's look of transcendence as she held Stacy in her arms for the first time; Mom, Stacy, and me puttering in Mom's herb garden; Mom's laughter and patient instruction as the three of us canned figs; Mom's sly grins as, together, we taught Stacy to play dominoes; Mom's gaze as she watched Stacy feed the ducks in Mallon Park. In every memory, Mom's face is glowing.

Mom and I had a difficult relationship—no doubt about it. But that wasn't the sum total of our time on this earth together, and it doesn't mean love wasn't there. Plus, Mom always held a fierce and true love for Stacy. She would have realized that, by cutting me out, she was also cutting Stacy out. I knew Mom never would have done that.

I recalled how thrilled Mom had been each time Stacy invited her and Dad to visit for Grandparents' Day in her classroom. With Stacy walking in the middle, holding their hands, the three of them would enter the school as Mom would invariably twist back to give me a wave and a grin. No joy?

Then there were all the holiday memories of Mom and Dad's visits for Christmases, Easters, and Halloweens. How could Judy know anything at all about our laughter as we sat around the table decorating Grinch and Santa cookies? How could she know about the glee Mom took in teasing Stacy with cryptic clues about where special eggs were hidden? And how could she understand Mom's delight in sitting by the fire while costumed Stacy dumped her trick-or-treat bag on the floor, anxious to share with her grandmother. No joy?

To imagine that Judy was right would have meant erasing all those memories. I couldn't. Then, even at the end of her life, there was Mom's misty-eyed look of radiant joy when I stepped to the side of her hospital bed. Body language seldom lies.

AGAIN AND AGAIN, in conversations with Judy, I felt myself drowning and recalling all the times she'd held me underwater as a kid. Her modus operandi was little more than displays of dominance, disconnected from any concerns about truth, fairness, or even kindness. At first, I struggled to maintain equilibrium. But then I remembered the dog poop.

One fall, years earlier, when Jim and I were scoping out Denver for a possible move, Judy invited us to have Thanksgiving dinner with her and her new partner, Jennifer. As soon as I crossed the threshold, I saw them: several piles of dog poop in her living room. As I stepped carefully around a pile, Judy just waved a hand at it, saying, "That's Jennifer's job. She's supposed to take care of cleaning the dog shit and I take care of paying the mortgage."

I laughed awkwardly, but Judy continued. "She's just in a tiff right now. But that's our arrangement and I'm holding her to it. Jennifer does all the shit I can't stand, and I pay the bills."

The more I pondered the dog poop, the more I saw the pitiful sadness of Judy. She and Jennifer split up a couple years after that, and as best I could tell from my infrequent visits with her, she never had another long-term relationship. It seemed she simply wasn't capable of loving someone—at least not in a way that wasn't transactional. Her desperate need for control had deprived her of true intimacy and human connection. Growing up in our household, she'd been so wounded that she had learned to view relationships strategically, and it had limited her.

RITA CLAIMED THAT Mom had cut me out because I'd blamed her and "made her feel guilty" for what the pastor did to me. Right away, Nancy saw that argument for what it was. "It's despicable," she told me. "Rita is using your abuse to justify her money-grab."

I pondered Nancy's word—"money-grab"—because Jim had used the same word. "Christa, you're trying to be too rational," he'd told me. "It's really simple. They wanted the money and they thought they could get away with it. It was a money-grab. Everything else—everything—it's just an afterthought. A rationalization."

Still, I was slow on the uptake. But then Judy took up the same refrain—"you made Mom feel guilty"—and did it on steroids. Repeatedly, she bludgeoned me with that line and berated me for being a "bad daughter," as if I had done something wrong. She insisted that what happened to me was "no big deal," that I'd made "a mountain out of a molehill," and that I'd deliberately hurt Mom in the process.

Ultimately, Judy overplayed her hand. The more she insisted that I'd made Mom feel guilty, the more I kept reflecting on it, until finally, I saw what I had failed to realize for so long. Mom's guilt wasn't just a normal sort of mom-guilt—the kind most moms feel when their kids are hurt. Rather, it was guilt because she'd *known* about what the pastor did to me. It was guilt because she'd been complicit in the church's cover-up. It was guilt of a far more profound depth.

When I finally allowed myself to see that, it gave rise to a pain so visceral I could scarcely say the words out loud: she had known.

How could I have failed to see it sooner? How could I have heard Mom say so many things that so obviously gave away her knowledge and still fail to understand? "Brother Hayden said you would forget about it. . . . Can you imagine what your father would have done? . . . We would have had to move. . . . We all did the best we could at the time. . . ."

I had blinded myself. Mom had *always* known. I just hadn't wanted to see. It was my own denial.

But simultaneously, what I also saw was that Mom, too, had been manipulated, convinced by Brother Hayden to keep things quiet. I still couldn't muster it up to blame her. She had trusted her pastor. And probably, she had lapsed into denial for much the same reason I had—because to open her eyes would have meant seeing more than she could then manage.

Not only would she have had to confront the way she had lent cover to those who victimized her daughter, but if she'd allowed *those* thoughts to rise to the surface, they may have triggered her own traumatic memories—about her own childhood abuse, the culpability of her beloved brother Jack, and the failure of her parents to protect her. Those were memories she'd spent a lifetime suppressing. It wasn't hard to understand how Mom had been unable to arrive at a place of empathy for the abuse I suffered when she had never allowed herself to see the abused girl that she herself had been.

APPARENTLY CHANNELING HER mother, Rita's daughter Molly sent an email to Stacy, saying how sorry she felt for her because she had such an awful, selfish mother—me. Molly ranted about how she'd always wished she could have her cousin as a best friend but that I had prevented that from happening by not letting Stacy grow up with her cousins and by raising her apart from the family. She ended the email with, "I'll pray for you."

"I hate that kind of passive-aggressive stuff," said Stacy when she told me about it. "There's just no point in talking to someone when they're like that. She's not trying to have any kind of dialogue; she's just being mean. Besides, who does she think she is? I *know* you. I've lived with you. I've grown up with you. Does she think she knows you better than I do? It's ridiculous. And if she really thought it was so important for us cousins to have a relationship, why didn't she come and visit with me when I was there at the hospital with Grandma? She was living just a few blocks away, and she knew I was there, and she didn't even drop by. And now she wants to tell me how awful it is that *you* didn't let us get to know each other better when we were kids?"

As I listened to my daughter, I wanted to applaud. Stacy hadn't spent endless hours doubting herself and weighing whether some part of what Molly was saying might be true. She hadn't made the kind of mistake I'd made so many times of trying to explain something to family members who'd already made up their minds. Stacy trusted herself and her own reality.

With Stacy's recounting of Molly's email, I saw how firmly Rita's bizarre claim had taken hold. I had previously heard the same story from both Judy and Nancy—about Rita's insistence that I had rejected family and refused to let the cousins grow up together. It was a claim belied by boxes of photos documenting holidays, birthdays, playground adventures, summer splash days, card games, Monopoly games, and trips to the zoo, the movies, pizza parlors, parks, and Six Flags. I even ran across a photo album that Rita herself had sent Stacy as a high school graduation gift. Rita had written "Cousins!" on the cover and filled it with photos covering a span of eighteen years. But apparently, none of those pictures were of any consequence once Rita decided to concoct a self-serving narrative to justify kicking me out of the family.

Hearing Rita's phony history from three sources made me realize it was one of the main things she had used against me. I took comfort in that. As Judy, Nancy, and Molly had all three told it, the basis for Rita's narrative was the fact that I had refused to let Stacy live with them that summer when Stacy was seven. And I knew with absolute certainty that if I had to do it again, I would make the exact same decision. Even if some seer had foretold that it would cost me $100,000 if I didn't let Stacy live with them, I would have still refused.

THE BALD FALSITY of Rita's "Christa didn't let Stacy grow up with the family" narrative raised questions for me about other family lore. What was true and what wasn't?

What about the "Grandma was crazy" story? She had dared to divorce my grandfather, but a couple of years later, remarried him. Was that her big mistake? Putting herself back in a position that afforded him power over her? Why exactly had she been stripped of all agency and warehoused for nearly twenty years in a psychiatric hospital? Who had she been *before* the awfulness of that place?

And what about Mom's story that her sister Ava's ex-husband had "destroyed the family" by getting custody of their kids? Maybe instead of trying to destroy the family, he was trying to protect his children. Maybe the reason he was awarded custody—something unusual for a father in those days—was because their daughter, Beatrice, had accused Uncle Jack of molesting her, and the whole family had pretended it was no big deal.

Mom herself had told me that Jack "messed with" Beatrice when she was a kid, but then she'd accused Beatrice of exaggerating the harm. And Judy had called Beatrice an "opportunist," apparently parroting Jack. It was the same slur a Southern Baptist Convention president had publicly flung at *me*. So I couldn't help but wonder if my family had done a similar wrong to Beatrice, shoving blame onto the victim so as to support the status quo and uphold the dominant male.

I yearned for more answers, but I tried to locate Beatrice and couldn't.

Then, on the other side of my family, Dad's last remaining sister, Aunt Opal, died, and yet another sordid piece of history came to light. Her son sent around an email to all the cousins, recounting that in one of Opal's last conversations, she had told a harrowing story of how her father—my grandfather—had been responsible for her mother's death.

Over the years, I'd often heard my grandfather described as a violent man. The details on exactly what that meant had always been vague. Mom had said he was "a strict disciplinarian" who "didn't believe in sparing the rod." From that, I'd always imagined that his violence was directed at his children and had never considered that it may have also been directed at my grandmother.

On the rare occasions when I'd asked Dad how his mother died, he had always mumbled something murky and turned away. Since he'd been eighteen when she died, I found it hard to believe he didn't know; yet it was something he would never talk about.

Years later, when I got a copy of her death certificate, I saw "ruptured kidney" as the cause of death, and Mom told me the story of how my grandmother's own brother, a small-town general practice physician, had tried to save her by doing emergency surgery. "Can you imagine?" Mom had asked. "He had to operate on his own sister, and she died on his table."

"How did it happen?" I asked. "How did she rupture a kidney?" I was imagining some accident with a farm tool or getting butted by a cow. But that was when Mom brought the conversation to an end.

"Oh, these things just happened in those days," she said and walked away.

Somehow, even with all these pieces, I had never allowed myself to put them all together—to see the picture they formed—until I got that email from my cousin. The picture was my grandfather beating my grandmother to death. And the three youngest children still at home—my dad and two of his sisters, Opal and Daisy—had probably seen it.

I had always known that Aunt Opal and Aunt Daisy had married young—at seventeen and fifteen—but had never thought much of it. Suddenly, the reason seemed obvious and ominous. They had both married within a couple months of their mother's death. They must have been terrified of being in the house with their father—my grandfather.

I DIDN'T GET every last detail nailed down, but from bank records and medical records, I uncovered enough to piece together a picture of what had likely happened during Mom's last days. Rita, the queen of control, and Judy, the queen of mean, had joined forces to shove me into exile. Afraid to risk their wrath, Nancy had ultimately gone along with things, and my sisters had split the bulk of the money four ways, with Richard replacing me as the fourth daughter. Perhaps most bizarre, funds had even been shifted a couple of days after Mom died. I knew for sure that Mom had not resurrected out of her casket for one last trip to the bank. And of course, the authority of any power of attorney ends when the person who granted the power dies. So, no one else should have been shifting funds either.

The whole scheme appeared as a calculated money-grab that had been in the making for months—a money-grab that they had then tried to legitimize by scapegoating me.

Scapegoating: It's a human pattern as old as time, used to marginalize and cast aside those who challenge the dominant social order. So it was with me. I had challenged the familial order by failing to "let it go," by rejecting Mom's "no big deal" narrative, and by refusing to apologize to Rita. And I had built an independent life for myself. So my sisters scapegoated me as a family defector and thereby relieved themselves of guilt for their underhanded money-grab.

When I read that ten percent of Americans experience elder abuse, including financial exploitation, I wondered whether abuse was what had really happened to Mom. It's the kind of abuse that's perpetrated by those who purport to love the victim, but it's a "love" that meshes conveniently with self-interest. I pray that, in my own last days, I will be surrounded only by those who know my heart and whose "love" crosses no lines with greed.

I THOUGHT I knew the worst of what had happened—that Nancy had simply gone along with things after the fact. This was what I wanted to believe, and it was easy to imagine. Having learned from childhood that disagreements could lead to terror, Nancy was so cellularly averse to conflict that she often rendered herself a doormat. With this view of the facts, I decided to make a final trip to Austin to talk with Nancy in person.

When first confronted with Rita's lies about the Chase Bank accounts, Nancy had railed about it and, all on her own, exclaimed how much she wished she could take back her consent for Rita to be administrator of the estate. So, taking Nancy at her word, I had quickly put together an easy half-page form that Nancy could sign and file in Rita's court case so as to withdraw her consent. Nancy never signed it. Instead, she told Judy what she was planning to do, and Judy "threw a fit." That's what Nancy herself had told me when she backed off from signing the document. And seeing how torn she was, I had chosen not to pressure her, hoping she would eventually do it on her own. She never did.

Over the course of two years, Nancy played it safe. She repeatedly told me how "appalled" she was by things Judy and Rita said and did. Yet she wouldn't speak up for me or do anything that might jeopardize her own relationships. Instead, she quietly fed me information, including a running tally of what Rita and her family had been spending the money on: paying off a second mortgage, a down payment on a condo for Bobby, cars, a truck, credit card debt, trips to casinos, and Disney World vacations. I knew that no Texas court would let me collect against cars and homesteads, and the rest of the money was simply gone.

At Nancy's house, as I carefully situated myself amid the clutter on her couch, I thought about how the instinct for clinging to stuff comes from a fear of scarcity. That's what I'd read somewhere, and if it was true, you could take one look at Nancy's house and see her fear. She was surrounded by it, cocooned in it, trapped by it. By then, Nancy was living on her own, her relationship with Tina having long ago ruptured—Jim had been the one to help mediate the property division for Nancy.

We made small talk for a while, until Jim got back from Home Depot. Then, while Jim set to work fixing the toilet in the adjacent half-bath, I tiptoed into more serious talk.

"But Judy said it wouldn't make any difference!" Nancy exclaimed, when I told her how much I'd been hurt by her failure to rescind her consent for Rita to be administrator.

"If it wouldn't have made any difference, why do you think Judy threw such a fit?" I asked. Nancy began to cry.

Then I asked her about the chart I'd sent several months earlier. Although I had talked on the phone with Nancy about what I discovered in bank records and medical records, Nancy had never seemed to latch on to what I was saying. So I had charted out the changes in Mom's credit union accounts with a time-line. Nancy had ignored it—always claiming to have not yet looked at it. That was another reason I had wanted to talk with her in person.

Suddenly, when I brought up the chart, Nancy's crying turned to outright blubbering.

"Rita made us promise we would keep it a secret," she blurted. "When we showed up at the credit union, we met her outside and before we went in, she insisted that we all three had to agree that we would always keep it a secret."

"Keep *what* a secret, Nan?"

"She said there was a lot of money in the account and that *you* weren't going to get any of it and that it would just be upsetting for you. 'You have to promise that you'll never tell.' That's what she said."

As I sat stunned, Nancy continued. "But I told her, you *know* she's gonna figure it out. She'll know Mom couldn't possibly have spent all the money she inherited from Jack. So where is it? She's gonna want to know. That's what I told her. But Rita said you'd never be able to trace it."

I looked at her. "And this seemed to you like something on the up and up? Nan, how could you not have realized that something underhanded was happening?"

"Well, I told her," she answered, "I told her you would figure it out. But she said no. She said there were too many accounts and it was too complicated and you wouldn't be able to sort through them. She said there was no way."

As Nancy kept talking—seeming almost to brag about how she'd "told her"—I bit my tongue, not wanting to interrupt her confession.

"So, I told her—I told her—that if you *did* figure it out, then I wouldn't flat-out lie about it. I told her. I wouldn't flat-out lie. I told her."

A lacuna of silence hung between us.

"Wow, Nan," I finally said. "Was that the best you could do?"

By then, Jim had stepped out of the half-bath and was standing to the side, screwdriver still in hand. From the sorrow in his eyes, I knew he'd overheard and could sense his unspoken grief for me. He had immediately realized the awfulness of what Nancy was saying, and he knew it would kill me—knew it even before I did.

I sat there quietly, remembering how the sun would glisten off Nancy's glossy hair as she held my hand when we walked to school together as children. My mind filled with pictures, like fluttering images from Dad's old eight-millimeter Brownie movie camera. I drifted back even as Nancy kept sobbing.

"Oh, Christa, I was just so overwhelmed. I didn't know what to do. And I'm so depressed all the time. I don't know what reason I even have for being alive anymore. If it weren't for taking care of my kitties, I wouldn't have any reason at all. They're the only thing that keeps me going."

I paused, trying to muster some compassion. "Well, Nan, if your cats are what's keeping you alive, then maybe you should get some younger cats." I just didn't have anything more in me.

I waited for Nancy to recover herself, and sure enough, she rallied. She was angry that I'd dropped my intervention in Rita's court case. Even though I'd notched a couple procedural wins, I had foreseen that, no matter how many battles I won, I would likely wind up with a moral victory but recover nothing financially. It would be an uncollectible paper judgment, and I would have to spend a bunch more of my own money and energy to pursue it. So, with little more to learn about what had happened, with the realization that there would be no Lazarus-raising for my relationships with Rita and Judy, and with little possibility for any financial recovery, I had chosen to walk away. In terms of money, it was a bitter pill. In terms of peace of mind, it was priceless.

But regardless of whether any judgment would have been collectible, and regardless of the emotional and financial cost of pursuing it, Nancy had wanted me to continue until there was a final judicial ruling. She'd wanted Rita to face consequences, but she hadn't wanted to risk anything to make that happen. She'd wanted the court to confront Rita and thought that with a court ruling, Judy would then see the truth as well.

"You just *let* them get away with it," Nancy complained.

"I didn't *let* them get away with anything, Nan. I learned what happened, and they know I know. And while I was spending months figuring it all out, turns out you knew all along what had happened. You fed me information on the sly but kept right on doing their bidding of keeping your little agreement a secret. *You* let them get away with it, Nan. *You.*"

"But I *promised*. I *promised* to keep it a secret."

"Nan, do you even hear yourself? You knew what was happening was wrong. Courts aren't a substitute for having a spine."

"But if you had evidence of fraud, you should have stayed in the case!" she exclaimed.

Mentally, I noted Nancy's use of the "fraud" word. I hadn't used that word, and had instead focused on Rita and Judy's weighty influence over Mom when she was frail. The fact that Nancy said "fraud" suggested to me what she was really thinking—what she'd probably been thinking for a long time.

"Nan, *you* had evidence of fraud," I responded. "An agreement for secrecy is primo fraud evidence, and you've just told me that you all had an agreement for secrecy. When people are doing everything aboveboard, they don't tend to need secrecy agreements."

"But you never had it in writing. It's not as if Rita signed something *saying* we would commit fraud."

I gazed at her. She was so obviously grasping against her own guilt. "No, of course not," I replied, shifting into a detached attorney gear. "That's just not how it usually happens. People don't draw up agreements to commit fraud and then have everyone sign them. It's usually proved by circumstantial evidence— by an accumulation of things—things that, put together, form a picture. And especially with all you've just said, Nan, I've got a pretty clear picture now."

"But you don't *know!*"

"Nan, I know enough. And you know too. You have for a long time."

Both of us sat quiet for a bit. Finally, Nancy asked, "What are you going to do now?"

"I don't know," I said. "I came here thinking I knew the worst of it, but now I have the image of all three of my sisters—you too, Nan—standing in front of the credit union, voting me out and promising to keep it a secret. You did that, Nan. You knew and you kept it a secret when, all the while, I was spending money on an attorney and endless hours trying to figure things out. That's a pretty ugly image, Nan, and I've gotta figure out a way to live with that."

"But what are you going to *do*?" she asked again.

I looked at her. "I don't know. The only thing I know for sure is what I *won't* do. I will *not* do what our family has done so often and just pretend like it never happened. I won't just wait for time to pass and then act like everything's fine. I'm not gonna pretend that I don't know what I know."

"But what about *me*?" she asked plaintively.

"That's up to you, Nan. The ball's in your court. I'm tired of trying to figure this all out."

I couldn't bring myself to try to make Nancy feel better or assuage her guilt. If she wanted to make things right, she needed to make some effort. But at the same time, I didn't want the interlude of truth-telling to be a fleeting moment. Jim had finished up the toilet project, and as I rose to leave, I invited Nancy to come visit us in Colorado for Thanksgiving—a month away—saying, "Maybe we can try to sort things out. I still think maybe we could."

I meant it. I was hoping that, with more dialogue, we could begin the process of building something new.

Nancy said she'd let me know. She never did. She didn't contact me ever again, and I didn't contact her. Even her drunken late-night phone calls finally came to an end.

AFTER NANCY'S CONFESSION, I felt as though every layer of my skin and all my past identity had been peeled away. It was my fourth death.

With the image planted in my head of all three of my sisters standing in front of the credit union, agreeing to split the money without me and to keep it a secret, the very bedrock of my sense of self was ruptured. Nearly sixty years of familial identity was shattered.

My sisters—all three of them—had erased me, as surely as if they had air-brushed me out of all those years of four-sister line-up photos.

Though our family had been almost dystopian in its dysfunctionality, and had certainly been unhealthy for all of us, it had nevertheless seeded within us roots that twisted tenaciously around one another. Though everything above ground had burned, my heart still wanted to cling to those roots.

"But Judy's *always* been mean," said Jim one day, trying to soothe me. "Good riddance. She's a sociopath."

"Yes," I said, "but she's the sociopath I grew up with. She was family."

24

The Do-the-Bare-Minimum Denomination

You see I've been to hell and back so many times,
I must admit you kind of bore me.

—Ray LaMontagne

WHEN DONALD TRUMP came on the scene, it felt like déjà vu with Southern Baptists. For years, I had listened to their self-righteous rhetoric as they shrugged off the reality of widespread sexual assaults committed by pastors against women and children. So when I saw the overwhelming majority of Southern Baptists championing a president who bragged about assaulting women, it felt like more of the same. Their minimization of horrific conduct was a pattern I had already seen up close. I had lived it.

Not only were many Southern Baptist leaders willing to turn a blind eye to a politician's sexual assaults—just as they did with pastors—but they were willing to overlook so much more for the sake of proximity to power. Even basic civility was given the boot. That, too, seemed a resurrection of how they treated clergy sex abuse survivors who dared to speak out—demeaning us, calling us names, and vilifying us.

After Trump was voted out of office, I watched as Southern Baptist leaders used their mantles of spiritual authority to amplify the big lie of a "stolen election." With that, the fraud of everything they professed seemed complete. As the country's second largest faith group—and as a mighty voting bloc—Southern

Baptists were willing to sacrifice democracy itself for the sake of an ends-justifies-the-means bargain for power.

"How could they?" many asked, as if Baptists' support for Trump was mysteriously incongruous with their morals. But for me, it seemed only one more illustration of their true selves, not some aberration. They had already shown themselves when they chose to sacrifice the safety of children to preserve their own institutional image and power.

Southern Baptists normalized and minimized the sexual predations of a president in much the same way they normalized and minimized the sexual predations of their clergy colleagues. Then, with nary a care, they left the rest of us—now the whole of our democracy—to deal with the fallout. With an identity and beliefs rooted in an authoritarian theology, they wound up supporting an authoritarian president.

MY QUEST FOR a system of clergy accountability in Baptistland was a sort of spiritual pilgrimage, and I never made it to the holy land. But the documentation on my *Stop Baptist Predators* website and blog helped lay a foundation for the work of others, including the 2019 "Abuse of Faith" series published jointly by the *Houston Chronicle* and *San Antonio Express-News*. Looking at a span of twenty years, they found more than 400 Southern Baptist church leaders and volunteers who'd been arrested for sex crimes, and more than 700 victims, nearly all of them children. It was an exposé that confirmed my own prior work, and over the course of months, I had spent oodles of time talking with the series' lead reporter, Rob Downen.

The publication of "Abuse of Faith" was a hallelujah moment when a big chunk of truth showed itself bright as day, and it seemed change might be possible. In addition to documenting hundreds of abusive pastors, the series implicated high-level Southern Baptist officials in ignoring and suppressing abuse reports, and it showed how the very structure of the Southern Baptist Convention enabled the quiet relocation of predatory pastors and stifled abuse reform efforts. The story was picked up by media all across the country.

Many Southern Baptist officials acted publicly as though they were surprised. But of course, it was all readily knowable long before, as my own website had documented. And an SBC Executive Committee member had written me, years earlier, saying that he checked my blog every day, as if he were bragging about how well informed he was. So I had no patience with their charade of surprise.

As what seemed little more than a performative face-saving measure, some SBC officials quickly organized what they called the "Caring Well" conference, as if, after all their years of uncaring do-nothingness, they suddenly had some wisdom to impart. With the conference's book sales tables and advertising lanyards, it almost appeared they were trying to generate a revenue stream off their sexual abuse problem. SBC officials also showed that they wouldn't hesitate to use survivors for public relations purposes and even for fundraising—a pattern that has continued.

SBC president J.D. Greear promised "bold steps" and tasked his "Sexual Abuse Presidential Study Group" with making recommendations. But as you might guess, "bold steps" never materialized. It was a Baptistland dog and pony show.

As part of the purported study, an SBC attorney "reached out," wanting me to share my experience, but I wrote back, stating bluntly that I thought it was a misstep for SBC officials to approach a clergy sex abuse survivor via attorney. As a retired attorney myself, I realized how inappropriate it was. Besides, it felt like déjà vu of the SBC's phony 2007 "study." And after having already shared my experience with so many other Baptist leaders—always with retraumatizing results—I recognized this tactic as part of their modus operandi: the use of private meetings to give survivors the illusion of being heard while simultaneously doing nothing to help. It was the showmanship of caring without the reality of caring, and I had no interest in their pretense.

Instead, I went to Birmingham. Together with other survivors and supporters, I stood outside the convention center where eight thousand Southern Baptists had gathered for the 2019 Southern Baptist Convention meeting. At a makeshift podium near a bus stop, with diesel fumes in the air, I gave a rallying speech to a crowd of about a hundred people. In the face of the cameras, I raised my fist and renewed my long-standing demand for a denominational database of clergy sex abusers, repeatedly asking, "How many more kids will it take?"

AFTER THE BIRMINGHAM rally, survivors and advocates gathered at a coffee shop to decompress. The event was filled with a sense of "beloved community," and it even included a lovely candle-lighting ceremony to honor me for my many years of advocacy against sexual abuse in the Southern Baptist Convention. I felt so appreciative of the event's organizers and of everyone who attended.

As the event drew to an end, one of the organizers called on a prominent Southern Baptist woman—an influencer who speaks at conferences and presents herself as an expert on sexual abuse—to close out the evening. Her presence there is an example of how, even in advocacy circles, there are those so enmeshed with the abusive institution that, functionally, they often serve the institution's oppressive ends. She walked over to where I sat, gripped my shoulder, and looming above me, launched into a too-long, too-loud prayer for me. Immediately, I felt myself going under into the roiling darkness, weighted by so many past weaponized prayers and reliving the terror of when Gilmore himself had done the same thing—stood over me, gripped my shoulder, and prayed aloud for God to cast Satan from me.

"Get your hand off me!" I wanted to yell. But instead, I froze as waves of panic overtook me. I focused my energy on breathing as I felt powerless, targeted, unsafe, and trapped.

As awful as it was, I initially assumed that the hurt of it was inadvertent, but a few weeks later, the two organizers of the event wrote me that they had actually talked with the woman about it ahead of time and had told her *not* to pray over me. Just days before Birmingham, *The Wartburg Watch* had published a piece in which I specifically described how Gilmore had stood over me praying to cast Satan from me, and they had realized how a prayer for me might traumatically mimic that. So they'd told the woman to just say "encouraging words" and "no prayer."

I was gutted by this news. "Was it really clear?" I later asked one of them. "You actually told her that praying over me like that would likely be hurtful?"

Her answer was simple: "Yes. I told her. She knew."

So, I'd been left with months of anxiety, ruminations, and renewed nightmares for no reason other than that this Southern Baptist woman wanted to do her showy prayer her way, regardless of its impact on me. The lesson of Baptistland was reinforced: *You are not safe here.*

Evangelicals evangelize, and sometimes they will do so even when it means hurting the real flesh-and-blood person right in front of them. Mission and evangelical agenda take priority. It's part of why so many churches turn a blind eye to clergy sex abuse: saving souls is viewed as more important than the safety of kids and congregants.

Perhaps it's hard for many evangelicals to understand how something they hold so dear could possibly be so hurtful. But for me, everything connected to the faith of my childhood is a tomb of trauma. Prayer, Bible verses, hymns, God-talk, and the faith of my own heart were all perverted into weapons for sexual assault.

I was a girl who loved God, wholly and simply, and it was all turned against me. So when I hear people say "Jesus never fails" and "put your trust in Him," sometimes I just want to scream. Because that's exactly what I did as a kid—I surrendered "all to Jesus"—and that's what placed me on a road that turned terribly dark.

When faith has been used as a sword, it doesn't serve well as a healing balm. You can't pick which edge of the faith blade you use. It's all the same bloody sword—the sword that eviscerated me.

IN 2021, A few weeks before the SBC's June convention, I publicly called for a federal investigation of sexual abuse and institutional enablement within the Southern Baptist Convention. Days later, a couple leaked letters from Southern Baptist official Russell Moore described the "spiritual and psychological abuse of sexual abuse survivors" and the "mafia-level intimidation tactics" used by the SBC's top leadership body, the Executive Committee. These descriptions weren't surprising to me—I had experienced the tactics in real life—but others were shocked, and the fact a white male elite insider had written those descriptions afforded them more weight in the SBC's male-dominant environment. These factors, combined with the continuing impact of the "Abuse of Faith" series, prodded SBC delegates—known as *messengers* in Baptistland lingo—to vote for the creation of a Sexual Abuse Task Force to oversee a third-party investigation of the Executive Committee's handling of sexual abuse reports and its treatment of abuse survivors.

Guidepost Solutions was the firm commissioned to conduct the investigation, and though many fought to stymie it, the investigation moved forward. I remained deeply skeptical for a host of reasons, not the least of which was the investigation's limited scope: it would consider only the conduct of the Executive Committee, not the SBC's churches, seminaries, or other entities. So initially I declined to meet with the investigators. It didn't seem worth the effort of traveling or the exhaustion of making myself vulnerable. But when they said they would come to *me*, I finally agreed.

I met with the Guidepost team for three days and exchanged numerous emails and phone calls. I spent weeks preparing a twenty-nine-page, single-spaced memorandum with over a hundred links, documenting what I knew of the Executive Committee's actions and inactions over the course of some twenty years, and I followed that up with an additional five-page memorandum with recommendations for action. All of it was draining and emotionally costly, but I gave of myself to the project in the hope that, with the aid of an independent investigation, the SBC might finally be prodded toward meaningful reforms.

In May 2022, Guidepost released its report—a total of nearly four hundred pages—documenting how, for at least twenty years, the SBC Executive Committee had allowed clergy sex abuse to go unchecked and had mistreated survivors. My name appeared in the report dozens of times, substantiating how the Executive Committee and its members had publicly impugned my integrity, smeared me in the *Baptist Press*, chortled at my in-person recounting of the pastor's abuse, and literally turned their back when I spoke.

"And then they lied about her." That was how the *Houston Chronicle* bluntly described SBC officials' treatment of me. They lied about me personally and they lied about the reforms I sought. And of course, they never did diddly-squat to help me.

In seeing my name "all over the sexual abuse report," one journalist described me as the "gadfly, instigator, lone voice, impetus . . . that harried the self-proclaimed holy men to pay attention to the horrors they overlooked." Unlike the ugly names I'd been called by so many Southern Baptists, these words gave me pride. And as countless media outlets picked up the story of all that the SBC had worked so long to conceal, those overlooked horrors were in the spotlight all across the globe. I talked with reporters writing for publications in English, Spanish, Arabic, French, Portuguese, and Hebrew as well as with radio and TV outlets, including a station in the Orlando area, where Gilmore resided, which even put his face up on the screen.

Through it all, I felt as though people were being made a tiny bit safer, not because the SBC had changed, but because the truth had been spread.

The Guidepost report validated everything that I'd been saying for two decades. It revealed that, time and time again, the SBC's Executive Committee had treated clergy sex abuse survivors with "resistance, stonewalling, and even outright hostility." It exposed ethical abdications beyond the bounds of human decency, including that "some senior SBC leaders had protected or even supported alleged abusers." And just as I had long believed, the report concluded that top leaders were "singularly focused on avoiding liability for the SBC to the exclusion of other considerations . . . even if it meant that convicted molesters continued in ministry with no notice or warning to their current church or congregation."

The truth was set forth in black and white: leaders of the Southern Baptist Convention had known about clergy sex abuse cases and had consciously chosen to protect the institution's dollars rather than to protect kids and congregants. It was a choice with a profound human cost, and for me, that cost was not abstract. In my mind, I could conjure names, voices, and stories. So, while the report brought vindication, it also resurrected a well of grief at the memory of so many lives decimated.

The report carried an additional bombshell, and though it was something I had long suspected, the proof still landed as a gut-punch. Contrary to all their public posturing about how "local church autonomy" precluded them from keeping a clergy abuser database, SBC officials had in fact been compiling a list of sexual abusers since 2007, but they'd been keeping it secret—"to avoid the possibility of getting sued." So, during almost the entire time I'd been tediously logging cases onto my old *Stop Baptist Predators* database, SBC officials had been quietly maintaining a parallel database, something they had incessantly proclaimed was impossible to do. Lo and behold, they could and they did. The duplicity was staggering. As the *Washington Post* pointed out, SBC leaders had "lied" about their "secret database"—for decades.

It was more than hypocrisy; it was moral bankruptcy. Their secret roster held the names of 703 pastors and church staff. Yet, according to the investigatory report, SBC officials had taken no action to determine whether the pastors were still in positions to do harm.

Immediately, I demanded that the secret list be made public, and within days, SBC officials did so. It was a singular victory and one that carried a weight of horror. As one reporter described it: "Reams of gruesome abuses were known, documented, and neatly organized in spreadsheet boxes."

Within minutes of its release, I was scrolling through the list. Many of the entries were names I recognized from my old *Stop Baptist Predators* database.

And then I saw it. Tommy Gilmore's name was there—his name along with the churches where he had worked. I stopped everything, closed my laptop, and wept.

They had known about him all along. They'd had him on a list, and they'd kept it a secret. The cruelty of it was inconceivable.

THE RELEASE OF the Guidepost report was a moment in time that cried out for accountability. But the Southern Baptist Convention responded with yet another committee, this time with the illustrious-sounding name of the Abuse Reform Implementation Task Force. And, at their 2022 convention, Southern Baptist messengers voted for the creation of a public database of clergy sex abusers. Superficially, it sounded good, and no doubt there were some who genuinely *wanted* to address the problem. But if there's one thing I've learned about Baptistland, it's that things are often not what they seem.

Baptistland is a giant Potemkin village, propped up for show.

In design, their proposed database was nothing like anything I had ever suggested. For determining if a pastor was "credibly accused," SBC officials planned to leave it up to each local church—forty-seven thousand of them—to commission an independent investigation. This would mean that to get a pastor's name onto the database, a survivor would have to rely on the very church that had previously been the site of sexual trauma, and often of re-trauma from church shaming, blaming, and intimidation tactics.

In other words, they were setting up a system designed to tell bloody sheep that they should trust in the den of the wolf who savaged them. Such a process would not only inflict more wounds on survivors but would render the database dysfunctional for gathering the data. When one survivor saw the proposal, he told me "Hell no. No way. No how."

EVEN THE HEAD of the SBC's own Sexual Abuse Task Force described their proposal as "the bare minimum of what can be called reform." Despite that, SBC people applauded themselves as though they'd launched a moon shot. Even some survivors cheered. People wanted a happy ending, and the SBC's 2022 convention seemed orchestrated to give them that—*cue the redemptive prayers, cue the uplifting music, cue the press conference.* I felt myself yet again as a voice in the wilderness crying, "Wait! We need deeds, not words!"

The next day, the messengers voted for a resolution "on lament and repentance for sexual abuse." It seemed designed more for show than for any genuine remorse. A Southern Baptist pastor had submitted a far more specific resolution that named both me and my assailant Tommy Gilmore, and that detailed the conduct of the Executive Committee in its awful treatment of me. But the Committee on Resolutions, chaired by Bart Barber, declined to present that resolution for a vote and instead substituted a broadly worded resolution that expressed appreciation for the advocacy of ten survivors, including me, but that didn't name any pastor-perpetrators and didn't detail the specifics of the conduct for which they were repenting. Barber claimed the substitution was made so as not "to leave people out." But as I saw it, the substitution allowed them to leave out the ugliness of the Executive Committee's own conduct. And if they really cared so much about repentance toward all the survivors, why didn't they do a separate resolution for each survivor, naming that survivor's perpetrator and the specific details of how that survivor had been mistreated by the Executive Committee? Why didn't they lament longer and repent more, rather than reducing it to one quick generality?

To me, it looked like yet another evasion of naming perpetrators and an avoidance of drawing attention to the Executive Committee's deplorable conduct. When the specifics are so egregious, it saves face to just repent of generalities.

At the conclusion of the 2022 convention, I was bereft. It seemed unfathomable that the SBC would do so little—even after a scathing investigatory report, global media attention, the sacrifices of countless survivors, and thousands of names on petitions. That it would do so little and then exploit that tiny bit for institutional image repair plumbed new depths.

It was David Clohessy who saved me from despair. Over the course of some thirty years of advocacy work against abuse in the Catholic arena, he had seen nearly everything, and his vision wasn't muddied by wishful thinking. So I shared with him about the survivor who had called me up from the convention center raving about the "goody bags" they were giving to survivors. She'd wanted to mail me one, and though I declined, I'd had to bite my tongue to avoid stepping on her emotional high. It felt as though I were listening to someone who'd been starved for years, and when a few moldy crumbs were tossed her way, she'd declared it a feast. That's how it goes with survivors sometimes. Church and denominational officials have treated us so terribly for so long that the smallest concession—even just basic decency—can wind up seeming like progress.

I unloaded on David. "Unless that goody bag has a check in it for all my counseling costs, I can manage just fine without their damned Chapstick and chocolate." David listened, and then with an air of utmost seriousness, he said, "Christa, I really have to disagree with you."

He paused, and I thought maybe I'd gotten myself too riled up. Then he continued. "I think you're way too easy on them. I wouldn't take that goody bag even if it had a check in it. I wouldn't take it unless it had cold hard cash. Because a check? I wouldn't trust them for the time it would take me to get it to the bank. That's how little *I* would trust them."

I laughed and laughed. Not only had David understood my frustration with the "goody bag" lunacy, but he held even more skepticism than me. In that laughter—founded on our joint truth and lived experience—I found fresh ability to carry on.

IT WAS MORE than apparent that the SBC's "bare minimum" of reform would be grossly inadequate, if they implemented it at all. And I had seen the SBC pattern repeat itself too many times: media, followed by promises and platitudes, followed by institutional inertia. Without outside, secular intervention, I believed the mass-scale abuses and hellish maltreatment of survivors would persist. So, only a couple weeks after the June 2022 convention, while many in the SBC were still patting themselves on the back, I renewed my public calls for a "Truth and Justice Commission," urging that the resources of the federal government and of state attorneys general should be brought to bear to investigate sexual abuse, church cover-ups, and institutional enablement in the Southern Baptist Convention. It was something I had previously called for, as far back as 2018. This time, however, someone seemed to hear.

Just a couple of months later, news broke that the United States Department of Justice had initiated an investigation related to sexual abuse within the Southern Baptist Convention. When I learned about it, I voiced my optimism on Twitter, now X: "Today ends with new possibility. Hope. And not just the fluffy, feel-good kind. It's the kick-ass kind."

As I'm finishing up this book, the DOJ investigation is ongoing. Hallelujah for whatever further flowering of truth it may bring.

A YEAR WENT by, and despite all their institutional self-applause, the Southern Baptist Convention added not a single credibly accused pastor to its new clergy abuser database. Not one. It didn't even add the names of pastors with criminal convictions—something that should have been easy. Survivors who had called the SBC's sexual abuse "hotline" contacted me, wondering why they'd been left hanging and why nothing was being done. *Was the "hotline" a sham? Was it just a data-gathering device for the SBC?* SBC leaders acknowledged that, in a year's time, the hotline had received "hundreds of unique submissions," yet they provided no information about who the reported pastors were, whether investigations were in progress, or whether congregations were informed.

I repeatedly urged that SBC officials should at least transfer to the new database all the pastors' names that were on that "secret list" of 703 that the Executive Committee had been forced to release. They didn't. Moreover, less than five months after releasing that secret list, the Executive Committee tried to downplay the horror of it by using its press arm to parse the meaning of "secret." It made about as much sense as saying it was "not a secret list" but rather a list kept secret. Far from owning their wrongs, the Executive Committee was back to its old tricks of spinning and minimizing.

More and more, it looked as though the SBC wasn't even going to do "the bare minimum" they'd proposed; they were just going to talk about it. Leaders spewed platitudes about patience and "not rushing things." They wanted to "get it right," they said—as if more delay added to decades of delay could yield rightness. Some spoke of taking "incremental" steps, apparently oblivious to how, in the face of ongoing immoral harm, incrementalism can be a form of complicity, and combined with hollow assurances of "wait, just wait," it amounts to continued cruelty.

With every vacuous word they spoke, they dug the hole of distrust deeper. And like many, I couldn't help but observe what a puny budget they'd allocated toward abuse reforms, how they were trying to address it on the cheap with volunteers, and how much greater energy they had for fighting their culture wars against women pastors, Critical Race Theory, and "wokeness."

In the end, the SBC Executive Committee stared into the face of its own documented cruelty, and effectively shrugged. Commentators and columnists all over the globe had read the Guidepost report, seen the obvious incivility, inhumanity, misogyny, and deceit, and responded with outrage. But the Executive Committee itself did little more than say "Meh . . . sorry." It made no amends; nor did it impose any consequence, even on itself as an institution.

For the Executive Committee, its reprehensible conduct was a mere blip. But for me, the absence of amends or consequences felt as yet another "You don't matter" message. Far from being a launchpad for accountability, the Guidepost report wound up as one more thing the Executive Committee could thumb its nose at. "See, this is how we can treat you and no one cares." *That* was the unspoken message.

I asked that they impose a nominal measure of accountability on Morris Chapman by stripping him of his honorary "president emeritus" title. Chapman had held top power during many of the years covered by the Guidepost report and had presided over the institution's horrific handling of abuse reports and maltreatment of survivors. Countless kids and congregants could have been spared dreadful harm if only he had acted. That realization haunted me, but apparently, it didn't haunt him or anyone else in Southern Baptist life. Not only did the Executive Committee fail to discipline Chapman, but at their February 2023 meeting, they *applauded* him. It felt as the continuing reverberation of the applause for his duplicitous 2008 speech in which he'd announced that the SBC couldn't possibly keep a clergy abuser database. It was as though the Guidepost report had never happened.

At the SBC's 2023 convention, a draconian, far-right effort at purging women pastors sucked the oxygen from the room. Far from earnestly interrogating how their authoritarian male-headship theology could be enabling abuse and cover-ups, the SBC doubled down on it, as if all their problems could be solved if only women would know their place.

During a break from railing against the evils of women in leadership, SBC officials purported to unveil the website for their new clergy abuser database. With much hoopla, they hyped it as a "historic" moment. But in reality, it was just an empty prototype website—a mock-up a teenager could have done—and it still didn't include a single name of any credibly accused pastor. Not one.

They also backtracked on what they had promised just a year earlier, announcing that whenever pastors' names would start to be added, they would include only those who had already "been convicted, confessed, or found liable in civil court"—in other words, only the easy ones. Since most clergy sex abusers never encounter the justice system—either civil or criminal—and seldom confess, this meant that the vast majority of predatory pastors would continue to remain under the radar.

SBC officials stalled on institutionally disclosing pastors determined to be credibly accused by independent investigation, which is the biggest category of what's needed and what I'd been advocating for since 2006. That still needed "further study," they said.

From the SBC's recalcitrance, you might imagine that holding credibly accused clergy institutionally accountable is something unprecedented. But it's not. Catholic dioceses across the country have, by now, released the names of 6,770 credibly accused clergy, not just those with criminal convictions, civil judgments, or confessions. The Catholic Church is an obviously low bar for addressing clergy sex abuse, yet the Southern Baptist Convention manages to fall far below it.

Thus, the SBC began by promising "the bare minimum" and then did not even fulfill that. Even though the SBC's national entities control about $1.1 billion in unrestricted funds, the SBC couldn't even manage to line up permanent funding or staffing for the database. And the idea of restitution for survivors dropped completely off the table.

To my eyes, it looked like institutional inertia dressed up in a clown costume. Southern Baptist leaders had put their priorities on full display: purge women pastors, placate the base, pull out all stops for institutional image repair, and do as little as possible about clergy sex abuse. But with a PR machine in overdrive, they spun their little bit of nothing as progress, which only seemed like still more gaslighting.

Months later, it came to light that even while SBC officials were putting on a show at this 2023 meeting—with their "we care" publicity schtick and their "historic" launch of an empty shell of a database—behind the scenes, they had filed a "friend of the court" legal brief in a case in which the SBC wasn't even a party, actively arguing *against* laws that would allow child sex abuse survivors to pursue civil justice and *against* the possibility that survivors could sue enabling institutions. The duplicity of it stunned many. The vast chasm between their deeds and their posturing was plain to see.

Not long after that, a former member of the SBC's Sexual Abuse Task Force emailed me with a stunning admission:

> I want to personally apologize if anything I did ever gave you hope for change in the SBC. I see now it was futile, and short of a miracle of God, nothing will change. The system as designed will not allow it.

It was a rare flicker of truth-telling from an SBC insider.

Eventually, maybe by the time this book sees print, I expect SBC officials will indeed stick *some* predatory pastors' names onto their flawed shell of a database. Continuing pressure will compel them. But they will persist in doing as little as possible for as long as possible. And the primary driver will remain the same as it has always been—protecting denominational dollars against liability risks.

When it takes massive media to get even the tiniest of baby steps, and when the pace of progress is so glacial as to resemble inertia, then the inescapable truth is that, institutionally, they really don't care.

This continuing uncaring reality was driven home yet again in August 2023 when the SBC Executive Committee installed a marketing and media professional, Jonathan Howe, as its new interim president, despite the fact that Howe was named in the Guidepost report in an illustration of the hostile culture that clergy sex abuse survivors face in seeking help from SBC leadership. In a 2019 email to another top SBC official, Howe wrote that survivors "just have to be ignored."

MANY SURVIVORS HAVE told me how grateful they are for my work—that my writings validated their own experiences and helped them see more clearly, and that my advocacy showed them they mattered. Some have told me that, even in their silence, they could see me fighting for them. "I'm alive because of you," said more than one.

For all of that, I am glad. But while I feel grateful that others believe I made some difference, and while I've certainly strived to honor the holiness of survivors' lives and traumatic stories, I have also felt the exhausting futility of my efforts at prodding institutional change. And the personal cost has been unfathomable.

Still, it gave me pause when journalist Sarah Stankorb profiled me and summarized my history with these words: "Using just her legal expertise, a Blogspot website and a Twitter account, she was fighting an institution . . . with what was then a $1.2 billion operating budget." That single sentence helped me put things in perspective. I thought about the stupefying odds of it—the holy defiance of it. I have stood as a raised fist in the face of this institution that callously and recklessly decimates so many lives.

When lies, abuses, manipulations, and cover-ups run rampant, then speaking truth becomes a form of resistance. Others see it. Others find their own voices. Others then also speak truth.

When the Religion News Association showed me at number five on their "Top 10 Religion Newsmakers" of 2022 list, I couldn't fathom it.

> **Christa Brown**, whose advocacy for fellow survivors of sexual abuse helped force a reckoning over the Southern Baptist Convention's history of mishandling cases of sexually abusive ministers and of mistreating victims.

I'm a quiet person—an introvert—and yet my name was there with people like Pope Francis, Thich Nhat Hanh, Justice Samuel Alito, and "the Iranian women who led protests against their nation's theocracy." On the one hand, it seemed tragic. We had gathered such massive global media about sexual predations within the SBC that an ordinary person like me wound up on a list like that, and yet the SBC had still barely responded. On the other hand, I know that truth does not reside in the determination of a recalcitrant institution to change or not change. Truth stands on its own as a moral force in the universe.

The Southern Baptist Convention's membership numbers have been in freefall. There are many reasons, but I believe one of them has to do with the wider dissemination of truth about sexual abuse and cover-ups. Maybe it's just coincidence, but the SBC's downward turn began the year I did my first sidewalk press conference outside Southern Baptist headquarters in Nashville. My efforts may have never succeeded in prodding meaningful reform within the SBC, but I hope they have at least contributed to the growing knowledge of the truth about this institution.

Resistance against oppressive forces is energy in the universe that is never wasted. Most days I still believe that. My task has been to bear witness and to speak the truth about the abuses and betrayals of Baptistland.

THE TENTACLES OF the Southern Baptist Convention reach long. Its influence pervades not only all of evangelicalism but also school boards, city councils, and statehouses across the country. As I was finalizing this manuscript, the US House of Representatives elected a Southern Baptist as Speaker. Mike Johnson, widely described as an election denier and Christian nationalist, is now second in line to the presidency. So, no one should underestimate the impact of this faith group's theologies and ideologies.

Yet Baptistland is even broader than the SBC. People who don't go to church at all may still find themselves in Baptistland, because Baptistland is also a belief system that permeates broad swaths of our nation's culture, affecting how we structure our relationships, how we raise our children, and how we view others and ourselves. It is a belief system that implicitly diminishes the inherent worth of human beings.

At its roots, the theology of Baptistland is a theology of domination. It focuses not on human flourishing but on the controlling of human beings through hierarchies of power and oppression. It proclaims as divinely ordered that some should hold dominion over those deemed lesser, and it invokes religion to rationalize categorizations of who should exercise authority and who should submit.

No one should ever forget that the Southern Baptist Convention has its very origins in a grotesquely depraved theology that sanctified the enslavement of human beings, consecrated the Confederacy, and birthed a bloody civil war. Those roots remain, and they continue to feed the branches of Baptistland. As William Faulkner said, "The past is never dead. It's not even past."

Without ever having fully reckoned with *how* the SBC got things so dreadfully wrong on race, Baptistland now uses similar religious rhetoric to legitimize a patriarchal hierarchy that subjugates women to authoritarian male power. Just as its leaders launched biblical proof texts to justify slavery and Jim Crow, they now use biblical proof texts to justify female submissiveness and male "headship." And in Baptistland's culture of unaccountable male clericalism, male pastors are the ones who claim authority to interpret those texts.

These Baptistland tactics of exploiting faith for domination have become more visible in the age of the internet. As more people see the twisted reality of it, more people are repulsed by it. Domination is not love. Domination limits all of us. Domination fosters abuse.

As another survivor said, it is as though Baptistland has encoded in its very DNA "a gene that is desensitized to humans." Baptistland built its wealth and power on the backs of the enslaved and it now protects that wealth and power by crushing the abused.

When religious leaders spend decades covering up the sexual abuse of children, refusing to protect others, and stonewalling survivors, they and their institutions forfeit moral credibility. No matter how much they cower behind proclamations of "biblical worldview," none owe allegiance to their self-serving, power-protective notions of authority and submission. They are the rotten fruit of polluted roots.

I died four times in Baptistland. Each death was, to some degree, derivative of Baptistland's high-control, male-dominant culture: an unaccountable pastor who twisted scripture for child rape, a brother-in-law who no doubt knew I would keep his destabilizing secret rather than risk being blamed, a church and denomination that cared only about silencing *me* rather than protecting others, and a mother who also trusted a pastor and whose guilt for it gave my sisters an excuse for scapegoating.

Through all four of those deaths, and the resurrected lives that followed, both family and church wanted me to be docile, muted, submissive, and deferential. That was my expected role—to not cause trouble—to be compliant. As an adult, it was a role I could not fulfill, a script I refused to follow. I would not sacrifice the self-determination of my own life.

Freedom isn't freedom if all it means is freedom to obey what authoritarian religious leaders proclaim as godly. We must all be free to pursue our own happiness and follow our own path. With the "one wild and precious life" we each hold, I pray we may all find freedom from the constraints of shallow expectations, narrow faiths, and oppressive hierarchies.

25

Into the Beyond

A life of wholeness does not depend on what we experience.
Wholeness depends on how we experience our lives.

—Desmond Tutu

AT THE OCEAN, I often catch sight of the beyond. On sunny days, the whole sea seems a cosmic mirror, reflecting sky and clouds, and stretching outward for infinity. Beyond every wave is another. Beyond every end is a beginning. Sometimes, at the death of day, the sea and sky merge, and moment by moment, they morph into fire.

I've come to see how intertwined they are—life and death—and how death transmogrifies into life. With each of my demises, seeds from the prior life were blown into the next one, where they took root and rebirthed me into a new life, nourished in the dirt and decay of the prior incarnation. Running beneath the soil of *every* incarnation has been the river of trauma that was Baptistland.

With long-term, repetitive sexual abuse in childhood, I know now that I will never be "over it." That is simply the truth; I accept it. In the words of poet Mary Oliver: "The child I was . . . is with me in the present hour" and "it will be with me in the grave."

In the blast radius of the pastor's sexual abuse, relationships disintegrated and my health deteriorated. But while truth-telling carried a heavy cost, it was for me the only way forward—the only way I could become healthy and whole.

My speaking out caused a seismic shift, and I had always imagined that Mom would eventually adjust to the altered terrain. I thought we would find our way back to one another in much the same way that Mom and Judy had eventually reconnected after Judy came out as a lesbian. But of course, I had spoken up for Judy, and none of my sisters had spoken up for me. And time was too short.

People sometimes ask how I can be so forthcoming about my life. It's because I grew up in a "what happened didn't happen" family and in a faith community enmeshed with denial, lies, authoritarianism, and shame. The toxicity of *that* way of life birthed in me an abiding commitment to love and truth-telling.

Sometimes the darkness still sneaks up on me, and I feel again its weight. Out of the blue, I'll feel yanked back out to sea and there's a storm brewing. But I am learning to make peace with the wildness of the sea. I have seen this roiling pattern often enough that when I feel myself going under in the darkness, I take a deep breath and wait for the waves to calm. Eventually, I float back to shore.

I've come to understand that wholeness does not derive from eradicating our wounds, our scars, our traumas; rather, wholeness emerges in the midst of these things.

"LIFE CAN ONLY be understood backwards." That's something Søren Kierkegaard said, and now that I'm older, the truth of it resonates.

I realize how lucky I am. Lots of people wind up with a life that is less than what they imagined in their youth. But perhaps because my imaginings were so limited, I wound up with a life far better than anything I could have contemplated. When I was younger, it wasn't that I imagined possibilities and assumed they were unattainable; rather, it was that it didn't even occur to me to imagine most possibilities. I lacked the capacity.

How did it happen that I wound up with a life beyond what I could have imagined? In significant measure, I think it stemmed from a mother who believed in reading aloud to her young children and a father who chose a house near a library. Books gave me a window to a bigger world.

In looking back, I see distinct times when my life transformed most profoundly: at seventeen when I went off to Germany, at twenty-one when I declined to marry Brad and instead took a job in France, at twenty-six when I rebuffed my mother's assessment that Jim was a dead end and chose to simply trust the love we shared, at twenty-seven when I left a teaching job and moved with Jim back to Austin, at twenty-nine when I rejected my mother's insistence that I could never cut it and launched myself into law school, and at thirty-eight when I catapulted myself into self-employment. All of these were times when I was beset by uncertainty and profoundly humbled by my lack of knowing, by my fear, and by my lack of a path. All of them demanded self-trust and brutal honesty. It was only by stilling myself long enough to see the truth of my own lived experience—and then placing trust in that truth—that I was able to take ownership of my life.

There is so much we don't know about who we are, whom we will encounter, and who we will become. The narrative line is never obvious, and likely doesn't even exist except in our heads. Not knowing is inherently frightening. But in the darkness of uncertainty, I saw the stars afar. My most transformative times were the times of not knowing.

IN THE MONTHS leading up to Stacy and Joe's wedding, I battled a sense of dread. As I fretted over whether to invite my sister Nancy—I didn't—old memories surfaced and the past curled up beside me. I kept trying to shoo it away, but it stayed and my body clutched up. I worried mightily that my distress would put a damper on the wedding celebration, but when the day actually arrived, the ghosts of the past grew smiles and the day held only love.

The wedding was at a small farm on the outskirts of town, and as I ambled around welcoming people, I could feel Mom and Dad's warm presence, so nearly real I could've almost sworn they were there, but absent any feeling of my mother's dismissiveness or my father's rage. It was easy to imagine them—Mom, the extrovert, chatting up the guests, and Dad, the introvert, strolling around, checking out the gardens, and looking up at the Big Dipper.

I can see so much of Mom and Dad in Stacy—the good in them—and it makes me smile.

Stacy carries within her the strength of ancestors who fled famine in Ireland and of others who walked from Tennessee to Texas, in hopes of a better life. A powerful intergenerational legacy of trauma resides in our family, but also an intergenerational legacy of resilience and endurance—ancestors who struggled against enormous odds, leaving behind the known for the unknown. In doing so, they forever altered the trajectory of our family, creating possibilities for their children and grandchildren that they themselves never could have imagined.

I give thanks every day that Stacy was not raised in Baptistland. Some of my childhood friends remain in that world, so I can easily imagine a life trajectory in which I, too, would have stayed. But my experience with religious abuse and authoritarianism propelled me in a different direction. Thank God. Stacy grew up safe from the destructive, misogynistic, fear-filled indoctrination of Baptistland, and so too will her children.

Though some of what I have told here reflects poorly on my family, I know that my existence in this world would not have been possible without the worlds that came before—those of my mother, my father, and my grandparents. We all grow from the roots of our ancestors, like redwood saplings around a charred trunk.

As difficult, slow, and painful as it might be, we must step over and around, to the side, and through the carnage of the past. This is life. This is love. Even with side steps and backward steps, we keep moving forward as we build new families and birth new generations, hoping that all the seeds of goodness in the past will find root in a new season.

I believe the greatest honor we can pay our ancestors is in doing better for the next generation. In that sense, I have tried my best to honor them by working to release the embedded patterns of darkness so that future generations might be freer. I believe my ancestors are cheering—for me, for Stacy, and now also for my grandchildren.

My life has transcended that of my ancestors, just as Stacy's life will transcend mine. I'm old enough that I think about what it means to be an ancestor, and I strive to be a worthy one. But I know that the next part of this intergenerational story will be Stacy's, and she will live it and tell it in her own way.

Stories of love and of family are simultaneously passed along and created in the telling of them. By love, force of will, boundless hope, and also self-deception, stories evolve. Indeed, all the powers of light and dark illuminate and shade the stories we tell to ourselves and to our loved ones. But still the stories continue and evolve because, within each story lies the seed of a different ending, an alternate destiny.

HANGING ON MY wall is a small ceramic daffodil plaque that Aunt Bonnie gave me when I was a kid. Bonnie was Dad's oldest sister, and she lived in a remote house, miles from anything, where she made ceramics with her own kiln. The few times we visited her, I was fascinated as she patiently answered all my questions and showed me everything she was working on. Since then, for over fifty years, I've hung the daffodil plaque in every place I've lived. It reminds me of the kind of women I come from. In the isolation of her home in the middle of nowhere, Bonnie worked to fill her life with beauty.

But there came a time when I was about twelve when we couldn't go see her anymore. Mom told me Dad had gotten into a huge shouting match with Bonnie's husband because Dad "didn't like the way he'd been treating his sister." They "nearly came to blows," Mom said.

"How was he treating her?" I asked.

"Oh, he just hits her sometimes," answered Mom.

Recalling Bonnie, and reaching backwards in time, I ponder the lives of my grandmothers, my mom, and my aunts—generations of women whose lives were circumscribed by violence, abuse, and trauma. All of it trickled into the present. I know that Mom did the best she could, given her life's difficulties and limited resources, but I also know that, with unaddressed trauma, sometimes a parent's "best" isn't enough to support the well-being of children. I don't fault Mom for that any more than I fault her mother or her grandmother. But we have to recognize reality. If we refuse to see the truth of the past, how can we hope to move beyond it?

As journalist Sarah Stankorb once asked: "How does a person, let alone an institution, heal without great, painful residence in the truth?"

The answer for me is that I don't think anyone can—not any person and not any institution. Destructive, multi-generational patterns are not easily broken, and it is likely flat-out impossible without radical and relentless truth-telling. For ourselves, our families, and our institutions, truth-telling can be transformative. But a failure of truth-telling is corrosive.

So many of the women in my family didn't get to have a voice. One grandmother lost all agency to her husband's guardianship and a psychiatric hospital. The other grandmother, by all indications, had all agency removed by being beaten to death. I hold gratitude that I was able to evolve into someone who was able to use my voice. I pray that I have used it well.

I think about the maternal deprivation that Mom must have suffered when, at age ten, her mother was committed to an institution. Then I think of how her mother—my grandmother—was just fourteen when *her* mother died. And when the grief of it all overwhelms me, I conjure the memory of Mom singing an Irish lullaby to Stacy—and it helps.

I wish that, through some magic of physics, I could reverse the natural order of things and mother the mother who so often didn't mother me. It's a crazy thought, but one that stirs compassion to my very core for the mother who so often failed me.

On a camping trip with Jim, I sat mesmerized by a host of fireflies, flashing lights that seemed to come from another dimension. It recalled to me the magical evenings in the backyard at Wichita, when Judy, Nancy, and I would run around in the dark, reveling in the wonder of what we called "lightening bugs," catching them, and putting them in jars. In one flash of a memory's moment, I was there again with my sisters, and in the next moment, I was weeping in the here and now.

I DREAMED OF Mom and Dad. Their presence was so real that, when I first awoke, I could have sworn they were sitting on the edge of the bed, smiling at me. It felt more like a visitation than a dream, and even now, I half-believe they were really there. Dad was in his prime, strong and vigorous, and Mom looked healthy and young, her hair a deep auburn. Their smiles radiated love as they held hands and told me how sad they were about what Rita had done. "We never wanted it to be like that," they said, as I pulled myself up to sitting, stunned at hearing their voices.

Mom began to cry. "Oh, Christa, I wish I had understood. I'm so sorry. I just couldn't say no to her. I don't know why I was so weak. But I never imagined she would take things so far."

I can't remember what I said. Maybe nothing. But I basked in their warmth.

The last thing Mom said was "Tell Stacy we love her." Then they both began to fade even as I reached to clasp their hands and hold them. Jim woke to see me sitting straight up in the bed, leaning forward with my arms outstretched.

I didn't tell Stacy what Mom had said, at least not right away. How could I tell her that I talked with ghosts? Yet, there they were. Even in death, Mom and Dad had both returned to me. It was an extraordinary gift.

I don't know what's on the other side. As Parker Palmer says, "We come from mystery and we return to mystery." That's all I know about what lies beyond. But what I always imagine is that there will be lots of good coffee. And if I'm lucky, I'll sometimes get to sit around a table again with Mom and Dad, sipping our coffee all together and watching the birds under a blue sky and green canopy.

WHENEVER I LOOK at childhood photos, I see the same eyes looking back at me. It's as though I can feel the whole of my life all at once: a little girl cowering in the pantry behind the dried beans, a teenager persuaded by faith to be a "helpmeet" for a predatory pastor, an in-love young woman ready to bolt at any instant, an idealistic law student learning how to be in a place she didn't belong, a mother constantly in awe of her daughter, a passionate appellate attorney arguing high-profile cases with creativity and confidence, and a past-middle-age writer trying to make sense of it all. They all reside in me simultaneously.

I know too well the dark strands of the family I came from. But I also know that, with every passing day, new strands are being woven into the eternal tapestry, bringing new colors and life to the fabric.

I wake in the dark, listening to Jim's breath beside me, and gratitude overwhelms me.

I see the light of love in Stacy and Joe's eyes, and I feel the rightness of the unfolding future.

I hold my grandchildren, and the world seems boundless.

I gasp at the sheer wonder of it all. Love is what makes us resilient.

AFTERWORD: LETTER TO CLERGY SEX ABUSE SURVIVORS

May you always know the truth
And see the light surrounding you.

—Bob Dylan

September 2023

Dear Survivors:

You are always in my heart. Your stories started me on this path, and your stories have inspired and guided me for two decades.

Will recalcitrant faith institutions ever really change?

Survivors often ask me this, and I would give my eyeteeth to be able to tell you that I believe the Southern Baptist Convention is finally reckoning with its clergy sex abuse problem. But I don't see any solid evidence that this is what's happening.

The SBC has had so many opportunities for reckoning, but in the words of Kristin Kobes Du Mez: "How many 'reckonings' can one have before we acknowledge that there is, in fact, no real reckoning to be had?"

That's where I'm at. I don't see genuine institutional repentance or reform. Mostly, I see performative public relations ploys.

My prediction for the Southern Baptist Convention is that it will persist in doing as little as possible and will continue to prioritize the protection of the institution over the protection of kids and congregants. That's not change; that's status quo. I hope my prediction is wrong.

And yes, Southern Baptists are the faith group to which I've directed most of my attention these many years, but I am acutely aware that many of you have traveled this bloody, awful road in *other* faith groups, and in nondenominational churches, with tragically similar patterns. You, too, are in my heart. We're in this together.

All of us deserve so much better. *All* of us. If we wind up building a movement that recognizes only "good survivors"—those who are white, cis, heterosexual, faith-filled in the "right" way, and "nice"—then we will have built it on the same authoritarian theological and ideological foundation that brutalized us.

Skepticism is warranted

With decades of entrenched institutional intransigence and duplicity, and with countless people who have been complicit in such systemic evil, the Southern Baptist Convention has rightly earned our skepticism. I hold to that skepticism without apology. I will look only to what SBC officials actually do and don't do—to expose and name clergy sex abusers, to hold accountable their colleagues who enable this travesty, to tangibly care for clergy abuse survivors, and to make amends for massive harms. Their words are virtually meaningless to me.

It is now *their* burden to *earn* trust, and they can do that only with deeds. They had the benefit of the doubt for decades, and they blew it, decimating countless lives in the process.

I hope you will cultivate your own skepticism, and never underestimate how easily those who hold power can distort the truth.

Where hope resides

My skepticism about the SBC does not mean that I see no hope. Because I do. Hope resides in you and in the truth of your stories.

Every time a survivor understands the truth of their own experience, there is hope. Every time a survivor is able to acknowledge that truth—even if only with friends or family—there is hope. Every time a survivor finds their voice and speaks out, there is hope.

When we tell the truth about something so painful as clergy sex abuse, it can empower us to tell the truth about a lot of other things. Strength grows. It's the kind of strength that brings hope for a different future for each individual, and collectively, with thousands of us, it brings hope for a different future for our children.

A better world is possible—a world in which these horrors will be far less pervasive. I may not see it in my lifetime, but on a good day, I swear I can almost hear that better world breathing.

As more survivors' voices rise, I believe we'll see more changes in statutes of limitation and in civil common law standards, which will allow more survivors to seek justice, not only against perpetrators but also against enabling institutions. These changes will eventually prod reforms within the SBC, because they'll bring more intense outside pressure and they'll cost the institution money. When the SBC sees financial incentives to change, then it will, belatedly and begrudgingly.

The work is slow—generations in the making—but always, survivors are at the forefront of pushing these changes to fruition.

I pray you will never doubt the value, and indeed the sanctity, of your efforts at bringing truth to light. You have faced overwhelming odds and formidable hurdles. I celebrate you—*all* of you. And though you may never see the sort of justice you yearn for—most survivors don't—that does not lessen the nobility of your efforts. What we do matters even if we never know the precise how and when of its mattering.

We survivors are deeply wounded people, but by our very resistance, we give evidence that evil does not wholly prevail and we embody human dignity. How do we resist? By surviving, by thriving, and by using truth to transcend the oppressive power of destructive unaccountable systems such as the SBC.

Transformation always begins with truth-telling, first to ourselves and then to others. Truth-telling holds value across time and it is the foundation for all reform—both individually and institutionally.

In solidarity

In the years that I've been working to shine a light on the SBC's patterns of abuse and cover-ups, my motivations have shifted. Nowadays, the reason I persist has less to do with "speaking truth to power"—because the powerful have long known the truth—and more to do with speaking truth with and for the powerless. I speak truth in solidarity with *you*.

As survivors, so many of us absorbed the lie that sexual abuse inculcates—the lie that says "You are a creature void of value." And we ingested the lie that the faith group's do-nothingness perpetuates—the lie that says "You don't matter." If nothing else, I hope my long persistence in this arena has served to communicate that you DO matter—that your lives, bodies, and spirits are of infinite value.

Even if the fight for clergy accountability is never won, *you* were always worth fighting for.

With you in spirit and truth,

Christa

ACKNOWLEDGMENTS

THANK YOU, BELOVED Jim. You have been my North Star and my companion in all things. For over four decades, the lived truth of your love, support, constancy, and goodness have sustained me and made me braver. Thanks for countless walk-and-talks together, for helping me navigate so many rough trails, for reading draft after draft of this manuscript, and for always being by my side. What an adventure it's been; I would not trade even one second.

Thank you, beloved Stacy. You are the greatest gift of all—a wonder. I am so proud of you.

Thank you, beloveds S, J, D, and H for the infinite joy you bring by your very beings. You are my sunshine.

Thank you, David Clohessy. Before I ever met you, your activism inspired me, and for two decades, you have been an ally and friend. I appreciate your unflinching willingness to stare into the face of what is real and to speak the truth of it. Thanks also for your work as an "alpha reader" and for giving such thoughtful suggestions.

Thank you, Jana Riess. As an editor, you gave advice with insight, compassion, candor, and grace. You made this manuscript so much better, and your words of encouragement kept me going at a time when I was on the verge of trashing it.

Thank you, David Morris and Lake Drive Books for partnering with me on this memoir, and pushing it forward. Thank you for taking a chance on it. And thank you, Ryan Stollar, for introducing me to David.

Thank you, Hannah-Kate. I am so appreciative of how you brook no bullshit from SBC officials and of how you look at the truth of their deeds, not the codswallop of their words. In you, I see the future of this movement for clergy accountability in Baptistland. Godspeed.

Thank you, Dave Pittman. I have bent your ear more times than I can count, and always you have listened and commiserated.

Thank you, Dee Parsons. Not only have you been a wise and trusted listener but you have told many survivors' stories. You gave me a moniker that made me feel proud—"Mother of all abuse bloggers"—and a moniker that made me laugh—"Daughter of Stan." (That's an inside joke stemming from a theobro who was intent on insult but misspelled "Satan.")

Thank you to all the clergy sex abuse survivors who shared their stories with me, both privately and publicly, in pieces big and small. All of you have helped to shift the collective story from endless silencing to voices in chorus.

Thank you to countless friends and advocates on Twitter, now X. Across time and space, your kindness and support have buttressed me on many a crummy day. You help me hold faith in the shared bonds of a caring humanity.

Thank you, Bob Allen. So much of the early history of advocacy efforts in the Southern Baptist Convention would have been lost if not for your journalistic body of work.

Thank you to *Baptist News Global* and its current publisher Mark Wingfield. I am grateful for your long-continuing efforts to document stories of abuse, cover-ups, unaccountability, and malfeasance in the Southern Baptist Convention. Thanks also for giving me a voice in your opinions section.

Thank you to Robert Downen, Liam Adams, Rose French, Peter Smith, Bob Smietana, Rebecca Sherman, Holly Meyer, John Tedesco, Sarah Pulliam Bailey, Adelle Banks, Michelle Boorstein, David Crary, Kate Shellnutt, Mark Kellner, Ruth Graham, Lise Olsen, Frank Lockwood, and so many other journalists who, for years, have worked to understand and document the Southern Baptist Convention's responses and non-responses to clergy sex abuse. Thanks also to the many local and regional reporters who documented clergy sex abuse stories, and in doing so, laid critical groundwork. All of you have furthered the flowering of truth.

Thank you, Boz Tchividjian. Your clarity and candor guided me through some difficult spaces.

Thank you, Sarah Stankorb. What an extraordinary journalist you are! Your work has made a difference and your words made me proud.

Thank you, Faithful America. When you sent me the bound "thank you" book with over five thousand of your members' signatures, I felt your care and it fortified me.

Thank you, Laura Duffy, for putting your creative edge into a fabulous cover design. And thank you to copyeditor Lauren Alexander for keeping order.

Thank you to Jason Hentschel and Wyoming Baptist Church outside Cincinnati. You actively listened and gave me a glimmer of "beloved community."

Thank you to Bruce Springsteen, Melissa Etheridge, the Chicks, Susan Tedeschi, Lucinda Williams, Laura Izibor, Johnny Cash, Bob Dylan, Mary Oliver, Wendell Berry, and many more lyricists and poets, past and present, whose work gave me a soundtrack for processing all the awfulness. You helped get me through.

Thank you to James Cone, Kristin Kobes Du Mez, Miguel De La Torre, Danya Ruttenberg, Judith Herman, Margaret Atwood, Barbara Kingsolver, and countless other writers, past and present, whose words have illumined truth and fought against injustice.

Thank you to the Rocky Mountains. Always, I look to the hills from whence cometh my help.

Thank you to the giant maple tree whose beauty through the seasons brought me respite.

I have been graced ten thousand times over by the goodness of so many who have crossed my path. My heart overflows with gratitude.

Notes

Chapter 2: God Loves You, Christa

In part, this chapter is adapted from my prior memoir, *This Little Light: Beyond a Baptist Preacher Predator and His Gang* (Cedarburg, WI: Foremost Press, 2009).

22. the youth pastor, Tommy Gilmore: Southern Baptist pastor Tommy Gilmore has not been criminally convicted. He has been publicly named on a list of credibly accused sexual abusers compiled by the Southern Baptist Convention's Executive Committee. SBC, "List of Alleged Abusers—SBC," 71, https://www. documentcloud.org/documents/22040155-list-of-alleged-abusers-sbc. And SBC attorney Gene Besen publicly affirmed that "Brown's abuse is well documented and uncontroverted." Sarah Stankorb, "The Southern Baptist Church Ignored Its Abuse Crisis. She Exposed It." *VICE*, January 4, 2023 (naming Gilmore). In addition, Gilmore has been publicly named by numerous news, media, and blogging outlets, including: Robert Downen and John Tedesco, "She Spent Decades Warning Southern Baptists About Abuse. This Week's Revelations Brought 'No Joy,'" *Houston Chronicle*, May 29, 2022; Robert Downen and John Tedesco, "75 Texas Ministers Named on Southern Baptist's Internal List of Offenders," *Houston Chronicle*, May 31, 2022; Nick Papantonis, "Southern Baptist Church Leaders Share Secret List of Ministers Accused of Abusing Kids," *WFTV9-ABC*, May 26, 2022; WSBTV.com News Staff, "At Least 40 Georgia Cases Listed on Southern Baptist Convention's Secret Sex Abuser Database," *WSB-TV*, May 27, 2022, https://web.archive.org/web/20220527164546/https:/ www.wsbtv.com/news/local/least-40-georgia-cases-listed-southern-baptist-churchs-secret-sex-abuser-database/YVSDNF3HVRAZ5J53VSOYYFOKKE/; Ryan Callahan, "More Than 50 Florida Pastors on Southern Baptist Church's List of Alleged Sexual Abusers," *Bradenton Herald*, May 27, 2022; Desiree Stennett, "Former Central Florida Church Leaders Appear on List of Southern Baptist Sex Abusers," *Orlando Sentinel*, May 27, 2022; Victoria Lara, "Southern Baptist Convention List of Accused Sexual Abusers Includes 13 East Texas Cases," *KLTV*, May 27, 2022; Andrea Watson, "38 GA Southern Baptist Pastors 'Credibly Accused' of Sex Abuse: Report," *Patch*, May 31, 2022; "Southwestern Seminary Releases List of 14 Individuals Connected to Sexual Abuse Allegations," *Southwestern Baptist Theological Seminary*, June 1, 2022; Dee Parsons, "Christa Brown Writes an Open Letter to Tommy Gilmore, the SBC Pastor Who Sexually Abused Her," *The Wartburg Watch*, June 7, 2019; Dee Parsons, "Open Letter to

the People of First Baptist Orlando: Do You Know That Tommy Gilmore Molested Me?" *The Wartburg Watch*, July 1, 2020; Harry Bruinius, "With No Verdict, How Survivors of Child Sex Abuse Find Own Sense of Justice," *Christian Science Monitor*, September 18, 2018; Eileen E. Flynn, "Crusader Confronts Baptists on Abuse," *Austin American-Statesman*, June 9, 2008; Bob Allen, "Group Asks Southern Baptist Leaders to Address Clergy Sex Abuse," *Good Faith Media*, February 19, 2007; Mark I. Pinsky, "Lawsuit Charges Sexual Abuse of Teen by Minister," *Orlando Sentinel*, October 22, 2005. Gilmore is also named repeatedly in this book: Sarah Stankorb, *Disobedient Women* (Nashville: Worthy Publishing, 2023), 70–76.

Chapter 5: Vomit-Cleaner

70. committed permanently to a psychiatric hospital: My maternal grandmother spent years as a patient at the Metropolitan State Hospital at Norwalk, a California institution that, in 1975, was made the subject of a documentary film called *Hurry Tomorrow*, showing abusive and dehumanizing practices.

Chapter 11: Mad Dog & Beans

128. Inherent to the trauma of childhood sexual abuse: Child USA, "Delayed Disclosure: A Factsheet Based on Cutting Edge Research on Child Sex Abuse" (Philadelphia, 2020), https://childusa.org/wp-content/uploads/2020/04/Delayed-Disclosure-Factsheet-2020.pdf; Rosaleen McElvaney, "Disclosure of Child Sexual Abuse: Delays, Non-disclosure and Partial Disclosure. What the Research Tells Us and Implications for Practice," *Child Abuse Review* (Dublin, 2013); Elizabeth L. Jeglic, "Why Children Don't Tell Anyone About Sexual Abuse," *Psychology Today*, February 28, 2022.

Chapter 13: Motherhood

157. babies routinely had surgery without anesthesia: *See* Linda Rodriguez McRobbie, "When Babies Felt No Pain," *Boston Globe*, July 29, 2017 ("It wasn't until 1987 that the American Academy of Pediatrics formally declared it unethical to operate on newborns without anesthetics."); Robert Lea, "When Did Doctors Start Using Anesthesia on Babies? Medics Thought They Couldn't Feel Pain," *Newsweek*, September 2, 2021.

Chapter 14: My Law Practice

167. the *Washington Post* described him: Joe Holley, "Personal-Injury Lawyer Pat Maloney Dies at 81," *Washington Post*, September 21, 2005.

Chapter 16: And Charlie Was a Happy Man

196. "That Lucky Old Sun": Haven Gillespie (lyricist) and Beasley Smith (composer), "That Lucky Old Sun," Robbins Music Corporation, 1949 (recorded by vocalist Frankie Laine, Mercury, 1949).

Chapter 18: The Do-Nothing Denomination

Parts of this chapter have been documented more extensively in my prior memoir, *This Little Light: Beyond a Baptist Preacher Predator and His Gang* (Cedarburg, WI: Foremost Press, 2009).

217. fifty-two is the average age: Child USA, "Why Parents Need a 'Window' to Protect their Kids from Sex Abuse" (Philadelphia, 2021), https://childusa.org/wp-content/uploads/2021/10/Parent-Guide-SOL-One-Pagers-10.12.21.pdf.

217. threatened to seek "legal recourse": Letter of Stephen N. Wakefield, Burford & Ryburn, LLP, August 9, 2004; Brown, *This Little Light*, 53; Stankorb, "The Southern Baptist Church Ignored Its Abuse Crisis. She Exposed It."

219. In 2023, when a reporter offered the above summary: Tzach Yoked, "She Was 16 Years Old When a Pastor Took Advantage of Her. She Went on a Crusade," *Haaretz*, January 20, 2023 (translated from Hebrew).

219. Ultimately, from Jimmy Moore: James A. Moore, Affidavit, Cause No. 05-06465 (192nd Judicial District, Dallas County, Texas, 2005).

219. From my childhood church: Mike Floyd (chairman of deacons, First Baptist Church of Farmers Branch), letter to Christa Brown, January 18, 2006. The letter begins: "On behalf of the deacons, the current ministers and the congregation of First Baptist Church of Farmers Branch, I express to you this church's most profound regret for the very serious sexual abuse that we have come to believe our prior youth and education minister, Tommy Gilmore, inflicted on you when you were a girl in the church youth group."

219. From the Baptist General Convention of Texas: Jan Daehnert (director of minister/church relations, Baptist General Convention of Texas), email to Christa Brown re "Confirmation of file listing," December 16, 2004; Bob Allen, "Southern Baptist Leaders Challenged to Get Tough on Sex Abuse by Clergy," *Good Faith Media*, September 27, 2006; Marv Knox, "Churches Must Act to Prevent Clergy Sexual Abuse," *Baptist Standard*, April 22, 2002 ("An accused minister's name may be submitted for inclusion on the list by a duly elected church leader. A case is placed in the file only when a minister (a) confesses to the abuse . . . (b) the minister is legally convicted . . . or (c) 'substantial evidence' points to the minister's guilt."); Brown, *This Little Light*, 61–62.

220. informing eighteen Southern Baptist leaders: Bob Allen, "Newspaper Story on Sexual Abuse in SBC Was a Long Time Coming for Activist Christa Brown," *Baptist News Global*, February 11, 2019; Bob Allen, "SBC to Consider National Clergy Sex-Offender Database," *Good Faith Media*, June 11, 2007; Allen, "Group Asks Southern Baptist Leaders to Address Clergy Sex Abuse."

220. Stanley ignored me: Adelle Banks, "Charles Stanley, TV Preacher & Southern Baptist Leader, Dies at 90," *The Roys Report*, April 18, 2023; Allen, "Group Asks Southern Baptist Leaders to Address Clergy Sex Abuse"; Allen, "Southern Baptist Leaders Challenged to Get Tough on Sex Abuse by Clergy"; Christa Brown, "Clergy Child Molesters Should Not Be Kept Secret: Are We Clear?" *StopBaptistPredators.org*, February 7, 2007; Survivors Network of those Abused by Priests, letter to First Baptist Church of Atlanta, February 6, 2007, https://www.snapnetwork.org/snap_letters/020607_baptist_atlanta.htm.

221. Media attention brought about Gilmore's resignation: Mark I. Pinsky, "Lawsuit Charges Sexual Abuse of Teen by Minister in 1960s," *Orlando Sentinel*, October 22, 2005.

221. "forty-five years in the ministry": Parsons, "Christa Brown Writes an Open Letter to Tommy Gilmore, the SBC Pastor Who Sexually Abused Her."

221. listed as a "church partner": Parsons, "Open Letter to the People of First Baptist Orlando: Do You Know That Tommy Gilmore Molested Me?"

221. He remained a music minister: Parsons, "Christa Brown Writes an Open Letter to Tommy Gilmore, the SBC Pastor Who Sexually Abused Her."

221. I wrote an op-ed column: Christa Brown, "No More Church Secrets About Sex Abuse," *Dallas Morning News*, April 28, 2006.

222. I started writing letters: Brown, *This Little Light*, 148–50; Survivors Network of those Abused by Priests, letter to Dr. Frank Page (president, Southern Baptist Convention), August 2, 2006, http://stopbaptistpredators.org/documents/SBCletter02.pdf; Guidepost Solutions, "Report of the Independent Investigation: The Southern Baptist Convention Executive Committee's Response to Sexual Abuse Allegations and an Audit of the Procedures and Actions of the Credentials Committee" (Washington DC, 2022), 49–50, https://static1.squarespace.com/static/6108172d83d55d3c9db4dd67/t/628a9326312a4216a3c06 79d/1653248810253/Guidepost+Solutions+Independent+Investigation+Report.pdf.

223. urging specific reforms: Anita Wadhwani, "Group Asks Baptists to Form Board to Track Clergy Linked to Abuse," *Tennessean*, September 27, 2006; Allen, "Southern Baptist Leaders Challenged to Get Tough on Sex Abuse by Clergy"; Survivors Network of those Abused by Priests, letter to Dr. Morris Chapman (president, Executive Committee of the Southern Baptist Convention), Dr. Richard Land (president, Ethics & Religious Liberty Commission), and Dr. Frank Page

(president, Southern Baptist Convention), September 26, 2006, https://www. snapnetwork.org/snap_letters/2006_letters/092606_southern_baptist.htm; Guidepost Solutions, "Report of the Independent Investigation," 50–52.

223. first sidewalk press conference: Allen, "Southern Baptist Leaders Challenged to Get Tough on Sex Abuse by Clergy."

223. On behalf of three of the SBC's top offices: Ruth Graham, "Southern Baptists to Release List of Ministers Accused of Sexual Abuse," *New York Times*, May 24, 2022; John Tedesco and Robert Downen, "Southern Baptist Leaders Will Publish Secret List of Sexual Abusers in Response to Scathing Report," *Houston Chronicle*, May 24, 2022; D. August Boto (Executive Committee Southern Baptist Convention), letter to David Clohessy, Christa Brown, and SNAP, September 29, 2006; Guidepost Solutions, "Report of the Independent Investigation," 52–53.

223. The denomination would not exercise: Stankorb, "The Southern Baptist Church Ignored Its Abuse Crisis. She Exposed It" (quoting and paraphrasing SBC's legal counsel: "Had SBC known about her abuse at the time and even now, the Convention cannot 'and will never attempt to exercise any authority over any other Baptist body' . . . even in case of child sex abuse."); Elizabeth Ulrich, "The Bad Shepherd," *Nashville Scene*, April 24, 2008 (SBC legal counsel says, "If we knew anything about it, we could not have provided any relief or prevention."); Bob Allen, "SBC Leaders Recommend Against National Database of Clergy Sex Offenders," *Good Faith Media*, June 11, 2008.

224. a phony excuse for inaction: Robert Parham, "Dismantle False Wall of Church Autonomy That Protects Child Predator Preachers," *Good Faith Media*, April 9, 2007.

224. one man literally chortled and another: Guidepost Solutions, "Report of the Independent Investigation," 57; Brown, *This Little Light*, 176–77; Stankorb, *Disobedient Women*, 77; Stankorb, "The Southern Baptist Church Ignored Its Abuse Crisis. She Exposed It."

224. But even as they treated me terribly: Guidepost Solutions, "Report of the Independent Investigation," Appendix D1, 34 ("Minutes of the SBC Executive Committee Bylaws Workgroup, February 2007").

228. In her groundbreaking book: Judith Herman, *Trauma and Recovery* (New York: Hachette, 1992), 1.

230. Baptist General Convention of Texas stopped keeping its file: Ken Camp, "Texas Baptists respond to clergy sex abuse," *Baptist Standard*, February 13, 2019.

230. the Baptist problem was more about: *See also* Robert Parham, "Catholics and Baptists Have Different Sacraments but Similar Child Abuse Scandals," *Good Faith Media*, April 4, 2010 (quoting Cal Thomas, who wrote that the sex scandals in Catholicism and Protestantism were different because, in Protestantism, the scandals were "between consenting adults").

230. Associated Press had gathered insurance data: Associated Press, "Data Shed Light on Child Sexual Abuse by Protestant Clergy," *New York Times*, June 16, 2007; Boz Tchividjian, "'Spotlight': It's Not Just a Catholic Problem," *Religion News Service*, December 7, 2015.

231. ABC *20/20* episode on "Preacher-Predators": ABC News, "Preachers Accused of Sins, and Crimes," *ABC News*, April 13, 2007; Bob Allen, "'20/20' Airs Report on Predator Preachers," *Good Faith Media*, April 13, 2007.

231. voted to instruct the SBC Executive Committee: Guidepost Solutions, "Report of the Independent Investigation," 62; Carla Hinton, "Pastor urges predator database," *The Oklahoman*, June 13, 2007; Elizabeth Ulrich, "What Would Jesus Say?" *Nashville Scene*, February 14, 2008.

231. no one bothered to bird-dog: Guidepost Solutions, "Report of the Independent Investigation," 63; Bob Allen, "SNAP Calls for 'Open and Transparent' Study of Sex Abuse by Clergy," *Good Faith Media*, September 18, 2007.

231. never even a budget: Ulrich, "What Would Jesus Say?"

231. Chapman stood before thousands: Allen, "SBC Leaders Recommend Against National Database of Clergy Sex Offenders"; Elizabeth Ulrich, "Save Yourselves," *Nashville Scene*, June 19, 2008.

232. in the next breath, he declared: Eric Gorski (AP), "Southern Baptists reject sex-abuse database," *Washington Post*, June 10, 2008; Ulrich, "Save Yourselves"; ABPNews, "SBC Officials Reject Idea of Sex-Offender Database," *Baptist News Global*, June 10, 2008.

232. Even Burleson: Adelle Banks, "Southern Baptists Elect President, Dismiss Abuse Database," *Religion News Service*, June 11, 2008; ABPNews, "SBC Officials Reject Idea of Sex-Offender Database."

232. SBC attorneys had specifically told: Sarah Pulliam Bailey and Michelle Boorstein, "Southern Baptist leaders say they will release list of alleged sex abusers," *Washington Post*, May 24, 2022.

Chapter 19: Hateful Faith

237. A public relations staffer: Robert Parham, "Does EthicsDaily.com Matter?" *Good Faith Media*, November 19, 2007.

238. it was Paige Patterson: Bob Allen, "SBC Seminary President Labels Clergy Sex-Abuse Victims' Group 'Evil-Doers,'" *Good Faith Media*, February 15, 2008; Ulrich, "What Would Jesus Say?"; Bob Allen, "SNAP Leaders Ask Patterson to Apologize for 'Evil-Doers' Remark," *Good Faith Media*, February 22, 2008; Stankorb, *Disobedient Women*, 78.

238. we had written to the seminary's trustees: Bob Allen, "SNAP Calls for Suspension, Investigation of Seminary President's Link to Accused Predator," *Good Faith*

Media, January 10, 2008; Ulrich, "What Would Jesus Say?"; Survivors Network of those Abused by Priests, "Clergy Sex Abuse Victims Want Seminary Head Ousted," January 9, 2008, http://stopbaptistpredators.org/press/southwestern_baptist_theological_seminary.html; David Bumgardner, "29-Page Memorandum Illustrates What the SBC Sexual Abuse Task Force Is Hearing," *Baptist News Global*, February 2, 2022.

238. trustees finally fired Patterson: Sarah Pulliam Bailey, "Southern Baptist seminary drops bombshell: Why Paige Patterson was fired," *Washington Post*, June 1, 2018.

238. "nothing more than opportunistic persons": Bob Allen, "SBC President Labels Sexual Abuse Critics 'Opportunists,'" *Good Faith Media*, April 20, 2007; Frank Page, "Guarding Against Sexual Abuse in the Church," *Florida Baptist Witness*, April 19, 2007, https://web.archive.org/web/20070824234751/https:/www.floridabaptistwitness.com/7229.article; Guidepost Solutions, "Report of the Independent Investigation," 59; Stankorb, *Disobedient Women*, 78.

239. a "morally inappropriate relationship": Jonathan Merritt, "In a #MeToo Moment, Will Southern Baptists Hold Powerful Men Accountable?" *Washington Post*, April 30, 2018; Holly Meyer, "Frank S. Page, Top Southern Baptist Leader, Resigns Due to 'Morally Inappropriate' Relationship,'" *Tennessean*, March 27, 2018; Bob Allen, "Southern Baptist Leader Steps Down Over Moral 'Indiscretion,'" *Baptist News Global*, March 28, 2018.

239. Page went on to pastor: Holly Meyer, "Top Southern Baptist Leader Finds New Church After Resigning Over Inappropriate Relationship," *Tennessean*, February 14, 2020.

239. Still another former SBC president: Allie Martin and Jenni Parker, "Former SBC president encourages local churches to prevent sexual abuse," *OneNewsNow*, February 28, 2007 (*see also* https://www.bishop-accountability.org/news2007/03_04/2007_02_28_Martin_FormerSBC.htm); Brown, *This Little Light*, 178–79.

239. And the *Baptist Press*: Staff, "SNAP apologizes to SBC Leaders, Admits Charges of 'Silence' Were 'Erroneous,'" *Baptist Press*, February 23, 2007; Guidepost Solutions, "Report of the Independent Investigation," 58; Stankorb, *Disobedient Women*, 78. Fifteen years after this *Baptist Press* smear, SBC official Jonathan Howe emailed me that *Baptist Press* was going to take down the 2007 story because it was an "error in judgment" and did not "represent what we desire to be as a news outlet." Immediately, I emailed back, requesting that the story stay up for the world to see, but with a statement added to the top acknowledging how wrong it was. I also informed Howe that I thought calling it an "error in judgment" was minimizing of what was done. *Baptist Press* then left the original article up with the addition of a May 24, 2022 "Editor's Note" stating, "We do not believe this story accurately represents the events . . . and does not meet our current journalistic standards." *See also* Brandon Porter, "First-Person: *Baptist Press* Makes Corrections to

Abuse-Related Stories, Issues Apology to Those Affected," *Baptist Press*, June 10, 2022.

239. SBC Executive Committee member maligned me: Guidepost Solutions, "Report of the Independent Investigation," 63; Bob Allen, "Clergy Sex-Abuse Survivor Questions Fairness of SBC Executive Committee Study," *Good Faith Media*, September 21, 2007; Ruth Graham and Elizabeth Dias, "Southern Baptist Leaders Mishandled Sex Abuse Crisis, Report Alleges," *New York Times*, May 22, 2022.

239. the most aggressive public scorn: Sarah Stankorb, "Reformers Notch a 'Fragile' Victory at Southern Baptist Convention Elections," *New Republic*, June 15, 2022; *see also* Stankorb, "The Southern Baptist Church Ignored Its Abuse Crisis. She Exposed It." ("Among their biggest targets was Christa Brown.")

239. a letter from an SBC insider: Sarah Einselen, "Southern Baptist Pastors Demand Investigation in Wake of New Russell Moore Letter," *The Roys Report*, June 7, 2021; Sarah Pulliam Bailey, "Newly Leaked Letter Details Allegations That Southern Baptist Leaders Mishandled Sex Abuse Claims," *Washington Post*, June 5, 2021; Stankorb, "The Southern Baptist Church Ignored Its Abuse Crisis. She Exposed It."

239. And an internal email: Sarah Einselen, "Former SBC Leader Says Abuse Survivor Advocates Are Part of 'Satanic Scheme' to Derail Evangelism," *The Roys Report*, June 8, 2021; Mark Wingfield, "SBC Executive Committee Declines to Entertain the Idea of Broadening the Scope of Its Investigation of Itself," *Baptist News Global*, June 14, 2021.

Chapter 21: Cancer

255. Data from a large-scale epidemiological study: Jane Stevens, "Traumatic Childhood Takes 20 Years Off Life Expectancy," *Lawrence Journal-World*, October 6, 2009; Carina Storrs, "Is Life Expectancy Reduced by a Traumatic Childhood?" *Scientific American*, October 7, 2009; Vincent J. Felitti, Robert F. Anda, et al., "Relationship of Childhood Abuse and Household Dysfunction to Many of the Leading Causes of Death in Adults," *American Journal of Preventive Medicine* 14 (May 1998); Joseph Brownstein, "Childhood Trauma May Shorten Life by 20 Years," *ABC News*, October 5, 2009.

Chapter 24: The Do-the-Bare-Minimum Denomination

286. the overwhelming majority of Southern Baptists: Sarah Pulliam Bailey, "White Evangelicals Voted Overwhelmingly for Donald Trump, Exit Polls Show," *Washington Post*, November 9, 2016; Justin Nortey, "Most White Americans Who

Regularly Attend Worship Services Voted for Trump in 2020," Pew Research Center, August 30, 2021.

286. who bragged about assaulting women: "Transcript: Donald Trump's Taped Comments About Women," *New York Times*, October 8, 2016 (On the *Access Hollywood* tape, Donald Trump said: "I just start kissing them . . . I don't even wait. And when you're a star, they let you do it. You can do anything . . . Grab 'em by the pussy. You can do anything.")

287. With an identity and beliefs rooted in an authoritarian theology: Sarah Posner, "The Southern Baptist Convention's Deal with the Devil," *The Nation*, September 12, 2022.

287. helped lay a foundation for the work of others: Stankorb, *Disobedient Women*, 249 (observing that many of the names on the SBC Executive Committee's secret list of abusers, released in 2022, "came from Brown's blog, *Stop Baptist Predators*"); *see e.g., BaptistAccountability.org*, crediting Christa Brown's work as the foundation and inspiration for their own database, https://baptistaccountability.org/about-us/; *see e.g.*, Andrew Denney, Kent Kerley, and Nickolas Gross, "Child Sexual Abuse in Protestant Christian Congregations: A Descriptive Analysis of Offense and Offender Characteristics," *Religions* 9, no. 1 (January 2018): 4, https://doi.org/10.3390/rel9010027 (stating that StopBaptistPredators.org was one of three websites it used for gathering its data).

287. the "Abuse of Faith" series: Robert Downen, Lise Olsen, and John Tedesco, "Abuse of Faith," *Houston Chronicle*, February 10, 2019.

287. more than 400 Southern Baptist church leaders: Downen and Tedesco, "She Spent Decades Warning Southern Baptists About Abuse. This Week's Revelations Brought 'No Joy'"; Ruth Graham, "Southern Baptists to Release List of Ministers Accused of Sexual Abuse," *New York Times*, May 24, 2022.

287. confirmed my own prior work: Stankorb, *Disobedient Women*, 198–99; Allen, "Newspaper Story on Sexual Abuse in SBC Was a Long Time Coming for Activist Christa Brown."

287. the series implicated high-level Southern Baptist leaders: Robert Downen, Lise Olsen, and John Tedesco, "20 Years, 700 Victims: Southern Baptist Sexual Abuse Spreads as Leaders Resist Reforms," *Houston Chronicle*, February 10, 2019.

288. SBC Executive Committee member had written me: David Bumgardner, "29-page Memorandum Illustrates What the SBC Sexual Abuse Task Force Is Hearing," *Baptist News Global*, February 2, 2022 ("Wilson stated that he checked Brown's website daily . . ."); Christa Brown, "Memorandum to Guidepost Solutions: Sexual Abuse and SBC Executive Committee Actions and Inactions," October 25, 2021, https://christabrown.files.wordpress.com/2021/11/guidepost-memorandum.pdf.

288. even for fundraising: Bob Allen, "Abuse Survivors Cry Foul Over ERLC's End-of-Year Fund-Raising Appeal," *Baptist News Global*, December 18, 2019.

288. "Caring Well" conference: Robert Downen, "Southern Baptist Group Overhauls National Conference to Focus on Sex Abuse Crisis," *Houston Chronicle*, May 1, 2019.

288. Greear promised "bold steps": Carol Kuruvilla, "Southern Baptists Share Strategic Plan to Address Sexual Abuse," *Huffington Post*, February 19, 2019; Meredith Flynn, "Greear Urges 'Bold' Steps to Prevent Abuse, Care for Survivors," *Illinois Baptist*, February 18, 2019; David Roach, "Greear Announces Sexual Abuse Study Group," *Baptist Press*, July 26, 2018.

288. an SBC attorney "reached out": Dee Parsons, "Another SBC/ERLC Dopey Move: Their Attorney Appears to be Contacting Victims," *The Wartburg Watch*, January 17, 2020.

288. Instead, I went to Birmingham: Stankorb, *Disobedient Women*, 201; Bob Allen, "Abuse Victim Advocates Pledge to Keep Fighting for Reform in the Southern Baptist Convention," *Baptist News Global*, June 12, 2019.

289. Just days before Birmingham: Parsons, "Christa Brown Writes an Open Letter to Tommy Gilmore, the SBC Pastor Who Sexually Abused Her."

290. I publicly called for a federal investigation: Christa Brown, "Justice for SBC Sexual Abuse Victims: A Call for an Investigatory Commission," *Religion News Service*, May 20, 2021; Guidepost Solutions, "Report of the Independent Investigation," 121 (noting this sequence of events).

290. a couple leaked letters: Paul O'Donnell and Bob Smietana, "Leaked Russell Moore Letter Blasts SBC Conservatives, Sheds Light on His Resignation," *Religion News Service*, June 2, 2021; Religion News Service, "Russell Moore to ERLC Trustees: 'They Want Me to Live in Psychological Terror,'" *Religion News Service*, June 2, 2021; Sarah Pulliam Bailey, "Newly Leaked Letter Details Allegations That Southern Baptist Leaders Mishandled Sex Abuse Claims," *Washington Post*, June 5, 2021; Sarah Einselen, "Southern Baptist Pastors Demand Investigation in Wake of New Russell Moore Letter," *The Roys Report*, June 7, 2021. As an off-beat note, Russell Moore even suggested that the SBC put up a statue of me in Nashville as "the abuse survivor who spent the past two decades fighting for reform." Sarah Pulliam Bailey, "Southern Baptist Leaders Covered Up Sex Abuse, Kept Secret Database, Report Says," *Washington Post*, May 22, 2022.

291. a twenty-nine-page, single-spaced memorandum: Christa Brown, "Memorandum to Guidepost Solutions: Sexual Abuse and SBC Executive Committee Actions and Inactions," October 25, 2021, https://christabrown.files.wordpress.com/2021/11/guidepost-memorandum.pdf; David Bumgardner, "29-page Memorandum Illustrates What the SBC Sexual Abuse Task Force Is Hearing," *Baptist News Global*, February 2, 2022.

291. Guidepost released its report: Guidepost Solutions, "Report of the Independent Investigation: The Southern Baptist Convention Executive Committee's Response to Sexual Abuse Allegations and an Audit of the Procedures and Actions of the Credentials Committee," Guidepost Solutions (Washington DC, 2022), https://static1.squarespace.com/static/6108172d83d55d3c9db4dd67/t/628a9326312a4216a3c0679d/1653248810253/Guidepost+Solutions+Independent+Investigation+Report.pdf; Deepa Bharath, Holly Meyer, and David Crary, "Report: Top Southern Baptists Stonewalled Sex Abuse Victims," *Associated Press*, May 23, 2022; Graham and Dias, "Southern Baptist Leaders Mishandled Sex Abuse Crisis, Report Alleges"; Kate Shellnutt, "Southern Baptists Refused to Act on Abuse, Despite Secret List of Pastors," *Christianity Today*, May 22, 2022; David French, "The Southern Baptist Horror," *The Atlantic*, May 23, 2022; Robert Downen, "Important Details You Might Have Missed from the New Southern Baptist Sex Abuse Report," *Houston Chronicle*, May 23, 2022; Bob Smietana, "Southern Baptist Leaders Mistreated Abuse Survivors for Decades, Report Says," *Religion News Service*, May 22, 2022; Liam Adams, "'Ignored, Disbelieved': Southern Baptist Convention Sexual Abuse Report Details Cover Up, Decades of Inaction," *Tennessean*, May 22, 2022.

291. "And then they lied about her": Downen and Tedesco, "She Spent Decades Warning Southern Baptists About Abuse. This Week's Revelations Brought 'No Joy.'"

291. one journalist described me: Talia Lavin, "Hopeless and Hopeful," *The Sword and the Sandwich*, May 31, 2022, https://theswordandthesandwich.substack.com/p/hopeless-and-hopeful.

292. The Guidepost report validated: Downen and Tedesco, "She Spent Decades Warning Southern Baptists About Abuse. This Week's Revelations Brought 'No Joy.'"

292. "some senior SBC leaders had protected": Bailey, "Southern Baptist Leaders Covered Up Sex Abuse, Kept Secret Database, Report Says."

292. "singularly focused on avoiding liability": Guidepost Solutions, "Report of the Independent Investigation," 3.

292. a choice with a profound human cost: Downen and Tedesco, "She Spent Decades Warning Southern Baptists About Abuse. This Week's Revelations Brought 'No Joy'"; Graham and Dias, "Southern Baptist Leaders Mishandled Sex Abuse Crisis, Report Alleges"; Susan Shaw, "Sexual Abuse in the Southern Baptist Convention Points to Subordination of Women and Girls," *Ms. Magazine*, June 6, 2022.

292. It was something I had long suspected: Ulrich, "The Bad Shepherd" ("Brown . . . says Guenther's statement implicitly suggests that the SBC must have some sort of internal system of tracking reports of clergy sexual abuse. . . . 'If people knew

that they actually kept track of this stuff—did nothing, but nevertheless kept some little record—I think people would insist on some action.'")

292. compiling a list of sexual abusers: SBC, "List of Alleged Abusers—SBC"; *see also* Willie McLaurin and Rolland Slade, SBC Executive Committee, "A Statement on the Release of a List of Alleged Abusers," May 26, 2022, https://www.sbc.net/on-the-release-of-a-list-of-alleged-abusers/; Graham, "Southern Baptists to Release List of Ministers Accused of Sexual Abuse"; David Bumgardner, "SBC Executive Committee Releases Previously Secret List of Convicted and Credibly Accused Church Sexual Abusers," *Baptist News Global*, May 26, 2022.

292. "to avoid the possibility of getting sued": Bailey, "Southern Baptist Leaders Covered Up Sex Abuse, Kept Secret Database, Report Says"; Guidepost Solutions, "Report of the Independent Investigation," 3 (Senior Executive Committee leaders were "singularly focused on avoiding liability for the SBC.").

292. SBC leaders had "lied": Bailey, "Southern Baptist Leaders Covered Up Sex Abuse, Kept Secret Database, Report Says."

293. SBC officials had taken no action: Guidepost Solutions, "Report of the Independent Investigation," 5; Bharath, Meyer, and Crary, "Report: Top Southern Baptists Stonewalled Sex Abuse Victims."

293. Immediately, I demanded: Stankorb, *Disobedient Women*, 249; Deepa Bharath, Holly Meyer, and David Crary, "Southern Baptists Face Push for Public List of Sex Abusers," *Associated Press*, May 23, 2022; Stankorb, "The Southern Baptist Church Ignored Its Abuse Crisis. She Exposed It."

293. SBC officials did so: Tedesco and Downen, "Southern Baptist Leaders Will Publish Secret List of Sexual Abusers in Response to Scathing Report"; Bailey and Boorstein, "Southern Baptist Leaders Say They Will Release List of Alleged Sex Abusers"; Liam Adams, "Southern Baptist Convention Leaders Decide to Release Long-Secret List of Accused Ministers," *Tennessean*, May 24, 2022. In these few days when the SBC Executive Committee was agreeing to publish its secret list, it's worth noting that the Executive Committee also repudiated Augie Boto's 2006 statement to me that "discourse between us will not be positive or fruitful." Sixteen years after the fact, and in the face of massive media pressure, the SBC Executive Committee finally issued a new statement saying that it "rejects this sentiment in its entirety and seeks to publicly repent for its failure to rectify this position and wholeheartedly listen to survivors." The hostile 2006 statement was also made on behalf of the SBC's Ethics & Religious Liberty Commission and the SBC president, but these offices have made no repudiation of it.

293. "Reams of gruesome abuses were known": Stankorb, "The Southern Baptist Church Ignored Its Abuse Crisis. She Exposed It."

293. Many of the entries: Stankorb, *Disobedient Women*, 249.

293. Tommy Gilmore's name was there: Robert Downen and John Tedesco, "75 Texas Ministers Named on Southern Baptist's Internal List of Offenders," *Houston Chronicle*, May 31, 2022; Stankorb, *Disobedient Women*, 249–50; Papantonis, "Southern Baptist Church Leaders Share Secret List of Ministers Accused of Abusing Kids"; Ryan Callahan, "More Than 50 Florida Pastors on Southern Baptist Church's List of Alleged Sexual Abusers," *Bradenton Herald*, May 27, 2022; Desiree Stennett, "Former Central Florida Church Leaders Appear on List of Southern Baptist Sex Abusers," *Orlando Sentinel*, May 27, 2022; Andrea Watson, "38 GA Southern Baptist Pastors 'Credibly Accused' of Sex Abuse: Report," *Patch*, May 31, 2022.

293. yet another committee: Stankorb, *Disobedient Women*, 251; Stankorb, "The Southern Baptist Church Ignored Its Abuse Crisis. She Exposed It."; Kate Shellnutt, "Southern Baptists Prep for Annual Meeting with Heavy Hearts, Cautious Hope," *Christianity Today*, June 10, 2022; Mark A. Kellner, "Abuse Survivors Call for More Action Than Proposed by Southern Baptists' Task Force," *Washington Times*, June 5, 2022.

293. voted for the creation of a public database: Deepa Bharath and Peter Smith, "Southern Baptists Agree to Keep List of Accused Sex Abusers," *Associated Press*, June 14, 2022.

293. some who genuinely wanted: No doubt there are good and well-intentioned individuals within the Southern Baptist Convention—people who sincerely want their faith group to do the right thing. Indeed, I believe the public relations efforts of SBC officials are, in part, oriented toward placating these good people in the pews with the illusion that the SBC is doing right. However, despite the good intentions of some individuals, when I look at what is actually done by the institution, I feel only dismay.

293. In design, their proposed database: Christa Brown, "Devil in the Details: The SBC and Sexual Abuse Reforms," *Good Faith Media*, August 2, 2022; Christa Brown, "What Southern Baptists Must Do Now to Address Clergy Sex Abuse," *Baptist News Global*, June 6, 2022; David Clohessy and Christa Brown, "Progress on Sexual Abuse in the SBC? Not So Fast," *Baptist News Global*, June 24, 2022.

294. "the bare minimum of what can be called reform": Bharath and Smith, "Southern Baptists Agree to Keep List of Accused Sex Abusers"; Rich McKay, "U.S. Southern Baptist Convention Tackles Sex Abuse at Annual Assembly," *Reuters*, June 15, 2022; Kate Shellnutt, "After Annual Meeting, Southern Baptists Begin the Hard Work of Abuse Reform," *Christianity Today*, June 17, 2022; Mark A. Kellner, "Southern Baptists Vote 'Bare Minimum' Steps Dealing With Sexual Abuse," *Washington Times*, June 14, 2022.

294. seemed orchestrated: *See* Stankorb, *Disobedient Women*, 250 (describing the "nearly inescapable praise music" and the "*awesome awesome awesome God* harmonies").

294. resolution "on lament and repentance for sexual abuse": ERLC Staff, "Key Resolutions from the 2022 SBC Annual Meeting," Ethics & Religious Liberty Commission of the Southern Baptist Convention, June 17, 2022, https://erlc.com/resource-library/articles/key-resolutions-from-the-2022-sbc-annual-meeting/; Stankorb, *Disobedient Women*, 252.

294. Barber claimed the substitution: Erin Roach, "Guidance in Lament Resolution Was 1 Corinthians 5, Barber Says," *Biblical Recorder*, June 21, 2022, https://www.brnow.org/news/guidance-in-lament-resolution-was-1-corinthians-5-barber-says/.

294. I was bereft: Christa Brown, "Skepticism Holds Seeds of Hope: The SBC and Clergy Sex Abuse," *Baptist News Global*, August 12, 2022; Mark A. Kellner, "Southern Baptist Panel Buries Compensation Demands in Recommendations to June Business Session," *Washington Times*, June 1, 2022; Bob Smietana, "Southern Baptist Abuse Task Force Requests $3 Million for Reforms, 'Ministry Check' Website," *Religion News Service*, June 1, 2022; Shellnutt, "After Annual Meeting, Southern Baptists Begin the Hard Work of Abuse Reform."

295. thousands of names on petitions: Faithful America and UltraViolet gathered more than twenty thousand signatures on petitions, urging the specific reforms many survivors sought and saying, "We stand with Christa Brown. Support SBC abuse survivors." https://act.weareultraviolet.org/sign/SBC_Survivors/?t=6&referring_akid=51380.626109.dh_ADp https://act.faithfulamerica.org/sign/sbc-reform/

296. renewed my public calls for a secular "Truth and Justice Commission": Clohessy and Brown, "Progress on sexual abuse in the SBC? Not so fast"; Bharath and Smith, "New SBC President Commits to Move Sex Abuse Reforms Forward."

296. It was something I had previously called for: Christa Brown, "Justice for SBC Sexual Abuse Victims: A Call for an Investigatory Commission," *Religion News Service*, May 20, 2021; David Clohessy and Christa Brown, "Clergy Sex Abuse: Why a National All-Faiths Inquiry Is Needed," *Religion News Service*, November 15, 2018; Stankorb, *Disobedient Women*, 254.

296. United States Department of Justice had initiated an investigation: Mark A. Kellner, "Justice Department Opens Sex Abuse Investigation into Southern Baptists," *Washington Times*, August 12, 2022; Holly Meyer and David Crary, "Southern Baptists Say Denomination Faces DOJ Investigation," *Associated Press*, August 12, 2022; Liam Adams, "What It Means for the Southern Baptist Convention to be Under Federal Investigation for Abuse," *Tennessean*, August 15, 2022; Anna Beahm, "'Long believed the day would come': Survivors Rejoice at News of Federal SBC Sex Abuse Probe," *Reckon*, August 16, 2022; Stankorb, *Disobedient Women*, 254–55.

296. "Today ends with new possibility": Christa Brown (@ChristaBrown777), X (formerly Twitter), August 12, 2022, https://twitter.com/ChristaBrown777/status/1558312583551062016.

296. added not a single credibly accused pastor: Christa Brown, "SBC Annual Meeting Reveals Little Progress on Sexual Abuse, Not Even 'Bare Minimum,'" *Baptist News Global*, June 16, 2023; Bob Smietana, "Southern Baptists Reaffirm Commitment to Abuse Reforms, Preview Database of Abusers," *Religion News Service*, June 14, 2023 (stating that "all the names to be added to the site are still being vetted").

296. SBC's sexual abuse "hotline": Christa Brown, "What We Know and Don't Know About the SBC's Sexual Abuse Hotline," *Baptist News Global*, February 10, 2023.

296. hotline had received "hundreds of unique submissions": Christa Brown and David Clohessy, "Five Things Southern Baptists Should Do Now to Address Clergy Sex Abuse," *Baptist News Global*, May 24, 2023.

296. urged that SBC officials should at least transfer: Brown and Clohessy, "Five Things Southern Baptists Should Do Now to Address Clergy Sex Abuse."

296. using its press arm to parse the meaning of "secret": Brandon Porter, "SBC President Bart Barber Featured on CBS' 60 Minutes," *Baptist Press*, October 9, 2022. It's worth noting that this was not the only way in which Southern Baptist leaders attempted to downplay the findings of the Guidepost report. *See* Kristin Kobes Du Mez, "Is This a Reckoning?" *Du Mez Connections*, June 3, 2022.

297. fighting their culture wars: Stankorb, "Reformers Notch a 'Fragile' Victory at Southern Baptist Convention Elections"; Bob Smietana, "Anti-woke Preachers Voddie Baucham and Tom Ascol to be Nominated as SBC Leaders," *Religion News Service*, March 22, 2022.

297. Commentators and columnists: *E.g.,* Michael Gerson, "The Report on Southern Baptist Abuses Is a Portrait of Brutal Misogyny," *Washington Post*, May 23, 2022.

297. It made no amends: Some might point to the SBC Executive Committee's settlement of a lawsuit as "amends." I do not consider it so. The SBC Executive Committee settled a viable legal claim brought by a single survivor and then used that strategic legal decision for its own public relations purposes, claiming their "bold and compassionate action" constituted "an intentional demonstration that we care for sexual abuse survivors (plural)." *See* Brandon Porter, "SBC Executive Committee Approves Resolution with Sexual Abuse Survivor," *Baptist Press*, February 22, 2022. And my response: Christa Brown (@ChristaBrown777), X (formerly Twitter), February 22, 2022, https://twitter.com/ChristaBrown777/status/1496278405456838667.

297. stripping him of his honorary: Brown and Clohessy, "Five Things Southern Baptists Should Do Now to Address Clergy Sex Abuse."

297. had presided over the institution's horrific handling: Kate Shellnutt, "Southern Baptists Refused to Act on Abuse, Despite Secret List of Pastors," *Christianity Today*, May 22, 2022.

297. they *applauded* him: Mark Wingfield, "Want to Understand Why the SBC Expelled Its Largest Church? Listen to W.A. Criswell," *Baptist News Global,* February 21, 2023.

298. draconian far-right effort at purging women pastors: Brown, "SBC Annual Meeting Reveals Little Progress on Sexual Abuse, Not Even 'Bare Minimum'"; Susan Shaw, "Southern Baptists Consider Women's Leadership a 'Threat,'" *Ms. Magazine,* July 6, 2023; Ruth Graham and Elizabeth Dias, "Southern Baptists Vote to Further Expand Restrictions on Women as Leaders," *New York Times,* June 14, 2023.

298. authoritarian male-headship theology: Stankorb, *Disobedient Women,* 255 (quoting me: "Authoritarian male-headship theology" welded together with a lack of accountability "is a Frankenstein monster that inflicts enormous harm"); Scott C. Ryan, "On Russell Moore's 'Apocalyptic' Moment for the Southern Baptist Convention," *Baptist News Global,* June 2, 2022.

298. hyped it as a "historic" moment: David Roach, "Sex Abuse Reforms 'Historic,' Task Force Says," *Baptist Press,* June 14, 2023; Smietana, "Southern Baptists Reaffirm Commitment to Abuse Reforms, Preview Database of Abusers."

298. just an empty prototype: David Roach, "ARITF Granted Additional Year to Fight Sexual Abuse," *Baptist Press,* June 14, 2023; Brown, "SBC Annual Meeting Reveals Little Progress On Sexual Abuse, Not Even 'Bare Minimum.'"

298. They also backtracked on what they had promised: Brown, "SBC Annual Meeting Reveals Little Progress on Sexual Abuse, Not Even 'Bare Minimum.'"

298. "been convicted, confessed, or found liable in civil court": SBC Abuse Reform Implementation Task Force, https://sbcabuseprevention.com (last accessed August 23, 2023). *See also* Shaw, "Southern Baptists Consider Women's Leadership a 'Threat'"; Smietana, "Southern Baptists Reaffirm Commitment to Abuse Reforms, Preview Database of Abusers"; Brown, "SBC Annual Meeting Reveals Little Progress on Sexual Abuse, Not Even 'Bare Minimum.'" A couple months later, in a September 1, 2023 update, the Abuse Reform Implementation Task Force backtracked still more, announcing that the initial "vetting" process wouldn't even include pastors who had confessed to abuse: SBC Abuse Reform Implementation Task Force, "Task Force Update (9/1/23)," August 31, 2023, https://www.abusereformtaskforce.net/updates/task-force-update-9123.

298. Since most clergy sex abusers never encounter: Smietana, "Southern Baptists Reaffirm Commitment to Abuse Reforms, Preview Database of Abusers" (quoting Marshall Blalock, chair of the SBC's Abuse Reform Implementation Task Force).

298. stalled on institutionally disclosing: Smietana, "Southern Baptists Reaffirm Commitment to Abuse Reforms, Preview Database of Abusers"; Brown, "SBC Annual Meeting Reveals Little Progress on Sexual Abuse, Not Even 'Bare Minimum.'"

298. 6,770 credibly accused clergy: Ellis Simani and Ken Schwencke, "Credibly Accused," *ProPublica*, January 28, 2020, https://projects.propublica.org/credibly-accused/ (last accessed August 23, 2023).

298. SBC's national entities control about $1.1 billion: Bob Smietana, "Who Will Pay for the SBC's Abuse Reforms Over the Long Term? No One Knows," *Religion News Service*, February 28, 2023; Brown, "SBC Annual Meeting Reveals Little Progress on Sexual Abuse, Not Even 'Bare Minimum'"; Smietana, "Southern Baptists Reaffirm Commitment to Abuse Reforms, Preview Database of Abusers."

299. Months later, it came to light: Christa Brown, David Clohessy, and Dave Pittman, "The Duplicity of an SBC Amicus Brief," *Baptist News Global*, October 27, 2023.

299. I want to personally apologize: Christa Brown, "'It Was Futile . . . Nothing Will Change,'" *Baptist News Global*, December 4, 2023.

299. SBC Executive Committee installed: Bob Smietana, "Executive Committee Names Temporary Leader, Deals with Fallout from McLaurin Deception," *Religion News Service*, August 18, 2023.

300. In a 2019 email: Guidepost Solutions, "Report of the Independent Investigation," 109–110; Mark Wingfield, "Guidepost Report Documents Pattern of Ignoring, Denying and Deflecting on Sexual Abuse Claims in SBC," *Baptist News Global*, May 22, 2022.

300. "Using just her legal expertise . . .": Stankorb, "The Southern Baptist Church Ignored Its Abuse Crisis. She Exposed It."

300. number five on their "Top 10 Religion Newsmakers": Religion News Association, "RNA Members Name Supreme Court's Roe v. Wade Decision Top Story of 2022," December 21, 2022, https://rna.org/news/rna-members-name-supreme-courts-roe-v-wade-decision-top-story-of2022; Religion News Association, "What story did journalists name as top religion story of 2022?" *The Oklahoman*, December 29, 2022; Kelsey Dallas, "The Top Religion Stories of 2022," *Deseret News*, January 3, 2023.

300. There are many reasons: Kate Shellnutt, "1 in 10 Young Protestants Have Left a Church Over Abuse," *Christianity Today*, May 21, 2019; Public Religion Research Institute, "Unveiling the Exodus: Americans' Reasons for Leaving Religious Traditions," *PRRI*, July 21, 2023; Ed Kilgore, "The Southern Baptist Church is Going to Hell in a Handbasket," *Intelligencer*, June 9, 2021; Staff, "Southern Baptists Lost Half A Million Members Last Year," *Relevant*, May 10, 2023.

301. The SBC's downward turn: Smietana, "Anti-woke Preachers Voddie Baucham and Tom Ascol to be Nominated as SBC Leaders" ("The denomination lost more than 2 million members since 2006, with no turnaround in sight."); Kate Shellnutt, "Southern Baptists Drop 1.1 Million Members in Three Years," *Christianity Today*, May 12, 2022 ("Membership in America's largest Protestant denomination has dropped from . . . a peak of 16.3 million in 2006"); Staff,

"Southern Baptists Lost Half a Million Members Last Year," *Relevant*, May 10, 2023 ("Back in 2006 . . . things started to shift"); *see also* Bob Smietana, *Reorganized Religion: The Shaping of the American Church and Why It Matters* (Nashville: Worthy Publishing, 2022), 29–31.

301. election denier and Christian nationalist: *See* Katelyn Fossett, "He Seems to be Saying His Commitment Is to Minority Rule," *Politico*, October 27, 2023.

303. "one wild and precious life": Mary Oliver, "The Summer Day," *House of Light* (Boston: Beacon Press, 1990).

ABOUT THE AUTHOR

NAMED AS ONE of the "top 10 religion newsmakers" of 2022, Christa Brown has persisted for two decades in working to peel back the truth about clergy sex abuse and cover-ups in the nation's largest Protestant denomination, the Southern Baptist Convention. As one of the first to go public with substantiated child molestation allegations against a Baptist minister—and documentation that others knew—she has consistently demanded reforms to make other kids and congregants safer. She's the author of *This Little Light: Beyond a Baptist Preacher Predator and His Gang*, a retired appellate attorney, a mom, a grandma, and lives with her husband in Colorado. Learn more at christabrown.me.

ABOUT LAKE DRIVE BOOKS

LAKE DRIVE BOOKS is an independent publishing company offering books that help you heal, grow, and discover. We champion books about values and strategies, not ideologies, and authors who are spiritually rich, contextually intelligent, and focused on human flourishing. We want to help readers feel seen.

If you like this or any of our other books at lakedrivebooks.com, we could use your help: please follow our authors on social media, subscribe to their newsletters, and tell others what you think of their remarkable books.

Printed in the USA
CPSIA information can be obtained
at www.ICGtesting.com
LVHW040332260424
778455LV00002B/2